PODCAST JOURNALISM

Podcast Journalism

The Promise and Perils of Audio Reporting

David O. Dowling

Columbia University Press New York

Columbia University Press
Publishers Since 1893
New York   Chichester, West Sussex
cup.columbia.edu
Copyright © 2024 Columbia University Press
All rights reserved

Library of Congress Cataloging-in-Publication Data
Names: Dowling, David O., author.
Title: Podcast journalism : the promise and perils of audio reporting / David O. Dowling.
Description: New York City : Columbia University Press, 2024. | Includes bibliographical references and index.
Identifiers: LCCN 2023032168 (print) | LCCN 2023032169 (ebook) | ISBN 9780231213301 (hardback) | ISBN 9780231213318 (trade paperback) | ISBN 9780231559829 (ebook)
Subjects: LCSH: Podcast journalism. | Online journalism. | Journalistic ethics. | Reportage literature. | Journalism—Technological innovations.
Classification: LCC PN4784.P56 D69 2024 (print) | LCC PN4784.P56 (ebook) | DDC 070.4—dc23/eng/20230803
LC record available at https://lccn.loc.gov/2023032168
LC ebook record available at https://lccn.loc.gov/2023032169

Printed and bound by CPI Group (UK) Ltd, Croydon, CR0 4YY

Cover design: Elliott S. Cairns

Contents

Acknowledgments   vii

INTRODUCTION
The Mainstreaming of Podcast Journalism   1

CHAPTER ONE
Podcasting the Pandemic: Beyond the NPR Revolution   24

CHAPTER TWO
The Perils and Promise of True Crime Podcast Journalism   48

CHAPTER THREE
Intellectual Culture   74

CHAPTER FOUR
Sound Transactions: Audience and the Advent of Paid Podcasts   99

CHAPTER FIVE
Charting the Far Right   124

CHAPTER SIX
Voices from the Margins   149

CHAPTER SEVEN
The Profit Motive: Brands as Publishers   175

EPILOGUE
Podcasting as Digital Literary Journalism   202

Notes   227
Selected Bibliography   273
Index   279

Acknowledgments

Of the many people and organizations that supported this book, my most immediate debts are to Kim Fox and Kyle J. Miller. Our collaborative research formed the foundation for much of this project. Anne F. MacLennan played a key editorial role in two early studies that established the basis of what later became the theoretical framework of this book. Jason Loviglio deserves credit for his support and editorial guidance. Collaborative research with Patrick Johnson and Brian Ekdale extended the purview of an important chapter. The influence of these individuals cannot be overestimated.

Melissa Tully, director of the School of Journalism and Mass Communication, and Christopher Cheatum, associate dean in the College of Liberal Arts and Sciences at the University of Iowa, provided vital financial support for this research. Academic associations and their subdivisions, including those of ICA (International Communication Association), AEJMC (Association for Education in Journalism and Mass Communication), BEA (Broadcast Education Association), and IALJS (International Association for Literary Journalism Studies), embraced initial research for this project bridging digital journalism studies and podcast studies. The panels I coordinated at the Detroit 2022 AEJMC meeting featured particularly rich exchanges offering powerful new understandings about podcasting's extension of digital longform storytelling.

I owe a debt of gratitude to Columbia University Press executive editor Philip Leventhal for his dedication, patience, and support of this project from its origin. Assistance with manuscript preparation from University of Iowa research assistant Kate C. Perez was invaluable. Thank you, Kate, for lending your expertise and generous contributions.

Finally, my deepest appreciation goes to my wife, Caroline Tolbert; daughters, Jackie and Ev; and son, Ed. Each in their own way energized this research with enthusiasm and compassion, enriching my appreciation for how politics and science shape intellectual culture in digital spaces.

PODCAST JOURNALISM

Introduction

The Mainstreaming of Podcast Journalism

Podcasting's ascent has drawn increasing attention to audio journalism as a form capable of entertaining and informing audiences in record numbers through investigative reporting and personal narrative. Since the milestone success of *Serial*'s debut season in 2014 transformed podcasting into a mainstream media phenomenon, media scholars have only begun to critically apprehend on-demand audio's capacity to perform as serious journalism. Whereas some have proclaimed this the golden age of podcasting, one that that remediates and revives the craft of oral storytelling that Walter Benjamin once considered obsolete due to the encroachment of modern mass media, others have found cause for concern with the industry's rampant platformization, corporate conglomeration, and manipulation at the hands of partisan pundits.[1] This book examines how new journalistic standards of nonfiction narrative reportage operate at the heart of the 800,000 podcast programs—up from 550,000 in 2018—amassing roughly 30 million episodes online.[2] Although news composes only 6 percent of the total programs listed, it accounts for 21 percent of the most popular episodes on the Apple Podcasts chart in the United States and 34 percent in France.[3] Podcasting is "our new front page," *New York Times* director of audio Erik Borenstein said in light of *The Daily*'s listenership reaching two million per day in 2019.[4] One year later, the *Times* cemented its commitment to the medium by acquiring Serial Productions, producers of *This American Life*, *Serial*, and *S-Town*, for $25 million. Among the most significant developments in digital journalism of the past twenty-five years, podcasting signals a promising and lucrative turn in a once beleaguered news industry. With its longform storytelling, binge-listening audience, and influx of sponsors, the medium has buoyed journalism from the wreckage of digital disruption seen in diminished attention spans, shallow online news templates, vanishing advertising revenue, and decimated newsroom staffs. Despite a plateau in podcast revenue reported by Spotify in 2023, a gold a gold rush mentality has ensued, raising this book's central question of the medium's industrial impact on journalistic practice: *To what extent can podcasting perform as principled, narrative journalism capable of fulfilling media's duty to democracy?*

Advances in podcast journalism have not come without their costs, ranging from a market increasingly dominated by fewer publishers and platforms, particularly Apple and Spotify, which have been vying for control over the medium since the late 2010s. In addition to big tech's corporatization of podcasting, journalistic principle has been severely compromised through improper reporting methods, as in the case of *Caliphate* by the *New York Times*, and in disinformation generated by Far Right podcasters led by Dan Bongino, the successor of firebrand Rush Limbaugh. Despite highly visible flaws in the short history of the form, podcast journalism's current phase of intense experimentation witnessed the first self-conscious attempt at the production of an aural literary masterpiece with *S-Town* in addition to upstanding service to democracy and social justice in shows such as Maria Martin's *Latino USA* and Madeleine Baran's *In the Dark*. Work such as Baran's—which defies the true crime convention of attempting to solve unsolved cases by instead examining the causes and consequences of failed investigations—allows for more fluid understandings of how media can serve democracy, particularly through radical experimentation with complex, large-scale narratives. As a circumventing technology that remains among the least censored of the world's media, podcasting transcends the expressive limitations of traditional categories separating news from entertainment, editorial from advertising content, and fairness from subjectivity.[5]

Nonfiction podcasts' unique intimacy and captivating storytelling typically associated with fiction are increasingly fueled by bold, rigorous reporting. Such rising standards for quality prompted the establishment of Audio Reporting as a new Pulitzer Prize category in 2020.[6] Eligibility for journalism's highest honor certified podcasting's credibility as news to match its status as the fastest-growing medium in digital publishing. Originally influenced by Ira Glass's *This American Life*, the form remediates predigital radio documentary and feature writing while extending online multimedia storytelling.[7] Such a sea change in storytelling, one uniquely adapted to the asynchronous mobile consumption patterns of twenty-first century audiences, has not occurred since the New Journalism of the mid-twentieth century unleashed the concept of news into the realm of richly textured nonfiction narrative.[8] As with the New Journalism, controversy has surfaced regarding the ethics of podcasting's deeply personal nature and capacity to preserve, transform, and threaten the core principles of journalism.[9]

As a potent extension of digital longform storytelling since the 2010s, audio journalism's narrative turn constitutes the central focus of this book. Its purpose is to provide a critical overview of the social contexts, genres, and industrial developments that have influenced podcast journalism's radical reformulation of production practices and redrawing of journalistic boundaries. This critical approach acknowledges the ambiguity of a complex set of tensions at the heart of an industry at once driving evermore powerful modes of storytelling and reporting while also opening space for platformization and the hijacking of the journalistic role by ideologues and corporate brands. Through examination of podcast content and industry data as primary source material understood theoretically at the intersection of podcast and digital journalism studies, this research addresses podcasting's reformulation of narrative journalism for the digital age. With the new premium on highly produced, absorbing audio storytelling, the industrial context for narrative journalism has become rife with competition, prompting distinctly monopolistic methods to emerge in the digital ecosystem.

With its dynamic content, expanding listenership, and aggressive business models, podcasting stands out as one of the most dramatic developments of the digital age, drawing major investments from platforms and publishers. Spotify, for example, has acquired exclusive rights to major shows with longstanding loyal listenership such as *The Joe Rogan Experience* and *Heavyweight*. As one of Gimlet Media's longest-running shows, *Heavyweight*'s transition to Spotify in 2021 stunned its fan base, which flooded social media with dissent.[10] Spotify's attempts at market domination are among many examples of platformization disrupting the organic development of podcast audience culture.[11] By locking listeners into streaming podcasts on their platform, Spotify prevents episodes from being downloaded, thus curbing the loss of revenue from dynamically inserted or baked-in advertising. Spotify's acquisition of such established shows gains the company exclusive access to listeners' personal data and drives traffic to its monetizing site to build subscriptions. Through streaming ad-insertion technology, Spotify seeks full dominion over the advertising pipeline, which is only possible if users stream exclusively on its platform. Spotify has achieved this objective by acquiring and contracting already popular shows for exclusive streaming on its platform. As Spotify makes a concerted effort to surpass Apple as the dominant platform of the podcast world, legacy media has also begun to develop its own digital spaces where listeners access shows. New York Times Audio, for example, is an audio-only app designed for *Times* podcasts as well as audio versions of its news and magazine journalism, including content from other publishers such as *Rolling Stone* and *New York Magazine*.[12] Although the *Times* generates highly acclaimed content fueled by *The Daily* and the newly acquired Serial Productions studio, the company faces a distinct competitive disadvantage due to Apple and Spotify's domination of the podcast app market. These big tech firms have effectively tilted the playing field in their favor by controlling the platforms where the vast majority podcasts are produced and consumed.[13]

As big tech companies and news media develop new ways of attracting audiences by acquiring appealing content in order to drive subscriptions, a new wave of investment in interactive audio has besieged the industry. Twitch's partnership with Warner Music Group, for example, leverages the popular streaming platform as a space for creators, including musicians and podcast hosts, to connect with their audiences. Amazon has also entered the market for livestreaming audio to compete with Spotify's Greenroom, a social audio app for podcasters to interact with their communities for exclusive experiences. As a massive global platform originally dedicated to uniting gaming communities online, Twitch and its highly coveted youthful demographic represent a major obstacle to Spotify's attempt to monopolize interactive audio. The object of this audio war is to become the main place users congregate, whether to listen to a podcast, engage in conversation with a respected professional, or stream music.[14]

Interactive audio has reintroduced the significance of the screen in the podcast industry. Listeners can interact with podcast content and advertising by tapping on their phone screens, a practice otherwise anathema to podcasting's liberation from screen-based consumption. Interaction with hosts during the shows themselves also extends to audio grouping via Spotify Greenroom, which competes with Facebook's Live Audio Rooms and podcasts for new podcast opportunities in distribution, discovery, monetization, and social connection all in one place. Companies in this sector compete to establish a single in-app experience for podcast selection, consumption, and social interaction with hosts and fellow listeners that comprise the podcast community. These tools for distribution, consumption, sharing, and interaction profoundly reconfigure podcast culture, illustrating how the medium is not neutral but affects the user. As Marshall McLuhan noted, the medium "does something to people; it takes hold of them, it rubs them up, it massages them, it bumps them around," shaping both the individual and collective experience of podcast culture firmly situated within the larger culture of the digital publishing industry.[15] Technology wraps the medium, transforming its conventions and production practices. Rather than determining the course of journalism into the twenty-first century in any prescribed way, podcast technology is socially constructed and highly responsive to its historical moment. Podcasting served the needs of quarantined audiences during the COVID-19 pandemic, for example, and offered intimate coverage of the protests following George Floyd's murder.[16]

PODCAST JOURNALISM IN DIGITAL CULTURE

Originally limited to independent startups at the fringe of digital culture, podcasting's pioneers Gimlet Media and Radiotopia are now joined by publishers invested in serious journalism, including such august brands as the *New Yorker* and the *Wall Street Journal*. Acclaimed podcasts hail from increasingly diverse sectors of the industry, ranging from hard news and investigative outlets such as WNYC and ProPublica's *Trump, Inc.* to the national and local daily press of *USA Today* and Reno

Gazette-Journal's *The City*. Nongovernment organizations and nonprofit organizations leveraging podcasts include the Brookings Institute for public policy, which earned the Academy of Podcasters' Best News and Politics Award in 2015 for *Brookings Cafeteria*. An expansive and increasingly diverse listenership encompassing both niche subcultures and mainstream audiences fuels what Pulitzer Prize administration calls a "renaissance of audio journalism" that has "given rise to an extraordinary array of nonfiction storytelling."[17] The medium's evolution toward longform investigative reporting has abetted deeper and more thorough journalistic checks on power in addition to coverage of underreported populations.[18]

The brief yet fierce evolution of podcast journalism has opened up space for progressive content produced by and about marginalized groups typically erased from headlines. A central argument of this book is that the diverse array of social and ethnic subcultures represented in podcast programs marks journalism's most significant advance of the digital revolution toward realizing—and refashioning—the Hutchins Commission's original guidelines for what society should demand of the press. Accurate representation of society's constituent groups, particularly underreported populations, is chief among these enduring standards for press responsibility.[19] Social representation is central to the Society for Professional Journalists' Code of Ethics charge to "boldly tell the story of the diversity and magnitude of the human experience," especially by seeking "sources whose voices we seldom hear."[20] As a form whose independent media and public radio genetic blueprint inclines it toward showcasing the authentic voices of grassroots subcultures, podcasting preserves and enriches sociocultural representation while extending the Hutchins Commission's timeless standards of context, a forum for discussion, the presentation of the goals and values of society, and full access to the latest intelligence.[21]

Among the most prominent of podcast journalism's evolving conventions is the self-reflexive and transparent representation of the process of production, highlighting rather than suppressing the ethical dilemmas of reporting. As Michael Barbaro of *The Daily* podcast explained, "podcasting is, by definition, a more vulnerable, transparent medium. You can *hear* the reporter's uncertainty."[22] Producers invite listeners to witness the ethically charged reportorial process, trading a polished portrait of news production for the open-minded quest for it. At the heart of the podcast medium is a complex paradox: in exposing the vulnerabilities of the reportorial process, the news product becomes more credible and trustworthy. Reporters' tendency to conscientiously question their own assumptions and verify sources has become a signature of the genre. Thus, journalists themselves appear more human in light of the complexity of their craft and the illusive nature of truth. At its best, podcast journalism espouses an unmistakably postmodern narrative sensibility, exposing and critiquing its own process of production and, by extension, the top-down black box (i.e., nontransparent) approach of traditional news media.[23]

As a digital space that can function as a site of resistance, podcasting remains among the least censored of the world's media, marked by its function as "liminal praxis."[24] The liminal, or in-between, space it occupies enables new aural cultures to leverage the medium to express and define subjectivity. Radiotopia's production practice for *Ear Hustle*, a #BlackLivesMatters podcast recommendation, exemplifies the integration of such subjectivity into audio storytelling. Their method is to eliminate "traditional scripted narration" and "intersperse tape with *conversation*—often between the hosts, or between the hosts and reporter, or between hosts and interviewees."[25] The unfettered use of first-person in podcasting is consonant with the liberating nature of the medium. Along with its relative lack of censorship, the podcast's aural and oral nature lends itself to community-building, especially among marginalized groups. Self-reflexivity is inherent in "liminal praxis" because it "imbues a questioning of the logics and effects of mediation itself," as evident in *Code Switch*, *It's All Journalism*, and *On the Media*.[26]

This book addresses how podcasting has developed as a phenomenon and critically examines how it variously fulfills and neglects journalism's role of providing a means of civic engagement in service to media's duty to democracy.[27] Key questions concern the medium's position at the forefront of journalism's digital future: How is the podcast situated industrially and culturally as a place where listeners increasing turn for information? How has podcasting retrieved and revived older forms of narrativity? In what ways are podcasting's current discourse conventions shaped by its independent media roots produced as a fringe amateur pastime? How has podcasting maintained or professionalized the amateur grassroots nature of that production practice during its transition into a major media industry? Where precisely has podcasting advanced journalistic excellence and where has it compromised the core principles of the profession? The movement from niche to mass media is evident in the growth of Libsyn, a company that provides podcast platforms. The company managed more than 2.6 billion downloads in 2014, a figure that grew to 3.3 billion in 2015 and 4.6 billion in 2016.[28] This explosive year-over-year growth is also reflected in how only 11 percent of U.S. users had ever listened to podcasts in 2006, a figure that quadrupled to 44 percent by 2018.[29] By 2019 the milestone of 50 percent had been passed, a watershed moment in the medium's evolution indicating that podcasting "has firmly crossed into the mainstream," according to the president of Edison Research.[30]

This book charts the ascent of podcasting into prominence as the fastest-growing medium in the digital publishing industry. As a journalistic form, the medium extends from live radio commentary and talk shows to edited documentary.[31] Its origins as independent media shape its journalistic function as information source, advocacy, activism, and watchdog roles while maintaining emphasis on entertainment. It should be noted that the categories of news and entertainment have always existed in tension with each other based on overlapping—and ever changing—formalized definitions. Due to its relatively low production costs and colossal capacity for audience reach into mobile user demographics, podcast journalism is now a staple of corporate media from broadcast and print to born-digital publishers. The movement of established brands into the market for audio forms of digital longform journalism has mainstreamed the podcast medium, in effect widening the gap between successful and obscure podcasts.[32] Podcast networks such as Gimlet and Radiotopia consisting of select independent and startup producers have responded to this development. This industrial context informs the typology of news and news-related podcasts, which ranges from longform serialized documentaries patterned after *Serial* to daily news bulletins, round-ups, and deep dives.[33] Each genre defines its past and current trajectory in terms of business model, sound design, narrative aesthetic, and journalistic principle.

TOWARD A "PODCAST CONSCIOUSNESS FOR JOURNALISM"

A key component of the mainstreaming of the medium's function as news source is what Martin Spinelli and Lance Dann call "a podcast consciousness for journalism" rooted in the "acceptance of attachment and impression" as a form of parsing the truth.[34] This self-reflexivity and transparency in the process of production—now signatures of podcast journalism—have been reshaped by corporatized media such as *The Daily*, produced by reporters from the *New York Times*. Newman notes that such deep-dive podcast journalism is the bastion of publishers with print and digital-born backgrounds due to their strengths in explanation and analysis, whereas broadcasters tend to focus on shorter forms such as microbulletins, which can be produced by repurposing radio news content.[35] Feature writing and reporting therefore represent the core journalistic skill set for longform news podcasting. The medium's unique affordances nonetheless deliver an aesthetic experience different from traditional print, broadcast, and screen-based digital journalism. Unlike print and video, whose media signify distance through sight, "sound envelops us, pouring into us whether we want it or not, including us, involving us."[36] Journalistic narrative, which represents the through line connecting each chapter of this critical overview of audio reporting in the digital age, elicits empathy in audiences through identification with others' pain and pleasure.[37] The reverse is also possible, which can be manipulated for niche audiences, thus potentially widening the ideological gap of hyperpartisanship as in the *Daily Wire*'s popular *Ben Shapiro Show*.

Podcasting is part of a wave of immersive longform storytelling that has taken over digital publishing, one characterized by business models predicated on engaged time rather than clicks.[38] The asynchronous on-demand technological affordances of podcasting are ideally suited to this industrial shift toward products designed to immerse user attention.[39] Podcasts function as journalism through the uniquely intimate quality of the medium that lends itself to coverage of communities and voices at the far reaches of the spectrum of cultural discourse—from prisoners to scientists—outside the breaking news cycle. Podcasts open up Black discourse on the meaning of Blackness in U.S. culture to an audience of unprecedented scope and diversity.[40] Podcasts now play host to the most sophisticated coverage and analysis of the Black experience in media history, a topic relegated less than a century ago to the equivalent of minstrel show amusement in radio shows like *Amos & Andy*.[41]

Other new spaces opened by the medium include scientific and intellectual culture previously limited to academia, revealing the human, lived experience behind abstract data. Podcasts epitomize our contemporary age's opposite trend from what communication theorist Walter Benjamin argued in 1936 was modern society's tendency to abbreviate storytelling. News feeds through the wire service during his time led to inverted pyramid writing according to what Ernest Hemingway called *telegraphese*, a clipped and truncated delivery that replaced the lavish and detailed narrative structure of the nineteenth century. Benjamin lamented the impact of mechanical reproduction on both art and news, observing that "by now almost nothing that happens benefits storytelling."[42] Jessica Helfand echoed Benjamin's lament in the early 2000s with her diagnosis of widespread "narrative depravation" endemic to digital culture's accelerated yet shallow pattern of online news consumption.[43] As with Benjamin's era, Helfand's early 2000s was characterized by abbreviated news that had yet to appear in distraction-free applications introduced in the early 2010s. Such somber—and premature—proclamations of the death of storytelling presume a deterministic evolution of media technology toward narrative depravation that is undercut by the rise of podcast journalism.

The storytelling Benjamin eulogized in 1936 and Helfand hungered for in 2001 was missing during those times due to the media technologies of the telegraph and the internet's homogenization of news. Podcast journalism now supplies the need for more deeply contextualized and complex storytelling in our accelerated digital culture. Although podcasting was available as a digital tool in the early 2000s, the masters of the craft had yet to bring them to their fullest expressive potential. The canvas was in place, but few had capitalized on its vast space for sound design, character development, setting, and scene construction. *This American Life*'s narrative formula for nonfiction remained on terrestrial radio separate from the podcast medium for nearly two decades, from *TAL*'s syndication in 1995 until the 2014 release of *Serial*'s blockbuster first season.[44] The instance recalls the invention of color television technology that preceded its entrance into homes by more than a decade.

The sudden deluge of quality longform content generated by podcasts has not been seen in media culture since the advent of cable TV movie channels in the 1980s (first HBO and Showtime, and later Cinemax), which introduced voluminous advertising-free, feature-length cinema into private homes. The ever-expanding selection of on-demand audio now brings rich longform content to audiences for asynchronous mobile consumption. Unlike on-demand streaming video, the podcast's screen-free status liberates users from the visual and tactile interfaces of their devices. Similar to how vision-impaired individuals cultivate acute sensitivity to cues and nuances in their audio environments, podcasts distill rather than scatter the attention of listeners, sealing them off from the visual noise of the internet's catacomb of distractions and advertisements.[45] In the spectrum of online media, attentional focus is relatively pure and unmitigated in a single audio stream. As such, public radio-inspired podcast journalism stands as one form of digital media to counter the tide of unintentional internet use driven by the attention economy and its distraction technologies.[46] If there is "little difference between habitat restoration in the traditional sense and restoring habitats for human thoughts," as Jenny Odell observes, podcasts can be construed as restorative digital space.[47]

Free from the visual noise of the internet, audio narratives draw listeners into "driveway moments" where they remain in their vehicles to reach the story's denouement.[48] Now smartphones and mobile audio devices allow for "driveway moments," only without physical captivity. Podcasting's unique power lies in the intimacy of voice and narrative, which Helfand calls the deepest link to our humanity.[49] As with the best feature journalism, abstract and scientific concepts have thus become more appealing and accessible. Intellectual culture now thrives on podcasts such as *The Skeptic's Guide to the Universe* and Neil deGrasse Tyson's *StarTalk*, both dedicated to science literacy for the general public. Audiences increasingly demand not only entertainment news but also rich cultural and social metacritique featuring rigorous research and reporting.[50] Programs such as *BhD: Black and Highly Dangerous* blur the lines between entertainment, activism, and criticism, leveraging both colloquial and intellectual discourse for progressive cultural analysis.

Introduction 11

Such content ranges from everyday experience to broader sociocultural constructs, often galvanized by long views into history and applications to politics.

The ascent of podcasting has been understood mainly in terms of its relation to other streaming-era media such as television, or its relation to radio history.[51] Publishing history and the spread of intellectual culture, however, is as significant a genealogy, particularly in the context of the digital news media industry.[52] Podcasting is part of an explosion of immersive storytelling in digital publishing whose success is a factor of not only developments in audio technology and delivery devices but also experimentation in reporting and storytelling for thought-provoking documentary narrative, longform content known according to industrial parlance as deep dives. This shift in digital publishing has transformed the principles of journalism in ways that resonate with both podcasting's current advances as well as its liabilities to the profit motive in some instances, particularly in the true crime genre.

Scholarship has mined the views of industry insiders for understandings of the ascent of podcasting that considers its relation to streaming video on-demand, explored the medium's intimate aural nature that predispose it toward personal narrative, treated it as a liminal space uniquely empowering to its producers, and examined the vast constellation of programs through selected titles from science to fictional dramas.[53] The industrial turn toward radical experimentation in nonfictional audio content affirms how "technological innovation must be fueled by the transformation and creation of additional content and services and other forms of expression," a process demanding "experimentation, imagination and creativity by professionals."[54] The literature on podcasting focuses on the development of new genre conventions by practitioners; motivations for consumption of true crime; podcasting's uses, evolution, and intersection with radio; approaches to longform audio journalism via genre; and convergence.[55] Michele Hilmes examines podcasting with respect to radio history, a perspective that complements this project's approach that situates the medium within the context of longform journalism and the digital publishing industry, as set forth in my recent study.[56]

Originally what Scott Eldridge II describes as "interloper media" within the field of journalism, podcasting's sheer scale and newfound critical acclaim now occupy and redefine the mainstream.[57] The technological context of digital publishing and the business models they foster—from partnerships and live events to content marketing and product placement—distinguish this research from the current literature. Podcasting's essence may be aural, but as a transmedia phenomenon, it is also increasingly consumed as streaming and YouTube video and read on any device as transcribed written text (as with *S-Town*) often accompanied by visual illustrations (as in the prisoner sketches of *Ear Hustle*) not unlike that of a transmediated screenplay. Transmedia scholarship therefore informs treatment of podcasts as digital media in a socially networked, cross-platform environment.[58]

NARRATIVE JOURNALISM'S AUDIO TURN

Taken together, the first four chapters of this book examine the most pivotal social, cultural, and industrial forces impacting narrative journalism's audio turn. They address podcasting's place within the NPR revolution, its key genre of true crime, and the intellectual culture it has spawned. The corporatization of the medium, its impact on storytelling, and developments in technology for production, distribution, and consumption continue to rewrite the rules of competition for market share, typically to the financial advantage of platforms. Platformization (a digital extension of corporatization) emerges as a key factor influencing the social and industrial context of podcast journalism.

The ensuing chapters explore the political uses of the medium by the Far Right and marginalized populations. After engaging how partisanship and identity politics of producers mitigate podcast content, the book's final chapter considers how brands have engaged in audio storytelling to promote their goods and services. Overall, these last three chapters showcase how the interests of producers—advancing the views and agendas of the political Right (chapter 5), Left (chapter 6), and corporate brands (chapter 7)—shape the narrative content of podcasts themselves. Finally, the conclusion coalesces the through line of the book on longform storytelling regarding emergent literary forms, such as the audio essay associated with The 1619 Project and the nonfiction audio novel, which has now gained both critical and scholarly attention for such works as *S-Town* (as in McHugh, 2021).[59] The following offers closer consideration of the major topics that comprise this book's critical examination of narrative journalism's audio turn, a movement that has redefined longform storytelling and the reportorial role.

The COVID-19 pandemic, as discussed in chapter 1, impacted the production practice and content of podcast journalism. With many top producers relegated to recording out of their bedroom closets, the medium's unique technological affordances enabled flexible, time-shifted, and remote production consumption during the crisis. The longing for human connection and updated information endemic to quarantine culture attracted new attention to daily news podcasts, particularly those in the deep-dive category ranging from twenty-five to thirty-five minutes, such as the *Guardian*'s *Today in Focus*. Downloads of news and news-related podcasts increased during the crisis, especially shows published by Public Media Marketing (which includes *This American Life* and *The Joe Rogan Experience*) and Vox Media.[60] During a time when most major newspapers dropped their paywalls, podcast content took a distinct public-service turn. NBC New Media's *Into America* addressed systemic ruptures exposed and intensified by the pandemic, the *Washington Post*'s *All Told* opened new opportunities for listeners to share their experiences, and Malcolm Gladwell's publication *Solvable* covered solutions to the economic fallout via innovations in mobile technology. The latter illustrates an apt example of solutions journalism as an alternative to the relentlessly negative coverage of the crisis and a relief from negative news fatigue. Due to strict stay-at-home orders worldwide, podcast journalism consumption during the pandemic shifted from the traditional morning commute to afternoons, when most shows were downloaded.

The pandemic accelerated the success of daily news podcasts in the deep-dive category, which leverage narrative journalism crafted according to the storytelling principles of NPR and Ira Glass's *This American Life*.[61] Producers manage degrees of subjectivity and opinion in their podcasts, using as a touchstone of comparison NPR's longer documentary programming that leveraged the inherent intimacy of the medium.[62] The "relaxed and personal" style of delivery cultivated by podcast hosts creates a "uniquely personal relationship between the listener and the content," thus foregrounding reportorial subjectivity.[63] Variations on NPR's revision of the traditional journalistic template for storytelling impact the way "stories have the power to influence minds and motivate actions."[64] To this end, the genres of solutions and advocacy journalism are examined in light of the past and ongoing NPR revolution in longform audio storytelling as well as the pandemic's influence on the news media's embrace of the public-service role.

Public radio and longform narrative were instrumental in popularizing the true crime genre. The second chapter examines two divergent trends in true crime podcasting, one at the leading edge of journalistic excellence and another willing to severely compromise reporting standards in pursuit of profit. The latter is examined in the debacle surrounding *Caliphate*, the investigative true crime podcast by the *New York Times*, which illustrates the dangers of real-time speculation regarding the veracity of testimony provided by untried suspects. The *Times*'s spectacular failure occurred in part due to the production team's attempt at a serialized true crime blockbuster, operating more like a book than a TV show or newscast, in the vein of high-end podcasts like *Reveal* and *S-Town*. *Caliphate* sacrificed fundamental reporting ethics in pursuit of meticulously designed narration—complete with metajournalistic performances of transparency—to heighten tension through scene-setting and character development in keeping with the true crime podcast genre's pivot from loosely structured interviews to longform narrative journalism.[65] In other shows, such as *Crime Junkie* and *Break in the Case*, reporters failed to explore potential flaws in police work, thus granting authorities exclusive control over the narrative.[66] In taking the word of authorities at face value, these shows veer dangerously close to what renowned Vietnam War correspondent Homer Bigart called *clerkism*, "the practice of uncritically accepting the official version of things" that turns the press into the dutiful scribes—and potential propagandists—of government officials.[67] By avoiding the risk and labor of investigating police corruption, these shows prioritize return on investment at the expense of the public interest. Such programs are "designed to elicit maximum sympathy for the police," in effect polishing their image to enhance public relations.[68]

In sharp contrast to these single-source investigations, progressive journalism informs *74 Seconds*, a 2017 production of Minnesota Public Radio, and American Public Media's *In the Dark*. As the antithesis of shows touting "exclusives" limited to authorized perspectives of crimes, progressive true crime reporting scrutinizes the accuracy and ethics of police work. Prompted to explore cases that closed without any convictions made, *In the Dark* host and lead reporter Madeleine Baran explained of the first season, "We didn't see ourselves as playing the role of detective . . . we saw ourselves as investigating the investigators."[69] This method of holding those in power to account builds on the tradition of Stephen J. Berry's *Watchdog Journalism*, which details the tenets of his Pulitzer Prize–winning probe of a sheriff drug enforcement unit's unjust seizure of millions of dollars from minority motorists.[70]

In this tradition of watchdogging the watchdog, such podcasts share the "fearless adversarial journalism" of *Intercepted*, the audio extension of *The Intercept*, founded by Glenn Greenwald (the former *Guardian* reporter who covered the Edward Snowden international surveillance scandal). *Reveal*, which showcases the work of the Center for Investigative Reporting, is central to progressive true crime journalism. Known for its Edward R. Murrow and Webby award-winning probe into voter suppression in advance of the 2016 presidential election, *Reveal* deploys systematic reporting in the public interest through aggressive checks on power. The show's legal impact is visible in one investigation that led to the shutdown of the use of drug treatment facilities as unlicensed work camps. *Serial* adopted a similar approach, shifting focus from the crime itself and the accused in season 1 to institutional failures in season 3. *Serial*'s third season examines the everyday machinations of criminal justice through the example of the Cleveland municipal court system, which granted Serial Productions full access, thus enabling the ensuing damning portrait of rampant corruption and institutional racism. Such content caters to an audience seeking podcasting not only as a means of civic engagement but also as an intellectual challenge.

Insofar as true crime audiences tend to be highly educated and inclined toward understanding the criminal justice system and journalistic practice by closely following experts, intellectual culture, the subject of chapter 3, emerges as a critical component of listenership. In the constellation of roughly three-quarters of a million podcasts online today, a significant portion have ushered intellectual culture into the mainstream. *Nobel Prize Conversations*, *Floodlines*, *The Last Archive*, and *Public Intellectual* are the case studies of the intellectually ambitious podcasts at the heart of this chapter. Intellectual culture in audio form, unlike written communication, "offers freedoms from disciplinary regimes and traditions, and from disciplinary modes of communication and knowledge production," providing a viable and liberating platform for public intellectuals.[71] With fewer constraints than TED Talks, the podcast medium affords greater independence and control over the production process that "offers a sense of status, and even power."[72]

According to Nic Newman's definition of the different types of popular news podcasts, talk and unscripted interview shows are among its four categories that include daily news / current affairs.[73] Talk and unscripted interview shows feature commentary in a format providing the sort of unstructured freedom that enables intellectuals to venture into topics otherwise considered off limits in traditional news media. Unlike broadcast television, whose intellectual range is severely limited by time constraints of scheduled programming and advertising, podcasts enable shows such as *Solvable*, published by Malcolm Gladwell and Jacob Weisberg, to explore uncharted territory with relative ease. Featuring "the world's most inspiring thinkers proposing solutions to the world's most daunting problems," *Solvable* bears Gladwell's intellectual influence that traces back to his *New Yorker* contributions and his books on the inherent biases of interpersonal and institutional judgment behind social and economic inequality. Such programming can bridge knowledge divides. "Thanks to the medium's wide accessibility—given its general affordability and portability—knowledge in diverse domains can be shared by individuals and groups around the world" thus directly abetting the mainstreaming of intellectual culture.[74]

The accessibility of densely produced content associated with various strands of intellectual culture is consonant with substantive, ad-free digital longform content. The increasing quality of such content has prompted the advent of paywalled and subscription podcasts. Chapter 4 examines the tension in podcast journalism between its potent appeal as entertainment capable of commanding a price from listeners and its function as a means of civic participation on behalf of democracy and social justice. News-related podcasts "offer the sometimes lurid satisfactions of story bolstered by the apparent rectitude of information."[75] Together, these forces enable podcast journalism "to outperform other types of content in terms of consumption," particularly according to the coveted metric of engaged time in digital publishing.[76] Previously associated with the consumption of live or recorded music in long sessions, binge listening now increasingly applies to podcasts. With the serialized content of podcasts, listeners can now indulge in the consumption of multiple episodes and entire seasons of programs. By nature, longform journalism performs according to the cultural tenets of slow media.[77] As audio longform, podcasts cannot readily "be checked, scanned, and rushed through," and instead are "designed to take up time," unlike most screen-based news.[78] The nonfiction podcast is the first journalistic form adapted to and produced for binge consumption on smartphones, yet it remains distinct from any other form of news media in its "commitment to a slow build, and to a sensual atmosphere," which draws on the textured narrativity of terrestrial radio dramas.[79]

When publishers package journalism for binge listening to win niche audiences, information silos can form, eroding public discourse on current affairs and civic participation. Such developments can lead to homogenization of news content associated with broadcast, print, and screen-based digital journalism, which is characterized by a decline of competition and domination of corporatized and legacy media, a process of increasing conglomeration by which fewer firms own more publications.[80] Large-scale products packaged in seasons can appeal to a decadent tendency in consumer culture toward instant self-gratification. An early wave of critics tracing back to the New Journalism of the mid-twentieth century argued that narrative journalism erodes the ethics of reporting by encouraging sensationalism and melodrama.[81] Certainly this is true in some sectors of the true crime genre, as previously noted. Additionally, the mainstreaming of subjective and immersive storytelling has enabled important investigative and advocacy reporting, in some cases carrying out justice as in the confession of an eleven-year-old boy's kidnapper and murderer in season 1 of *In the Dark*. Serialized structuring, furthermore, does not always imply one mode of binge consumption, primarily due to the medium's on-demand, asynchronous nature. "Podcast listeners, like Netflix viewers, might prefer to 'stack' episodes, delve into archives, skip episodes, or revisit favorites."[82] But the serial structure and slow narrative unfolding of unresolved cases can prompt active listener participation. Civic participation is often direct via tips sent by listeners sparking and aiding investigations, as with John McLemore's solicitation of Brian Reed to produce *S-Town*, and with the citizen whistleblowers revealing the Mississippi district attorney's racial profiling of Curtis Flowers in season 2 of *In the Dark*.

New patterns of consumption inclined toward consigning listeners to a greater commitment via payment for their podcasts finds its political analogue in highly charged, extremist political podcasting. Chapter 5 charts podcast journalism's Far Right through the legacy of talk radio's Rush Limbaugh. Whereas personal expression has become a core practice of journalism whose merits can include greater attention to context and interpretative analysis, these freedoms from the constraints of traditional broadcast conventions can pose serious risks, including the ideological hijacking of journalism by partisan actors.[83] In popular right-leaning podcasts such as those hosted by Ben Shapiro and Dan Bongino, the element of opinion amplifies the tendency of the podcast medium to relegate news to a secondary concern behind emotional impact. Not only do podcasters like Shapiro and Bongino contribute to a fractured media environment of hyperpartisan news and commentary, they also use social media platforms and transmedia networks to undermine traditional journalism and replace it with an alternative conservative media ecosystem—a multiplatform, full-service clearinghouse of news and commentary afforded by the publishing capabilities of the internet and the distribution algorithms of social media platforms like Facebook. Conservative audio production is traced from the influential work of talk radio star Rush Limbaugh through the latest innovations by conservative podcasters as exemplified by Shapiro and Bongino. Scholarship on metajournalistic discourse and conservative media frames discussion of how Far Right podcasters cast doubt upon the value systems of traditional journalism and position themselves outside of the institution of journalism in order to, first, delegitimize it and, second, position their journalism as the only acceptable replacement.[84]

Whereas left-leaning podcasts share the Right's intimacy and anecdotal first-person voice, they distinctly depart in terms of a greater emphasis on self-questioning metajournalistic discourse—that invites rather than evades self-critique—of the sort spearheaded by Sarah Koenig in *Serial*. The journalism of affirmation has been the cornerstone of right-wing podcasting since Rush Limbaugh's predigital talk radio days in contrast to the more heterogenous array of views encouraged and explored on left-leaning podcasts. Podcasting has been celebrated for its ability to provide a space for marginalized voices, as discussed in chapter 6, a characteristic that has been shown to engender specific forms of community-building and foster "subaltern counterpublics" that challenge and resist mainstream sociopolitical discourses.[85] In 2017 more than one-third of podcast listeners were non-white, an increase of 6 percent over the previous year. Two years later, in 2019, non-white listenership rose to 43 percent, with Latino and African Americans, respectively, at 15 and 13 percent, leading this sharp rise in audience diversity.[86] Although the 2014 blockbuster podcast *Serial* is routinely credited as initiating the rise of podcasting as a cultural phenomenon, Black podcasting's ascent took place roughly six years earlier. Through his pioneering podcast network This Week in Blackness (also known as TWiB!) established in 2008, Elon James White created a digital space for free-flowing spirited discussion associated with African American barbershops, beauty salons, and churches.[87] Intimacy and authenticity are vital ingredients in leading-edge podcast production, particularly for African American–hosted programming featuring outspoken views on race.[88] Escalating listenership, following *The Read*'s 2013 launch, was instrumental in expanding Black podcasts from six programs in 2010 to hundreds by 2015, including "must-listen" lists indicative of the genre's reach.[89] By 2016 Gimlet Media's *The Nod* took a different approach to *The Read*'s commentary on popular culture by systematically anatomizing race-related subjects and their larger sociocultural implications.

African American and Latino podcasting's ascent is among the most potent articulations of ethnic and gender identity and experience in media history, one reaching an unprecedented range of audiences, dialogues, and online communities. The cultural impact of ethnicity and race on the mainstream is also integral to Latino podcasts touting powerful journalistic storytelling, as in *Highly Relevant with Jack Rico*. *Latina to Latina* operates at the intersection of gender and ethnicity via the rigorous and unrelenting reporting of Alicia Mendez, "the new gladiator of radio journalism."[90] Podcasting's roots in public media is evident in *Latino USA*, which represents NPR's investment in the burgeoning community of listeners. Minority voices have become a major force in the digital publishing industry with programs that illustrate "the multi-social relationships that podcasts enable: relationships that cross socio-cultural boundaries, as well as international time and distance divides," as Lukasz Swiatek notes.[91]

The views and agendas of both right- and left-leaning producers and hosts shape podcast content, enabling a deep channel for articulating interests across the political spectrum. The interests of corporate brands are also powerfully articulated through podcasting. In addition to attracting more diverse listeners than any sector of digital news media, the podcast industry continues to be one of the most lucrative in online publishing, with advertising revenue projected to exceed $1 billion in 2020 and reach $3.3 billion by 2025, as discussed in chapter 7.[92] According to the tenets of digital marketing, podcasting epitomizes long-tail economics. Its proliferation of topics and subjects has followed a set of marketing strategies that views niche audiences not as liabilities and high-risk ventures but as lucrative opportunities. The extraordinarily diverse array of subcultures targeted by podcasts testifies to the sense that no audience is too small or remote to be cultivated through programming that captures and celebrates its dialect and discourse community. Podcasting is currently in a phase of radical experimentation regarding business models and potential revenue streams, beginning with the *Nerdist* podcast's live events and extending to metapodcasts, partnerships, product placement, and content marketing such as *Inside Trader Joe's*, evidence that brands have become podcast publishers.

The profit motive, however, may pose a potential threat to the principles of journalism, particularly for podcasts operating on behalf of brands as sponsored content or in partnership with supporting advertisers. Due to the relatively nondistracting nature of podcasts, product placement and content marketing have become prominent in the medium. Younger audiences are being targeted by brand-produced podcasts including *iHeartRadio First Taste Fridays with Coca-Cola*, which reports on the latest in the music scene including interviews with popular artists. *The Sauce*, from McDonald's, is structured as a mockumentary parody of *Serial* investigating the cause of the fast-food chain's widely publicized failure to stock enough Szechuan sauce at the behest of zealous online fans. *The Sauce* broke into iTunes' top 100, a milestone only previously achieved by *Inside Trader Joe's* among branded podcasts. The grocery store chain's show reached the fifth spot on iTunes with its series that has received popular and critical acclaim.[93] Host Matt Sloan begins the opening episode with the questionable disclaimer that "This isn't going to be a commercial."[94] Audio content marketing was established in 2013, one year before *Serial*'s debut, by a manila envelope producer whose *Keeping You Organized* is the first-known and longest-running branded podcast. A major consideration of this chapter is the blurring of the boundary between journalism and public relations / advertising, one that has raised questions since the rise of digital native advertising and content marketing production studios such as T Brand Studio of the *New York Times* and WSJ Custom Studios of the *Wall Street Journal*.[95]

THE PROSPECT OF A "NEW HUMAN JOURNALISM"

Despite the perils of podcast journalism, a growing number of programs have not only transformed digital culture but have also impacted the criminal justice system in unprecedented ways.[96] Through the use of methods that align with advocacy literary journalism, the podcast medium has emerged as a powerful channel for justice characterized by what Spinelli and Dann call "a *new human journalism*." Podcast journalism's personal storytelling modes acknowledge "the tension between fact and truth (or the tension between objective expression and narrative)" and "the inclusion of subjects and audience in the construction of journalistic narratives."[97] Its chief method is the rescuing of "all nuance, all the shadings that a realistic judgment of reality requires," as Arthur Miller described of precisely what was lost in Cold War culture.[98] Detractors of longform audio journalism often point to its unbridled pursuit of the ethic of empathy in journalism, which others defend as urgent and necessary for an industry that often dehumanizes both reporters and their subjects.[99] The debate echoes that surrounding the New Journalism of the 1960s and, more recently, the digital longform movement of the early 2010s.[100]

If "literature is an act of radical empathy," as Ayana Mathis believes, podcast journalism performs precisely this function, particularly through its fulfillment of the Hutchins Commission's original mid-twentieth-century charge for media to cover marginalized and underrepresented groups in society.[101] As a form of radically empathic aural literature, podcasting has developed a distinctive and unmistakable journalistic practice and discourse as "a genre of nonfiction that adheres to all the truth-telling covenants of traditional reporting, while employing rhetorical and storytelling techniques more commonly associated with fiction."[102] Emotion plays a crucial role in journalism, which is amplified in nonfiction podcasts.[103] Just as poetry became remediated through the aural medium of popular music, as illustrated by Bob Dylan's Nobel Prize for Literature, serialized nonfiction harkening back to the triple-decker novels of the Victorian era flourishes online through the world of podcasting. As Sarah Koenig quipped in response to the unprecedented success of *Serial*, episodic storytelling "is as old as Dickens."[104] Now episodes take on a daily rhythm, with shows like *The Daily* bringing all the medium's highly evolved and nuanced storytelling back to *jour*nalism's original diurnal principle as a record of the day, or *jour*. This responsiveness and adaptability of the medium is considered in the next chapter's examination of the newfound public-service mission of the daily news podcast during the darkest days of the pandemic in March of 2020.

CHAPTER ONE

Podcasting the Pandemic

Beyond the NPR Revolution

At the height of the COVID-19 pandemic outbreak in the United States, the cable television station MSNBC aired an interview on the evening of March 29, 2020, with journalist Trymaine Lee, host of the podcast *Into America*. In an effort to promote NBC's news network as a reputable, digitally adept journalistic outlet, the exchange publicized *Into America* as the network's transmedia storytelling extension into the world of podcasting, providing viewers a sampling of its content to convey the purpose and scope of the new program. It also offered a reflective pause from the dizzying procession of updated statistics and breaking news regarding the spread of contagion, its death toll, the battle to "flatten the curve," and risks faced by health workers on the front lines of the crisis. At that stage in the pandemic, public discourse had only begun to fathom the soaring unemployment rates that neared 30 percent by the first week in April, approaching levels not witnessed since the Great Depression.[1] Thus, Lee's report on the pandemic's exposure and intensification of systemic socioeconomic inequality, delivered via split screen with the interviewing anchor, supplied what had been missing from the TV broadcast up to that moment: highly personal narrative journalism drawn directly from *Into America*, underscoring the podcast's unmistakable advocacy reporting and progressive political agenda.[2]

Epitomizing the core characteristics of transmedia storytelling—especially content expansion, continuity, diversity, and immersion[3]—Lee told MSNBC viewers the story of Penny Wingard from his *Into America* podcast episode titled "Into Coronavirus for the Uninsured."[4] Wingard's predicament speaks to those of the many living below the poverty line during the pandemic, and whose experience has largely gone unreported both in print and broadcast news. The North Carolina resident's ill fate began with the termination of her position as an after-school teacher followed by a stage II breast cancer diagnosis. The ensuing bout with the disease left her immunocompromised. Once her chemotherapy treatments ended, she discovered she no longer qualified for Medicaid and also could not afford coverage available through the Affordable Care Act. Despite showing symptoms associated with the SARS-CoV-2 virus, and without proper coverage for testing and care, Wingard was forced to work to sustain herself, worried that she might be infecting others.[5] Her dilemma points to the vicious cycle of the pandemic's threat to the safety of the uninsured, who continued working while ill out of acute economic necessity. As an African American, Wingard was at an even greater risk given the well-documented racial disparities in COVID-19 cases. Blacks in Michigan, for example, were 133 percent more likely to contract the disease than whites, suggesting broader inequities in structural health conditions tracing back to redlining, according to the Brookings Institute.[6]

Lee's reportage of Wingard's moral conundrum and analysis of its political implications showcase the rich journalistic content surfacing in the latest wave of podcasts shaped by the coronavirus pandemic. This new generation of audio reporting bears a lineage in media history tracing back to the NPR model of highly contextualized, analytical longform storytelling driven by personal narrative.[7] With the category of Audio Reporting eligible for the Pulitzer Prize for the first time in 2020, podcast journalism has risen in prominence due to the quality of its reporting now matching, and in some cases exceeding, the entertainment value of its absorbing narrations.

The global pandemic has sparked renewed commitment to media's public-service mission and duty to democracy, core principles often subordinated to the pursuit of profit.[8] Public opinion surveys worldwide reflect a declining public trust in the news media as "journalists labor under constant criticism that they do not adequately serve their publics."[9] Yet during the crisis, that trend reversed suddenly as 70 percent of

Americans said the news media were doing well in their coverage of the pandemic.[10] Almost all newspapers removed paywalls—with the notable exceptions of the *Boston Globe* and the *Los Angeles Times*—to serve the public interest.[11] Many online news outlets nobly offered their products for free precisely when demand skyrocketed, a gesture unimaginable in other industries that routinely thrive on rampant price gouging in times of crisis, as with Florida hotels at the onset of hurricanes. News media thus demurred at the opportunity to recover a portion of its decades-long revenue decline precipitated by lost advertisers and consumer resistance to paying for online news.[12] It was in this climate that the quarantined audience downloaded news and news-related podcasts in record numbers. Podcast content pivoted with few exceptions toward advocacy, public service, and solutions journalism as the crisis occasioned serious investigations of unresolved systemic ruptures and the plight of those most vulnerable in the global crisis.

In keeping with this book's main concern for audio journalism's narrative turn, this chapter industrially and culturally situates podcast journalism with respect to the dual influences of the past and ongoing NPR revolution in longform audio reportage and the COVID-19 pandemic, forces shaping the medium's current use of narrative storytelling for public service. It explores how the crisis impacted news podcasting by accelerating its brief yet rapid evolution to meet rising demand for both breaking news and immersive storytelling. As a genre of audio reporting, daily news podcasting had already established itself among the fastest-growing sectors of the digital publishing industry for roughly eighteen months prior to the peak of the outbreak.[13] The sharp rise in demand for political and news-related podcast content in the spring of 2020 bolstered the burgeoning industry for podcast journalism, particularly in shows patterned after *The Daily*, the blockbuster *New York Times* program hosted by Michael Barbaro that reaches a colossal 2 million listeners per day.[14] The following section establishes the theoretical framework for understanding the industry for podcast journalism as immersive media that extends beyond the NPR revolution to the digital publishing industry and the rise of longform storytelling. Attention then turns to the impact of the pandemic on daily news podcasting, transmediation, and the medium's unique delivery of public-service reportage through personal narrative and progressive social critique.

THEORIZING THE PODCAST INDUSTRY

Although many new daily podcasts have entered the market, those earning the largest market tout a pedigree tracing to legacy media brands (whether broadcast or print), many with connections to celebrity journalists. As Richard Berry aptly observes, podcasts hailing from independent producers disconnected from this nexus of power are rare since "podcasts require an advantage, which often comes from being a brand, such as being associated with a familiar producer, brand or personality," including connections to powerful institutions.[15] Many successful shows bear news brands such as the *New York Times* and the *Guardian*, with formally trained hosts like Michael Barbaro, winner of the prestigious Alfred I. duPont–Columbia University Award in 2018, one of the most coveted prizes in the world of journalism. The market for daily news podcasting thus does not favor small and independent producers, an industry-wide trend established prior to this particular genre's ascent.[16] Despite the precipitous decline of local news during the pandemic that saw experts calling for a journalism stimulus due to a mass exodus of advertisers, podcast journalism, particularly among corporatized and legacy firms, has remained relatively stable, in many cases thriving on its renewed public-service mission.[17] The crisis shifted emphasis from content targeting niche listeners toward more general audiences, breaking down the silo effect of the media environment.

Although corporatized and legacy firms have increasingly entered the field, in effect widening the gulf between the popular and obscure producers in the world of podcasting, those powerhouse publishers have not established a complete monopolistic stranglehold of the market.[18] Corporate media continues to compete with born-digital companies such as Vox Media and independent producers that have combined to form networks of their own such as Gimlet, Radiotopia, iHeartRadio, Wondery, and Barstool Sports. Although less than 1 percent of podcasts are associated with these networks, their influence is considerable as they attract lucrative advertising deals and rank high on charts measuring audience reach.[19] The commercialization of podcasting impacts independent content as well. As part of a larger process of what John Sullivan calls the formalization of podcasting into a cultural industry, "commercial-style production values, audio quality, content genres, distribution methods, monetization structure genres now begins to inform the production practice of independent podcasters."[20]

Timothy Havens and Amanda Lotz's framework detailing the industrialization of culture is useful in contextually situating newly emerging nonfiction narrative conventions and tropes in podcasting content.[21] Various industrial circumstances constitute the forces that have the effect of circumscribing production autonomy, suggesting that the narrative renaissance in deep audio storytelling, which Berry calls the "golden age of podcasting," is not the result of autonomous creativity alone.[22] Such creativity in approaching deep journalistic storytelling for podcasts occurs within specific industrial parameters and with respect to certain overt company protocols made in response to the broader industrial context. Shifts in the digital publishing industry, led by innovative products, market competition, and external forces such as the pandemic, have shaped the trajectory of podcasting's increasingly immersive journalistic narrative content. As a result, a specific set of production practices and listening behaviors converge podcasting's immersive online storytelling modes with daily news formats, particularly deep dives reaching up to thirty-five minutes per episode, as with the *Guardian*'s *Today in Focus*. Daily podcasts are increasingly adopting the signature NPR genre conventions of personal narrative, absorbing editing, dramatic sound design, and reflective interludes for sociopolitical critique.

Podcasts deepen the way we engage with narrative, raising nonfictional storytelling to new heights. The medium contributes to digital longform journalism's appeal to younger, mobile audiences.[23] This chapter's focus on the expanded formatting and increasingly diverse listenership of daily news podcasts answers to Guy Starkey's call for more research into "the case of longer-form radio journalism," initially an ethical subject of critical debate in mainstream media, which has become a burgeoning academic topic.[24] Because of time-shifted consumption, news updates and bulletins were previously understood as ill-adapted to podcasting as radio interviews and discussion programs.[25] Past critical consensus understood the best-suited journalistic genre for podcasting to be the serial documentary, which leverages absorbing nonfiction narrative to expand on the stories behind headlines and probe deeper than breaking news. Now the signature conventions of the serial documentary genre have won a massive daily audience by performing precisely that function for daily news podcasts in the category of the deep dive.[26] Additionally, demand for podcasts produced as news roundups and microbulletins is also soaring (as detailed later in this chapter), sparking new innovation in production of these short-form genres.

The journalistic technique of humanizing the reporter draws on older forms associated with literary journalism that honored rather than restricted the narrator's subjectivity or presence in the story as a character influencing events. Martin Spinelli and Lance Dann call this a *"new human journalism"* rooted in "an *effort to understand* something, and at a deeper level, an *effort to heal* something rather than a desire to simply tell a tale."[27] This healing component was particularly evident in longform podcasts such as *The Liturgists* and *WTF* helping listeners—met by profound suffering and waves of uncertainty—cope with the grieving process during the pandemic. Humanistic journalism's characteristic dynamic is to explore how human bonds form "and what effect they have on both the investigation and the way the story ... is processed."[28] In the cases of Barabaro's *The Daily* and Vox's *Today, Explained*, narrative suspense and subjectivity are showcased in the reporting and writing process, and with journalistic rigor and an ethical commitment to drawing forth justice through the full exposure of criminal behavior. Programs such as Radiotopia's *Ear Hustle* and the *Washington Post*'s *All Told* extend into new territory the qualities of interactive storytelling and transparency that has characterized the development of digital journalism over the last decade. *The Daily* and a host of similarly structured daily news podcasts now build on these methods. Thus, narrative suspense, subjectivity, a commitment to justice, interactivity, and transparency drive podcasting's industrial evolution toward sticky content: material designed to attract and engage audiences, particularly mobile ones, who make up 69 percent of listeners compared to 31 percent on laptops and desktops.[29]

The rapid expansion of podcast journalism is reflective of the medium's evolution toward increasingly sophisticated narrative content. Podcasts have gained prominence as a powerful form of journalism vital to transmedia storytelling, a process clarified by Havens and Lotz's framework for media industry analysis directed at company protocols, market contexts, and production practices.[30] Production practices leveraging new podcast-specific journalistic reporting and writing shape program content as distinct from terrestrial radio broadcasting, print, and television news. The foregoing discussion addresses categories highlighted in Mia Lindgren's case study methodology for podcast analysis, including storytelling, emotiveness and empathy, craft and industry, ethical impact, and innovation.[31] The impact of these industrial and aesthetic factors frame the rhetorical analysis of selected podcast content. New methods of narrative technique, particularly metanarrative self-reflexivity, have emerged in daily news podcasting, which reflect innovations upon traditional reporting and writing with immersive storytelling methods drawn from literary journalism. New conventions rooted in public service and daily breaking news with an eye toward advocacy now intersect with podcasting's evolution toward immersive narrative storytelling, determining a new set of conventions and distinguishing set of characteristics of this emergent and suddenly dominant medium in digital culture.

"OUR NEW FRONT PAGE"

Barefoot in his cramped bedroom closet, wedged between clothes on hangers pushed aside to clear space for his laptop and bulky podcast microphone, Ira Glass narrated *This American Life* in March of 2020 at the onset of the COVID-19 pandemic. "Recording this week's show," he tweeted, "(well I closed the closet doors while I read my narration)."[32] Despite this rare moment of comic relief, the shadow of the pandemic loomed over news organizations. Initially, many "newspapers, television, radio, and other media services" listed as "essential businesses" were exempt from work-from-home orders mandated March 2020, such as one impacting six counties in the San Francisco Bay Area.[33] Soon after, news media employees began testing positive for SARS-CoV-2, such as ESPN's Doris Burke, CNN's Chris Cuomo, and a Vox Media staff member, which prompted the closure of all Vox offices as well as company-owned and-operated studios.[34] Self-recording in-home environments by *Slate* entailed distributing equipment to employees at their residences. Nilay Patel, host of *The Vergecast,* interviewed the FCC Commissioner Jessica Rosenworcel from a closet in his home, the results of which delivered surprisingly high production values. The hosts of *Grier and Leitch,* the

New Republic's podcast dedicated to film criticism, produced their show from opposite coasts in Athens, Georgia, and Los Angeles, California. Aided by rudimentary yet effective recording and editing technology, production required no more than laptops, the requisite software (a combination of Audacity and Adobe Audition, in their case), and microphones, with edited results sounding "like we were in the same room together."[35] Circumvention of bans from studio production during the pandemic was aided by what Berry identifies as podcasting's low technological bar for entry.[36] As with the smartphone technology's democratizing impact on photojournalism, the podcast medium originally eliminated the need for prospective publishers to receive specialized training in how to use complex broadcasting equipment while also opening up consumption from set schedules to time-shifted, on-demand listening.[37]

Remote podcast production outside of studios reached one of its widest audiences during the pandemic in the instance of *Solvable*, when host Jacob Weisberg recorded "Solvable Presents: Help in a Crisis" from his bedroom closet. The episode ranked second among Global Trending Podcasts for the week March 30–April 5, catapulting up 571 spots from the previous week, according to Chartable. The release of this unexpected introductory episode to season 2 of *Solvable*, published by Weisberg and Malcolm Gladwell's Pushkin Industries, responded to negative COVID-19 news fatigue with solutions journalism, a form of rigorous, evidentiary reporting responding to social problems. Solutions journalism augments the watchdog role of the press by providing avenues of citizen action that might bring about a resolution to a crisis.[38] Investigative news stories in this mode adopted by *Solvable* present evidence that entrenched problems can in fact be solved. The show's premise is that people want to know answers and have a clear sense of how seemingly insurmountable problems might be solved.

On this episode of *Solvable*, Michael Lewis interviewed Jimmy Chen, producer of the Fresh EBT app for individuals on food stamps, which provides users immediate updates regarding their current cash balance. Chen's initial investigations revealed that the essential problem with the food stamp system in the United States was not hardware but software. Many aid recipients owned smartphones with internet access, he discovered, but were still forced to wait in long lines for data that could be delivered directly to their mobile devices. Correcting for the class bias among Silicon Valley software designers, Chen's app met this demand, one exhibited by the fact that the most commonly called phone number in the United States is the 1-800 number for EBT card balances.[39] Chen noted that the pandemic's impact on food stamp recipients was particularly severe, as 88 percent had lost jobs, a situation in which the "pandemic for people already struggling financially is compounded."[40] This segment of the working class does not have the purchasing power to stock up on supplies. "People effected by disasters need cash more than anything else," he explained, encouraging listeners to donate to www.givedirectly.org/COVID-19, an instance of public-service journalism with a clear channel for audience contribution to a tangible solution.[41]

With a major shift from studio to remote podcast production taking place during the pandemic, including interviews with tech innovators and high-profile public figures, the industry was capable of not only maintaining but in many cases expanding its market share of the daily news media audience. Podcast journalism's investigative reporting through personal narrative storytelling is no longer the exclusive domain of serialized longform dominated by the true crime genre investigating past murders (as in *Serial*'s first season) or profiles of obscure individuals (*S-Town*) only tangentially related to daily headlines. As in a time of war, worldwide national emergency declarations shifted attention to daily news, which the podcast industry had fortuitously invested in roughly eighteen months prior to the outbreak. Once the fledgling sector of the podcast industry, daily podcasts have now risen to prominence, bringing with them the conventions of storytelling handed down from public radio and Ira Glass. Those conventions consist of narrative (defined as plot and human experience), analysis played out in moments of reflection on the plot's larger meaning, and commentary from experts capable of providing a critical edge.[42] The NPR template for journalistic storytelling was always integral to daily audio reporting. During the 1990s, for example, Glass reported stories "for NPR's daily news programs" that "had scenes and characters and plot twists, funny moments and emotional moments," as he recalled.[43] Now such narrative methods are vital to the success of *The Daily* by the *New York Times*, the *Serial* of daily podcasts.

The pandemic is likely to leave a lasting mark on the podcast industry and the world of journalism. During the pandemic in late March 2020, for example, Spotify noted "an increased interest in news podcasts" on its audio streaming platform.[44] In response, Spotify created a pandemic hub featuring podcasts separating pandemic facts from fiction produced by the BBC, CNN, and Foreign Policy, among others. Acast, the most powerful global podcast company, noted that during the pandemic it showed "record breaking listens (+8.4% globally) during the past two weekends" from late March to early April of 2020. This, of course, is a global estimate not specific to the United States, where morning commute (between 5 a.m. and 10 a.m.) listening plummeted 20 percent due to stay-at-home orders. Early morning downloads all but vanished during the crisis, shifting mainly to the afternoon.[45] Acast observed that the medium occupies "a far stronger position than many other channels—not least because the outbreak is having no impact on people's ability to listen to podcasts." Although Acast admitted that it was too early to foresee the future of the medium, it was "fortunate that podcasting is predominately a digital medium and that Acast products and services will remain unaltered."[46]

Quarantine culture actually lent itself well to established podcast listening patterns reported by Reuters in 2019 indicating that "the majority of podcast usage is at home (58%)," followed by "commuting on public transport (24%) or via private transport such as car or bike (20%)."[47] Across all nations, the Reuters study found "the main reasons for listening to podcasts are to keep updated about topics of personal interest (46%) and to learn something new (39%)."[48] A majority audience that previously consumed podcasts at home with the desire to keep updated and expand their knowledge was ideally situated to increase podcast journalism consumption during the extended quarantine. That is, the home-bound condition of the COVID-19 pandemic, coupled with the spike in demand for both news updates and edifying content, played directly into the strengths of daily news podcasting. Thus, the loss of commuters during the crisis may not have had the deleterious effect on the podcast listenership that many assumed.

Up First does not employ the sort of narrative longform storytelling *The Daily* has become renowned for but instead relies on a relatively direct adaptation of its *Morning Edition* aired on terrestrial radio through NPR affiliates nationwide. *The Daily* is crafted by an audio team of fifteen, including reporters, hosts, engineers, and sound design technicians, making it the largest production unit in the daily news podcast industry.[49] The significance of this unit increased dramatically with the onset of the pandemic from February to April of 2020, a time that saw visitors to the *Times*'s homepage where the podcast is linked rise from 328 to 569 million.[50] With respect to format, *Up First* lies in the middle of the spectrum of daily news, with spots ranging from six to fifteen minutes. *The Daily*'s twenty-five-minute program thus bears more in common generically with the *Guardian*'s half-hour daily podcast *Today in Focus*, produced by ten dedicated audio employees. The *Guardian* and *Times* podcasts not only share similar formats but also derive their predilection for narrative journalism from their backgrounds as legacy newspapers renowned for feature reporting and writing.[51]

Nic Newman categorizes *Up First* as a news roundup (six to fifteen minutes), double the length of the shortest genre of microbulletins (one to five minutes), which is designed for voice devices and new platforms such as Spotify Drive.[52] At over twenty-five minutes, *The Daily* and *Today in Focus* are classified as deep dives that share company with titles such as *Code Source*, *The Journal*, and *Beyond Today*. These podcasts attract "younger and better educated 'latte drinking' audiences," which are the envy of major advertisers.[53] Engaged time on these shows is much higher than with screen-based multimedia longform features, which struggled to maintain audience attention with the myriad distractions on the open Web. The *New York Times* broke records for engaged time when viewers averaged twelve minutes per visit to their milestone interactive documentary achievement "Snow Fall: The Avalanche at Tunnel Creek" in 2012.[54] The figure still towers over the current average engaged time on the company's homepage of just under three minutes.[55] By comparison, in 2019 podcast listeners engaged single stories between twenty-four and twenty-eight minutes on average in the case of the *Guardian*'s 80 percent listening rate for *Today in Focus*, the longest of daily podcasts at thirty to thirty-five minutes, according to Christian Bennett, *Guardian* director of audio production.[56] Podcast listeners thus remain with stories significantly longer than with even the most immersive screen-based counterparts.

Podcasting's roots in digital longform journalism innovation toward longer engaged time are further evidenced by the convergence of the 2012 breakthrough appearance of "Snow Fall" with audio reporting's efflorescence during the early to mid-2010s. The period from 2012 to 2017 marked major advances in digital design for journalistic storytelling. The renaissance in podcast journalism, particularly for longform documentary, is highlighted by the publication of *Serial* in 2014 (by *This American Life* staff in collaboration with NPR affiliate WBEZ Chicago) and *S-Town* (by Serial Productions, the producers of *Serial* and *This American Life*) in 2017. The year 2017 marked a milestone for podcasting, as *S-Town* took only four days to reach 10 million listeners compared to *Serial*, which took four months to reach the 1 million mark.[57] It was in 2017 that *The Daily* quadrupled its listenership from 500,000 to 2 million per day, just below the mark reached by *S-Town*. Programming aimed at sustaining audience attention has coincided with the sharp increase in engaged time with digital longform content among mobile users.[58] As the fastest-growing medium in digital publishing, podcasting was originally fueled by the success of public broadcasting, whose listenership has exploded since the early 2000s.[59] Nonfictional and journalistic narrative has never seen a larger and more versatile canvas than during the current digital revolution. From 360 VR to highly produced audio features, immersive online content is now capable of entertaining and edifying audiences with increasingly complex self-reflexive narrative content.[60]

Reading and interacting on the Web through a screen either on a mobile device or laptop of course bears the liability of distraction with other visual media and platforms, all of which are pitted in direct competition for the user's attentional focus. Capitalist competition in the digital ecosystem plays itself out through an attention economy in which the most coveted asset is the user's attention. As such, visual digital design for competing websites, articles, and news interactives function as technologies of distraction vulnerable to disruption by other similar media products, applications, or any of the myriad native, pop-up, and banner ads. Audio media, however, bears a more immersive quality due to its passage through a single channel that it completely fills without sharing space with other sources vying for the listener's attention.[61] The podcast medium thus extends the "cognitive container" the *Times* established with its app-like multimedia features that other news organizations, such as the *Guardian* and the *Wall Street Journal*, as well as brands such as Netflix, created as sponsored content.[62] Now audio has emerged as the leader of news media in engaged time.

In addition to attracting coveted advertising revenue through greater quantities of user attention, daily news podcasts also deliver a unique listening quality that speaks to the medium's depth. Attentional focus is requisite to a growing number of podcasts touting sophisticated content. Programs offering quality listening through deep dives in the world of audio journalism include *Against the Rules*, hosted by Michael Lewis, *Moneyball* author and former White House correspondent to the Obama administration. The show investigates the bias of adjudication, exposing the politics behind the committees who determine success and failure in the worlds of finance, art, philanthropy, and sports. Its publisher, Pushkin Industries, is led by *Blink* author and *New Yorker* celebrity journalist Malcolm Gladwell and *Slate* founder Jacob Weisberg, creators of the aforementioned *Solvable* podcast. The podcast *Intercepted* also offers deep dives featuring world-class journalism. The program is an extension of the investigative digital-only outlet *The Intercept*, founded by Glenn Greenwald, the *Guardian* reporter who broke the Wikileaks–Edward Snowden Five Eyes international espionage scandal. In addition to such investigative podcasts testing the limits of access, other narrative reportage leverages historical research, which looks to the past to identify future trends, as with *The Secret History of the Future*, hosted by journalists for *Slate* and the *Economist*.

IMMERSIVE AUDIO STORYTELLING

Research on daily podcasting by Newman indicates that deep dives tend to be adopted with greater frequency by publishers with backgrounds in print or born-digital media because the form plays to the strengths of specialists in feature and longform journalism.[63] Shorter genres such as news roundups and micro bulletins are instead the bastion of broadcasters, who tend to redistribute their content between news programs and podcasts. The case of MSNBC's borrowing of their own *Into America* content, as discussed earlier, epitomizes such repurposing among broadcasters. Interestingly, Newman's Reuters report deploys what I would argue is a necessarily broad and inclusive purview for what constitutes news in the medium of podcasting. That purview encompasses five categories: daily news and current affairs; talk/interview unscripted; narrative series, single topic; other documentary, many topics (which can be native or catch-up, or both); and audio long read (a native podcast that is a reading of a newspaper or magazine feature article).[64] *Still Processing*, a show dedicated to commentary and analysis of African American culture and politics by *New York Times* critics-at-large Jenna Wortham and Wesley Morris, would thus qualify as journalism according to this schema. Although the show ostensibly consists of commentary, it is not without a solid foundation in research and reporting that sustains conversation between hosts who dissect topics from white fragility and the politics of *Black Panther* to the logics of blaxplaining in blaxploitation films of the 1970s. As with most podcast journalism, these genres are not rigid, discreet, and mutually exclusive. *Still Processing*, for example, displays elements of both talk/interview unscripted and documentary categories. NBC, the *New York Times*, and the *Economist* all have invested in transmediating their news products into podcasting, in some cases commissioning born-digital programs to attract younger more diverse demographics who are difficult to reach through their home media.

Podcast journalism's extended listening times have important implications for the mindfulness the medium demands, suggesting a level of attention previously unheard of in the digital ecosystem. As podcast listeners actively discuss and share their favorite stories through social media, listening takes on a dialogic function in the discourse of online communities. That process underscores how "listening is essential to the engagement with most of our media, albeit that the act of listening which is embedded in the word 'audience' is rarely acknowledged," a point often lost on conceptualizations of "the public sphere, where the objective of political agency is often characterized as being to find a voice—which surely implies finding a public that will listen, and that has a will to listen."[65] Podcast journalism attuned to its audience represents a countermovement in current news media characterized by the perpetual decline of print sales and access to content by the news organization's homepage. These access points of print and publisher home page have been largely replaced by mobile strategies and "the ever-changing parameters of Social Media that directly affect the access and distribution of media content, the rise of podcasts, personalized news and content, video and add-blocks [sic] as well as the unstable ambient of apps."[66] Now podcasting, once a peripheral means of reaching audiences in a sea of social media and video apps, has become as important as the front page of any major newspaper or cover of a national magazine.

Podcast journalism now finds a prominent place, both sheltered from the visual noise of the online "marketplace of attention" and standing atop its leaderboard in the race for engaged time.[67] A growing number of companies have invested in attracting and sustaining audience attention through immersive media. Their texts aim not only to "surround users completely in a space of visual illusion" but also to achieve a sense of "being there" in audio environments.[68] In sound studies, audio immersion usually refers to the multichannel sound environments that artists and technologists favor in cinemas and installation artworks. In online media, technological dimensions typically define the concept, while in podcasting, immersion alludes to consumer interface, especially headphone-oriented listening. Previously limited to documentary serials, podcasts have developed new narrative techniques for daily news designed to leverage innovations in sound design, making immersion not only a factor of technology but also of journalistic storytelling. The higher levels of engaged time in this category, however, mean that it "outperforms other types of content in terms of consumption," as Newman observes.[69] According to Chartable, a company that measures podcast performance through analytics combining all major ratings systems for the medium, news comprises 21 percent of the most popular episodes on the Apple Podcasts chart despite making up only 6 percent of the 770,000 programs listed in Apple's catalog.[70] In France, an even greater portion of 34 percent, more than one in three, of the most popular podcasts across all genres is news.[71]

Like other digital longform media, podcasts often refer to their own journalistic process of production.[72] Self-reflexivity and transparency establish the critical distance and intellectual absorption associated with deep reading and the literary mind.[73] Sensory immersion combines with intellectual stimulation in "a context of cultural and linguistic exchanges, referring to the feeling of being enveloped by different social norms and engaged in an intense learning situation."[74] This challenge-based dimension of immersion refers to a "particularly engrossing state of mind, a concentration of mental resources in the course of a specific activity."[75] Building on the tradition of documentary narrative, daily news podcasts of twenty-five minutes or longer such as *The Daily* and *Today in Focus* feature probing investigations that challenge listeners, often confronting them with a moral dilemma of timely cultural significance. The core medium of podcasting is the human voice, with which "the best audio storytellers spark vivid movies for the mind's eye."[76] The podcast's power to captivate audiences for extended periods is attributable in part to how "people convey what they feel both through their words and the sounds of their own voices."[77] Its strengths accentuate the features Kern identified in documentary radio, which include intimacy, mobility, and space. Without space limitations, podcasts can deliver fully realized narratives without yielding to advertising interruptions and restricted arbitrary program scheduling.[78]

The concept of "the driveway moment" is central to the operational definition of immersive audio storytelling: a story so "inherently dramatic" and "compelling that it keeps you in your car listening to the radio."[79] Axiomatic of audio documentary's immersive turn, "the driveway moment" now extends beyond the car to mobile podcast listeners, whose screen-free digital consumption "doesn't demand that you point your eyes at it."[80] Just as "users often stay within the 'walled gardens' of apps" on smart phone and tablets, podcast listeners tend to remain engrossed for extended periods.[81] Listeners receive audio content through a distraction-free medium that encourages their absorption in it; there is no portal to the open Web via hyperlinks or other visual incentives to leave it. Witmer and Singer's seminal study on virtual environments found that "when experiencing a novel environment, people are typically more aroused and broadly focused," a condition necessary for a high level of presence in a virtual environment.[82] Immersive storytelling via audio documentary operates similarly to produce "the novelty, immediacy, and uniqueness of the experience."[83]

NPR PRINCIPLES IN A CORONAVIRUS AGE

At issue in podcasting's overwhelming impact on the world of journalism is the principle of fairness and balance in a medium rooted in "capturing and sharing stories that deal with deeply personal experiences," one that "carries a great risk of exploitation, especially when the lines between fiction and nonfiction are blurred."[84] Such concerns are attributable to podcasting's predilection toward intimate confessional modes that often combine with advocacy agendas openly pursuing the ethic of compassion and empathy in journalism.[85] The impulse to monitor such methodological liabilities is the forebear of narrative reflexivity—pauses for moments of reflection and genuine emotion—originally established in the 1990s on NPR and the work of Ira Glass, the luminary behind Chicago Public Media's *This American Life*.[86] This convention has since opened up new journalistic metanarrative self-reflexivity made famous by Sarah Koenig in *Serial*'s debut season in 2014. The method of opining out loud, following hunches, and reaching tentative conclusions should not be muzzled, Ryan Engley argues; rather, "it needs to be considered on its own merits and ultimately, pushed to inhabit its own ethical territory" that stretches traditional notions of journalistic responsibility in pursuit of truth.[87] Particularly conducive to the new ethic of transparency for journalism is the aural medium of podcasting, which foregrounds and discloses journalistic uncertainty in the cadence and valence of the reporter's voice. Such serial uncertainty characterizes the pandemic's daily news cycle, with its day-to-day proclivities of unresolved anxiety and tension.

The unique affordances of podcast journalism lend themselves to audio longform narrative, deep dives that are rigorously reported and edited according to the public radio longform documentary tradition. Music and sound design not only enhance dramatic effect but also support two key principles of audio reporting Glass identified as forming the foundation of radio documentaries for NPR. The first is to offer listeners a mystery or puzzle to solve, or "the *hermeneutic*, or *enigma code*," according to Roland Barthes, whose *S/Z* influenced Glass's early development. The best stories, according to Glass's formula, step out of the narrative and address what he calls "big ideas," concepts typically rooted in the culture's most salient learned debates, or "*the cultural code*," according to Barthes's schema.[88] These interludes of abstract theoretical consideration engage a macro level of awareness, emerging out of storytelling dense with data and delivered through self-reflexive, highly transparent humanistic narrative.

During the current era of unprecedented experimentation with the medium, not all podcasts have executed either this or a unique set of machinations for quality content. Deep technical and thematic flaws, for example, marred presidential candidate Joe Biden's *Here's the Deal with Joe Biden*.[89] Although many major figures in public life host their own shows, from former Democratic National Committee Chair James Carville's *2020 Politics War Room* to former ESPN celebrity journalist Bill Simmons, not all are comfortable in the role of host. Michael Barbaro's halting delivery, although ripe for satire on *Saturday Night Live*, exudes intelligence and careful inquiry, a sense of quiet yet determined journalistic probing that characterizes *The Daily*'s award-winning investigations. Vocal performance specific to the medium and comfort with interview sources are by comparison noticeably absent from Biden's podcast, which habitually relies on Zoom discussions, whose delayed rhythm and poor sound quality degrade production values. Leitch suggested Biden should turn over control to a cohost—"whatever [the producers] do, don't let Joe drive the car"—who might be more adroit at steering discussion.[90] The rhetorical mode of the campaign speech is not appropriate to the medium, and Biden typically falls into that pattern while speaking past his guests.

A major advantage of masters of the medium such as Barbaro and Trymaine Lee is a background in journalistic reporting and writing, one in which the art of narrative and interviewing coalesce with the appreciation for expanding on documentary evidence, a process by which the minute particular takes on greater significance. The arc of Bill Simmons's career toward increasingly literary and narrative journalistic forms, for example, mirrors the ascent of podcasting's status as the chosen medium for the world's most renowned journalists. His career began as an obscure blogger in Boston known as "The Sports Guy" prior to his adoption by ESPN, where he flourished as a broadcaster. He then pivoted toward print journalism on *Grantland*, the cable television station's boutique literary sports-writing website and quarterly journal targeting intellectual culture associated with the indie bookshop set.[91] *The Bill Simmons Podcast* is now the central outlet for his work, which continues *Grantland*'s tradition of reaching beyond the world of sports to politics and cinema through the audio medium.

Podcast content has reached a standard of quality rivaling the print feature, as seen in the regular transcription of content for reading on the Web available for programs such as *S-Town* and *Into America*. Testifying to the ascendance of podcast journalism as a source for quality reportage is its spread across media, a process of media convergence defined by Henry Jenkins as media merging in an ongoing process at the intersection technologies, industries, cultures, and audiences.[92] This process is evident in the appearance of *Into America*'s host on parent company NBC's cable television programming, referenced at the beginning of this chapter. In *Into America*'s transmediation of podcast content for cable television, host Trymaine Lee leveraged Glass's principles of narrative audio journalism.[93] In particular, he told the story of Penny Wingard as an emblem of the human experience behind a flawed political economy. Her life changed when her state, North Carolina, elected not to expand Medicaid, leaving her among the state's five hundred thousand uninsured. That population represents a tiny fraction (one-sixtieth) of the 30 million nationwide who faced the pandemic without proper medical coverage.[94] When asked for a final word before ending the interview, Lee emphasized that the current crisis exposed the urgent need for structural change to the current system's neglect of its most vulnerable citizens. Lawmakers and the medical insurance industry, through pressure from the public, can begin by placing "people over profits, people over politics."[95] Such analysis fulfills the podcast's mission of "connecting the dots between policies and voters across the legal system."[96] Personal narrative delivers what Glass would call the "big idea" in this case, rooted in plot and critical reflection.[97]

Building on the success of the *Dateline NBC* podcast, which ranked second in Global News for audience size across twenty countries according to Chartable, NBC News Media's *Into America* debuted in February 2020 with an episode on Michael Bloomberg's stop-and-frisk policies as mayor of New York City. It then visited the topics of Lindsey Graham's reelection bid against African American contender Jaime Harrison, a figure who had raised more money than any candidate for U.S. Senate in South Carolina's history yet remained largely unknown and missing from headlines. Resonating with these keynote themes at the intersection of race and politics, the topic of democracy pivoted toward its intersection with the pandemic via decisions in mid-March of 2020 to delay state primary elections. The next episode, on citizens such as Wingard lacking health insurance, was then followed by a third consecutive show dedicated to the pandemic's impact, focusing specifically on the physical distance now required at birth and death, the inexorable passages into and out of life usually attended physically by loved ones. Such abiding commitment to diversity is an essential tenet of journalism handed down from the Hutchins Commission guidelines that proved instrumental in emboldening coverage of alternative perspectives and marginalized social categories.[98] It illustrates "the tension between a classical journalistic ethics of impartiality and detachment versus a new human journalistic acceptance of attachment and impression."[99] The latter foregrounds rather than reigns in subjectivity, a sensibility tantamount to "a podcast consciousness for journalism more relaxed about its humanity" and more willing to leverage human emotion as an asset rather than a liability in the social matrix of reporting and storytelling.[100]

Into America demonstrates several important points about the viability of the podcast medium as principled journalism. The producer's intent, as described in the introductory segment, was ostensibly to be "a show about politics, about policy, and about the power it has over people," an aim clearly designed to leverage the medium's uniquely affective power to immerse audiences in personal narratives of the individuals from across the electorate to illustrate the human consequences of larger systemic forces.[101] This resonates with a key function of transmedia journalism to generate alternative forms of storytelling for the public to delve deeper into the story.[102] The medium's fluidity allowed for adjustment to the historic life-changing effects of the pandemic, as three of its last six episodes centered squarely on COVID-19 topics. The pandemic nearly subsumed all public discourse, including this podcast's original agenda as a series of investigations into the political system prompted by the 2020 presidential election. By cross-referencing its pandemic coverage with its relatively new podcast, NBC brought a Web presence to the story to encourage its spread through user sharing, in addition to offering more details about the news through content expansion, a feature known as drillability.[103] With the television audience exposed to the podcast, the dimension of continuity and seriality was introduced to maintain engagement within the same NBC news brand.

The cottage industry of pandemic podcasts responded proactively to the views and experiences of the public. The *Washington Post*, for example, dedicated its podcast series *All Told* to the pandemic. The program had previously consisted of feature stories ranging from the true crime genre (via a two-part reinvestigation of the infamous Rolling Stones concert murder at Altamont in 1969) to social issues (a living case study of universal basic income recipients in Mississippi) and the refugee crisis (a German city that refused to turn away Syrian immigrants in 2015). As with NBC's *Into America*, the *Post*'s *All Told* embraced its public-service role along with many news organizations. *All Told* recast itself from this eclectic blend of features well outside of the breaking news cycle to "sharing a special, ongoing series of firsthand stories from Americans living through the coronavirus pandemic." The podcast invited the public to share "how your life has changed due to the coronavirus outbreak" in order to "help us share first-person accounts of life during the pandemic," according to the *Post*'s online promotional material.[104]

As with the howling citizens engaging their nightly vocal ritual from the porches of Marin County, California, and with New York City's collective cheer of appreciation for its hospital workers and first responders, podcasts enabled the human voice to connect individuals in our physical isolation in ways richer and deeper than a 500-word print news story, single photo, 90-minute film, or 140-character tweet.[105] Although listenership for true crime podcasts declined during the COVID-19 outbreak, Public Media Marketing brands, including *The Joe Rogan Experience, Serial, This American Life,* and *Finding Your Roots with Henry Louis Gates, Jr.*, along with *Slate* and podcasts owned by Vox Media all reported significant increases in downloads.[106] Sports podcasts, faced by the dilemma of finding content in the wake of most sports ceasing, reinvented themselves as feature and investigative journalism covering topics of social and political significance of the sort associated with the feminist Title IX advocacy journalism of *Burn It All Down*. The WNBA draft, for example, took on new significance as mass audiences began embracing alternative, diverse sports coverage like that curated by *Longreads*, the digital longform aggregator for connoisseurs of narrative nonfiction. The pandemic sparked a new wave of genre boundary-crossing between news formats, prompting a power surge in creative approaches to public-service journalism. Narrativity regained credibility as a means of providing context and analysis to document the historic pandemic, building on *Serial*'s earlier "negotiation of new journalistic values more native to podcasting" initiated in 2014.[107] Six years later a new podcast movement emerged out of a state of medical and fiscal catastrophe, one whose new production practice and guiding principles maintain the "rigorously transparent" and self-reflective quality of the medium's origins in public radio, breakthroughs that established "a new set of ethical criteria for podcast journalism."[108] That ethical criteria uniquely equipped podcast journalism to reveal how the coronavirus crisis exposes and intensifies social inequality.

As the world stood still due to the outbreak of the COVID-19 global pandemic, the realm of digital culture boomed. *Slate*'s audio media division reported a 47 percent increase in downloads for the month of March in 2020, and Vox Media podcasts reached 50 percent more listeners for their shows, which include *Recode*'s *Recode Decode*, hosted by Kara Swisher, and *Recode Media with Peter Kafka*, *The Vergecast*, *Vox*'s *The Weeds*, *The Ezra Klein Show*, *Today, Explained*, and *Trumpcast*.[109] The pandemic's transformation of public life was evident in the disappearance of human presence from public spaces. Mandates to practice social distancing and maintain strict isolation in home quarantine occasioned the March 30, 2020, cover of the *New Yorker* depicting an artist's rendering of a cavernous Grand Central Station, vacant except for a lone custodian sweeping in the foreground as shafts of spring light stream in through high massive windows. The haunting image of this normally frenetic crossroads along with surreal *Times* video footage of New York City's empty streets resembling a bad, yet real, science fiction film signaled the sudden retreat from public life.[110] The *New Yorker* released a special *Radio Hour* podcast episode "featuring voices and other sounds from across the city" in an effort "to encapsulate this moment at the epicenter of the crisis."[111] Quarantine culture applied tremendous pressure on digital media to keep populations connected, informed, and engaged with the democratic process. As this chapter demonstrates, the internet and digital journalism were particularly influential during the global pandemic of 2020, with work, education, and leisure activity taking place online more than at any single stage in the history of digital culture. Podcast journalism's ascent in the years prior to the crisis ideally positioned it to provide richer understandings of not only the scientific process and social implications behind the spread of contagion but also the politics of managing closures, delays, cancellations, and myriad digital alternatives to in-person meetings and events.

The pursuit of an ethic of empathy in audio narrative journalism that began with *This American Life* in the 1990s now extends into the heart of the digital age's global pandemic, diversifying a medium previously dominated by true crime serial documentaries (the subject of chapter 2) with highly responsive public-service journalism. Just as the terrorist attack on the Twin Towers of New York City on 9/11 inspired new uses of mobile phone technology as a tool for citizen journalism, the COVID-19 pandemic occasioned new uses of the medium of podcasting, bringing it more relevance as a channel attuned and responsive to daily breaking news than ever in its brief yet precipitous rise. Podcasting in spring of 2020 became relevant as daily news, a medium originally known for its epic expansion of the audio journalism template associated with deep dives into remote lives and events deliberately drawn from outside of the purview of daily headlines. Quarantine culture dramatically increased dependence on digital media technology for human communication as audiences in extended physical isolation yearned for the connection, reassurance, and social intimacy of the human voice. Media history helps explain the rise of podcasting during the pandemic. Audio media's crucial role during national emergencies in the United States traces back to war-time fireside chats narrated by President Franklin Delano Roosevelt. The seriality and continuity of his thirty informal talks from 1933 to 1944 were instrumental in informing and reassuring Americans through the unique intimacy of audio narrative. During a time of despair and uncertainty, the medium allowed the president to quell rumors and clarify his policies through a channel directly connecting him to citizens, one unmitigated by newspaper owners' bias. Yet CBS executives, not Roosevelt, coined the phrase *fireside chat*, which the president eventually adopted.[112] Publishers continue to exert influence on the framing of audio programming and, thus, public opinion. Today's leading-edge podcast journalism, while bearing the imprimatur of its parent company, extends beyond the NPR revolution with its new connection to current headlines and public service.

Popular media's capacity to perform as public-service journalism is evident in podcasts addressing emergent and ongoing crises. Public service also plays a role in many true crime podcasts—the medium's key genre and product of public radio—that have informed court decisions and led to the resolution of unsolved cases. Inherent in the true crime genre are tensions between informing and entertaining, and between news and narrative, presenting serious risks that extend to the most reputable publishers. The following chapter thus considers the Icarus-like fall of *Caliphate* in attempting to claim the mantle of serialized true crime documentary in light of Madeleine Baran's *In the Dark*, among other true crime shows that uphold the journalism of verification in service to democracy.

CHAPTER TWO

The Perils and Promise of True Crime Podcast Journalism

Building on her previous successes in the field of investigative journalism for the *New York Times*, Rukmini Callimachi seized the opportunity to expand her work on ISIS into the world of podcasting. Unlike Sarah Koenig, who first approached the documentary true crime podcasting project *Serial* in 2014 as a career audio reporter with a vast repertoire of experience and skills honed on the team of *This American Life*, Callimachi had no significant broadcast experience. Callimachi's exemplary credentials in investigative reporting, however, traced her ascent from being named Pulitzer Prize finalist in 2009 for her Associated Press projects on exploited children in Central and West Africa, and again in 2014 for her work on al-Qaida, to her hiring that year by the *New York Times* to cover global terrorism. By 2016, Callimachi was named the winner of the coveted Integrity in Journalism Award by the International Center for Journalists. Her stratospheric ascent took her into the heart of ISIS, where she seized 15,000 internal files from the terrorist organization while embedded with the Iraqi Armed Forces, publishing the leaked documents conjointly with the *Times* and George Washington University in 2018.[1] During these years, she began interviewing Shehroze Chaudhry for a longform documentary podcast titled *Caliphate*, a project released precisely when *The Daily* had emerged as "the modern front page of *The New York Times*," the most downloaded podcast on Apple Podcasts in 2018, occupying the number one or two spot on Podtrac the entire year.[2]

Daily news podcasts drew on the conventions of narrative and feature journalism casting the reporter in the story.[3] The *Times*'s aggressive pursuit of podcasting converged with Callimachi's rise to prominence, situating her as the next Sarah Koenig and *Caliphate* as the next *Serial*. By 2020 the *Times* had acquired Serial Productions to form a strategic alliance with the producers of *This American Life*. What appeared to be a natural convergence of investigative talent and a legacy daily newspaper reinventing itself in the digital age, however, would soon end in disaster.

The exposure of *Caliphate*'s main source as a fraud occurred when Canadian officials arrested Chaudhry in September of 2020 for falsely portraying himself as a former member of the Islamic State. *Caliphate* illustrates how true crime podcast journalism can strategically deploy the genre's signature self-reflexivity established by *Serial* into transparency as a "metajournalistic performance" in which "self-celebratory transparency strategically performs boundary-setting, definitional control, and legitimizing functions."[4] The reporters' willingness to continue the investigation in the face of overwhelming evidence undermining Chaudhry's credibility—along with editorial's willingness to publish it—points to other similar breaches of journalistic principle throughout the industry. Producers often bend reporting in pursuit of thrilling narrative at the core of the true crime genre. Through overreliance on single sources leading to confirmation bias, which undermined foundational journalistic principles for sourcing, *Caliphate* marked the most significant lapse in the medium's precipitous ascent toward respectability as a form of serious journalism, one that promised to inspire new confidence in journalism in the face of waning trust in news media.[5]

More than just human error contributed to the fall of *Caliphate*. In addition to the aforementioned professional pressures and expectations Callimachi personally faced, institutional and industrial demands led the production team to sacrifice accuracy for a gripping story, a telling instance of the risks intrinsic to audio journalism's narrative turn. Industrially, legacy news organizations have traditionally approached podcasts within its larger web of cross-platform storytelling as ancillary or supplementary to the main print and digital newspaper publication.[6] Institutionally, *The Daily*'s status as the new front page of the *Times*, however, represents how the ontological reality of the massive podcast audience fueled by mobile and new media technologies has advanced beyond epistemological approaches to editorial news production.[7] The "tendency toward sensationalism and privileging narrative over journalism appears symptomatic of a gold rush" on intellectual property in audio media, prompting what one *Times* reporter called "a profound shift from stodgy paper of record into a juicy collection of great narratives, on the web and streaming services."[8] Podcast journalism's medium-specific pressures intensify within its unique position in the digital ecosystem, especially in the absence of an industrywide set of best practices tailored to such demands.

Beyond legacy media's increasing investment in true crime podcasting, an influx of publishers specializing in the genre sort into two categories. *Crime Junkie* (ranked third in audience size for U.S. podcasts in 2020 according to Edison[9]) and *Break in the Case* (produced entirely by the New York City Police Department) represent copcasts, a subgenre of true crime podcasting written and produced primarily from the vantage point of police. Copcasts thus function as a form of promotional / public relations media on behalf of law enforcement that undermines core tenets of journalistic principle and practice regarding sourcing.[10] By contrast, *Reveal*, *In the Dark*, and *Serial*'s third season represent a second category of meta-investigative true crime podcasts that perform the reverse function by investigating the investigators.

This chapter explores both successful true crime podcast journalism exhibiting exemplary investigative methods for bringing about justice and cases that violate core journalistic principles, often in pursuit of absorbing narrative intrigue. The following section profiles the audience for true crime podcasting to establish an understanding of the genre's aesthetic, reportorial, and editorial dimensions. It culturally situates the highly differentiated journalistic practice of true crime podcasting to highlight the ways in which credibility and verification are not universally homogeneous but are shaped by specific industrial contexts that reflect and refract audience expectations. Case studies then follow, the first of which focuses on how industrial context and publisher situatedness expose gaps in journalistic integrity, particularly in the *New York Times*'s *Caliphate*. The second showcases how true crime podcasting can fulfill its duty to democracy through the public service of holding authorities in the criminal justice system to account in *Reveal*, *In The Dark*, and *Serial*'s third season, meta-investigations anathema to copcasts engaged in "perpetuating a myth of an effective criminal justice system."[11]

THE TRUE CRIME AUDIENCE AND GENRE

Research indicates that true crime podcast listeners are "predominantly female, active, involved, and interested in the material covered."[12] With 66 percent of listeners holding a college degree or more, the demographic is more educated than podcast consumers in general, 51 percent of whom have earned a degree in higher education.[13] Female survey respondents were more likely than men to agree with the statements, "Listening to true crime podcasts educates me about the criminal justice system" and "I listen to true crime podcasts so I can learn about what could happen to me."[14] Civic engagement offers a means of psychological reassurance because "women have a desire to avoid becoming the victim of a crime and they want to educate themselves for a worst-case scenario."[15] Hae Min Lee, the eighteen-year-old Baltimore murder victim of *Serial*'s first season is representative of the genre's tendency to focus on female victims, a pattern tracing back to Dan Zupansky's *True Murder*, which pioneered the first wave of true crime podcasting in the early 2000s.[16] Print journalism continues to reinforce this tradition, as seen in the *Little Village*'s reinvestigation of Michelle Martinko's 1979 murder in an article that won the Best Feature Story Award from the Association of Alternative Newsmedia in 2020.[17]

Producers cater to this intellectually inclined audience by maintaining "extremely detailed websites, posting court documents, case files, and photos of evidence and people related to the case."[18] With 63 percent of users participating in "online podcast-specific communities," true crime podcasts invite direct involvement in solving cases, a participatory cultural practice that began with *Serial* in 2014.[19] Beyond entertainment, news and information are major motivations for listening to podcasts. The type of civic information true crime podcast listeners seek is much deeper and systemic—probing the core function of criminal justice institutions—than such data as Civil Service test information and traffic closing updates sought by visitors of police websites.[20] A 2018 survey of true crime podcast listeners showed 60 percent were employed full time, 62 percent were eighteen to thirty-four years of age, 66 percent held a college degree or more, and 28 percent held graduate degrees.[21] The extensive attention span of true crime listeners suggests that demand for these media products places pressure on producers to weave lengthy narratives in serial installments for longform documentaries to appease binge listening habits. The aforementioned 2018 survey indicated that one-third of listeners were "extremely likely" and 31 percent were "somewhat likely" to listen to at least three episodes to a full season of a true crime podcast at a time.[22]

The overzealous attempt to reach this well-educated audience of critical and active listeners derailed the process of production for the *New York Times*'s *Caliphate*. Pakistani-Canadian Shehroze Chaudhry showed signs of fabricating the story of his participation in terrorist activities, especially two chilling murders of hostages he said he committed in 2014 while with the Islamic State, leading to his 2020 arrest by OINSET (O Division Integrated National Security Enforcement Team) of the Royal Canadian Mounted Police. *New York Times* executive editor Dean Baquet, due to what he described as "an institutional failure," largely retracted (but did not remove) the twelve-episode podcast series and returned the Pulitzer Prizes and Peabody Awards that Callimachi and audio producer Andy Mills received in 2019.[23] Baquet explained that the *Times*'s senior editorial staff had failed to scrutinize the content of each episode with the kind of precision and thoroughness it routinely applies to its most ambitious projects.

With its peerless reputation in podcast journalism, *The Daily* provided an ideal platform for a public explanation to signal the *Times*'s established credibility in audio reporting. However, Michael Barbaro's interview of Baquet—his employer and the supervisor controlling his salary—represented a potential conflict of interest. Ideally, the interview should have been conducted by an individual who was not an employee of the institution being held to account, a core principle further compromised by the fact that *Caliphate* executive producer Lisa Tobin is also Barbaro's partner. In further efforts to mitigate the public relations crisis, Barbaro also privately contacted journalists critiquing the *Times*, including NPR's David Folkenflik, to request that they "temper their framing of the story."[24]

Media history informs the tensions and risks of delivering a credible investigative report packaged in the genre conventions of true crime, a process that played a major role in the demise of *Caliphate*. True crime is medium-specific, taking on different meanings in each of its historical moments. True crime magazines of the 1920s and 1930s, for example, had different audiences and cultural functions as texts than true crime books of the mid-and late-twentieth century, which still carried meanings distinct from the true crime cable TV and on-demand streaming video of the current era.[25] Although Callimachi had written investigative features using narrative techniques, she had not hosted a true crime podcast and thus had no experience in the genre's inherent medium-specific tension between crime fiction and investigative journalism. "We fell in love with the fact that we had gotten a member of ISIS who would describe his life in the caliphate and would describe his crimes," Baquet explained. "We were so in love with" this opportunity to construct a true crime audio narrative "that when we saw evidence that maybe he was a fabulist . . . [and] making some of it up, we didn't listen hard enough."[26] The siren song of sensational narrative in this case compromised the journalism of verification. By contrast, Koenig leveraged the epistemological instability of evidentiary truth and the pursuit of accuracy—even at the expense of narrative closure—as the keynote of *Serial*'s first season.

Ian Case Punnett builds on Jean Murley's concept of true crime as carrying meaning based on the technological features, affordances, and consumption practices of its users by noting that true crime stories bear a tension between pulp crime fiction at the one extreme and public-service driven investigative journalism at the other.[27] The latter is responsible for serving the public interest by narrating a version of real events to the public, particularly through "moral messages and social truth" as epitomized by the podcast *Suspicious Activity: Inside the FinCEN Files*.[28] Launched in 2020, this collaboration between BuzzFeed, Pineapple Street Studios, and the International Consortium of Investigative Journalists accompanies a milestone exposé of global money laundering, a project fulfilling podcasting's role in public interest journalism, which is vital to the function of democracy.

True crime serial podcasts, especially those in the documentary tradition of *Serial*, operate on a continuum between frothy sensationalized pulp on the one hand and sober forensic investigation on the other. The host's neutral, reportorial role often shifts to one of advocacy, particularly on behalf of victims. However, true crime podcasts can also focus on perpetrators, as in the classics *In Cold Blood, Helter Skelter,* and *The Stranger Beside Me. Caliphate* was crafted as precisely such a perpetrator-focused narrative.

Historical perspective illuminates true crime's operation at the edges of journalistic accuracy. *Caliphate*'s breach of principle can be traced to the *Times*'s relative newness to the serialized medium in which podcast episodes function like the successive chapters of what Tom Wolfe called the "nonfiction novel" at the height of the New Journalism movement. The true crime genre has enticed accomplished and decorated veteran journalists like Callimachi into exactly this conundrum of delivering a narrative according to the aesthetic of true crime fiction while attempting to adhere to the truth-telling covenants of traditional investigative reporting. Tracy Kidder faced precisely this dilemma with *The Road to Yuba City: A Journey into the Juan Corona Murders*, a book based on his MFA thesis for the famed Iowa Writers' Workshop. It disgusted the author so deeply over time that he bought the rights to the book to have it removed from circulation. In his youthful fervor to call into question the moral ambiguities of the crimes, he had grossly underestimated the risks of following too closely the killer's story for the sake of generating a book that read like irresistible fiction. The pulp fictional techniques, he realized in retrospect, had prevailed over the better judgment of his responsibility as an investigative journalist.

Callimachi's fall into a similar trap was not simply due to human error; her fall reflects a liability unique to podcasting in the true crime genre. In a series of interviews with true crime podcasters, Kelli S. Boling found that although the news function as a form of public education was paramount in the production values of the industry's top producers, including *In the Dark*'s Madeleine Baran, "none of the informants expressed any concerns regarding journalistic objectivity and advocacy," nor did they perceive any risk in "the likelihood that they might misinterpret the cases or manipulate audiences in a particular way."[29] Boling's podcast producers indeed took a defensive posture—not unlike that of the young Tracy Kidder in 1974—alluding to "the months of preparation that went into their podcasts and how seriously they considered their job of presenting the facts of the cases in a clear and concise manner to the audience."[30] Such noble aims to educate the audience on the criminal justice system, however, downplay the real risks of journalistic reporting and writing for the true crime genre.

Both Callimachi and Chaudhry succumbed to those risks by overreaching for the podcast audience, which is among most coveted in the entire online news industry. According to a 2020 Pew survey, those who depend on social media for their political news possess lower levels of political knowledge (with only 17 percent who are highly knowledgeable about major current events) than most other groups, second only to local TV news. Those with the highest levels of political knowledge (with 45 percent in the highly knowledgeable category) instead rely upon a news website or app such as the iOS podcast app that comes preinstalled in new Apple iPhones, slightly ahead of radio (42 percent) in second place.[31] Podcast producers have more control over their messages than producers of text and video. "With social media, journalists and editors have lost the ability to control the context in which stories are consumed, interpreted and commented upon," a situation in which "the imagined audience, as journalists and editors were able to envision it, has collapsed."[32] Because audio never appears in a disaggregated visual context, it can inform and educate at deeper cognitive levels, whether as news websites, podcast apps, or radio.

This broad canvas for richer storytelling and undivided listener attention promises lucrative revenue streams. "The need to make money," however, "has been a central consideration for journalists and news media from the very beginning of modern journalism" and thus "is not some nefarious plot."[33] Commercialization of the news has nonetheless diminished trust in the press.[34] Sensationalized gore has a long history of profitability in the news media, a pattern whereby "as the American press became more commercialized, media coverage became more sensationalistic."[35] Although true crime podcast producers cite the education and well-being of society as the driving force for their work, which is part of a broader attempt at restoring declining authority and public trust in news media, the profit motive looms large as evidenced by the growing number and popularity of true crime's more than 169 shows.[36]

THE ECONOMY OF NEWS LABOR

The profit motive drives an economy of labor in the *Times* that entails pre-scripting stories—particularly large-scale ambitious narratives demanding significant investment of time, resources, and staffing—in order to win the backing of editorial. Former *Times* reporter Kendra Pierre-Louis, now employed by the podcast producer Gimlet, alluded to an instance in which a colleague alleged Callimachi had "pre-reported in her head" a major story, "looking for someone to tell her what she already believed."[37] Although Pierre-Louis had "no insight" on the details surrounding *Caliphate*'s production, she confirmed that reporters of ambitious longform stories are particularly at risk for confirmation bias because of financial pressure to return the approved story rather than an alternative based on discovery of new evidence. She noted, it "is true of my experience working at NYT [that] you had to write a very detailed reporting memo to get your trip approved and God help you if you came back with a story that deviated."[38]

For *Caliphate*, financial pressure impinged on the accuracy in precisely this way. The key journalistic standard of accuracy, which entails "reliance on legitimate sources," was compromised due to the failure to maintain "checks on pure profit maximization."[39] Such economic pressure within the media system can prevent media from delivering what democracy requires.[40] *Caliphate* is the most prominent instance in the short history of podcast journalism of the media falling short of its social and democratic responsibility to serve as a means of civic engagement. The standard of checks on profit maximization entails that "decisions of which stories to cover, how to play them, how much to follow up, and the like are made more on grounds of professional news judgment than on immediate profit calculations."[41]

The decision on how to frame the *Caliphate* scandal was largely a campaign of strategic communication aimed at protecting the publisher's deep investment in podcast journalism. The editor's note and podcast interview with Barbaro on the special episode of *The Daily* titled "An Examination of Caliphate" amended to *Caliphate* explores the *Times*'s "institutional failure."[42] Without explicitly addressing market pressure and medium-specific properties of documentary podcasting that may help explain the flawed reporting, Editor-in-Chief Dean Baquet answered Barbaro's question, "Why the post-fact-check fact-checking?" a phrase itself that suggests a fastidious and unnecessary layer of editorial approval, implying that perhaps the *Times* had been excessively self-critical in their mea culpa. Baquet replied that there was insufficient "fact-checking, source accumulation, and source confirmation."[43] Mark Mazzetti, a correspondent specializing in international espionage and leader of an investigation of the *Times*'s handling of the story, found that Chaudhry had been under investigation for being an impostor since 2016 and that ample evidence of his fabrications appeared in posts on Facebook, which included photos posted by other people in Syria that he repurposed as his own. The *Times* story was reported while the Canadian law enforcement was conducting its investigation, which would end in its 2020 arrest of Chaudhry. Following Chaudry's arrest, his attorney announced that he would plead not guilty because intent to sow fear of terrorist activity among Canadians must be proven for a conviction. The plea does not claim he was actually a member of ISIS in Syria, nor does it attempt to refute that he perpetrated the hoax. It simply claims he never intended to propagate confusion and fear.

The Daily's inclusion of this detail regarding Chaudhry's plea contributes to the overall function of the episode as an appeal on behalf of the *Times*—a defense cloaked as a confession—highlighting that the perpetrator who duped Callimachi proved difficult to unmask even for Canadian law officials. Baquet explained that subsequent information researched after publication of *Caliphate* exposed the lack of follow-up regarding Chaudhry's credibility that should have taken place during the reporting process, a different level of indiscretion compared to a refusal to divulge information already gathered. "I don't think there was any fraud or deceit on our part," Baquet claimed; instead, "confirmation bias" meant "we didn't listen hard enough to the stuff that challenged the story, and to the signs that maybe the story wasn't as strong as we thought it was."[44] In the *Times*'s defense, Barbaro noted, "two—not one but *two*—government officials independently confirmed that Chaudhry had been in ISIS. Isn't that convincing?" Baquet responded, "Our sin was not paying enough attention to the counter-evidence we had," specifically that "his whole account was based on his having been in Syria committing these crimes when he said he did."[45] Chaudhry's social media posts exposed inconsistencies in the timeline revealing that he was not in Syria committing the crimes he claimed he did.

Not mentioned in *The Daily* episode addressing *Caliphate*'s violation of journalistic principle was that Chaudhry had been interviewed in 2016 by Callimachi, convincing her that he was prepared to divulge the stories of the atrocities perpetrated as a member of an ISIS terrorist cell because he was "in this window of time when he essentially thought he had slipped through the cracks," as she told the Canadian Broadcast Company (CBC) in 2018.[46] Callimachi maintained that Chaudhry recanted his claim that he committed murder to avoid prosecution. In Chaudhry's May 2018 CBC interview, he confesses that "I was being childish. I was describing what I saw," particularly acts of violence, "and basically, I was close enough to think it was me."[47] The subject's story clearly changed during the two years subsequent to Callimachi's 2016 interview when he claimed to have committed murder. Yet as early as 2017, the year following his initial claims, Chaudhry described in a CBC report only witnessing violence and not committing it. These warning signs occurred prior to the 2018 publication. Due to its status as "deep, big, ambitious journalism," *Caliphate* demanded greater editorial scrutiny.[48] Callimachi was not fired from her position as reporter for the *Times*; she was reassigned from her international terrorism beat.[49]

The newly won credibility of podcast journalism reflected in the inaugural Pulitzer Prize for Audio Reporting in 2020 received a serious setback with the spectacular fall of the *Times*'s award-winning podcast. The most ambitious podcast project in the publication's illustrious history appeared poised to capitalize on the medium's advance to the leading edge of digital journalism. Interestingly, anxiety about the tenuous credibility of the form at this early stage in its development toward becoming a universally recognized medium for world-class journalism is built into the signature storytelling convention of documentary podcasting known as transparency.

PERFORMING JOURNALISTIC TRANSPARENCY

Caliphate strategically performs its transparency "in response to today's authority crisis in journalism."[50] Podcast journalism is distinct from other forms of journalism in that the host/reporter is often positioned as an expert, thus building on the self-reflexive turn unique to true crime podcasts that began with *Serial*.[51] As with the murder mystery genre's emphasis on the epistemological instability of evidence for deductive reasoning, the evidentiary status of journalistic sources is central to documentary podcasts such as *Serial* and *Caliphate*. True crime's narrative convention typically begins with a body, which then sparks an investigation of the circumstances to identify the perpetrator of the crime. The drama in crime fiction aligns with true crime podcasting in showcasing the interpretive process that engages psychosocial, historical, and forensic considerations.[52] The detective is thus the main character in crime fiction much in the way the reporter appears as a character in narrative podcasts directly interacting with sources and mulling the veracity of evidence.

Crucially, journalistic podcasts diverge from crime fiction and nonfiction magazine and true crime narrative in the sense that scenes are often constructed through reporters interviewing or dialoguing with other reporters.[53] Those reporters often take over as experts, shifting narrative control and decentering journalistic authority from the individual reporter to a collective voice more representative of the industry at large. This convention appears in "heavily produced episodes" such as those of *Caliphate*, when "the reporters position themselves as a main character in the story by giving background information about how they came to interview a certain person or setting the scene through the use ambient sound."[54] The host may share their personal struggles with covering the case, offering a revealing glimpse inside the process of journalistic production for audiences.

The performative aspect of the true crime narrative rooted in deducing meaning from a tangled array of evidence lies in the reporting itself. This is conveyed either as a series of questions over whether to act on a variety of hunches and leads or as the culmination of them in a major conundrum, such as the one Brian Reed faced when his subject, John C. McLemore, took his own life at the end of the second episode of *S-Town*. The drama shifted from unsolved murders to Reed's own dilemma regarding whether to proceed or cease production. *S-Town*'s narrative arc turns on the process of reporting and writing itself through Reed's agonizing decision over whether to proceed. His decision drew criticism for exploitation of the story's central subject, which then led to a lawsuit filed by McLemore's estate against the publisher, Serial Productions, LLC. The suit (eventually settled out of court in 2020) claimed Reed and Serial Productions violated McLemore's right to publicity via the use of his name for commercial purposes (in the form of revenue drawn from the podcast's ads) without the subject's approval. The defense contended that the podcast is exempt from needing subject approval because it is "a public interest documentary work" of journalism.[55] According to the estate, details of McLemore's personal struggles with mental illness and life as a homosexual in rural Alabama (including his affair with a married man, which Reed divulged despite agreeing to keep it off the record) did not constitute "matters of legitimate public concern, nor were these matters that McLemore contacted Reed to investigate or write about."[56] McLemore became Reed's main subject, an enigma presenting a mystery of identity to decipher in itself.[57] At stake in this dispute over whether true crime podcasting can perform as journalistic public interest documentary was the lucrative revenue from *S-Town*'s 80 million downloads since its 2017 launch. Although the podcast ostensibly profits from the disclosure of private details—bordering on sensationalism packaged for lurid fascination—in McLemore's personal life, it was deemed a work of journalism in the settlement. Serial Productions CEO Julie Snyder noted the settlement affirmed that McLemore was "absolutely an active and consenting participant" in the podcast.[58]

True crime lends itself to psychological intrigue in which the reporter signals the listener's appropriate emotional response. Risk assessment is weighed through the reporter's decisions on whose story to believe and which clues to pursue. This first-person narrative approach featuring personal anecdotes and contemplative asides dramatizing such decisions is central to re-edits of broadcast radio news stories for the podcast format.[59] In *Caliphate*, audio reporter / producer Andy Mills operates as a stand-in for the uninformed listener, asking for explanations from Callimachi, who is cast as the expert. *The Daily* consistently draws on expert interviews from the *Times*'s own stable of print journalists who have written influential stories on the episodes' chosen topics. In essence, this turns print stories into podcasts precisely through the metajournalistic performance of transparency, a process by which the reporter's findings and their subjective—often highly emotional—experience of producing the story are of equal importance.[60] The listener can then enter the tumultuous world of reporting on high-stakes stories through the host's interview or dialogue on their reporting.[61] Self-celebratory transparency "omits as much as it conceals, carefully constructing a form of faux-revelation meant not so much to let the audience into the newsmaking process as to construct the appearance of legitimacy."[62]

The performance of transparency through podcasting is not without its commercial appeal, one strengthened by the authenticity that hosts convey through parasocial relationships with audiences.[63] Walter Benjamin's "Art in the Age of Mechanical Reproduction" provides a helpful way of understanding the commodification of transparency as an attempt to package and sell podcast journalism as a uniquely humanized, hand-crafted alternative to industrial-scale news media. That feel of humanized production is facilitated in podcasting by a sense of a relationship between the audience and the host. The illusion of two-way communicative intimacy is achieved through parasocial interaction that "intimates conversational give-and-take" between the persona of the podcast host and the unseen listeners. As with broadcast television, "the persona accomplishes this by insinuating the absent [listener] into his talk, thereby simulating conversation between himself and them."[64] Because "the conversational tone of the host can mimic a social interaction," listeners can feel as though they are being directly addressed, "causing the audience to automatically engage in mindreading, resulting in the development of these intuitive feelings and assumptions about the current mental state of the host."[65] Michael Barbaro has openly wept on *The Daily*, for example, a moment occasioned by the realization that his own personal biases had prevented him from reporting the full story of a conservative laborer toiling in coal mining industry in Appalachia. In this case, as with *Caliphate*, the power of the human voice conveys the reporter's emotional encounter with the demands of the profession.[66]

This uniquely powerful parasocial dimension of the podcast medium brings the additional affordance of brand lift and amplification. The performance of transparency in this sense provides reporters a way to "proudly advertise the quality of their performance" and "market the merits of their journalistic identity to potential audiences."[67] Transparency can be a way for journalists to reassert the boundaries of their profession and establish themselves firmly within them.[68] As David Ryfe points out, transparency has been tactically deployed since the nineteenth century to show journalism can be trusted and that the story is true.[69] As a key mechanism for managing the problem of certifying the truth of the story, the performance of transparency can define the uniqueness of the news brand to distinguish it from competitors.[70] To this end, professional print journalists actively resist the label of *blogger* and thus adopt storytelling conventions that elevate their professional products over those of amateurs.[71]

The recursive examination of evidence in true crime podcasting thus establishes professional credibility while also offering an opportunity to promote the publisher's brand. The news product not only delivers a story but also serves as an advertisement of the publisher.[72] *Caliphate* strategically appropriated a trope originally meant to disclose journalistic vulnerability as a means of building trust, particularly as used by Sarah Koenig in the first season of *Serial*. According to Koenig, building trust is "the main thing that you're doing as a reporter on any story," which entails "asking the audience to trust you: that you're being fair, that you're not cherry-picking information, and that you're not building something up to make a better story."[73] Although Callimachi made copious and emphatic observations about her own reporting and the documentation in the case, confirmation bias led her to cherry-pick those moments to build confidence in her source.

Transparency in news stories allows the audience to glimpse news culture's principles in action, particularly bearing witness on the ground, norms of objectivity, and the verification of sources and data gathered.[74] In addition to this exposure of journalistic culture, the serialized documentary podcast genre also entails self-disclosure, a ritual of personal confession that reflects on the individual reporter within that larger cultural milieu. This constructed meaning of the reporter's work within journalistic culture generates "greater respect for their work and will to concede epistemic authority." To reinforce this effect, especially through the intimate and highly parasocial medium of podcasting, "reporters can project their journalistic culture *inward* through audible or visible moments of self-reflexivity."[75] Transparency can perform a false self-check on journalistic credibility and method, yet one profoundly convincing given the high degree of parasocial intimacy in podcasts. Whereas moments of transparency in traditional journalism tend to be unusual, they have come to be expected as the narrative template for true crime podcasts. These performances of transparency expose audiences to internal practices in order to justify norms in the journalistic culture at large and the reporter's adherence to them in particular.[76] Deviation from this formula would threaten to unhinge the story's truth claim as well as the reporter's reputation and the publisher's credibility.

Caliphate draws back the curtain on the investigation—but only partly—to offer what appears to be a full behind-the-scenes revelation of Callimachi and Mills's reporting. Jokes, sound tests, and expletives humanize the reporters and invite the listener into a parasocial relationship as a quasi-production team member, particularly when journalists "talk about themselves, the behind-the-scenes of the investigation or journalism in general."[77] These imperfections signal to audiences that although this may be serious journalism, it still bears the markings of a podcast, once an evolving form of journalism emerging from the periphery of the media ecosystem.[78] *Caliphate* epitomizes how legacy media, once threatened by the advent of digital forms, is "reclaiming its place at the center" while also paying homage to the form's conventions of informality.[79] By inviting the listener into the investigation, the challenges and difficulties of reporting generate the scene-by-scene tension that builds throughout the narrative. Small hurdles such as losing contact with their main source, whose alias is Abu Huzaifa al-Kanadi in the podcast, are included to cast the journalists as the protagonists of the narrative. "The whole enterprise may ring more credible to listeners precisely because exposing momentary failures of the journalistic process seems more authentic than pretending that it is an infallible machine."[80]

Two momentary failures illustrate how *Caliphate*'s strategic editing allowed for Chaudhry's story to appear credible. The first, in chapter 9, "Prisoners Part I," depicts Callimachi and Mills entering an Iraqi prison in an effort to interview confirmed ISIS members among its detainees. After saying under her breath, "I'm now breathing through my mouth" due to the revolting smell of sweat, Callimachi noted in her request for interviews from the prison official that "I made clear that I *only* wanted to see confirmed ISIS members. And I do that because, according to Iraq's counter-terrorism law of 2005, there are only *two* outcomes of confirmed members of terrorist groups—life sentence, or capital punishment."[81] She wishes not to turn this journalistic endeavor into a death sentence. "The reality is that once you're taken into a prison like the one we're in, your chances of coming out are close to none," she adds, underscoring the brutal code of law that necessitates treading lightly with her reporting. In a confessional tone, she recognizes that boundary and the ethical dilemma it poses. "There are some people out there who would say we have no business doing what we're doing. The very action of coming into a prison and speaking to a prisoner could compromise that person's fate."[82] But she asserts that she has compensated for that risk through interviewing only those who are confirmed members of ISIS, thereby avoiding inadvertently inducing a life sentence or, worse, capital punishment. The journalist in her would wish to interview both confirmed and unconfirmed detainees, but she upholds reportorial principle here by recognizing the legal ramifications of work on a human life. The momentary failure here bears the legitimizing function of defining the boundaries of journalistic practice in order to situate Callimachi firmly within them.[83]

In the second strategically presented momentary failure, we join Callimachi in medias res covering a flurry of terrorist strikes that take her from London to Jordan and Turkey, her voice breathless at the front step of the home of one suspect and finally on a return flight to the United States. In the role of indefatigable reporter, her work is not done on the return flight. "After pulling up my notes and *methodically* going over what Huizega had told me, it was at *that* moment that I suddenly got a sinking feeling in my stomach—something was off with his passport." To the ambient sounds of Callimachi's team discussing the details of his passport with boxes of evidence shifting ("all right; oh, boy," one member grumbles), they examine its stamped dates as she says, "We went over *every* detail of what he told us." She explains that after interviewing "three dozen" of these informants, what is essential is "to find corroboration" because their stories are not always consistent. Searching his flight record, she finds that he never arrived in Turkey. "This completely blows a hole in his story," she proclaims, appearing to arrive at what we now know to be the correct conclusion.[84]

But this revelation is quickly covered. Mills sighs deeply and asks, "What is going on?" Callimachi, exasperated, answers, "I don't know, let's keep looking." With overlapping audio of their chatter dramatizing their scramble to untangle Chaudhry's story, the statement "let's make two timelines . . . to see where the inconsistencies are" surfaces to the sound of dry-erase markers squeaking on a whiteboard, with the scent of ink and copious notations evoked in the sound design. The journalistic process of production then becomes palpable as the scene unfolds in a "glass walled–in conference room at the *New York Times*," the reportorial equivalent of a forensic lab featured in TV crime dramas. Color-coded with fifteen entries covering Chaudhry's travel since 2014 with every single entry and exit, the team begins this thorough documentation. To reinforce their visual reconstruction of the event, Callimachi says "let's put everything we know on the—what do you call it?—squeegee board." Mills corrects her: "No, whiteboard," he says, reestablishing the visual focal point of their performance of transparency. Callimachi then pivots from the whiteboard to call a *Times* technology expert to attempt to pinpoint the exact geographical coordinates of a video of a man firing a weapon that Chaudhry identified as himself. They determine that Chaudhry claimed he was there much later than the time he indicated. Mills then ruminates on the ramifications. "What if this turns out to be the weirdest case of catfishing?" only without the romantic interest, but certainly a case of "someone online pretending to be someone else" by sharing details that rope others into actions with intense consequences. If this were such a case, he comments, it would be "the most strange and profound one I had ever heard of," implying that a hoax would be unlikely given its elaborate construction. Callimachi quickly counters that the felt details in their source's story suggest its authenticity because only someone who had committed these acts could describe them with such powerful immediacy.[85]

At this stage, Mills and Callimachi commit the unpardonable sin that undermines the credibility of the investigation. After certifying their reportorial credentials through the metajournalistic performance of transparency in the whiteboard scene, they undo the overwhelming evidence they amass from his passport data—and that of the visual expert's forensic work on a video, from which Callimachi confirms "he was there far later than he told us he was"—verifying that the source's timeline was consistently inaccurate. She abandons this evidence to instead rely on her intuition that Chaudhry struck her as more grim and serious than a self-promoting charlatan falsely claiming, "Oh, yeah, yeah, I was there when Baghdadi [the leader of the Islamic State] announced . . ." She speculates that he had been a member of ISIS and indeed committed the crimes he claimed he did but had simply altered his timeline. But this conclusion is refuted by the color-coded timeline on the whiteboard and the complete travel records that clearly indicate he never entered Syria at all. This is the precise moment at which the podcast embraces lurid pulp over verifiable fact, revealing the liabilities in true crime podcasting's tension between investigative reporting and crime fiction, between journalistic principle and a sensational narrative. "But not going there at all and making up all those ugly details about the tribesmen, about this execution, what it's like to hold a gun, to whip somebody," she insists breathlessly, her cadence accelerating, "about the fact that *the blood splashes back up on you.*" She then pauses for reflection. "That's a level of invention that's too much," she concludes, grossly underestimating the widespread availability of such atrocities—not limited to these but also including tortures and beheadings—easily accessed online. "He's providing details that nobody knows," she assumes, asking for validation from Mills, "you know?" He replies, "Yeah." The scene ends with synthesizer notes matching Callimachi's tone of intrigue.[86]

Callimachi then determines that "this is a person that needed help," and since she insists it is not the job of a journalist to turn individuals over to police, she instead refers Chaudhry to "a former Islamic extremist turned undercover operative," a reformed former ISIS member dedicated to deradicalizing individuals associated with terrorism.[87] "We are journalists; we are not an extension of law enforcement," she claims, invoking the principle of an independent press in this gesture of self-legitimating transparency. The episode concludes with a reaffirmation that his "*deep* insider, in-the-weeds knowledge" of the terrorist group was utterly convincing; Callimachi noted that Chaudhry said things "I initially didn't know, but later upon reflection and upon research, I realized were actually true about the group." Mills's question, "So what do we know?" is answered resolutely by Callimachi, who affirms that her subject's story matches the pattern of radicalization in Islamic terrorist groups.[88]

Captivated by the detail of Chaudhry's testimony, Callimachi's confirmation bias acknowledges he lied about the time he entered Syria but falsely assumes the question remains regarding when, rather than if, he had ever set foot there. She suspects he was in Syria and that likely some evidence will emerge to prove it, and until then, her "notebook remains open."[89] In essence, the narrative proceeds under the assumption that his story is true, yet without corroborating evidence. This is indeed permissible within the self-reflexive storytelling conventions of true crime documentary podcasting that candidly disclose the process of pursuing journalistic truth as dynamic, ongoing, and provisional. However, corroboration remains incomplete to the end of the season, in effect upholding the validity of his narrative.

Caliphate remains available in entirety for listening with a disclaimer voiced by Barbaro stated at the beginning of each episode. In it, Barbaro refers listeners to yet another journalistic performance, which is his interview with Baquet. User comments beneath the podcast's table of contents expressed shock that the publisher had not removed the story altogether. Callimachi's own confession appeared in a concise, prepared statement posted on Twitter in December of 2020. She alludes to transparency in the second sentence, interestingly, as a performance of transparency itself referencing her failure to be sufficiently transparent in her work on *Caliphate*. "As journalists, we demand transparency from our sources," she writes, "so we should demand transparency from ourselves."[90] Her personal anguish is foregrounded as "humbling" and "gutting," particularly in "thinking of the colleagues and newsroom I let down." The statement itself describes her process as being fully complicit with requisite journalistic principle in kind ("I caught the subject of our podcast lying about key aspects of his account and reported that"; "I added caveats to try to make clear what we knew and what we didn't") if not degree ("I also didn't catch other lies he told us" and, regarding the caveats, "it wasn't enough"). This *meta*-metajournalistic performance of transparency operates as a validation of methodological soundness while also confirming the extraordinarily demanding nature of the profession. The apology's function as a confession of flawed practice is clearly overshadowed by its disclosure of the overwhelming rigor demanded of investigative reporting.

Caliphate failed due to narrative priorities—aimed at preserving the established story through its seemingly valid and rich main source—that abrogated reportorial integrity. The *New York Times*'s own lack of editorial oversight of audio production allowed for excessive narrative latitude and creative license, which was compounded by pressure to set the new standard for serialized true crime documentary podcasting. The pursuit of prestige and profit took precedence over accurate reporting. These professional, institutional, and industrial factors profoundly influenced Callimachi's decision to trust her main source. Genre expectations for true crime also played a key part.

INVESTIGATING THE INVESTIGATORS

Callimachi's confirmation bias sought to reinforce the veracity of Chaudhry's story because it provided a rich supply of material for *Caliphate*'s central narrative while also bolstering its status as true crime saturated with horrifying violence. Since 2005, true crime storytelling has increasingly shifted from contextualization toward the "heightening of emotion and suspense, the juxtaposition of good and evil through the repetition of sticky words, and the details of horrific violence."[91] The more mundane reality of Chaudhry as a disaffected youth, immersed in online terrorist data and videos, threatened to undermine the *Times*'s expectation of a high-profile, revelatory investigation. For Chaudhry, the podcast presented an opportunity to tell lies to an individual with no authority to make an arrest. The rising popularity of the podcast medium makes it susceptible to a wide array of opportunists seeking an open mic. Crime suspects, for example, often seek out podcasters to defend themselves against potential charges when they discover someone has been investigating their case.[92]

Deceptive testimony plagues true crime podcasts, particularly those relying on single sources or institutions for the main narrative. This is exhibited not only in the *Times*'s case of publicizing a false confession but also in podcasts relying solely on the perspective of police. The principle of a free press is violated when the police—rather than independent reporters—provide the bulk of the evidence. *Crime Junkie* and *Break in the Case*, for example, tend to polish the image of law enforcement and "oversimplify complex, tragic cases" such that "the good guys find justice for the victims and the bad guy gets what he deserves."[93] These are "more summary than investigative" because they rely upon "official accounts of law enforcement as the factual backbone of a story," thus perpetuating the myth of a functional criminal justice system beyond critique. Shows such as Madeleine Baran's *In the Dark*, published by American Public Media, instead "investigate the injustices of the criminal justice system rather than extending the myth of its competence."[94]

True crime's historical roots in pulp fiction shape its latest digital incarnation in podcast form, raising the risk of compromised reportorial standards when serious journalism migrates into that online space. Audiences are more easily deceived by unprincipled podcast journalism because they are less skeptical of entertainment media, particularly publications premised on absorbing nonfictional narratives, which bear higher rates of trust than traditional news media.[95] The structural bias of true crime podcasts that reinforces the judicial system is abetted by the audience's parasocial relationship with the host whereby listeners are conscripted in the cognitive challenge of assisting their investigation. The host plays the role of detective in an absorbing narrative that can polish the image of the criminal justice system, especially if told predominantly from the perspective of one source representing law enforcement. Such storytelling is blind to the multiple perspectives of various stakeholders and institutional contexts of crime solving. Journalism's migration into true crime podcasting, a potent form of popular culture, can instead function in the public interest when the investigators are investigated, as in *Serial*'s third season and Baran's *In the Dark*.

Whereas *Crime Junkie* and the NYPD-produced *Break in the Case* are produced in collaboration with law enforcement rather than as independent journalism, which conceals rather than exposes injustices in the criminal justice system, *In the Dark* and *Reveal* represent how the true crime genre can strengthen the public-service function of podcast journalism. *Reveal*'s accolades include Webby and Murrow Awards and a commendation from the Center for Investigative Reporting for its report that eventuated in the closure of illegal work camps. The title, *In the Dark*, alludes to a lack of transparency in law enforcement, particularly among sheriff's departments. Host Madeleine Baran, an investigative reporter for APM Reports and recipient of a 2016 Peabody Award, has significantly advanced the public-service function of true crime podcasting. She avoids "rehashing gruesome details and psychological trauma" according to the "titillating, voyeuristic, and occasionally exploitative" tone of many true crime podcasts and instead questions the accountability in the American legal system in a more journalistic, subtle tone that shocks the listener without sensationalism.[96] Her work defies the common assumption that true crime should be dedicated to solving unsolved cases. As with her first episode on the abduction of eleven-year-old Jacob Wetterling, an investigation that led to the Wetterling Act requiring registration of violent sex offenders in the United States, Baran's method deliberately avoided assuming the role of crime detective and instead aimed to investigate the investigators.[97] "We weren't trying to solve the case," she noted, "we were trying to figure out why it hadn't been solved, and the consequences of the failure to solve it."[98] This approach runs counter to the convention of true crime podcasts focused on solving isolated cases treated as intellectual puzzles for the listener's gratification. "We shouldn't all become like amateur sleuths," she explained, "and forget there's an institution that we should be holding accountable, whose job it is to solve crimes."[99] As with The Marshall Project, a digital news organization dedicated to reform of the criminal justice system, Baran is less concerned with performing self-reflexive acts of transparency to justify her own methods than with revealing flaws endemic to police investigations, particularly at the county sheriff's level in the United States.

This focus on institutional reform is explicit at the end of episode 8 of *In the Dark* in the list of the least productive sheriff's departments in the United States, places where perpetrators of the most heinous crimes routinely go unpunished. The list implores audiences to check their own local clearance rate (meaning charges were filed without necessarily ending in convictions) of Part 1 crimes (defined as the most violent including homicide, arson, sexual assault, and robbery). Boling explains Baran's method of criminal justice reform through podcast journalism as a back-door approach in which "educating the public is the first step towards being aware of and/or initiating change," primarily by proposing and supporting new legislation through the electoral process for judges and sheriffs.[100] This brand of citizens' rights advocacy is voiced through solutions journalism in the work of Baran, an approach exhibited in Malcolm Gladwell's *Solvable* podcast that dives deeply into some of the world's most perplexing problems in order to propose viable solutions.

Epitomizing the spirit and practice of independent reporting, Baran's work pursues a higher standard for investigative journalism than true crime catering to lurid fascination for commercial gain. Serial Productions embraced Baran's approach in season 3 of *Serial*, which eschewed unusual, isolated cases (a forgotten murder in its first season and an AWOL soldier in the second) for an investigation of the broader criminal justice system, with the locus of operation centered on the Cleveland municipal court system. The shift from the traditional deductive logics of true crime opens space for inductive reasoning, particularly through consideration of deep structural inequalities within legal institutions. In addition to *Reveal* and *In the Dark*, a new wave of podcasts has entered this progressive, reform-driven branch of true crime podcasting including *Somebody*, a seven-part series published by *The Intercept*. The show follows Shapearl Wells's investigation, launched with the aid of journalists from the Invisible Institute, into her son Courtney Copeland's murder. Distrust of the official explanation for his death prompts her confrontation of Chicago law officials, in the process revealing racial disparities in volatile relationships between police and citizens. The institutionally embedded racial bias of the criminal justice system also surfaces as a major theme in season 3 of *Serial*, illustrating "the arbitrary nature of power at every level from street cops to judges."[101] As Charley Locke notes, "the oft-touted abilities of the medium—to bring a listener into a host's perspective, to tailor length to what a story calls for, to find an audience without a production company or a book deal—make it possible for podcasts to challenge our preconceptions," particularly in ways that "acknowledge uncertainties within the flawed criminal justice system."[102]

Among the most powerful permutations of true crime podcasts is their evolution beyond the self-reflexive performance of journalistic transparency, one that might transcend the presence of journalists as protagonists in the dramatic throes of solving individual crimes. Indeed, understanding the criminal justice system's institutions requires humanizing those whose lives are impacted by it, from the courts in *Serial*'s third season to carceral space in *Ear Hustle*. The latter represents one of the most enlightened innovations of true crime that leverages the unique affordances of the podcast medium to render a humanizing portrait of convicted and imprisoned criminals themselves. In *Serial*'s third season, the focus on investigative journalism forgoes the potential benefits of true crime's stickiness premised on storytelling that drives toward the possible resolution of a mystery. Season 3 of *Serial* thus operates "according to a completely different set of terms" than the conventional true crime podcast formula. Koenig readily admits that the lack of closure for *Serial*'s first season defied expectations. "It would have been great to have answered the question, solved the crime [laughs]," she admitted. "I think we held out hope for quite a while, and then slowly, we were like, 'We're not going to solve it.'" Koenig's producer explained that, in sharp contrast to Callimachi, "[Koenig] can live there, in the uncertainty, because it's the responsible place to sit." Koenig notes that this may have been the result of choosing "the right story, or that we just aren't the crackerjack reporters we hoped we were."[103] That realization turned season 1 of *Serial* into a meditation on "the shortcomings of information gathering" and the epistemological confrontation of "what's a human error, a mistake."[104] The position of uncertainty that frankly admits the inability to solve the crime may have been tolerated and even encouraged by *Serial*'s production team. However, no such result would have likely sufficed at the *New York Times* for *Caliphate*—especially if Callimachi had delivered a story of true crime in which the crime was anything but true—given the publisher's industrial protocol for ambitious stories to come out as originally pitched in order to ensure a safe return on investment. Callimachi, unlike Koenig, faced an industrial context, specifically as a *Times* reporter of an ambitious prestige project designed to build its reputation in the podcast market, that pressured her into pretending to know that her source was credible. By contrast, Koenig "didn't pretend to know what was solid, what was true," even if it resulted in an unsolved case.[105]

The public interest can be served by reinventing the true crime genre as an investigative journalistic form capable of educating and informing listeners not only about inequities and failures in the criminal justice system but also about their impact of human lives. *Ear Hustle* engages in no forensic explications of complex interconnected webs of evidence and launches no explicit argument on behalf of any of its subjects as victims of "bad raps" but instead aims to evoke daily life at San Quentin Prison. Along with Baran's aggressive advocacy approach, such innovations "serve as a check on oversimplified TV crime narratives, drawing back the curtain on systemic abuses of power," a process that advances beyond "the bingeable formula" of the innocent victim, nefarious suspect, and the satisfying denouement of the case closed.[106] Journalism suffers when the formula becomes ossified and succumbs to commercial pressure; it flourishes in its most publicly edifying forms when it deconstructs the power structure of institutions. As journalism increasingly explains its editorial decisions to counter decreasing levels of trust, drawing the curtain to reveal its own processes of production has become as important as unveiling the machinations of society's most powerful institutions.

The intellectual predilection, cemented by Ira Glass and Sarah Koenig, to confront ambiguity at the epistemological edges of evidentiary fact is consonant with the expansion of shows directly appealing to challenging questions in and beyond the realm of true crime. Intellectual culture's development through the podcast medium is thus the focus of the following chapter, which traces longform storytelling's cognitive range beyond traditional explainer journalism.

CHAPTER THREE

Intellectual Culture

Among the many forms of journalism that encourage intellectual thought, podcasting has emerged as one of the most potent in the digital ecosystem. Under various names including *analytical, explanatory, deep-dive,* and *solutions journalism,* audio reporting has provided a platform for intellectual culture that has undergone a renaissance beginning in the mid-2010s.[1] Prominent titles attracting active, engaged listening include *Vox*'s *Worldly,* which builds on the digital publisher's brand of explanatory journalism specializing in geopolitical longform storytelling augmented by historical perspective. Magazines catering to educated audiences engaged in learned debate have achieved popular and critical acclaim with notable podcasts such as the *New Republic*'s *The Politics of Everything,* which dissects the power dynamics of a wide array of subjects, and the *Atlantic*'s *Floodlines,* a documentary history of the aftermath of Hurricane Katrina. Independent startups have also entered the podcast market for intellectual discourse, as exhibited by *Public Intellectual,* which examines a new topic in each episode from the perspective of prominent scholars featured on the show. The embarrassment of riches in sophisticated content continues to import topics typically reserved for academics into mainstream media culture, offering listeners an avenue for public education—from science and technology in *Nobel Prize Talks* to musicology in *Switched on Pop*—previously inaccessible to news consumers.

The metacritical turn of podcasting that Dario Llinares identifies as inherent in the "liminal praxis" of the medium has opened up new space for examinations of the process of media production, particularly longform journalistic storytelling and its kinship to fiction writing as addressed in the *Longform Podcast* and *Always Take Notes*.[2] Media criticism is common among a host of intellectually inclined podcasts. Jill Lepore's *The Last Archive*, for example, lends the insight of an Ivy League historian in examining the interplay between epistemology, the past, and evidentiary documentation. Nicole Hemmer, among the world's most influential media historians, hosts *This Day in Esoteric Political History*, a show consisting of broad and lens histories depending on the episode, using shorter installments of ten to twenty minutes to examine American politics. *Citations Needed* deconstructs popular media coverage in weekly one-hour episodes, unveiling how unnamed sources shelter the powerful from criticism. Among other topics, the show examines how bias against powerless populations such as the homeless is woven into the language of news stories in "Incitement Against the Homeless," a two-part series including episodes 85 and 86, "The Infestation Rhetoric of Local News" and "The Exterminationist Rhetoric of Fox News," published in September 2019. Such criticism is consonant with Antonio Gramsci's portrait of the ideal intellectual as one who applies their intellectual pursuits to the criticism of the status quo and its maintenance of power over society's marginalized groups.[3]

The broad movement toward longer, more immersive media products that has marked the evolution of journalistic storytelling in the twenty-first century has brought richer cognitive challenges to audiences.[4] Among them are not only cultural-critical opportunities to examine media production itself and the formulation of historical knowledge but also scientific information that has enabled new understandings of energy, climate change, and psychology at far deeper levels than traditional journalism has allowed. The podcast *Nobel Prize Conversations* (formerly *Novel Prize Talks*) details scientific issues through interviews with recent winners of the prize, in the process humanizing intellectuals themselves while making their findings more approachable to a general audience. The show has performed the ambassadorial and diplomatic mission of the Nobel Prize by providing opportunities for social capital building via bridging disparate groups and organizations within, across, and beyond academic networks.[5] This emphasis on humanizing intellectual labor through compassionate reporting also drives the podcast *Beyond the Microscope* on the lives of women researchers in science, technology, engineering, and mathematics (STEM) fields. The show celebrates the accomplishments of women researchers in these traditionally male-dominated fields by showcasing their achievements and casting them in light of broader advances countering gender inequity in these areas of academic culture. African American intellectuals holding PhDs are presented according to a similar aim in *BhD: Black and Highly Dangerous*, which spotlights the scholarship and careers of figures such as University of North Carolina–Chapel Hill's professor Christopher J. Clark at the leading edge of academic research in race and politics.

This chapter examines the techniques by which scientific and historical podcasts leverage intimate narrative storytelling associated with feature writing, often through podcast-specific script/tape editing, to animate and foster intellectual culture for a broad audience. The first section examines such podcast editing methods in the case of *Invisibilia*, whose aesthetic repertoire rooted in *This American Life* and *Radiolab* established the standard for podcasts dedicated to explaining and exploring scientific concepts and their influence on everyday lives. Hybridizations of feature profile and explanatory genres of journalism inspired by *Invisibilia* appear in a wave of powerful scientific podcasts including *Science Vs*, *Nobel Prize Conversations*, and *Beyond the Microscope*. Podcast editing techniques developed for *Invisibilia* shape this sector of podcasts dedicated to illuminating the work of scientific communities as part of the larger project of fostering intellectual culture. Lukasz Swiatek's concept of podcasting as an intimate bridging medium capable of connecting disparate discourse communities informs discussion of the Nobel laurates featured on *Nobel Prize Conversations*.[6] The show effectively deploys personal narrative in ways that capitalize on what Mia Lindgren identifies as the unique affordances of podcasting for intimate storytelling.[7]

These podcasts explain and define scientific work capable of bridging knowledge barriers and sociocultural divides in ways that imbue "a questioning of the logics and effects of mediation itself," particularly by exposing gaps in mainstream media representations of scientific concepts and the experience of scientists themselves.[8] Such inequalities are made explicit in shows that simultaneously carry an intimate bridging function while drawing attention to inequalities that surround it. Next is a consideration of how historical podcasts perform a similar function by drawing listeners into the process of intellectual production and inquiry. *Floodlines*, the acclaimed *Atlantic* podcast dedicated to revisiting Hurricane Katrina from the perspective of surviving community members whose testimony often clashes with that of elected officials, is the first case study examined in this light. Attention then turns to *The Last Archive*, a podcast that also treats history in order to render critical insight into social and political processes, particularly as a means of dispelling the hoaxes, disinformation, and conspiracy theories that exert undue influence on public opinion. Jessa Crispin's *Public Intellectual* similarly unmasks media's role in generating public hysteria. The final section treats the podcasts of slow media publisher *The Slowdown*, which use the principle of time to deconstruct dominant discourse on industry, technology, and the environment perpetrated by government, mainstream, and legacy media.

COMMUNICATING SCIENCE THROUGH THE PODCAST MEDIUM

As traditional forms of journalism increasingly migrated into digital spaces previously understood as entertainment media, such as streaming video on-demand, the end of the 2010s witnessed a sharp increase in audience demand for what Nic Newman and colleagues term *constructive, solutions-based*, and *explanatory journalism*.[9] The explosion of demand for the documentary category of titles on Netflix coincided with the rise of on-demand audio in the form of podcasts. Like their video counterparts, longform constructive, solutions-based, and explanatory journalism are typically published according to the Netflix model of episodes packaged as seasons or released at consistent (often weekly or biweekly) intervals. This Netflix-inspired publishing model provided the template for podcasts delving into the long tail of intellectual culture. The niche topics of Netflix documentaries—from the probing exposé of the advertising industry in *Art and Copy* to the revelatory meditation on competition and human striving in obscure subcultures in *We Are the Champions*—now see their audio analogue in the long tail of podcasts that increasingly encompasses serious topics of learned debate offering a means of civic engagement. Science podcast production is consonant with the embrace of explanatory, constructive, and solutions-based journalism by slow media outlets such as Zetland, Tortoise Media, and *Republik* online magazine, which seek to "provide more meaningful, inclusive, coverage" for engaging alternative forms of civic participation, according to Reuters Digital News Report.[10]

The commitment to personal narrative at the heart of the most effective science podcasts has revived dull and stuffy nonfictional media forms of the predigital era associated with scientific radio reporting. Reporting abstract data through audio media risks alienating audiences, particularly if presented without attention to its historically specific context in which scene setting and human agency can animate its process of production and role in everyday lives. As one news consumer commented, traditional science journalism "doesn't get into my brain, because there's something about the story shape that just sticks."[11] Science radio programming has also been described as "dull," "boring," and "condescending," in part because "it lacks an awareness of human relationships that drive scientific work and that shape the way people experience science," in addition to the larger impact of scientific findings on the social, political, and economic exigencies of everyday life.[12] Compared to its terrestrial broadcast radio counterpart of the predigital era, science journalism has flourished in the podcast form, drawing large audiences that are curious, highly engaged, and riveted by narratives in popular shows such as *Astronomy Cast, The Guardian Science Weekly, The Science Magazine Podcast,* and *The Naked Scientist.* Science journalism clearly takes on the dual function of both entertaining and edifying audiences in podcasts such as *The Lonely Idea.* Host Rich Wolf interviews six Caltech scientists, for example, with one episode dedicated to each. Subjects engage consequential topics of social and economic importance bearing immediate relevance, such as the episode on Colin Camerer's research into how neuroscience can explain what physiological processes influence decisions on stock market trading and in other financial contexts.

The recent renaissance in science journalism enabled in part by podcasting primarily dates from 2010. Prior to 2010, inadequate coverage of scientific topics represented a major shortcoming of legacy media that potentially misled the electorate.[13] When reporting of climate change finally commenced, for example, many news stories carried the "detrimental effects of 'balanced' media coverage that depict climate change as an open debate between 'skeptics' and 'warners.'"[14] The journalistic norm of balance has played a major role in obscuring the scientific truth behind climate change and issues such as vaccination, which are often approached in traditional media as matters of open debate, neglecting the overwhelming consensus among the scientific community. Due to the temporal demands and the rapid rate of production dictated by the norms and routines of daily newspaper reporting, most journalists lack the necessary time and expertise to assess conflicting scientific claims. Competing views on scientific issues, therefore, often receive equal weight. Science podcasts catering to intellectual audiences correct for this problem by eschewing an undue emphasis on balance, instead situating scientific findings within the field of academic research on the topic. Early research on media coverage of climate change has shown that environmental and science journalists lacked fundamental awareness or a conceptual grasp of what climate experts considered basic common knowledge.[15]

In 2020 podcasts about climate change went mainstream, according to *Grist*, an online journal dedicated to the subject in its myriad forms from policy and activism to laboratory research and meteorological events. Also corroborating this claim was *Fix Solutions Lab*, a digital publication specializing in solutions journalism tied to networks of problem-solvers and innovators across industries. The "deficit model of communication" for scientists is no longer effective as a paradigm for communicating scientific discoveries to a mass audience. The deficit model, according to Faith Kearns, PhD in environmental science from University of California, Berkeley and specialist in science communication, operates under the assumption that "if people are given enough facts and data about" topics such as climate change, "then they would accept the science—in a logical, rational way—and decide to take action."[16] Although the deficit model accurately portrays the situation in the most stark terms of volume of scientific data available to the public, it elides the question of method, or approach toward remedying that deficiency. Scientific knowledge is not inert and neutral, but like any evidentiary fund of information, is more or less readily absorbed by audiences depending on how it is communicated. Beyond lexical choice for verbal or written expression, the choice of medium and platform profoundly impact not only knowledge acquisition but also the affective response that may prompt political action. The deficit model neglects the importance of nuanced storytelling in delivering scientific findings to a general audience, which entails an acute awareness of the "messiness of the world and the role that emotions play in guiding decisions," particularly, Kearns explained, the "other pieces of communicating that don't have to do with providing information."[17]

Beyond the data itself, other elements vital to the effectiveness of science communication relate to how, rather than what, information is being conveyed. Media framing refers to the emphasis of certain aspects of news stories, establishing causal inferences that can imply assignation of blame and culpability.[18] Tone is a literary concept that refers to the author or speaker's attitude toward the subject through the use of rhetorical devices such as simile, synecdoche, and metaphor at the sentence level, and ellipses and sliding perspectivism among others at the story level. Rhetorical devices associated with fiction are often leveraged in narrative journalism according to the tenets of literary journalism. In podcasts, tone modulation is both a function of audio intonation through voice, music, or ambient sound. Such manipulations of sound can enhance narrative tone through both literary devices at the linguistic level and through audio editing. The podcast medium can avoid the stereotypically dry delivery of scientific journalism through these techniques for adjusting tone in conjunction with engaging the host and narrator in novel ways. Kearns aptly observes that scientists have often assumed a condescending attitude toward the press, which results from the situation of describing highly technical and specialized information to a general audience.[19] The expectation that scientists are dispassionate intellectuals who occasionally agree to speak with the press neglects that scientists are also public citizens experiencing the effects of their research subjects. Climate scientists personally experience floods and wildfires just as immunologists are subject to mask wearing during the COVID-19 pandemic. Kerns points out that scientists, like journalists, bear a duty to democracy to inform the public of their findings, and in the process reveal their own personal experience and potential biases.

Rather than a strategic ritual of transparency deployed as a self-celebratory legitimation of the speaker's narrative (as discussed in the previous chapter of true crime podcasting), the frank disclosure of the researcher's cultural and political situatedness provides the listener valuable context for a more thorough grasp of the data's origins and uses. Skeptics of science advocacy claim that breaking the veneer of objectivity in science is an act of heresy, despite the fact that "true objectivity is impossible." Further, "the debate over science advocacy," much like that of advocacy journalism, "regularly glosses over that there are at least as many ethical concerns with standing on the sidelines as there are with engaging."[20]

The societal benefits that accrue from science journalism were originally touted by Benjamin Franklin in the United States, particularly in the interest of public health through reporting on the quality of urban water supplies in the early republic. Since Franklin, E. W. Scripps, founder of the Science News Service and Scripps Institute of Oceanography in 1907, was dedicated to ways of improving life through an understanding of science. He believed "the way to make democracy safe is to make it more scientific."[21] This tenet views the integration of scientific knowledge into society as a measure of strength and safety of democratic nations. Insofar as civilization is only as evolved as its scientific data, he urged the importance of building society based the most recent and highest quality information. "Modern civilization," he claimed, "is founded upon known data far inferior in quality and in quantity to what science can furnish today."[22] His Science News Service and the multiple scientific institutes he founded aimed to improve life through the understanding of science and therefore to promote the public mission of science as a form of service to democracy. In his view, a safe democracy is an intelligent democracy, and the key to intelligence is high-quality scientific data.[23] The current renaissance in environmental and scientific journalism, a movement that has coincided with the rise of digital longform and its expanding mobile audience now dominated by podcasting, traces back to the vision of Scripps predicated on the principle that civilization is only as good as the data its citizens can access. To strengthen democracy, it is essential to fortify journalism with sound scientific knowledge, a point Walter Lippmann emphasized in *Public Opinion* in 1922.

THE EDITORIAL CRAFT OF SCIENCE PODCASTS

Scientific podcast journalism is the latest, and perhaps most influential, expression of the vision of E. W. Scripps to furnish the electorate with the most advanced findings from the scientific community. One of the earliest podcasts offering deep dives into scientific phenomena was *Invisibilia*, originally hosted by Alix Spiegel, one of the founders of the iconic NPR show *This American Life*, and Lulu Miller of *Radiolab*. The show engages scientific topics that comprise "the invisible forces that shape human behavior," as Spiegel describes it, particularly the processes of "thoughts, emotions, beliefs, [and] expectations."[24] Prior to its 2021 relaunch, *Invisibilia*'s episodes consistently intersected with science as a means of accessing topics related to immortality, expectations, reality, emotions, and the impact of authoritarian tactics on the concept of trust. The show has since replaced hosts Spiegel and Miller with the duo of Yowei Shaw and Kia Miakka Natisse, both of whom were previously members of the show's production team. The move coincided with a relaunch of the show from pure psychological subject matter to a more sociological and structural focus in response to the new urgency that emerged from the social discord and political strife of 2020.

Invisibilia's original subject is perhaps best understood as what Ralph Waldo Emerson called "the infinitude of private man," as the show grapples in a deeply human way with nothing less than the meaning of inner life itself. With each episode focused on a specific category of psychological experience, Spiegel's approach is deliberately nondidactic, closer in treatment of evidence to the questing agnosticism that Sarah Koenig would make famous on *Serial* in 2014. The show's deliberate refusal to fabricate a false sense of closure invites readers to continue exploring according to an open-minded quest for meaning rather than resting content on easy answers. According to Spiegel, "a typical *Invisibilia* ending ... doesn't have a strong authoritative position about what to think, it simply describes." She admits, "it's not that I wouldn't *love* to have clear answers to tell people what to think and believe, but I simply don't have them."[25] This honest intellectual predisposition combined with a thirst for knowledge—which has made Spiegel after decades of reporting "humbler about what I feel like I know rather than less"—is evoked in the editorial process for the show, particularly the innovative orchestration of scripted material with recorded tape, ambient sound, and music.[26]

Among the most important developments in the evolution of science podcasting was the editorial method for the production of *Invisibilia*. The approach transformed otherwise obscure and abstract psychological concepts into accessible concepts through narratives rooted in lived experience. The show effectively humanizes cognitive, neurological, and behavioral science through the immediacy of the podcast medium via the transitions between script (prewritten material delivered by the host) and tape (unscripted interview material). These transitional techniques are instrumental in shaping each episode's narrative tone unique to its subject while also capturing and communicating the spirit of restless intellectual curiosity that refuses the complacent stance provided by pat answers to complex psychological phenomena. The emotional tone of the writing puts a human face on facets of psychosocial behavior science, bringing nuance and felt detail through intimate portraits of subjects in their natural environments. One *Invisibilia* episode about the psychological disorder of touch synesthesia is particularly effective at modulating narrative tone through editorial transitions between tape and script. Traditional hard-news reporting uses a formal tone for the script in order to distance the reporter from the subject. That distance is further reinforced in the transition to tape, when the reporter introduces it by announcing the full name of the speaker. The script then takes over at the completion of the tape, continuing primarily on this alternating pattern between the two, with formal introductions. The episode, which is representative of most on *Invisibilia*, instead uses less formal and more intimate script writing in order to align with tape that probed "deep inside people's heads and heads and hearts." The use of first-person "brought the reporter closer to the listener" to hear their "real reactions, their wonder, their laughter, their anger," as Spiegel explains of a technique drawn from Ira Glass's *This American Life*.[27]

In addition to *Invisibilia*'s Ira Glass–inspired approach to informal script writing to humanize reporters and hosts—combined with tape gathered to reveal the emotional depth in subjects—is the use of music, pauses, ambient sound, and tape-to-tape intercutting techniques also developed on *This American Life*. These transitions enable greater control of pacing for dramatic effect. *Radiolab* innovated upon this method further by using improvised conversation only (or scripted to sound as if improvised) rather than traditional prewritten scripted narration. *Radiolab* functions like a radio drama in that the major figures of each episode are introduced in the opening segment as a play would its dramatis personae. This enables a "seamless interweave between their voices without feeling the need to always reidentify which person is talking," as Spiegel notes.[28] Unmitigated interaction in this manner in effect repositions the host and reporter into the mix of characters, as their voices are not marked as different from those of the subjects in the story. This allows their intellectual reactions to be central to the story, particularly as a tool for dramatizing the jagged fits and starts of intellectual inquiry. *Radiolab*'s radical innovation therefore positions the reporter as a character in the story precisely by liberating them from the role of introducing tape. On *Radiolab*, the tape bursts through and ruptures the improvised speech of the host. Spiegel makes explicit that the spectrum between traditional scripted hard-news reporting and the radio drama formatting of *Radiolab* all contain potential to navigate and explore the inner lives of subjects. The fantasies and personal lives can be treated even in a traditional format as long as the subjects are covered with the same attention to psychological and emotional nuance that Gay Talese made famous in his feature writing. Modulating tone is the key to literary journalism in podcasting, "a matter of finding a way into the viewpoint of the person whose story you're telling, like fiction writers do."[29]

The *Invisibilia* episode "Entanglement" on mirror-touch synesthesia operates in precisely this manner, diving deeply into the inner life of its afflicted subject, referred to as Amanda. Suffering from a neurological disease that manifests itself as a bizarre form of excessive compassion, Amanda cannot see another individual being touched without feeling it on her own body, a situation akin to a science fiction scenario.[30] The challenge in the episode was to capture the human experience of Amanda while also delivering the hard scientific data on the disease's function and effect. In addition to *This American Life* and *Radiolab*-inspired editing techniques, humor and informality provided vital tools for the *Invisibilia* production team to disarm potential skeptics and to explain complex scientific concepts as "unthreatening, accessible, and easy to track for a general audience."[31] Mirror-touch synesthesia occurs as a form of quantum entanglement (hence the episode title "Entanglement") at the atomic level. After introducing Amanda, attention turns to the question of whether this bizarre inner life—in which a child falling from a grocery cart will send her into excruciating pain—is actually sensory or purely imagined.

The episode's script-to-tape editing deftly transitions to the science, which casts the explanation of this rare condition in clear light. After splicing in a brief side comment from a neuroscientist at the University of London on the matter, the hosts joke that they were "*yearning* for the authority of a British person right now." The scientist then points out that whereas mirror neuron systems operate in all people, in Amada's case, they are overexcitable and overreact when activated. The moment of scientific insight bears as much meaning for the human condition and the universality of compassion as a fact of human neurophysiology. When the University of London team observed subjects with Amanda's condition watching others being touched, "the touch centers of their brain go wild."[32] The tape cuts to the scientist confirming that since we all have mirror neurons, "we do kind of automatically slip into the shoes of other people, and we're not consciously aware of that," bringing emphasis to the episode's controlling metaphor of compassion, as defined through science, narrative, and humanistic audio reporting in the tradition of *This American Life* and *Radiolab*.[33] Amanda's extraordinary power of perception that according to a cursory understanding might be construed paradoxically as a gift is something of a curse that hampers this woman's ability to function in normal society. Mirror neurons evoke the core function of personal narrative in podcasts themselves; we feel *her* feeling the sensation of others too much, a point that highlights by implication the power of podcasting to perform its own version of touch synesthesia, only through audio rather than visual cues.[34]

The longform interview format of *Nobel Prize Conversations* shares *Invisibilia*'s aim of making complicated scientific concepts unthreatening and accessible. The show first launched in 2013 as *Nobel Prize Talks* with thirty episodes through 2017. After its relaunch as *Nobel Prize Conversations* in January 2020, nineteen episodes appeared in only eighteen months, nearly doubling the rate of release time from roughly five or six episodes per year to more than ten per year (as ten-part seasons). The producers thus doubled their investment in the show precisely when demand for intellectual podcasts exploded. Due to this podcast, the general public can access more intimate and nuanced renditions of the research of Nobel laureates than during previous eras of media history. In this portrait gallery of world-class intellects, interviews render subjects with nuance and complexity typically reserved for feature profile journalism. Listeners are made to feel as though they are part of the interview through the intimate conversation between host Adam Smith and an award-winning scientist. Access to the inner thoughts of Nobel laureates on the show is achieved through a dynamic referred to as double articulation, which is talk between both a person and the person spoken to *and* between this talk and the audience.[35] Headphone listening, which is more common to podcasts than radio, enables technological immersion for a sense of presence or "being there" with the host and interviewee.[36]

Due to "their intimate, personal and often-conversational nature, podcast episodes can help individuals of different educational levels cross disciplinary boundaries easily," an attribute that lends itself well to the public outreach program protocols behind the production of *Nobel Prize Conversations*.[37] As Robert C. McDougal observes, just as "viewing experiences can be attended by a powerful sense of *being there*, it can be even more enveloping with words spoken to us through a pair of earphones."[38] Unlike visual media that always signals its artifice through the noticeable mediation of delivery device technology via the screen, audio delivered through earbuds is both frictionless and invisible, literally words whispered in the ears of the listener. The sense of "getting inside someone's head" makes mobile listening extremely adept at approximating "having someone speaking to/with you while walking, sitting, or standing next to you."[39] This uniquely intimate affordance of the podcast medium is particularly potent as a means of fostering intellectual culture when the head the listener enters is that of a Nobel laureate.

Nobel Prize Conversations effectively performs as a form of public pedagogy. Along with other newer media forms, such podcasts can increase "the efforts of individuals, groups, and institutions to deploy the pedagogical potential of the new media in constructing new knowledge."[40] The podcast brings elite scientific research into "those public spheres" that Henry Giroux describes as digital spaces "where the formative culture necessary for creating educated and informed citizens can develop and flourish."[41] The parasocial relationships of *Nobel Prize Conversations* transcend the individual level of the personal consumer's experience with the show's function as a bridging medium, a process in which "parasocial relationships become multisocial relationships."[42] Connections are encouraged within and across intellectual communities, mainly through the practice of linking the podcast or individual episodes of topical interest on various websites. For example, websites for advocacy groups on behalf of public health and immunology research (such as the American Association of Immunologists and the Australian Academy of Science) provide links to 1996 Nobel laureate Peter Doherty. The biomedical researcher's interview was featured on *Nobel Prize Conversations* during the height of the COVID-19 pandemic, given the pertinence of his work on how immune systems recognize virus-ridden cells. Although dedicated primarily to showcasing the lives and works of newly named laureates, *Nobel Prize Conversations* uses the flexibility of podcast content programming by featuring past prize recipients based on the salience of their work to urgent current affairs. Host Adam Smith and his production team's decision to interview Doherty, for example, arose during the long, pre-vaccine winter of the pandemic in February of 2021. The decision to feature Doherty on the show at that time can be construed as a form of solutions journalism, defined as reporting that "contributes to a more accurate and balanced media landscape by informing the public about growth and progress as much as conflict and tragedy."[43] The show circulated widely through social media, enabling listeners "to connect with new, and even difficult, subjects beyond their regular areas of interest and expertise, by engaging them in easily digestible material through the intentional and conscious social act of listening."[44]

Donna Strickland, the featured Nobel Laureate of a March 2021 episode, is distinguished as the first woman to win the prize in the field of physics. Host Adam Smith's interview of Strickland proceeds without the elaborate tape/script transitional techniques of *Invisibilia*, instead allowing Strickland to express her personal and professional narratives without editorial intervention. This episode is representative of how the show bridges intellectual sociocultural divides by demystifying the lives of elite scientists. We learn, for example, that Strickland's father saved a newspaper on the day she was born as a kind of time capsule kept in a sealed bag with other memorabilia. As her career in physics began to take shape in graduate school, her mother discovered that the issue of the newspaper contained a feature story on a woman graduate from an elite scientific program, yet the story was framed patronizingly according to retrograde gender politics of the time. The story foretold the considerable cultural barriers Strickland would face while motivating her to defy such assumptions regarding women's aptitude for scientific research. She never deviated from her desire to earn a doctorate in physics despite being told upon entrance to graduate school that if she had any other ambitious to pursue them instead.[45] Her most significant research discovery regarding short-frequency laser transmission, she revealed, appeared in the first paper she published as a graduate student thirty-three years prior to her award. The passage of time thus placed her in the odd predicament of championing a decades-old finding, deep in the past of her laboratory experimentation. As a whole, the interview demystifies her elite status, simultaneously connecting her experience to the mass of mainstream listeners and offering a rare glimpse into the exigencies of intellectual history at the intersection of knowledge and the experience of its production.

Extended interviews like *Nobel Prize Conversations* and highly edited documentary podcasts such as the "Entanglements" episode of *Invisibilia* display the curiosity, engagement, conversation, narrativity, and awareness of human relationships constituting the core elements of science podcasts identified by Spinelli and Dann.[46] Those elements counter the didactic tone and lack of relatability inherited from twentieth-century science radio programming, typically featuring voice-of-God narration in the documentary tradition. The humanizing approach to science journalism contributes to intellectual culture not only complex concepts but also an epistemology of news coverage that departs from black-box top-down traditional news coverage. Such programming acknowledges "the tension between raw material and story shapes (and the unavoidable impact of representation on what is being represented)," an awareness that "is quite sophisticated in the world of podcasting."[47] Science podcasts achieve this by revealing the lived experience of scientific discovery whereby the creative lynchpin of science journalism becomes a form of intellectual culture itself through verbal storytelling. Devices, techniques, and tropes employed in highly produced and edited documentaries tend to support the narrative architecture while also paradoxically calling attention to its constructedness.

Storytelling for science podcasts thus presents itself as a matter of recording unscripted conversation, as with *Nobel Prize Conversations*, and editing tape to animate abstract research discoveries, as in *Invisibilia*.[48] A visceral nearness to invisible scientific processes can be achieved through what Spinelli and Dann call "the breathless edit," or the "seamless interweave" of tape-to-tape transitions, according to Spiegel. Such editorial "processing, selection, inflection, and manipulation" is particularly adept at capturing and communicating the drama of intellectual discourse.[49] In documentary shows, listeners have come to expect more edits and layers of narrative as the quality of production rises at a precipitous rate. Of the many uses of tape Spiegel has identified are four editorial techniques for audio that have accelerated the evolution of intellectual culture through podcasting: (1) imperfections and outtake material strategically left in to remove listeners from the smooth veneer of narrative and to highlight its constructed status; (2) sonic synecdoche providing a brief audio leitmotif that functions as shorthand for a larger theme (such as the sound of clocks signifying the obsessive intellect of the protagonist in *S-Town* and the sound of chimps alluding to primitive origins of concepts in *Radiolab*); (3) reference to a past interview whose content is paraphrased and contextualized by the reporter; and (4) repeat iteration in which a key phrase is taken from different conversational contexts, each carrying different intonations and inflections and lined up in sequence without transitions bearing the effect of an audio montage.[50]

Science Vs uses these editing techniques to communicate complex scientific concepts that debunk conventional assumptions about a wide range of topics from personal health to climate change. The show's conceptual focus aligns it with explanatory journalism in contrast to the sociological approach of *Beyond the Microscope*, for example, which profiles women specialists coping with gender inequity in STEM fields, or the biographical frame of *Nobel Prize Conversations*. Australian biomedical research specialist Wendy Zukerman, the host of *Science Vs* since 2015, has written for the magazines *Popular Science* and *Psychology Today*, which were among the few media outlets dedicated to mass communicating science to nonscientists prior to the digital revolution. The podcast's function as public service journalism is evident in Zukerman's insistence on resisting false balance in reporting, urging that "if there's a 95% consensus among scientists, you report the consensus."[51] *Science Vs* thus corrects for the journalistic tendency to "present competing points of views on a specific scientific question as though they had equal scientific weight, when actually they do not."[52] Commercial pressure in mainstream media encourages false balance reporting in part because "conflicts create news value and thus stories that grasp audience attention." Application of the norm of balance without proper attention to consensus in the scientific community "amplifies the views of contrarians (which may attract audience attention) and distorts coverage of the issue."[53] Such flawed reporting opens space for conspiracy theories and the weaponization of podcasts for the Far Right. Election- and climate-denying conspiracy theories have misled a significant portion of the electorate, prompting Jill Lepore to ask, "Who killed the truth?" the central question of season 2 of her podcast *The Last Archive* examining "the rise of doubt over the last 100 years."[54]

HISTORICAL ANALYSIS AND MEDIA CRITICISM

As with scientific concepts and the researchers who develop them, specialized academic work in the field of history has proliferated through mainstream culture via podcasting, a process abetted by the editorial techniques unique to the medium. As a staff writer for the *New Yorker* and host of the podcast *The Last Archive*, the renowned Harvard historian Jill Lepore has played a key role in sophisticating public discourse on complex historical issues. Like Wendy Zukerman, her objective, especially in season 2 of *The Last Archive*, is to unearth the archival morgue of "lies, fakes and hoaxes" to deconstruct their dissembling logic in light of reliable evidence. This critical angle poses an important and edifying intellectual challenge for listeners in a culture beleaguered by conspiracy theories and election denial. Lepore's journalistic work was first produced for audio on the *New Yorker Radio Hour* in 2016 before she launched her own show with Pushkin Industries, the podcast publishing firm established by her *New Yorker* colleague Malcolm Gladwell and Jacob Weisberg, the former *Newsweek* writer who left his position as founding editor of *Slate* in 2018 to become the company's CEO. *The Last Archive* builds on the success of Lepore's book, *These Truths: A History of the United States*, which NPR heralded as "nothing short of a masterpiece" that treats "our country's painful past (and present) in an intellectually honest way."[55]

Pushkin produces both solutions journalism with the podcast *Solvable* as well as explanatory journalism with *The Last Archive*. Whereas the former advances solutions to seemingly intractable problems, the latter explicates ongoing news stories by providing greater context than commonly found in traditional news reporting. Explanatory journalism is a form of reporting that Michael Schudson describes as inherently analytical.[56] Explanatory and analytic journalism "explain a complicated event or process in a comprehensible narrative," which entails "intelligence and a kind of pedagogical flair, linking the capacity to understand a complex situation with a knack for transmitting that understanding to a broad public."[57] Bearing such narrative and analytical attributes, the podcast medium has contributed to what *Poynter* described as a "golden age" of explanatory journalism during the 2020 pandemic.[58] What began as a product of the *Tampa Bay Times* during the 1980s, the current revival of "a kind of enterprise reporting that made sense out of a more complex, technical and cluttered world" inspired the Pulitzer Prize category for explanatory journalism.[59] In the contemporary digital publishing industry, *Vox* has become synonymous explanatory journalism as well as celebrity journalists like Nate Silver, Bill Simmons, Michael Lewis, and Deborah Blum. This type of journalism has always been central to the *New Yorker* and *Atlantic*, both of which have spawned podcasts by their more prominent contributors who have made powerful contributions to intellectual culture.

Explanatory journalism is ideally suited to Lepore's strengths as a Harvard history professor and celebrated *New Yorker* contributor. Whereas the first season of *The Last Archive* reprised *Serial*'s convention of examining the circumstances of a forgotten murder in the distant past, the second is dedicated to "the vault of fakes."[60] It begins with the episode "Believe It," which dives into the veritable morgue of potential story leads the production team considered and rejected for the first season. To the melodramatic sounds of *The Shadow*, Lepore notes, "1930s radio was good, but so over-the-top. So be skeptical, very, very

Intellectual Culture

skeptical," intoning the intellectual keynote for the metacritical investigation into the untruths of the last century for a long view of disinformation's checkered past.[61] "The role of radio in the history of doubt" constitutes this exploration of radio's carnival barkers selling falsehoods in the tradition of P. T. Barnum. As such, the podcast features archival audio from *Ripley's Believe It or Not* to contextualize social media driven disinformation on the internet. "Any time I use the word *radio* on this episode," she tells listeners, "you can substitute the word *internet*."[62] This apt analogy begins with the premise that "with the right copy and announcer, everything could be *made* to sound like news" as with today's multimedia storytelling. As with online news, "radio sounded so authoritative, so easy to believe." The episode then pursues the equivalent of a research question: "What is the relationship between belief and doubt in democracy and the radio, if . . . there's something of conflict between majority rule and freedom thought?" Further refining the focus, she asks, "What if the majority starts telling you what to think? Then, radio is potentially pretty dangerous, because it can lead you to lose your sense of what's true and what's not." Setting the keynote is the question of whether radio was potentially powerful enough to destroy democracy by leading listeners to "unknow things."[63] Whereas Ripley and other audio hucksters comprise the focus of the second episode, the first examines the famous Scopes Monkey Trial addressing the teaching of Darwin's theory of evolution in public schools. Such media history is rendered fresh and important in light of political polarization, particularly events such as the formation of the Federal Communications Commission to prevent manipulation of the mass audience, since radio reached 78 million listeners by the 1930s, twice the number of telephones at the time.

In terms of production practice, *The Last Archive* stands out among other podcasts treating intellectual subjects for its use of 1930s radio drama motifs, particularly musical interludes and transitions. These knowing, self-reflexive, metacritical signatures are well suited to the show's serious examination of 1930s radio topics such as the banning of foreign language stations, an act of sociocultural xenophobia. In "Episode 2: Believe It," Lepore interviews Dolores Inés Casillas, University of California, Santa Barbara media scholar and author of *Sounds of Belonging: US-Spanish Language Radio and Public Advocacy*, to tell the story of

Pedro Gonzáles, a pioneer of Spanish-language radio broadcasting in the mid-twentieth century. Gonzáles was falsely accused of rape—a milestone lie in media history—and sentenced to fifty years in prison. After serving six years on Alcatraz Island, Gonzáles was deported to his native country of Mexico. Casillas notes that Gonzáles brought "listeners together and gave them a sense of power," an opposite effect of Ripley's exploitative charlatanism.[64] After learning that Gonzáles had been assisting listeners in organizing and resisting against deportation, the Los Angeles district attorney became concerned that he would start a revolution. Gonzáles was eventually arrested on trumped-up charges of rape in 1934 following several failed attempts to indict him on false charges. Casillas breaks down in tears during her commentary. The unregulated creative power of radio, Casillas notes, can save lives of a people "who are so"—her voice cracking with emotion—"legally vulnerable." In this way, "radio becomes so important."[65] Radio continues to provide a safe resource for immigrants desperate for information without being identified. Podcasts indeed operate in a similar way for current immigrants, as discussed in the following chapter. History is revealed in this episode to be a potent force for explanatory journalistic coverage of the current issue of immigration. Compared to editing for the radio format, podcast editing is racier and bolder, foregrounding intimacy and empathy as its rhetorical foundation. Hard-news broadcasters typically restrain rather than openly express intense emotion. Momentary emotional outbursts are indeed so rare in radio history that they represent milestones of the medium, as with Herbert Morrison's report of the Hindenburg disaster in 1937. Lepore's empathy for Casillas when she breaks down is palpable.

The Gonzáles story of *The Last Archive* exhibits podcast-specific intimacy and its four implications identified by Spinelli and Dann as (1) the technological affordance of the "aural mechanics of podcast listening" through headphones or earbuds, (2) the modeling of "intimate listening practices" by showcasing intimate listening in action, (3) trust established through the interpersonal nature of the podcast medium, and (4) empathy as material for generating podcast content.[66] Certainly Casillas's emotional response to Spanish-language radio's capacity to save lives represents intimate listening that builds trust between host, reporter, and audience. Empathy in the scene clearly provides the material for the scene. In this case, a sense of anguish in the plight of

Mexican immigrants in Southern California emerges from critical thinking about media processes. While the episode "Believe It" explicates the ways in which lies are perpetrated in the example of Ripley, the application of audio media misinformation through social and legal channels is exhibited in the false accusation that led to Gonzáles's indictment. Attention to how these lies and hoaxes are constructed and deployed empowers listeners with the critical tools for decoding disinformation in their own media diets.

A show similarly concerned with "how we know what we know, and how we used to know things" is the historical documentary podcast *Floodlines*.[67] It similarly evokes empathy not only as a dramatic device but as a way of deconstructing dominant media narratives. The eight-part series published by the *Atlantic Monthly* magazine is hosted by Vann R. Newkirk II, a journalist with training in the field of public health. The show's premise is that "Hurricane Katrina was not the disaster; the disaster was what happened after."[68] Regarded by critics as the best podcast of 2020, *Floodlines* captures the significance of the large-scale event in the personal, intimate plight of the survivors and victims. Unlike *The Last Archive*, the historical trajectory of *Floodlines* mainly follows the experiences of New Orleans native Le-Ann Williams, who was fourteen when Katrina struck. The narrative through line is the course of her life prior to the disaster, survival of the storm itself, escape from the disaster area, life after relocation, and finally return home. Compassion for her plight is driven by a powerfully written script and deft use of tape to bring a sense of temporal coherence to the story. Music is essential for placing the listener in the setting of New Orleans, evoking the rich jazz history of the city in what Nicholas Quah calls "a melancholic haze" that brings "a dreamlike quality to the proceedings, except we're dealing with the recollection of a nightmare."[69] The struggle to access any help that may have been available was stymied by failed media communication to inform survivors of where and how to access aid. Racialized rumor and misinformation precipitated what should have been avoidable confrontations with police.

Newkirk's interview with Michael Brown, the FEMA director at the time of the disaster, revealed that communication is the "number one thing we are supposed to do. We didn't do a very good job of it."[70] Brown explained that due to the focus on the response, "when it came to things like press relations, media relations, acknowledgments, I think we completely dropped the ball." Although Brown could not empathize enough to apologize for his errors, he did express personal sorrow for Le-Ann, who recalled feeling as though she might perish while awaiting aid. Revisiting Michael Brown's legacy occasioned both Newkirk's reflection on his scapegoating in the media and the psychology of his response, one that performed transparency in a clear admission of errors due to his own incompetence. Yet "the paradox of Michael Brown," Newkirk concluded, "seems to be this: All of his efforts to defend himself, to not be made the scapegoat . . . seem to make it impossible for him to perform empathy."[71] Importantly, Brown's exercise in self-disclosure seemed to prevent him from "understanding why an apology from him might mean something," particularly as a broad gesture to the city of New Orleans and not only to Le-Ann. As a public health official, Brown's dubious place in American history should not be relegated to that of a scapegoat. Instead, his flawed approaches to public safety crises surfaced in the decade following Katrina, when he refused to wear a protective mask and be vaccinated against COVID-19 until the relatively late date of February 25, 2021 (nearly one year into the pandemic), when he recanted his position on his radio program, *The Michael Brown Show*.[72] Media distortion comes under close analytical scrutiny in *Floodlines*. During the height of the Katrina disaster, the lack of credible information from FEMA or any other government organization meant that "all information was credible information." This void rapidly became filled by news that "painted the people left behind as violent and dangerous and turned them into monsters in the eyes of the people in charge," according to Newkirk.[73] With no concerted public relations strategy in place, "even the police chief and mayor started to repeat misinformation." In the spirit of explanatory journalism, Newkirk aptly characterizes the situation as "a feedback loop. If the media were reporting that mobs of armed looters were roving the streets, if the police chief was saying it too, the people thought it was real."[74]

Critical perspectives on media are also offered in *Public Intellectual*. In the context of a discussion about the paradoxes of manipulatively persuasive figures in history such as Jim Jones, guest Chelsey Weber-Smith told *Public Intellectual* host Jessa Crispin, "The heart of our show is complicated; but neither side of the political spectrum wants [ideas to be] complicated." After a brief pause, she captured the spirit of intellectual podcasts: "But we're not moving forward without nuance and understanding of how culture moves forward in different ways or whether we like how it does or not."[75] Such commentary suggests intellectual culture has taken on a new life bearing a distinctly different posture—one capable of tolerating ambiguity and sitting with complexity while also rooting out truth and unmasking frauds—than in predigital generations while also manifesting many of its core principles. In the nineteenth century, Ralph Waldo Emerson called for intellectuals to take a public stand, using the press to amplify their ideas, which he and his followers regularly did through Horace Greeley's *New-York Tribune* during the antebellum era on behalf of women's rights, abolition, wage labor, and public health.[76] Just as Emerson protégé Margaret Fuller declared the press as the only efficient instrument for the education of the masses, particularly the editorial pages of the *Tribune* and weekly newspapers that featured the serial fiction of Harriet Beecher Stowe and spawned publications run by Frederick Douglass, now podcasting carries that torch. Only since the 1980s and 1990s has science embraced the role of public intellectual. By contrast, popular histories date back to the weekly press of the mid-nineteenth century. The Harvard physicist Alan Lightman recalled writing popular press articles and encyclopedia entries when he began his scientific career in the mid to late 1970s. During this time "it was considered a taboo, a professional stigma, for scientists to spend any time at all in writing for the general public." The scientific community then considered such projects "a waste of precious time, a soft activity" because "the proper job of a scientist was to penetrate the secrets of the physical world," and anything less was considered "a dumbing down." Lightman noted that "the stigma was real and I could feel it."[77] Undaunted, he proceeded according to the models of Rachel Carson, Carl Sagan, and Stephen J. Gould in serving the public interest through scientific knowledge.

The current podcast industry for intellectual content now finds itself with an embarrassment of riches for resource material. The podcast *Time Sensitive* counters the notion that digital spaces constitute highly distracting environments anathema to deep reflective thought on challenging concepts. One year after the launch of *Time Sensitive*, the show was rebooted as *At a Distance* precisely at the onset of the COVID-19 pandemic in March 2020 without its screen counterpart. This version of the podcast distinctly sought out high-caliber intellectuals for its guest interviews, in the process adhering to the tenet of slow media that enacts a critique of mainstream media predicated on a manic, Twitter-driven news cycle, an approach detailed in the research of Jennifer Rauch, author of *Slow Media: Why Slow Is Satisfying, Sustainable, and Smart*, and Peter Laufer, known for his book *Slow News: A Manifesto for the Critical News Consumer*. In addition to featuring episodes dedicated to Rauch and Laufer, specialists who helped pioneer the field of slow media as a countercurrent to the highly distracting digital news media ecosystem first identified in Nicholas Carr's *The Shallows: What the Internet Is Doing to Our Brains*, *At a Distance*'s debut episode featured renowned activist environmentalist public intellectual Bill McKibbon. Only weeks after the onset of the pandemic, McKibbon, who writes the foreword to the most recent edition of Henry David Thoreau's *Walden*, spoke about the links between the climate crisis and the pandemic, offering rich insight into how biology and physics cannot be negotiated with. McKibbon explained that our ability to learn from the pandemic will be contingent upon how much carbon we continue to throw into the atmosphere and how we continue to respond to crises. "Can we get our heads around inequality that makes response difficult?" He anticipated that after the pandemic, "we are not going to be looking for things we sought prior to COVID-19 in our economy such as *speed*; not the ability to grow rapidly, but stoutness, resilience, reliability, hardiness—not a racehorse, a draft horse."[78] The point invoked the notion of sustainable and responsible production, an ethos consonant with the slow media production practice of *At a Distance*, built on the foundation of Rauch, Laufer, and Thoreau.

McKibbon's intellectual contribution to *At a Distance* underscored not only the importance of slow, sustainable production for richer, more lasing products but also the importance of recognizing scientific consensus. The Donald Trump White House denied the scientific warnings of Dr. Anthony Fauci, insisting that church pews would be filled by Easter of 2020. McKibbon then connected the current pandemic to the climate crisis, explaining that "the notion that science is optional, that it's ok to dismiss reality as a hoax if it's inconvenient to your economic or political aspirations, is one of the things that's kept us form dealing seriously with the climate crisis." He noted that precisely such regard for science as a matter of partisan belief "hampers us from thinking as clearly as we could about the current pandemic."[79] Such a perspective has delayed prompt action on climate change, which could have controlled the current crisis through moderate emissions restrictions beginning thirty years ago. McKibbon noted that lack of prompt action on the COVID-19 virus led to a similar catastrophe, adding that technological hubris may have contributed to a sense of invulnerability. "No matter how shiny your technology, the world continues to be a biological place, a chemical place, a place where the very small CO_2 molecule can take over the world."[80] In just under thirty minutes, McKibbon captured the common foundational flaws in government, politics, and industry, offering a wide-ranging cultural critique of the detrimental impacts of anti-intellectualism, resource allocation, and economic production for sustainability. Just as Carl Sagan and Rachel Carson leveraged the popular media of their predigital eras to foster intellectual culture offering a critical perspective on the fate of our planet, we now see figures like McKibbon continue their legacy through the podcast medium.

The public radio roots and narrativity of podcasting accelerated by the pandemic provided the foundation for podcasting's signature genre of true crime and the wide-ranging intellectual culture it helped inspire. With demand for intellectually rich podcast content in the fields of science, history, and media criticism sharply rising due to the approachability of complex subjects through longform narrative, the industry standard for quality has increased significantly. With this higher standard, publishers now turn to subscription and paid business models in response to the shift in digital culture whereby audiences increasingly show a willingness to pay for quality podcasts. This brings us to the topic of our next chapter detailing the advent of paid podcasting.

CHAPTER FOUR

Sound Transactions

Audience and the Advent of Paid Podcasts

The rise in quality of journalistic content that has increasingly migrated into the world of intellectual culture has effectively elevated the standard for podcasting, in the process raising the prospect of paid and subscription business models. This marks a major departure from the previously held expectation that podcasts should remain available online for free. In the digital news industry, "original sin" alludes to online users' refusal to pay for their news, an expectation established when newspapers originally offered content free on their earliest websites.[1] The paywall debate ensued in the mid-2010s, pitting proponents of the existing advertising-driven model such as *Slate* founder and then-editor Jacob Weisberg against print-based legacy media figures like *Harper's* publisher John MacArthur. Prior to paywalls, the prevailing online business model that provided free news to users served a similar democratic purpose to that of the penny press in the nineteenth century. Dependence on advertising as the main source of revenue draws on the rich financial resources of commercial industry compared to the relatively limited support offered by subscriptions or government subsidies alone. The sale of newspapers at or below the cost of production expanded readership to an unprecedented scale beginning in the 1840s, in the process opening a vast range of opportunities for literacy and civic engagement well beyond the reach of the prior generation's patron-supported partisan papers.[2] Echoing the Industrial Revolution's new printing technologies and distribution channels that democratized the press with affordable and readily accessible news, the digital revolution brought similar effects with its primarily free news. Digital ads, however, were not initially concentrated into the pages of news publications at the dawn of the digital age as they were at the onset of the penny press. Instead, advertising dollars diffused across the internet to platforms like Craigslist, where print classified advertisers eventually migrated. This financial challenge for print news publications navigating the shift to digital during the early 2000s was then met in a variety of ways. To remain profitable during the transition online, legacy media such as the *Guardian, Atlantic, Washington Post, New Yorker,* and *New Republic* drew on an array of resources and tactics, including charitable trusts, wealthy owners, and dramatically higher subscription prices.[3] In 2009 only 9 percent of Americans paid for online news, a figure that more than doubled to 21 percent by 2021.[4] *New York Times* editor Jodi Rudoren declared in 2020 that "the new business model is about subscription" aimed at "reaching readers where they are, understanding their needs, and filling them."[5]

HISTORICIZING PODCAST PAYWALLS

During the early 2010s the influx of newcomers into the market for online news media stimulated greater competition, particularly toward data-driven, substantive journalism epitomized by figures such as Ezra Klein and Nate Silver. "Rather than too much competition in too small a niche," the scenario held great promise in the eyes of Weisberg and media critics such as Felix Salmon, who saw "the supply of high-quality journalism creating its own demand."[6] Detractors described free content as "a race to the bottom in which more and more traffic becomes less and less valuable."[7] Critics lamented that the resultant ad-laden news formats had become increasingly cluttered and distracting, leading to shallow reading habits characterized by scanning and skimming.[8] Rather than bemoaning the oversupply of content, Weisberg pointed to the benefits that accrue to publishers in an increasingly competitive digital ecosystem. "Competition from digital newcomers has been good for *Slate*" and the larger digital publishing industry, he noted, by encouraging the development "of a culture around data, analytics, and testing." The unique voices of born-digital news brands, he argued, enabled a culture of journalistic production that "lets individual contributors shine."[9] Curiously, Weisberg's own faith in advertising as the main source of revenue appears somewhat unsteady. His appeal on behalf of the internet's power to revive journalism mentions *Slate Plus*, his paid membership program offering premium content designed to open a new source of subscription-based revenue directly from users. "It's like Amazon Prime," he said, comparing it to the streaming on-demand video platform rooted in a subscription-based business model.[10]

For all his digital utopianism in 2014, Weisberg nonetheless disclosed his fundamental mistrust in the future integrity of exclusively free online news by mentioning his own outlet's adoption of subscriptions. Paid news, as Peter Laufer notes, is correlated with higher quality news produced according to a more painstaking, and often slower, process.[11] The credo of slow media and journalism has since its origin depended on direct revenue from its audience, through both online startup donation portals such as Kickstarter—as in the case of *De Correspondent*, the world-record holder for most contributions received by a startup news organization—and relatively high-priced single issue and subscription rates.[12] Only by charging readers for their news can the standard for journalistic quality be maintained, according to *Harper*'s publisher and hard paywall proponent John McArthur.[13] But just as Weisberg amended his free-news stance by offering payment options on *Slate*, McArthur admitted to benefiting from the digital and advertising sectors despite his staunch opposition to online news accompanied by ads.[14] One of his most memorable achievements for the august journal, whose contributors include major figures in intellectual history such as Noam Chomsky and Norman Mailer, was in securing a contract with Steve Jobs of Apple for the Macintosh PC "Think Different" advertising campaign—paradoxically in a print monthly. For all his misgivings about the internet and digital media's erosion of journalistic principles, McArthur still championed the rich financial resources of advertisers—even in the computer industry—and their capacity to support journalism more effectively than governments and subscriptions alone.[15]

The 2010s paywall debate revealed a false binary in the rhetorical construction of a mutually exclusive dichotomy of advertising versus subscription business models, a debate with profound implications for the posterity of journalistic quality. In light of the current movement toward subscription podcasts, which Apple and Spotify have embraced with new programs, protocols, and digital tools, it is clear that both digital utopians like Weisberg and traditionalist print publishers like McArthur shared the common ground of recognizing the need for both advertising and subscription revenue sources to mutually sustain the financial viability of journalism in the twenty-first century. Just as the quality of television evolved from its vast wasteland of the 1950s to the relatively sophisticated content enabled by on-demand streaming video according to the Netflix model, podcasting enters maturity as a medium through the advent of subscription. This shift, enabled by user gravitation toward longer, more immersive storytelling, bears significant implications for podcast journalism, as users increasingly show a willingness to pay for news.[16]

This chapter explores the advent of the subscription-based business model in the podcast industry with respect to podcast user preferences and motivations. In 2021 major investments by Apple and Spotify in subscription tools for podcast publishers marked a milestone in digital culture, specifically toward normalizing paid podcasts, thereby expanding the overall market in terms of the medium's profitability. This development raises profound implications for the quality of the news and its manner of consumption. By expanding the industry's opportunities for profit through the monetization of latent revenue streams, subscription and direct listener payment promise to transform the culture of podcast consumption by increasing demand for higher quality content, particularly for users drawn to information and current events. This shift toward paid podcasts is in part a cause and consequence of the rise of audio reporting quality concurrent with the diversification of longform narrative documentary and true crime genres into daily news.[17] The availability of subscription tools for publishers on Apple Podcasts and Spotify may encourage a wider diversity of news startups and audiences that the industry has previously not accommodated. Perhaps most telling of the new prominence of the Netflix-inspired subscription approach to podcasting appears in the new wave of entrepreneurs siphoning from subscriber-only podcasts. Castbox, for example, allows listeners to access subscriber-only shows. In addition to such industrial intermediaries poised to profit from this sea change in podcasting, the normalization of paid podcasts thus brings a wide array of implications for producers, consumers, and content.

The following section profiles the motivations of podcast news users in order to establish an understanding of audience demand targeted by platforms and publishers. Specifically, motivations for news-related podcasts include the desire for high-quality audio content to be experienced as a stand-alone activity. Online radio users, who are more active listeners compared to traditional radio audiences, increasingly turn to podcasts for their journalism. Information-related motives lead to more continuous engagement over time, which can be measured through the willingness to pay for podcasts.[18] Following this is a discussion of the slippage in user perceptions of what it means to pay for news. The overwhelming majority of Pew survey respondents, for example, said they do not pay for news.[19] But when subsequently asked if they had any subscriptions, many acknowledged that they did. The lack of conceptual clarity regarding payment for news hinges on the definition of news itself, which has also been in radical flux during the height of the digital revolution. Then a comparative case study examines the new subscription programs offered by Apple Podcasts and Spotify, illustrating the next phase in the platformization of the podcast industry.[20] In this light, the subscription movement represents the latest development in the industry dominance of podcasting by these two companies, one that raises the bar for entry by startups and threatens to segregate listeners into media silos. Analysis also treats the benefits that accrue to the evolution of journalistic quality via longform storytelling associated with the normalization of paid podcasts. Apple Podcasts and Spotify platform users represent a different audience demographic characterized by raised expectations for frictionless access to high-quality audio experiences compared to listeners who access and subscribe to shows on the open Web via RSS (Really Simple Syndication) feeds through the standardized system for the distribution of content from online publishers. The conclusion considers how these developments in the technology and consumption of podcasts are fostering shifts in the function and meanings of news as well as the exchange value between publishers and their audiences.

UNDERSTANDING PODCAST LISTENERS

Podcast listeners have been the envy of advertisers since the breakthrough publication of *Serial* in 2014. In the early 2010s the prevailing expectation among online users was that digital content, including narrative journalism and daily news, should be free with some exceptions.[21] Certainly *This American Life*'s capability of commanding this mass audience suggested an equally massive potential for profit, prompting Ira Glass to proclaim that public radio was "ready for capitalism," much to the consternation of NPR purists and aficionados.[22] In 2014 podcasting's main revenue source was sponsorship and advertising. Once the listening audience expanded to the scale of *Serial* and to the colossal reach of *S-Town* by 2017, publishers began to entertain new approaches to monetizing this following. The narrative longform revolution in audio reporting helped establish podcasting as a stand-alone activity for many listeners at the time. Since then, the increasing sophistication and artistry of shows has demanded more attention and cognitive focus from listeners. This trend is apparent not only in the true crime genre but also in complex cerebral podcasts such as *Hooked on Pop* (hosted by ethnomusicologists) and *Who? Weekly* (a perspicacious examination of celebrity culture). No longer audio wallpaper, post-*Serial* podcasts are a stand-alone activity for 70 percent of listeners.[23] Such attention is warranted by the greater number of shows invested in reaching a higher aesthetic standard through carefully orchestrated sound design.

Recent research on podcast consumption measures audience by width, depth, and routine. Width, which is the oldest and most rudimentary metric, measures the amount of downloads for each show. On an individual level, width refers to consumption quantity, which is the number of podcasts an individual listens to during a given period.[24] Depth addresses the intensity of engagement, typically measured as engaged time, which is more revealing of consumer behavior than frequency alone. Together with engaged time, frequency takes on greater significance in capturing the nature of podcast consumer patterns.[25] Listeners commonly immerse themselves in three or more episodes or entire seasons at a time, a consumption pattern previously associated with on-demand streaming video.[26] Routine is revealed in the number of shows to which a listener subscribes and the length of time they maintain those subscriptions. Often referred to as *loyals* in the television industry, long-term subscribers counteract churn, or audience turnover. Churn has been a major concern for digital publishers competing in the attention economy for capricious online news consumers.[27]

Compared to streaming music, podcasts require more attention from the listener and thus carry higher value as engaging media.[28] Kris M. Markman notes that unlike traditional radio, which is linear and standardized, podcasts are personalized, time-shifted, and consumed on-demand.[29] The podcast's unique appeal distinguishing it from terrestrial radio lies in its combination of entertainment, information, and audio platform superiority, which are the most prominent motives for podcast consumption. Sylvia Chan-Olmsted and Rang Wang conducted a revealing two-thousand-person study of regular podcast users, roughly half men and women with a mean age of 40.3 years.[30] Of the total, 31.4 percent earned an annual household income greater than $70,000, with only 4.4 percent of listeners earning below $39,000. This demographic's relatively high educational attainment is evident in the 37 percent who hold a college degree or higher, followed by 28 percent with some college and 13.2 percent with an associate degree. Kelli S. Boling and Kevin Hull also found that the vast majority of podcast listeners are college educated, with many holding graduate degrees. The sophistication of the podcast audience suggests that the nature of binge listening has increasingly become an intellectual endeavor rather than strictly escapist entertainment.[31]

The affluence and educational attainment of the podcast audience mitigates criticism originally raised by *Serial*'s success "about the ethics of using real people and events in a format that resembled fictional television dramas."[32] Mindless, prurient fascination has been associated with "the way many listeners 'binge listened' to the twelve episodes further mirroring our viewing habits."[33] Objections to the consumption of digital on-demand longform journalism formatted in seasons echo earlier resistance to the literary journalism movement that borrowed the structure and devices of the novel for nonfiction storytelling. The influence of the New Journalism's incorporation of narrative techniques associated with fiction reached deep into the heart of daily news reporting in the late twentieth century.[34] The extension of narrative journalism into the realm of podcasting formatted and consumed like fictional television dramas divides content into interrelated chapters not unlike the novel. Indeed, *Serial* host Sarah Koenig noted that *Serial*'s achievement may have leveraged a new medium to reach a mass audience, but its storytelling, she insisted, was as old as the triple-decker Victorian novel.[35]

Intrinsic to these absorbing storytelling structures is the paid-subscription model. As on-demand digital media, narrative journalistic podcasts assembled in a serialized episodic format share the same genetic code as streaming video on-demand documentary series. Cinema and the novel are genres that have always been sold to audiences rather than offered for free based on an advertising-dependent revenue model. Similarly, the antebellum weekly press's serialized fiction—including *Uncle Tom's Cabin* by Harriet Beecher Stowe and *Franklin Evans* by Walt Whitman—always commanded a price from readers, depending more on subscription for profit than advertising. Indeed, one of the most lucrative newspapers in media history, the *New York Ledger*, featured celebrity contributors in an ad-free format. Thus, experimentation with the paid-subscription model for podcasts as a way of monetizing the vast listening audience is the latest iteration of the long history of media production rooted in sophisticated narrativity commanding a price. A new wave of apps including Stitcher Premium, for example, now offer ad-free content and bonus episodes for paid subscribers.[36]

Despite the rise in online paid content, many users do not associate their subscriptions with purchased news. According to a 2020 Pew survey, only 17 percent of respondents saying they "paid for news in the past year" and the overwhelming majority (83 percent) claimed to not have paid for news.[37] Yet a follow-up question revealed that among those 83 percent, roughly 20 percent said that they or a household member purchased a subscription to a newspaper, magazine, or news website within the last year. An additional 6 percent indicated that they had made donations to public news organizations during the same period.[38] Among other transactions respondents overlooked as occasions in which they actually paid for news were the subscriptions to cable or satellite TV and satellite radio. Although these escaped the awareness of users as instances of paying for news, such subscriptions clearly constitute "payments [that] do result in increased financial resources for some news organizations."[39] Despite the cord-cutting revolution that saw a mass exodus from cable

TV subscriptions, 57 percent who said they do not pay for news do indeed subscribe to a cable TV package. As cable television's audio counterpart and the first form of paid audio content in media history, satellite radio such as SiriusXM accounted for 18 percent of respondents. Satellite radio represents an important step toward the normalization of subscription podcasts. Yet, unlike satellite or free radio, podcasts resist churn. "Because people have gone to an effort to choose the podcast, they are more likely to stick with it because they know and trust the brand and have invested a little more in it," according to Claudia Taranto, co-executive producer of *Earshot*.[40]

As *Inside Radio* observed, "podcasting perceptions seem to be lagging behind perceived usage, with some listeners not thinking about podcasts as news sources per se," which is a similar phenomenon to social media and online search.[41] This lack of recognition of paid news is a vestige of 2000s digital culture when free news prevailed online. The consumer expectation for all content to be free on the internet has since gradually yielded to metered payment, freemium, and soft paywall approaches. In addition, news publishers now thrive on cross-platform transmedia publication.[42] Since "many news outlets no longer stay confined to producing content on only one platform," now newspapers such as the *New York Times* produce audio content on podcasts that also airs on radio stations accessible through smart speakers, video series, cable TV, streaming devices such as Fire TV Stick, or Roku smart television. The lines between platforms are further blurred by the presence of this content on social media such as Facebook, YouTube, and Twitter.[43] The ubiquity of news in the digital ecosystem, which is fueled by its radical transmediation, may have become so commonplace that users do not recognize it. As Clay Shirky reminds us, media only become socially significant when they are so widely adopted that they become invisible to those who use them.[44] Indeed, the common practice of sharing and circulating media content across platforms, services, and devices makes it difficult for users to identify which platforms and publishers produce original news content, as many survey respondents incorrectly believed Google News produced its own stories and *Huffington Post* did not.[45] Since radio broadcasts can be accessed through podcasts and smart speakers, ambiguity arises with respect to the notions of paying for news, helping explain why users might overlook the extent to which they purchase journalism.

The podcast medium's emergence into maturity has outpaced perceptions of it as a news source. The medium's hybrid nature at the intersection of the novel, cinema, and streaming on-demand video might contribute to its lack of recognition as a news source. Combined with its multiplatform transmediation through myriad delivery devices, the podcast becomes even more chameleonic.[46] Users' lack of awareness of their payment for news may stem from journalism's complete integration into the media ecosystem, including forms traditionally not considered sources of information. The prevalence of users consuming more paid journalism than they realize suggests journalism's pervasiveness in the digital ecosystem. These findings suggest binge listening can be more edifying and informative than the indulgent guilty pleasure stereotypically associated with streaming video, as podcast listeners increasingly seek information in addition to entertainment through news-related shows. The information motive for podcast listeners, which helps to explain the rise of podcast journalism as a genre, is defined by Chan-Olmsted and Wang as users' need to learn new things and acquire knowledge about the world around them.[47]

Instrumental podcast listening for information-seeking audiences correlates with deeper engagement. Ritualized consumption, by comparison, is more casual, passive, and less selective. A podcast may accompany a routine activity such as exercise or commuting and thus serve as part of—or ancillary to—another ritual. Instrumental listening instead describes listeners who are seeking specific types of information, whereas ritualized consumption is integral to a pastime or habit.[48] John Biewen, producer and host of the podcast *Scene on Radio* and director of the audio program for the Center for Documentary Studies, explained that active and selective listening increases intimacy for both listener and host. Compared to an audience of passive radio listeners, for example, podcast intimacy is enhanced by "knowing your listeners have deliberately chosen your show."[49] The intentional selection of a podcast, especially for nonfictional and documentary content, is often instrumental in the sense that listeners seek more than diversion from the show but also some specific data or insight to satisfy the need for a particular type of knowledge. The alignment of the audience's background knowledge and interests is therefore more precise when intentional selection occurs. As a host, Biewen prizes such listeners because "they've pressed click on the episode as opposed to having it show up unbidden on their radio. That can mean less need for introductory and contextual chatter," he notes. Additionally, it can mean that hosts are free to develop far richer and more dense content for exploration. As a stand-alone product asynchronously consumed in a time-shifted manner, podcasts liberate hosts from the predicament associated with radio programming by which reporters and producers must "shape the tone and sound of [their] work to fit other people's radio shows."[50] Instead, the medium enables them to shape content to their audience's expectations through a variety of narrative techniques such as first-person storytelling and a blend of attributed and unattributed assertions. Instrumental listening thus aligns with production practice relatively free from the formats and time-constraints of radio that mitigate the host–listener relationship.

The question of the listener's location bears important implications for podcast journalism's evolutionary trajectory toward increasingly sophisticated content. According to Chan-Olmsted and Wang, use at home tends to be more intentional as opposed to ritualized mobile use associated with exercise and commuting.[51] For nonfictional content, the at-home podcast listener is less motivated by escapism or a pastime activity than information seeking.[52] The active and instrumental listening that characterizes at-home podcast audiences contrasts sharply with at-home radio passively consumed as "aural wallpaper" to accompany routine domestic tasks.[53] Significantly, the home is the most common site of podcast consumption, which suggests a different experience than radio listening, which predominantly occurs out of the home.[54] Furthermore, the cognitive focus demanded by highly produced nonfictional podcasts extending to twenty minutes or longer is analogous to the print journalistic features appearing in high-caliber publications such as the *Atlantic Monthly* and the *New Yorker*. Major contributors to those publications, such as Malcolm Gladwell and Jill Lepore, have capitalized on this trend by developing successful podcasts. Binge listening has now taken on new meaning beyond escape and entertainment toward intentional information seeking. This pattern directly aligns with the current shift toward a paid subscription (and à la carte) business model.

PRIMING PAID PODCAST LISTENING

During the 2020 pandemic *Apple News Today* became the first platform to publish a daily news podcast. The podcast represents the closest Apple has come to producing its own original journalistic content. Although the show is hosted by audio reporters Shumita Basu and Duarte Geraldino, who have public radio backgrounds, the show does not feature its own interviews. Instead, it "showcases the best and most interesting stories from a range of U.S. publications."[55] Lauren Kern, editor-in-chief of Apple News, explained the podcast "as an extension of the work we already do in the Apple News App in terms of curation." The innovation in this case is that the curators are not faceless algorithms but embodied hosts, representing a gesture toward greater transparency regarding the platform's key role in journalistic production. Kern explained, "We're now putting faces and voices of Apple News editors out in public and talking more about journalism and why we think a story is good," offering a rare instance of humanized curation as a balm for its automated algorithms.[56] The Apple algorithm's colossal influence on the news industry has received criticism as an unaccountable, machine-generated aggregator distanced from the journalistic role. Apple's decision to respond to such criticism by investing in the podcast series *Apple News Today* speaks to the growth of the podcast industry during the pandemic, one that opened the possibility for paid subscription and à la carte approaches.

The dramatic increase in at-home podcast consumption was consonant with quarantine stay-at-home orders during 2020, which presented an avenue toward reaching younger audiences and "engaging them more deeply with their brands."[57] Reuters's study of daily news podcasts during the 2020 pandemic revealed a sharp rise in news organizations pursuing subscription business models out of a desire to leverage the medium's capacity to increase loyalty and decrease churn.[58] The younger audience, which in the United Kingdom includes an under-thirty-five audience four times greater than those over fifty-five, spends a significant amount of time listening to podcasts and tends to listen to the majority of each episode.[59] The rise in podcast listening correlates with a decrease in reading news on phones, prompted in part by an appreciation for a digital news experience liberated from the screen. With its high educational attainment and long attention span, this younger audience's preferences for digital on-demand media are ideally suited to a subscription model. *Apple News Today* was devised to appeal to this younger demographic in an effort to drive subscriptions to Apple News+, Apple's premium product. As part of this campaign to use podcast journalism to drive subscriptions, Apple published twenty audio stories per week during 2020, each drawn from an article in a leading journal and read by a celebrity actor.[60]

Many top news organizations are well positioned to adopt a subscription model to augment lucrative gains in advertising revenue made during 2020. Robust investments in audio have dramatically increased across the news media industry. In 2019 the *Wall Street Journal* (*WSJ*) launched *The Journal*, a deep-dive podcast—modeled after *The Daily* by the *New York Times*—to supplement *What's News*, its successful roundup of financial and tech news published twice daily. *The Journal*'s prime position within the industry is due in part to its sound design and editing managed by its co-producer, Gimlet, the podcast specialist. Spotify's ownership of Gimlet additionally provided *The Journal* with coveted privileges, including early access to Spotify advertisers and prominent billing atop its recommendations, especially under the category of "Your Daily Drive." *The Journal* remains free of charge to better fulfill its primary purpose of driving a younger demographic to the monetizing site to sell subscriptions. The show adds value for *WSJ*'s current subscribers, deepening listener connection to the brand and reducing churn. As Drew Stoneman, vice-president of commercial strategy at *The Journal* noted, the podcast sits outside of the paywall because "we always need to be providing our members with products that are worthy of the subscription price that they pay us every month."[61] Unlike a prestige project appealing only to niche audiences, *The Journal* instead seeks audio to appease the paper's advertisers. "All the ad categories traditionally associated with the *WSJ* are investing in audio," according to Stoneman. Along with other news organizations, the *Guardian* enjoyed a 48 percent increase in listens during a nine-month span of 2020.[62] As discussed in chapter 1, over 90 percent of weekly podcast listeners during July 2020 matched or exceeded total listening time since the onset of the pandemic, a milestone in the medium's emergence into mainstream digital culture.[63]

This widespread investment in audio could be construed as a "defensive strategy" designed "to meet the challenge of changing audience habits," particularly to reach younger audiences seeking "more informal and less confrontational types of content."[64] But as the podcast medium now enters maturity, this surge in creativity is positioned less as a defensive strategy than a means of commanding a price from an audience willing to pay. With advertisers of august legacy brands such as *WSJ* already pivoting to audio, the prospect of a paying audience promises to build the base of the most committed sponsors. A paying audience represents to advertisers a far more appealing and easily profiled demographic than the less selective free audience. The demand for quality audio drives the justification for charging for news, making news consumption potentially richer than superficial online skimming of headline-driven news.[65] Podcast publishers and platforms now attract listeners from online radio. At-home podcast users tend to also be heavy users of online radio such as iHeartRadio and streaming music.[66] Given the significant overlap between the two audiences, listeners are drawn to online radio for many of the reasons they prefer podcasts. The information motive for podcast listening's positive association with music streaming services "signals a complementary relation between the two seemingly competing audio formats in the information sphere," as Chan-Olmsted and Wang aptly observe.[67] Streaming music listeners turn to podcasts for their information because the audio format is ideally matched to their media consumption preferences. iHeartRadio, Spotify, and Pandora have thus invested heavily in podcasts to capitalize on this trend.[68] In addition to regarding on-demand audio as superior to other audio forms, streaming music aficionados are intentional and selective about curating and sharing their lists of preferred artists. Similarly, podcast listeners find the medium provides superior content compared to other formats.[69]

In addition to building on established listening practices of internet radio and online streaming audiences seeking quality audio experiences, the highly intimate nature of podcasts lends itself well to justifying a financial commitment from listeners. The bond between programs, listeners, and personalities leads to affective and cognitive consequences that include greater identification, enjoyment, engagement, and loyalty. User perception of the mental and social benefits of shows can be predicted by the nature of their parasocial relationship with the host.[70] The power of parasocial relationships has led social media influencers and celebrities to enter this digital space as a means of expanding their reach and impact.[71] Whereas affective, entertainment-related motives linked to a charismatic host increase the amount of consumption (the actual usage level), information-related motives lead to more continuous engagement over time, which can be measured by subscription. The following case studies of the 2021 subscription programs introduced by Apple and Spotify examine the normalization of paid podcast listening as a key phase in the transformation of audio journalism in digital culture.

CASE STUDY: APPLE PODCASTS SUBSCRIPTIONS

Given the complexity of cross-platform consumption, podcasting is not a simple digital, on-demand, mobile extension of radio. Not only is it consumed differently than radio, but its audience consists of many nonradio listeners. The rising popularity of nonradio podcast platforms and amateur (nonexpert) podcast production speak to the uniqueness of the medium's affordances, technologies, and audiences. Since Apple's introduction of the preinstalled Podcasts app on all new iPhones in 2012, the concept of a subscription was understood by users not as a financial transaction but as a means of curating a favorites list, much like the subscribe option on YouTube. For Apple's first dedicated Podcasts app, the act of subscribing simply added the podcast to a grid or list on the app's main interface. From the grid, any episode could be streamed or downloaded to a device for offline listening. No direct payments were possible on the app until 2021. With the advent of prosumer culture came a wave of self-produced amateur podcasts. Apple responded to this trend by offering creators the opportunity to post their own podcasts on the platform, complete with the option of charging listeners for access. With its new set of features introduced in 2021, Apple Podcasts Subscriptions thus offered podcast creators the ability to generate premium or freemium subscription products in direct competition with Spotify.

The actual features of the Apple Podcasts Subscriptions program reflect an aggressive attempt to alter the established culture of podcast production and consumption. In particular, they appear in most instances to lock both creators and listeners into Apple's media ecosystem, as design details reflect the company's terms and conditions that serve its platformization of media production and consumption.[72] The new subscription model comes as a direct competitive response to its rival Spotify, whose market share threatens to take over Apple's once-dominant position in what has become the fastest-growing sector of the digital publishing industry. Apple's accidental cultivation of the medium as an on-demand online extension of the iPod—hybridized with the concept of the internet broad*cast* as the *pod*cast—gives the company additional incentive to protect its brand's inherent association with podcasting. Thus, financial and brand identity factors loom large in Apple's aggressive entry into paid-subscription listening. Apple's tilted marketplace speaks to platformization's economic dominance over creators, particularly with its standard annual charge of $19.99 for use of its subscription program.[73] Creators additionally must pay Apple 30 percent of their revenue from each transaction facilitated within the first year, which drops to 15 percent beginning with the second year. The first-year 30 percent figure poses a potential barrier for entry for new podcast creators, thus attracting shows that have already established a solid audience and financial base.

Such uneven terms for competition not only place startups at a distinct financial disadvantage but also contribute to the funneling of profits to an increasingly limited number of top publishers. This exacerbates the plight of smaller publishers concerned with struggling for greater prominence on the third-party platform's promotional hierarchy. Interestingly, these exorbitant revenue cuts that are also integral to Apple's App Store prompted Epic Games to develop its own method of circumventing such payments required of in-game transactions for *Fortnite*, the popular battle royal video game. Apple responded by suing Epic Games, which expressed its dissent through a satirical recreation of Apple's iconic *1984*-themed Super Bowl advertisement announcing the release of the first Macintosh personal computer. In Epic Games' version, the totalitarian, media-controlling figure of Big Brother—from which citizens yearn for liberation—is refigured as the Apple Computer Company. Apple's high revenue cuts have generated criticism of the company's monopolistic tactics, which now extend the creative content interests of Apple TV+ into original audio.[74]

Epitomizing platformization in the Apple Podcasts Subscriptions program is the stipulation that Apple owns publishers' listenership on its platform. This condition prevents publishers from engaging their listeners on the app through any means of communication other than the shows themselves. This arrangement creates friction for publishers, who must migrate outside of the app to communicate with their audience. Host–listener communication outside of the show's content is considered a vital component of the podcast medium. Direct, unscripted, and frictionless communication with the audience functions as one of the most important "triggers that encourage heightened engagement," particularly as "shifts in the technologies of media distribution and production have elevated fandom from the fringes of audience activity to a central role in the production of media texts."[75] Markman notes that podcasters continue to produce in order to foster relationships that benefit a community of listeners.[76] Without ownership of listenership, publishers on Apple Podcasts Subscriptions also lack access to valuable demographics, which help guide production practice and serve audiences' needs and interests. The app therefore hijacks the publishers' listener data—a lucrative commodity in the digital ecosystem—by making it the exclusive property of Apple. This enables Apple to unilaterally adjust promotional privileges for any given show on its platform. The lack of transparency in this feature of the subscription tool package is consistent with the company's lack of transparency in its algorithms and curation, informing a business model in which "Apple is not forthcoming with information about how they decide which shows to feature or how their charts are calculated."[77] Any podcast built with Apple Tools remains on the Apple Platform, thus forcing publishers to re-create their work from scratch in order to place it on another podcast platform. This condition discourages producers from reaching the Android market, which directly competes with the Apple iPhone, via distribution throughout the wider digital publishing industry.

Publishers on Apple Podcasts Subscriptions intent on building a comprehensive subscription program must replicate their work in order to distribute paid episodes on other platforms. The closed subscription system on the Apple Platform undermines the concept of open-source software sharing, the original principle guiding internet pioneer Tim Berners-Lee's release of HTML code for public use and innovation.[78] Apple Podcasts Subscriptions is therefore anathema to the open Web's principles of free sharing of software tools as practiced on platforms such as GitHub. As Apple Podcasts assumes greater control of the industry, it also threatens to erode the standard of production, especially by minimizing publishers' access to distribution networks and choking off communication with listeners, the lifeblood of the podcast medium. Further, nonfictional and journalistic content according to this model will become less responsive to audiences, which may result in a widening divide between producers and consumers. In-app podcast creation on Apple's platform thus profoundly changes the nature of the host–listener relationship, creating a more distanced, prepackaged product. Apple Podcasts Subscriptions' most significant threat to the digital culture of the open Web lies in the app's design that discourages publishers from expanding their work through RSS, the Really Simple Syndication characterizing the standard system for the distribution of content from all manner of online publishers. RSS feeds represent a key method for creators to allow users outside of Apple's platform to subscribe to their shows. The third-party platform, in this sense, interferes with the supply and demand of the podcast industry. These competitive forces, which have sparked unprecedented innovation in the medium, may be truncated by Apple's anticompetitive, monopolistic interventions.[79]

The overall lack of publisher autonomy in Apple Podcasts Subscriptions is not to be underestimated. In addition to discouraging wider distribution outside the app, charging 30 percent of subscription revenue, and seizing ownership of listenership for shows it did not produce, Apple also owns the transcripts of every show. Apple's terms and conditions of the program agreement claims that its possession of full transcripts is necessary for machine learning to generate preview clips for better discovery. This clause clearly aligns with the company's policies designed to assume rights to products themselves, in addition to the revenue they earn on their platform. Conversely, the benefits of Apple Podcasts Subscriptions share much in common with tethered content in the app economy, which offers frictionless access, ease of payment, and a self-contained, more intuitive system for navigation compared to relatively complex RSS feeds.[80] The listenership will build on those already in the Apple ecosystem rather than drawing on the more diverse audiences on the open Web. The company's protocol to monetize casual listeners by converting them into paid subscribers entails normalizing payment for access to podcasts in a digital culture accustomed to listening to shows for free.

CASE STUDY: SPOTIFY PREMIUM SUBSCRIPTIONS

In February of 2021 Spotify announced its premium subscription tools, which together provide an important point of contrast to Apple regarding approach and policies that condition the production and consumption of podcasts. Since its foray into the podcast industry, Spotify has positioned itself as the upstart capable of wrestling dominance away from Apple. Unlike Apple, Spotify's subscription tools are provided by Anchor, acquired by Spotify in 2019, which specializes in podcast creation, distribution, and monetization through premium or freemium subscriptions. Prior to its acquisition by Spotify in 2019, Anchor was an independent company with its own policies designed according to the principle of open-source and unrestricted distribution on RSS. Spotify elected not to severely restrict such publisher autonomy established by Anchor. Spotify accordingly allows publishers to distribute their shows to other platforms as paid listening experiences, as Anchor had prior to acquisition. In this sense, Spotify's use of Anchor positions it as more of a direct competitor with other open Web podcast platforms such as Supporting Cast and Patreon than with Apple, which does not allow for open redistribution through RSS and other platforms. Spotify's market share, however, does position it as Apple's direct competitor.

Unlike Apple, Spotify instituted the constraint of three price points ($2.99, $4.99, and $7.99) publishers can charge for subscriptions to their shows. This measure of controlling prices impedes the organic fluctuations of supply and demand in the free market, setting unnecessary limits in an effort to regulate the low and high ends of the spectrum of subscription pricing. It also bears the potential of artificially generating a kind of caste system of upper, middle, and lower tiers. This system risks stigmatizing podcasts in the lowest price bracket and may prevent listeners from agreeing to subsequent increases in subscription rates. Already successful shows with the strongest followings might feel restricted by a fixed price ceiling. Apple's flexibility in allowing publishers to set any price for subscription therefore may be preferable to publishers. Conversely, a distinct advantage for creators on Spotify is that the platform allows free access to its subscription tools, with only 5 percent of revenues required in 2023 compared to Apple's 30 percent for the first year and 15 percent thereafter. Another key distinction between the two platforms' subscription models is the location of transactions, with Apple's restricted to in-app payments only. By contrast, Spotify subscribers are directed out of the iOS app for their transactions to prevent Apple from charging a percentage of the payment. Spotify's need to circumvent such charges speaks to Apple's ubiquitous hold on the digital marketplace, one that can potentially force its competitors into the role of customers.

With the exception of fixed subscription pricing, these details underscore the built-in autonomy Spotify has granted its publishers compared to Apple's expensive and limited arrangement. Apple's frictionless payment system may prove seductive to listeners seeking a faster and easier payment method than Spotify's. From the perspective of the publisher, however, Spotify's main advantage lies in the expectation that users of its subscription tools maintain unmitigated control of their relationships with their audiences. Unlike Apple's publishers, those on Spotify may provide paid podcasts even if that paid-subscription base is managed by a third party off site. The Open Access Platform on Spotify allows creators of podcasts on their platform the option to provide paid content for their audience through Spotify, a feature strictly prohibited on Apple. This major difference, as with most in Apple's terms and conditions, aims to prevent all creation, publication, payment transactions, and consumption from leaving its platform, enabling the company to profit from every stage, from publication to reception, as well as ownership of the audience and full text of podcast episodes.

The tectonic shift in the industry that these subscription programs potentially represent is best understood in terms of their impact on the open standard for Web publication. The question remains whether the adoption of subscription by the two largest podcast platforms in the industry will render RSS for the medium increasingly irrelevant to the point of becoming obsolete. This development points to the erosion of the open standard, along with its ethos of disintermediated enterprise. Even in the case that Spotify's more autonomous, laissez-faire subscription program prevails over Apple's, the ecosystem for podcast creation stands to become increasingly dependent on a major platform—with explicit aims at controlling the entire industry—to facilitate publication, thus profoundly reshaping the context for consumption and audience–host communication. Although there are scattered instances of podcasters who help monetize their shows through direct payment from their listeners, mostly in the form of membership programs, the dependence on advertising as the main source of revenue remains the prevailing business model for the medium. Advertising may remain the industry's dominant revenue source because successful publishers with a thriving base of listeners will not see an immediate need to abandon their lucrative brand partnerships and sponsors. The paid podcast will thus likely converge with the advertising model by complimenting rather than supplanting it.

THE PUBLISHER–AUDIENCE EXCHANGE VALUE

As with the advent of paywalls in the early 2010s, the mainstreaming of paid podcasts raises the question as to whether enough consumer dollars exist to sustain this business model. It is naïve, of course, to assume that the capital resources for consumer spending for online news is infinite. It is plausible, however, that users will recognize the overall benefit and value of including purchased news—particularly longform podcast journalism—in their media diets. Laufer recommends that consumers purchase at least some portion of their total news media intake to inculcate more mindful selection and gain exposure to higher quality journalism than free content alone can provide.[81] The base of consumer spending on podcasts has great potential for expansion, particularly as the audience grows in response to the medium's evolution. As the shows increasingly justify payment, both startups and transmedia publishers such as the *New York Times* can potentially allocate more resources into production and editing. Operating on the free model, the *Times* revealed the severe cost of editorial neglect in their early bid for a documentary true crime blockbuster with *Caliphate*, as discussed in chapter 2. The compromised editorial oversight that destroyed its credibility may not have occurred on a subscription model. Although paid podcasts may have the effect of enhancing journalistic quality for principled producers, they risk abuse in the hands of those who prioritize profit over journalistic integrity.

As subscriptions to podcasts increase, advertising will likely become more targeted and tailored to the paying audience, as with paywalled, screen-based digital journalism. This streamlining of advertising on podcasts may remove what many observe as excessive commercials, both in the form of interruptions for hosts to pitch products and as pre-recorded ads appearing at the beginning and end of episodes. Even the most dedicated fans show disdain for awkward interruptions for endorsements, as in the case of Ben Shapiro suddenly promoting waffles in the middle of the most urgent and politically efficacious episode of his career the day following the insurrection on the U.S. Capitol in January of 2021. Free of such intrusive and distracting advertising, the quality of the listening experience for podcast journalism will likely improve. Although it is unlikely to become the dominant model immediately, subscription-first podcast businesses now have a more viable future due to the introduction of subscription options for Apple and Spotify creators. Integrated subscription tools inject new diversity into business approaches for podcasters, effectively raising the standard for content quality, but in the process also introduce the risk of expanded platformization. Perhaps most importantly, the shift of consumer expectations prompted by these new tools initiates the process of mainstreaming the notion of paid podcasts, not only raising but substantively transforming consumer expectations. Paid podcasts may also expand the pool of potential revenue as a whole. The news media industry has not seen such an opportunity for increased revenue since the advent of the digital revolution. Factors to monitor closely in this development include whether paid podcasting will enhance or diminish news quality and whether it will break down or reinforce existing information silos.

The normalization of the notion of paid podcasts in mainstream media culture is historically informed by the introduction of paywalls for screen-based news media. The original paywall debate in the 2010s did not anticipate how fluid the notion of a paywall could be, ranging from freemium and metered to soft and hard designs. Further, few anticipated how common it would be for publishers and editors such as *Slate*'s Jacob Weisberg to explore revenue sources beyond advertising, including a variety of forms of direct payment from users.[82] The power of paying for news lies in the elevation of news consumption that places the user in a position of valuing the content. The monetary transaction places the consumer in a better position to appreciate and understand the labor, technology, and craft of the product itself. "Getting paid a fair price for the hard work of writing and reporting," as *Harper's Magazine* publisher John R. MacArthur has argued, is integral to saving the craft of journalism from depreciating in value as "free content" under the advertising-dependent digital publishing model.[83] The practice of offering content free in the quest for more advertising, MacArthur notes, devalues the work of the writer and the editor "by feeding it—with little or no remuneration—to search engines, which in turn feed information to advertising agencies."[84] Publishers have indeed lost substantial advertising revenue to Google and Facebook on the free model, which does not promise to sustain high-quality journalism.

For readers, advertising on screen-based digital news encourages scanning and skimming through interfaces anathema to deep reading. Readers "cannot absorb information well on devices that buzz, flash and generally distract" with their myriad windows and notifications that can simultaneously be open.[85] Paywalled podcasts answer to both of these dilemmas by offering a screen-free, immersive news experience with little or no advertising. In the process, what promises to be restored is "the exchange value between news publishers and their readers," according to the editors of the subscription-only French magazine *XXI*. The opportunity to produce poised, reflective journalism increases with greater exchange value between publishers and their readers, and the reverse occurs as that value declines. Advertising's presence will remain, but it may be less obtrusive in cluttering content and in functioning as a domineering presence mitigating the relationship between writer, publisher, and reader. Paid audio content has drawn interest from legacy media. The *New York Times*, for example, acquired Audm in 2021, "a subscription narrated article product." As of the writing of this chapter, NPR confirmed plans to launch a podcast subscription service allowing "listeners to directly support their favorite podcasts and receive sponsorship-free versions of individual podcasts for a small fee."[86] NPR plans to share the revenue with local member stations in order to introduce podcast listeners to local radio and vice versa. This measure attempts to bridge the gap between radio and podcast audiences, which do not consistently overlap. NPR continues to provide free content in addition to its subscription products, which it develops in partnership with Apple and Spotify, and declared that its implementation of paid podcasts does not interfere with its public service mission.[87] Given NPR's importance in setting the standard for the evolution of documentary longform audio journalism via *This American Life* and Serial Productions, this development provides further evidence of the potential industry-wide adoption of paid podcasts in the future. Subscription options expand the return on investment that has yet to be fully realized throughout the industry, offering creators a new way of drawing revenue. The normalization of paid podcasts has already begun to take shape in digital culture with the spread of paid podcasts and "as consumers show a willingness to pay for premium audio experiences without ads."[88]

The lessons of the first paywall debate of the early 2010s now bear significance at a time when audio reporting comes of age. The least distracting digital medium now becomes relatively ad-free to augment its advances in storytelling and sound design. Improved content promises to expand the paying audience for news while also offering users a more intentional and meaningful media diet.[89] As John V. Pavlik notes, "paying for news in some form is an increasing norm for most Americans and it is a pattern likely to grow in the years ahead as advertising dollars continue to flow toward digital companies such as Google and as news providers increasingly require other forms of user payment to access the news."[90] Although a paid news ecosystem potentially closes off access to quality journalism for lower-income users and makes their concerns less relevant to the format and coverage options of news executives, the range of payment options already established remains quite broad. The normalization of paid podcasts does not pose an existential threat to inclusive and democratic governance as many publishers such as NPR will continue to offer free or nominally priced products. Journalism's service to democracy is therefore more directly threatened by podcast subscription becoming subsumed by Apple and Spotify, whose algorithms, terms, and conditions continue to favor a limited number of publishers with established audience bases, in effect tilting the playing field against smaller podcasters seeking to gain traction in the increasingly competitive podcast market.

In this industrial context, platforms exert influence over content by controlling and conditioning the digital space for podcast production, distribution, and consumption. Also of profound influence over these processes are the political and commercial interests of producers, which is the focus of the next three chapters. The rise of paid podcasts and platformization sets the stage industrially for the following exploration of Far Right podcasting, which thrives on media ownership patterns supporting its political agenda through an elaborate conservative media ecosystem.

CHAPTER FIVE

Charting the Far Right

The February 2021 death of conservative talk radio icon Rush Limbaugh occasioned a moment of deep reflection among listeners and critics alike on the meaning and origins of conservative media in the United States. Having won the Presidential Medal of Freedom just months before his passing, an honor President Donald Trump bestowed in unprecedented fashion during a State of the Union Address, Limbaugh's legacy drew renewed attention. WBUR Boston's obituary was representative of many in the news media refusing to eulogize Limbaugh, instead laying bare his corrosion of public discourse via vitriolic tactics aimed at dehumanizing and annihilating political opponents, a legacy that set the stage for the insurrection on the U.S. Capitol.[1] Opposite responses appeared in the elegiac tones of Fox News and the flags flown at half-mast throughout the state of Florida at the behest of Republican governor Ron DeSantis. First through terrestrial broadcast radio and later through podcasting, no figure in the history of audio media has made a greater impact on modern American politics.[2]

Despite its emancipatory promise to abet free speech as one of the world's least-censored media forms, podcasting's democratic function is uneven and highly contested, as noted by media scholars who have questioned its progressive potential.[3] Podcasting's greatest assets of aural intimacy and expressive power delivered through the human voice can alternately become its most dangerous liability, one that "carries a great risk of exploitation" with grave implications for democracy.[4] As Walter Lippman pointed out, any crisis in Western democracy should be understood as a crisis in journalism.[5]

THE ORIGINS OF THE RIGHT-WING PODCAST

The history of right-wing podcasting traces directly back to Limbaugh and his unique brand of pugilistic populism that drew on the rise of shock jock radio during the late 1980s, spawned in part by the repeal of the Fairness Doctrine in 1987. Originally established by the FCC in 1949, the Fairness Doctrine mandated the balanced, equitable, and honest treatment of controversial issues. Its legislation aimed to control an unwieldy pattern in manipulative radio content, the most dangerous voice of which resounded in the brutal antisemitism of Father Charles Coughlin, the Nazi sympathizer who commanded a colossal 15 million listeners in the mid-1930s.[6] The National Association of Broadcasters (NAB) originally banned Coughlin from radio in 1939, two decades before the federal mandate. At the time, the capacity for radio networks to act swiftly in defense of democracy was enabled by a leaner, more centralized industry capable of reaching consensus for developing, amending, and enforcing its own professional code of ethics. Such decisive self-regulation in the public interest would be inconceivable in the current highly corporatized information ecosystem.[7]

The NAB initially removed Coughlin and other radio ideologues in the late 1930s by closing the industry's financial loophole that allowed the sale of airtime to entities intent on presenting controversial issues in an uncompromising, doctrinaire, or propagandistic manner. In the wake of the NAB's amended code of ethics, "the ability to pay was no longer enough" for extremist and fringe figures like Coughlin to gain airtime, as radio historian Michele Hilmes explains. "Now broadcasters had an obligation to restrict all those outside the broad mainstream of political views."[8] Coughlin's banning was also prompted in part by Orson Welles's elaborate *War of the Worlds* radio hoax that underscored in 1938 the medium's persuasive power to influence public opinion and potentially alter the course of civil society.[9] The fictional scenario of an alien invasion of New York told through a series of news bulletins was believed by hundreds of thousands of listeners who took to the streets to escape.[10]

In the wake of Welles's hoax and Father Coughlin's hate-fueled propaganda, The Fairness Doctrine effectively prevented ideologues from winning an undue share of the radio audience, as witnessed in the culture of civil on-air political discourse that prevailed from 1949 to 1987.

Among President Ronald Reagan's widespread cuts to federal programs and government regulations, the repeal of the Fairness Doctrine in 1987 stands out for its lasting and profound impact on the media climate, the nature of political discourse, and the trajectory of the Republican Party, or GOP. Originally spearheaded by Republican lawmakers who argued that the regulation served to silence conservatives, the removal of the Fairness Doctrine ushered in conservative talk radio, the core conventions of which now drive the billion-dollar right-wing podcasting industry.[11] Without responsibility for equitable treatment of controversial issues, hosts such as Limbaugh were unleashed to foment against liberals, leveraging extremist rhetoric that became the keynote for conservative talk radio. The effort to make politics entertaining drew on a base element in the listening audience that savored meanspirited attacks and crass humor. Analysis and independent critical thinking were willingly abrogated for blind compliance, as Limbaugh's followers dubbed themselves "ditto-heads." Cable television had less tolerance for Limbaugh, who was forced to resign from his position as ESPN commentator on *NFL Countdown* after he insisted that African American quarterback Donovan McNabb's talent was overrated by liberal media members who "wanted to see a Black quarterback thrive."[12] Decades later, in the role of a podcaster, Limbaugh would downplay COVID-19 as no worse than the common cold, alleging the pandemic was being weaponized by the liberal media against Trump.[13] The month prior to his death, Limbaugh hailed the Capitol insurrectionists as patriots worthy of the reverence bestowed upon American Revolutionary War veterans.[14] All amounted to gross distortions worthy of P. T. Barnum himself and his preposterous Fiji mermaid, packaged and sensationalized as a spectacle for a demographic desperately wanting to believe.

Open racism and assaults on the mainstream press as a liberal propaganda mill were staples of Limbaugh's show that would inspire innumerable imitators in the podcast industry, particularly those advancing conspiracy theories.[15] Limbaugh's 1992 book *The Way Things Ought to Be* cemented his credo that recast the GOP's self-concept toward a more extreme and unrelenting posture readily apparent in his 1994 "Address to Incoming House GOP Freshmen" solicited by Speaker of the House Newt Gingerich. Moderation, Limbaugh claimed, was a sign of weakness, and no quarter should be given to liberal values such as compassion for the working class.[16] "This is not the time to get moderate," he urged in his address. "This is not the time to start gaining the approval of the people you've just defeated." Appealing to the manhood of House members, he exhorted them to "stay rock-ribbed, devoted in an almost militant way to your principles" in order to "continue to be sent back here until you're term-limited out."[17] Specifically, he advised them to anticipate and actively resist appeals to their humanity—especially from liberal female journalists such as NPR's Cokie Roberts, whom he names in the speech—in phrases like "The war on the poor" and in allegations that the removal of social programs is "cold hearted, cruel to the poor." All are tactics, he warned to the newly elected GOP House members, "designed to get you to moderate, to maybe not follow through as you intended to on welfare reform and other cultural issues."[18] This reinvention of the GOP as entrenched and militant resonated with a wave of extreme conservatism that denigrated the feminist and environmental movements, a movement visible in 1990s-era tracts such as William A. Henry III's *In Defense of Elitism*, which fulminates against the alleged evils of affirmative action and accommodations for the disabled. Such caustic bipartisan public debate has a polarizing effect on the public, according to research in political communication. "When citizens are exposed to media coverage depicting mass polarization, they dislike members of the opposition more, and rate them more negatively on a number of dimensions."[19]

Contemporary podcasting's Far Right derives directly from Limbaugh, embodying the toxic strains of digital culture endemic to online commentary on platforms such as Twitter and Reddit, both of which figured prominently in the 2021 Capitol insurrection. This chapter argues that whereas "speaking personally" has become a core practice of journalism whose merits include greater attention to context and interpretative analysis, serious risks arise from these freedoms from the constraints of traditional broadcast conventions.[20] The most prominent of risks include "alienation and personal attacks online" in addition to the concerning pattern identified by the American Press Institute in which more than half of internet users reported that they could not easily tell the difference between news and opinion, particularly on social media.[21] In popular right-leaning podcasts such as those hosted by Ben Shapiro and Dan Bongino, the element of opinion amplifies the tendency of the medium to relegate news to a secondary concern behind that of format. As Nee and Santana explain, "an outcome of the emphasis on form and storytelling" in podcast journalism "is that the dissemination of new news becomes less important than the packaging and emotional impact."[22] Such podcasts deploy talk radio's signature convention whereby the host trades the role of impartial journalistic observer for that of a highly opinionated pundit whose commentary is accessorized with "live-to-tape conversations between reporters and some guests with very little editing."[23]

The following section provides a theoretical framework for understanding how the industrial context has accommodated and encouraged Far Right discourse to flourish on news-related podcasts, which encompass opinion and commentary.[24] This leads to an examination of platformization as a function of media ownership and conglomeration that impacts moderation interventions and, thus, norms for allowable content.[25] It is followed by case studies of two of the most influential conservative podcasts of the early 2020s. Analysis focuses on how the technological affordances of the podcast medium combine with shifts in industry ownership and regulation to provide fertile ground for Far Right–leaning content fueled by conspiracy theories and social intolerance. Findings on Bongino's and Shapiro's January 7 episodes in the wake of the 2021 Capitol insurrection reveal a spectrum of responses among podcasting's Far Right ranging from reactionary denialism to constitutional conservatism. The concluding section explores the future trajectory of Far Right podcasting in the context of conservative media.

THE JOURNALISM OF AFFIRMATION

The effort to make political content entertaining in audio media raises the question of the boundaries between journalism and other forms of media.[26] Entertainment media has a long history of carrying journalistic content, particularly in the form of engaging personal narrative and editorial modes featuring highly subjective commentary.[27] Personal narrative's migration into audio media is most readily apparent in long-form serialized documentary tracing back to Ira Glass's *This American Life* on NPR.[28] In contrast to this highly edited form characterized by carefully orchestrated sound design, the more discursive *extended chat* is identified by Reuters Digital News Project as roundtable discussions delivered in an informal style with a flexible format that takes on single or multiple topics and frequently features extended monologue.[29] Conservative daily news podcasts such as *The Ben Shapiro Show* prefer the extended chat because they enable a form of reporting that Bill Kovach and Tom Rosenstiel identify as the journalism of assertion.[30] As a mode of broadcast journalism that flourished on both talk radio and cable television news shows such as those hosted by Bill O'Reilly and Sean Hannity, the journalism of assertion places a premium on publishing information as quickly as possible, with less concern for vetting information items prior to releasing them to the public.[31] Outlets trafficking in the journalism of assertion have been places "where news sources could more easily assert whatever they wanted with less vetting or filtering."[32] Political insiders and media strategists such as Roger Stone have manipulated the proliferation of news outlets engaging in the journalism of assertion, a movement enabled by the rapid publication cycle that accelerated with the advent of digital communication technology. Stone has made a career of shaping public opinion through baseless rumor and innuendo that drive headlines.[33] Hence, one of Stone's preferred outlets was Alex Jones's *InfoWars*, the notorious purveyor of "alternative truths" whose host has been removed from all major social media platforms for amplifying misinformation.

For audiences interested in reinforcing their own preexisting political perspectives, the journalism of affirmation—working in tandem with the journalism of assertion—lends color, theater, and even valor to their ideological self-concept. In his address to Congress in 1994, Rush Limbaugh described his method accordingly. "What happens on talk radio is real simple: We validate what's in people's hearts and minds already."[34] Radio's original public service ideal of "mixed programming designed for the listener to encounter something unheard of" has yielded to "increasing specialization and formatting" often "tailored to fit the most precise personal tastes."[35] Spotify's success at microtargeting music listener demographics through its sophisticated playlist algorithms, for example, has its corollary in political podcasts. Listeners seek affirmation of their own preexisting political values as "an expression of a desire to have the world reflect back and echo the listening subject, either as some sort of narcissistic extension and self-confirmation, or an expression of anxiety about difference or the unknown."[36]

Extended chat podcasts are particularly adept at performing as an ideological echo chamber. Like television talk shows, they transform politics into an entertaining spectacle for audiences according to the journalism of assertion in which "what were once the raw ingredients of journalism—the rumor, innuendo, allegation, accusation, charge, supposition, and hypothesis—get passed onto the audience directly."[37] In this sense, journalistic leads become subject to speculation and are delivered directly to audiences as published content, in the process removing the importance of reporting. This method is anathema to the journalism of verification, an approach steeped in documentary and interview evidence that entails thorough fact-checking prior to publication.[38] Instead, the journalism of assertion is prone to factual errors because "it is easier to assert misinformation" in this mode of discourse, a tendency that grows with the number of outlets practicing it as the norms of the profession shift.[39] The birther conspiracy alleging that Barack Obama was not born in the United States was originally an innuendo, for example, that became amplified on Limbaugh's show.[40]

The journalism of assertion is "less of a filter and more of a conduit" relying on a "postpublication vetting process" that bears serious risks much like those associated with crowd-sourced and citizen-produced data.[41] The amplification of innuendo and rumor, such as voter fraud following the 2020 election and antivaccination conspiracy beliefs, can inspire online users to actively seek out evidence (however fabricated or misrepresented) to support those claims. The journalism of assertion thus leverages the immediacy and liveness of the extended chat form of daily news podcast. In the process of prioritizing speed, volume, and sensational appeal, the liabilities to inaccuracy escalate. When conjoined with a platform operating according to the journalism of affirmation, such inaccuracies increase exponentially.[42]

Among the main types of daily news podcasts identified by Reuters Digital News Project, which include the news roundup, the microbulletin, and the deep dive, the extended chat stands out as a branch of opinion journalism, which, at its most principled, contemplates news events after they have occurred and features careful consideration of evidence.[43] In print journalism, *The National Review*, *The Nation*, *Harper's*, and the *Weekly Standard* represent this tradition of opinion writing rooted in rigorous reporting and research, a process that also drives longform documentary podcast programs. When legacy media publishers such as the *New York Times* established themselves in the world of podcast journalism, it became apparent that the subjective style of reporting could provide greater context around the news issues of the day rather than operating according to the primary objective of reinforcing and potentially radicalizing listeners' ideological perspectives.[44]

Listeners generally turn to podcasts with the intent of being informed and entertained.[45] The intimacy and informality of the podcast medium reaches listeners at deeper emotional levels than traditional radio reporting due to freedom from constraints of time, format, and content regulations. Freedom from such constraints "presents both opportunities and dilemmas for news podcast producers within the context of journalistic norms," posing challenges to the storytelling process.[46] The first-person perspective can be used as a tool of propaganda wielded by persuasive and charismatic hosts, thus "creating tension between podcast journalism and the boundaries of traditional journalistic practices."[47] Due to the lack of digital tools for searching and flagging audio content, podcasting has remained largely unchecked by government regulators as well as media watchdogs operating on behalf of the public interest.

Podcast journalism's deviation from traditional journalistic practice, however, can be executed according to highly evolved principles that challenge audiences with intellectually rich content generated by a process of production rooted in self-reflexivity and transparency.[48] Longform podcast interviews of the sort popularized by Bill Simmons on The Ringer, for example, exemplify how the extended chat form can be executed in a principled and carefully documented manner. Documentary longform podcasting operates at precisely the opposite register of the journalism of assertion due to its slower, more painstaking production process. The convention of on-air self-questioning and transparent assessment of reportorial ethics made famous by Sarah Koenig in *Serial*, for example, takes an opposite approach to knowledge-seeking compared to the journalism of affirmation. "To approach a more nuanced conception on truth on *Serial*... requires us to slow down our thinking to close analytical listening," an understanding of "truth as a *process*" between journalist, audience, and events of the ontological world.[49] This perspective is antithetical to the prepackaged dogmas of right-wing podcasts. As a genre, right-wing podcasting is technologically and intellectually mired in a predigital talk radio form anathema to the self-aware epistemological advances in journalistic practice at the vanguard of digital longform storytelling.[50] As part of the shift from news to opinion detailed by Kimberly Meltzer, the ranting monologue is thus the staple of conservative podcasts, a blunt approach to the medium as a megaphone rather than a carefully orchestrated series of interviews with complex editing and highly produced sound design according to the Koenig and Barbaro schools of production practice.[51] A decade before blogging, the rant began as a comedic form developed by Dennis Miller on *Saturday Night Live* during the 1980s before it transformed into a staple of conservative political expression. The form was instrumental in Miller's own career transformation into an increasingly serious right-wing pundit with a regular segment on Fox News's *The O'Reilly Factor*. Unlike in traditional journalistic forms, such affective polarization is packaged as entertainment media treating politics and current affairs, resulting in "polarized media coverage [that] causes citizens to view the opposing party less positively."[52]

PLATFORMIZATION AND CONSERVATIVE PODCASTING

The journalism of affirmation derives from media ownership and digital publishing structures. Longer episodes are essential to the generation of such huge currents of conservative thought in the information ecosystem, as exhibited by *The Ben Shapiro Show*, which is the leading daily news podcast in the extended chat category and fourth overall, according Podtrac's September 2020 ranking. Its episodes are twice the average length of those in the next longest category, which is the deep dive.[53]

Emotionally charged media content consumed in massive quantities over longer time intervals results in stronger media effects, including narrative transportation and knowledge retention.[54] Compared to effects from one-time exposure, the accumulation of individual media effects is more capable of leading to macrolevel societal effects.[55] In presentations about public affairs, variations in news quality measured through completeness, accuracy, and objectivity mean individual news knowledge gain "may not necessarily be functional for society."[56] The social impact of low-quality news is a factor of its pervasiveness. *The Daily Wire*, which publishes *The Ben Shapiro Show*, is by far the most prolific rightwing publisher on Facebook. Its social media saturation campaign drives traffic to the publisher's monetizing website in part by cannibalizing its own content through the reformatting of older stories.[57] This massive wave of conservative podcast journalism, which functions as a daily news source for tens of millions of listeners, has been enabled by a system of platformization.[58]

Within the podcast industry, "platformization may be the biggest change on the horizon."[59] As with games and film, podcasts tend to be located on platforms that the publishers of these media products do not control.[60] Platforms such as Google Play, Amazon Prime, and Apple condition the creative environment for media producers in order to generate monopolistic network effects. In their heated competition to control the podcast market, Spotify and Apple prioritize profit maximization over serving media's duty to democracy, which is a core principle of journalism.[61] Both companies engage in data harvesting through universal surveillance and the centralization of power.[62] Platformization has effectively raised barriers for entry for upstart podcasters while offering advantages to industry insiders.[63]

The most significant shift in the podcast industry toward platformization occurred in 2015 when Spotify announced it would include podcasting in its offerings. With over 217 million active users drawn to its services for music storage, discovery, and consumption, Spotify has taken the podcast industry by storm with acquisitions of podcast producers including Gimlet Media and Higher Ground productions, owned by Michelle and Barak Obama.[64] The latter acquisition included exclusive publication of *The Michelle Obama Podcast*. Gimlet also made a contractual commitment to produce original and exclusive podcasts for Spotify's subscription and advertising-supported platform.[65] In 2019 Spotify acquired Megaphone, formerly known as Panoply, for $235 million. Originally launched as a podcast extension of *Slate* in 2015, Panoply pivoted to hosting and advertising technology in 2018 and then rebranded itself as an amplifier under the moniker Megaphone. These initial acquisitions generated momentum for Spotify in their quest to acquire the most lucrative products in podcasting, leading them directly to the perennial chart-topping show, *The Joe Rogan Experience*. The acquisition placed this popular program under the editorial auspices of Spotify, thus allowing Rogan significant creative latitude.

Two months after signing a $100 million exclusive distribution contract with Spotify, Joe Rogan invited the notorious Alex Jones on *The Joe Rogan Experience*. Despite Jones's highly publicized removal from several major social media platforms in recent years, Spotify allowed him to be Rogan's featured guest on a three-hour show in late October of 2020. In it the conspiracy theorist argued, among other similar claims, that liberals were attempting to damage the economy to remove Trump from office, that masks were not effective in preventing the spread of COVID-19, and that vaccines caused polio.[66] Spotify's defense for allowing Jones on the show was that Rogan had fact-checked his information. However, Rogan's fact-checking merely consisted of drawing an article from a digital news publisher addressing the probability of vaccines causing polio. Further, Spotify argued that if they had banned Jones from the show, "then other news organizations would not theoretically be free to engage Jones in a 'properly' fact-checked appearance, should they wish to do so, and get distributed on the platform."[67]

Just as Meta CEO Mark Zuckerberg has repeatedly defended his decision to allow for disinformation on Facebook in defense of free expression, Spotify delivered a similar defense, which served the company's larger goal of dominating the podcast market.[68] Without the even application of policies, the platform risks losing certain content producers. According to Spotify CEO Daniel Ek, "We are a creative platform for lots of creators. And it's important that they know what to expect from our platform. If we can't do that," he explained, "then there are other choices for creators to go to, so that consistency is super important."[69] However, rather than operating in the role of supplier of neutral infrastructure, Spotify's function as publisher is apparent in its direct payment of Rogan's salary under contract for exclusive rights to his original content.

Spotify's business model assumes that hosting deplatformed figures such as Jones is justifiable because the vast spectrum of voices they host makes regulation moot. This argument was similarly made with reference to the internet in its earliest stages of development as government regulation and media monopolization threatened the grassroots online communities that thrived without interference, a position advanced by high-profile entertainment media celebrities. Grateful Dead lyricist John Perry Barlow, for instance, penned "A Declaration of the Independence of Cyberspace" to defend the free speech rights of the Electronic Frontier Foundation, which fostered online networks Henry Jenkins would later describe as affinity spaces, or online communities where mutual learning and meaningful cultural exchanges occurred.[70] Now, with increasing abuse online, original principles on internet freedom have shown the limitations of the electronic frontier. Digital spaces for interaction typically begin with such idealism defending neutrality against industrial and government interference only to end in excessive abuses of free speech, which devolves into hate speech.[71] The gold rush phase of newly scaled platforms leads to pressure to implement restrictions on problematic content, a scenario that also arose during the advent of Twitter. Spotify's core function, like that of Netflix and YouTube, is to offer subscription services for exclusive original content, as seen in the contracts proffered to talent such as Joe Rogan, and to host other platforms, such as Anchor.

Although YouTube and Reddit eventually banned white supremacist channels, Spotify has been reluctant to institute such measures.[72] Spotify's bid to lead the podcast market seeks to reap the benefits of unprecedented growth in digital on-demand audio media. Based on the YouTube model, Anchor built its status as the most popular space online for independent creators to distribute their products for free and draw 30 percent of advertising revenue.[73] Spotify's purchase of Anchor for $150 million in 2019 opened up their platform to millions of creators, thus escalating the risk of abuse, particularly in creators deliberately distorting current affairs to build an audience.[74] The move from streaming music into podcasting entailed confronting journalistic standards and ethics in ways the company never encountered when it launched in 2015.

Since its aggressive entrance into the world of podcasting, Spotify now functions as the primary app for 25 percent of podcast listeners, eclipsing that of Apple at 20 percent.[75] This marks a sea change in the industry, which began with Apple's early control of podcast distribution in 2005, when the company first allowed users to download shows. Since then, Apple built a seemingly insurmountable lead in the industry, mainly by offering its podcast app predownloaded free of charge on its new devices. As Spotify's most important creative tool, Anchor was the engine generating an expansive array of content to be promoted through Megaphone, the industry's leading podcast brand-builder.[76]

Prior to its acquisition by Spotify, Anchor stood atop the competition for creative tools as the audio version of YouTube, while Megaphone dominated the market for podcast promotion, advertising, and marketing aimed at monetizing these massive audiences. Acquisition of the leading creative tool and advertising companies alone might have catapulted Spotify past Apple in the race for the podcast market. However, Spotify sought a complete takeover of the industry by acquiring *The Joe Rogan Experience*, which boasts the largest listenership in the world, at 200 million monthly downloads, vastly exceeding that of the second-most-downloaded show, *The Daily*, at 60 million.[77] By harnessing this and other leading shows, Spotify secured its takeover of the most lucrative sectors of the industry, galvanizing its dominance with the acquisition of Parcast, Gimlet (one of the earliest startups specializing exclusively in original podcast production in the digital publishing industry), and The Ringer, Bill Simmons's podcast company spawned from his critically acclaimed *Grantland*, the former ESPN boutique literary sports journalism site.[78] The total investment to acquire these three producers was $400 million, with Simmons's The Ringer carrying the highest value at $250 million. Gimlet and Parcast were thus worth $150 million combined.

When asked about the pivot from *Grantland* to the podcast-heavy digital outlet The Ringer, Simmons alluded to the podcast medium's suitability to extended chat, particularly as a means of covering daily news. "We've had so much success on the website [The Ringer], and even more on the podcast side, by reacting and being there when something happens."[79] He explained that "It's something we didn't do at *Grantland* because we didn't have to—we had ESPN.com covering news and reacting right away, so we positioned ourselves as levitating above that, taking our sweet time, doing bigger pieces." The slow journalism of *Grantland* that operated on extended news cycles thus yielded to daily news coverage through the extended chat format on The Ringer. Video was then ruled out as an option because podcasts outperform televised longform interviews. The immediacy and creativity of podcasting prompted Simmons to specialize in audio sports journalism, despite having an extensive oeuvre from books and print to digital and television that afforded him a future in any medium he desired.[80] His embrace of podcasting speaks to the medium's power to meet the moment of breaking headlines, yet without sacrificing the depth of coverage that longform interviews allow. The Ringer demonstrates how extended chat can be produced without succumbing to the liabilities of misinformation endemic to the journalism of assertion.

Simmons's adoption of on-demand audio for his brand of sports journalism speaks to the ascent of podcasting beyond its early 2000s origins as a fringe, grassroots digital community into a big business that favors leaders through consolidation and corporatization. Spotify's flurry of acquisitions of podcast producers and creative tools endows it, along with Apple, with "monopolistic capabilities that go far beyond the platform-as-intermediary."[81] The business model that seeks ad revenue through data mining tends to outstrip and disincentivize the maintenance of journalistic standards, especially for shows that intersect with current affairs and news content. Instead, with fewer shows taking up a greater share of the market, more creative license will be granted to hosts such as Joe Rogan to retain the exclusive rights to publication.[82] Howard Stern's exit from terrestrial radio to SiriusXM, the satellite digital audio provider, similarly circumvented responsibility for offensive content flagged by the FCC.[83] Platforms now function as regulators of creative content, placing big tech in what has been traditionally a government role. This process has opened unprecedented space for Far Right–wing podcasts, the most prominent of which are treated in the following discussion.

THE RIGHT-WING PODCAST INDUSTRY

Advances in digital media have shaped journalistic coverage of politics in ways that have influenced policy change and directly inspired political action, from the Twitter-driven Arab Spring uprisings of 2011 to the insurrection on the U.S. Capitol in 2021. For much of its first decade, podcasting was primarily a liberal-leaning media space. Indeed, the serial documentary form that propelled podcasting into the mainstream with the publication of *Serial* in 2014 traces back to NPR and the work of Ira Glass, who set the template for such longform audio reportage with *This American Life*. Glass and his team won the first-ever Pulitzer Prize for audio journalism for the "The Out Crowd," a series detailing the compromised lives of rejected asylum seekers on the Mexican side of the U.S.–Mexico border during the Trump administration.[84] The award was both a fitting tribute to the legacy of *This American Life*, whose dedication to journalistic principle dates back to the 1990s, and a clear signal that podcast journalism's coming of age has occurred under the mantle of reportage for social justice steeped in the journalism of verification.

Podcasting is no longer a predominately liberal-leaning media space. A large and rapidly expanding number of the top 200 titles on Apple Podcast charts openly brand themselves as right-wing podcasts. In addition to shows by Republican elected officials such as *Verdict with Ted Cruz* and *Hold These Truths with Dan Crenshaw*, the most downloaded conservative podcasts include *The Dan Bongino Show, The Ben Shapiro Show, The Glenn Beck Program, The Sean Hannity Show, The Rubin Report, The Michael Knowles Show,* and *Bill O'Reilly's No Spin News and Analysis*.[85] Many lean Far Right and embrace extremist ethnonationalist perspectives. *The Rush Limbaugh Show* signaled the keynote with its self-described "combination of serious discussion of political, cultural, and social issues along with satirical and biting humor, which parodies previously 'untouchable' personalities and topics."[86]

Several right-wing podcasts broke into the top rankings after the 2020 U.S. presidential election. *The Mark Levin Show*, for example, originally ranked in the 70–100 and 100–150 ranges, varying from month to month. One week after Election Day, the show skyrocketed to number 10, fueled in part by allegations of voter fraud and the Stop the Steal movement Trump supported on Twitter, which eventually discontinued his account for spreading misinformation. In the final months of 2020 leading up to the election, *The Ben Shapiro Show* held the number 4–7 spots. *The Dan Bongino Show* typically hovered between 20 and 40 on Apple Podcast charts, suddenly bursting into the top 10 and eventually remaining one of the top 2 most-downloaded shows since the 2020 election.[87] Bongino's popularity surged on Facebook, driven by his uncanny ability to drive headlines and set the agenda for the Right on the national debate. The social media connection proved vital to Bongino's ascent.[88]

The ascent of right-wing podcasts is due in part to their unique historical moment during the buildup to Election Day 2020 and the ensuing firestorm of conservative voter fraud allegations that followed, eventually fueling the insurrection on the Capitol. Listeners commune with conservative talk show personalities from four to five hours per week, heightening the parasocial relationships fostered by the medium's unique technological affordances.[89] A senior executive at Westwood One, which manages and represents sales of *The Daily Wire* that distributes these publications, revealed that "right-wing podcasting nowadays seems purposefully integrated with the broader right-wing infrastructures, and are themselves individual assets of much larger multi-platform presences."[90] Figures like Dan Bongino marshal "attention between his multiple media outputs, from his broadcast radio show to his social media feeds to his podcasts to his various media appearances."[91] In 2018 Westwood One repackaged *The Ben Shapiro Show* for radio broadcast, an instance of a born-digital podcast expanding its audience through terrestrial radio. *The Mark Levin Show* took the opposite trajectory, beginning as a radio broadcast program before eventually undergoing minor reformatting edits and entering the podcast world.

As acquisitions and vertical conglomeration increase, more nonjournalistic firms with no experience in the news industry—Spotify was originally a platform for storing, discovering, and sharing music rather than publishing or distributing news-related content—find themselves in the position of gatekeeper for public information on current affairs. As podcasting scales, "it has some features that become attractive to many more players without any public service mandate."[92] The old guard of conservative talk radio has risen to prominence through elaborate layers of media ownership, corroding journalistic principle and coarsening political discourse. When faced with the question of how it administers to the dubious speech content on *The Dan Bongino Show*, Westwood One's executive could only affirm, "We have a very, very strong policy on content," and "We feel strongly that we have the ability to uphold the truth."[93] A strong policy on content, however, would have certainly helped to mitigate the conspiracy theories and allegations of fraud surrounding the 2020 U.S. presidential election. The Stop the Steal movement reached its most deadly moment in the storming of the U.S. Capitol on January 6, 2021, which comprises the subject of the following case studies.

CASE STUDY 1: *THE DAN BONGINO SHOW*

In the wake of the insurrection of the U.S. Capitol, Dan Bongino, the former Secret Service agent and erstwhile guest on Alex Jones's ultraconservative *InfoWars* who also once hosted his own cable television program on NRA TV, vigorously defended the mob on his popular podcast. The day following the storming of the Capitol met with a flurry of commentary online, some placing the event in the category of 9/11 and the attack on Pearl Harbor in terms of its national significance. Bongino instead framed the riot as an extension of political violence normalized by the Left. He specifically targeted those who supported the #BlackLivesMatter protests and demonstrations in the wake of the George Floyd killing. On the January 7, 2021, episode titled "About Yesterday," Bongino asserted that the "media hypocrisy regarding political violence is impossible to watch" because violent efforts to disrupt the congressional certification of Electoral College votes cementing Joe Biden's victory were denounced by liberal media who, he claimed, hypocritically celebrated violence committed by protesters on behalf of racial justice in cities such as Minneapolis and Portland during the summer and early fall of 2020.[94]

Defenses of the Capitol insurrection fell far outside the editorial purview of most news organizations. Bongino alleged a liberal media plot apparent in its self-serving casting of heroes and villains in political protests.[95] But unlike the social justice demonstrations, the insurrection involved the forcible entrance into a federal building to impede the democratic process. Placing the blame squarely on the liberal media for the violence, Bongino extended the conspiratorial premise to include big tech—in this case, Twitter—which he excoriated as a liberal organization bent on destroying conservative values.[96] In the show, he casts Twitter as ruthlessly blocking then-president Trump's account "after he calls for peace." Calling for a virtual uprising through social media, he rhetorically asked, "Is the digital media revolution coming? They're trying to whack-a-mole when they just can't do it, especially when you're the distribution channel," he declared, exhorting his listeners to rebel against media totalitarianism.[97]

Although Bongino made explicit on the show that he does not endorse political violence, he nonetheless lay blame for the insurrection on liberal media's alleged support of the antifa riots on behalf of racial justice in Washington, D.C.[98] He reported that his former Secret Service colleagues feared that the liberal protesters would storm the Capitol. These agents were "legitimately concerned that the White House would fall . . . if 100 or 200 people stormed the fences of the White House, they wondered what would happen." He claimed to have "never heard that conversation before, even as an active agent," suggesting that liberals had normalized political violence first and thus were the true cause for the insurrection. "There are liberal media people," he insisted, "who say don't you bring up BLM [#BlackLivesMatter] and Antifa. We're going to keep the conversation solely on what happened with a limited group of people yesterday." Relishing the occasion for defiance, he lashed out at the collective enemy in a voice rising to a shout, "If you've been in the media and have been dismissing political violence for the last four years, you should sit down and shut up!"[99] He then spotlighted the antifa assault on the Federal Courthouse in Portland during racial justice protests in this fifty-eight-minute inadvertent exemplar of the logical perils of whataboutism, all cast in the pugilistic tones of partisan counterpunches in keeping with the boxing bell that signals the opening of the podcast.

Bongino's criticism of Twitter and Facebook for discontinuing Trump's account underscores the podcast host's own colossal presence on social media—and dependence on it for his massive listenership. His total number of Facebook interactions nearly doubled that of Ben Shapiro and Sean Hannity in October of 2020.[100] The monthly engagement on Bongino's Facebook page is greater than that of the pages for CNN, *Washington Post*, and *New York Times* combined. During one twenty-four hour period in October of 2020, he accounted for eight of the top-performing link posts by U.S. Facebook pages.[101] The content of these posts echoes his podcast, which has argued against mask wearing as an effective means of preventing the spread of COVID-19, spearheaded election fraud conspiracies, and inculcated fear of a coup led by Democrats. He has functioned as one of the most potent agenda-setters on the Far Right, generating more viral headlines and misinformation than any conservative podcaster. Kevin Roose observed that "he is skilled at a certain type of industrial-scale content production, that is valuable on today's internet, flooding social media with a torrent of original posts, remixed memes and videos and found footage."[102] His *Bongino Report* aggregates right-wing news stories—supporting QAnon and the Hunter Biden laptop scandal, among others—as an extremist alternative to *The Drudge Report*. PolitiFact has flagged Bongino's Facebook page several times for disinformation, a text-based affordance for fact checking not yet available for the more evasive audio content of his podcasts, most of which are not transcribed.[103]

CASE STUDY 2: *THE BEN SHAPIRO SHOW*

Ben Shapiro's podcast is an extension of his online news publication *The Daily Wire*, which the analytics service NewsWhip identified as "by far" the top right-wing publisher on Facebook.[104] Shapiro's commanding following on Facebook depends on a network of *Daily Wire*–affiliated Facebook pages to generate traffic. The clandestine network consists of "14 large Facebook pages that purported to be independent but exclusively promote content from *The Daily Wire* in a coordinated fashion."[105] The method entails identifying incendiary news items preying on bigotry and fear, stories that are months or years old and thus out of the current daily news cycle. Shapiro's *The Daily Wire* is actively promoted by the rewriting of these stories (with no indication that they are old) for right-wing pages titled "Mad World News," "The New Resistance," "The Right Stuff," "American Patriot," and "America First." What appear to be new links to *The Daily Wire* on these sites are actually repurposed to both readers and Facebook's algorithm, thus artificially inflating its numbers. In the attention economy of social media, the tactic is tantamount to printing money. At typically no more than five hundred words in length with no original reporting, these stories propelled *The Daily Wire* to the seventh spot among Facebook's top publishers.[106]

The ethical and ideological agenda behind Shapiro's podcast is best understood through the combined function of social media distribution and media ownership. Bentkey Ventures's Farris C. Wilks owns *The Daily Wire*, which Shapiro launched in partnership with Jeremy Boreing in 2015. Wilks, who made his fortune through the sale of his fracking company to a Singapore firm, is a GOP supporter.[107] The Texas fracking billionaire donated $10 million to GOP super PACS during the 2016 election and runs a politically conservative Jews for Jesus church. Wilks served as the minister of his church, which adheres to a literalist reading of the Old Testament as scientifically and historically accurate, one that supports his views of abortion and homosexuality as crimes.[108] These perspectives may intersect with the political principles of Shapiro's podcast.

Shapiro's podcast episode published the day after the Capitol insurrection offers an illuminating contrast to *The Dan Bongino Show*'s episode of the same day. After dubbing January 6, 2020, "the worst day in American history since 9/11," Shapiro stopped short of condemning Trump for inciting the riot to pressure Congress. In his signature rapid-fire staccato delivery—displaying far more sheer verbal agility and intellectual precision than Bongino if not the brute force of the former Secret Service agent—Shapiro urged that "Trump is not guilty of directly causing or directing violent actions."[109] However, Shapiro then adopted a distinctly more centrist stance than Bongino by claiming Trump was guilty of "raising the temperature" through his accusations that Congress was stealing the election, "falsehoods" that set the stage for insurrection.[110] His lack of loyalty to Trump in this case did not mitigate his partisan fervor, as he lashed out at the way "the Left blames all Republicans for the insurrection."[111] Shapiro, who supports constitutional conservatism, openly criticized Trump, unlike Bongino, who has consistently played the role of his apologist and arm-chair defense attorney to the masses. Shapiro did not cast his vote for Trump in 2016 but did so reluctantly in 2020 mainly out of support for the GOP. Although Shapiro's show reflects his anti-gun-control and antiabortion stances, and his staunch opposition to the LGBTQ community rooted in his belief that gays are mentally ill, he condemns alt-right ethnonationalist and extremist groups such as the Proud Boys and has been a vocal critic of Trump's Stop the Steal voting fraud movement.

Shapiro's episode titled "The Worst Day in Modern American Political History" thus marks a distinct departure from Bongino's more extremist rhetoric. The day after the insurrection, the vitriolic tenor of the Far Right response on social media reached a fever pitch, prompting the Apple and Google App stores to deplatform Gab and Parler, conservative havens for toxic speech and misinformation, especially among those seeking an outlet after being banned from Twitter. Some of the more vocal and extreme conservatives, such as Ted Cruz, have more followers on Parler than Twitter.[112] Like Telegram and Spreely, Parler is less moderated than mainstream platforms such as Twitter and Facebook. Platforms like Parler hosted the internet's most dangerous speech, which included fantasies of committing violent acts and details regarding the most effective methods of smuggling arms into Washington, D.C., to evade its strict gun-control laws. Far Right provocateurs banned from mainstream social media congregate on these platforms, which are fueled by links to news stories on One America News Network and Newsmax, news outlets promoting outlandish views of contemporary politics and current affairs. The domain provider GoDaddy and the payment service PayPal both withdrew from their contracts with Gab when a man who committed a massacre at a Pittsburgh synagogue was revealed as an active user. Hate speech and networking abetting violence thrive on platforms such as Gab and Parler, yet they may be construed as less dangerous than Far Right podcasts because their most egregious expressions are more easily accessed and flagged in time-stamped writing than the nonvisual (screenless) audio content of right-wing podcasts.[113]

THE FUTURE OF RIGHT-WING PODCASTS

The right-wing editor and podcaster Matthew Sheffield commented on the loss of journalistic credibility among many conservative news media producers, observing that "they don't see journalism the way that more traditional journalists do."[114] Instead, "they see their media enterprise as [being] about activism and about supporting whoever is their top Republican." He added, "they see [this] as their duty," a dedication tracing "from the very beginning of conservative media in this country," one "heavily linked to political electioneering."[115] Nicole Hemmer, author of *Messengers of The Right*, explained that the radicalization of certain strains of conservative America occurred when "Rush Limbaugh and Fox News appear on the scene and they bring not just conservative politics, but entertainment and this totalizing conservative media," which would later develop into a fully realized alternative information ecosystem.[116]

Conservatives now have an array of choices, from Bongino to Shapiro, and thus "have no reason to interact with any other media sources."[117]

A major challenge exists in holding right-wing media accountable, particularly in the new digital space of interpretive, extended chat, and opinion-based podcast journalism. Sheffield urged that "the funders of right-wing media need to face social business consequences for what they do."[118] Ownership with doctrinaire leanings in the age of conglomeration raises the specter of figures such as Rupert Murdoch, who "has been enabling a growth of a fanatical movement in this country," according to Sheffield.[119] "Anybody who is funding these far-right publications needs to be exposed," he added, prescribing a shift in conservative media ownership toward "funding mainstream Republicans." Conservative media owners need to counter the current trend, "otherwise," he warned, "they are just going to grow radicalization over and over."[120]

Conservative media ownership may not be capable of playing such a gatekeeping role, however, since in several instances it is indistinguishable from the on-air personalities. This increasingly self-serving system now places hosts in a supervisory role with the editorial power of a publisher, as evidenced by Dan Bongino's co-ownership of Parler and Ben Shapiro's editorial oversight of *The Daily Wire*, which he founded. Rush Limbaugh's 15 million listeners per week who tuned into his three-hour-per-day show have been readily absorbed by Bongino, Shapiro, and, for older listeners, Sean Hannity. This generation of podcasters is the latest remediation of conservative talk radio, particularly Limbaugh's legacy that Hannity credited for the development of Fox News.[121] The extraordinary reach of conservative media's conglomerated ownership structure, as well as the proliferation of voices in the podcast universe directly patterned after Limbaugh's, is evident in the ownership of Limbaugh's show by iHeartMedia, which also syndicates Glenn Beck and Sean Hannity's programs. There are myriad conservative provocateurs in podcasting that have followed Limbaugh's lead. Limbaugh "created the genre, which then flooded the market with competitors, some less talented, some more," conservative pundit Ann Coulter observed.[122]

The intersection between old-guard talk radio and the new wave of conservative podcasting is perhaps best captured in Bongino's dedication of an entire episode to Limbaugh. In a Fox News interview, Bongino reprised his sentiments from that episode, paying homage to Limbaugh and crediting him for setting the standard for conservative podcasting. Identifying the origins of contemporary conservatism in Limbaugh's show, Bongino commented that "every conservative I know . . . has had that Rush Limbaugh moment where they were listening and heard an idea for the first time ever."[123] Acknowledging that he now works within the same space Limbaugh "created," Bongino explained that "Rush Limbaugh invented the national conservative talk radio space—he invented the game."[124] It is fitting, therefore, that *The Dan Bongino Show* was slated to take over Rush Limbaugh's radio time slot on May 24, 2021.[125]

Bongino's allusion to conservative podcasting as contiguous with "the game" of "conservative talk radio space"—one as carefully attuned to the ideological hyperbole as to market share—captures precisely how its rhetorical conventions of caustic, pejorative attacks on rivals and overt misinformation have become normalized.[126] The journalism of assertion and affirmation in this instance has fueled partisan extremism capable of inverting reality to rally support. Brian Rosenwald observed that "without Rush Limbaugh, there is no way you get from the party of George H. W. Bush to Donald Trump."[127] The Trump presidency—through the final stages of denial of the election result and support for the insurrectionists—could be understood as the political apotheosis of Limbaugh's legacy.[128] Over the thirty-two years Limbaugh was on the air, "he conditioned his audience as to what they wanted to hear and what they had an appetite for," Rosenwald explained. "And it thrilled them to hear someone who said what they might have thought, but felt uncomfortable saying."[129] That sense of affirmation galvanized the Far Right, particularly through emotionally charged conservative news-related podcasts, a fervor that Trump directly applied to politics. For YouTube users, the intellectual dark web has been proven to be a gateway to its Far Right sector.[130] Far Right podcasting also plays a key role in the Republican Party's transformation into a counter-majoritarian party, one increasingly less interested in appealing to the majority of the public.[131]

As with advances in its evolution, threats to podcast journalism are attributable in part to its blurring boundaries of forms. Far Right podcasters not only undermine journalistic values but are exploiting a lack of standards missing for some time in this space. They do this specifically by taking advantage of podcasting's freedom from the constraints of traditional broadcast reporting standards, which has opened new channels of personal expression, yet at the risk of the ideological hijacking of journalism by partisan actors. The implication is that a wide range of interest groups and political movements engage in self-legitimizing metajournalistic discourse through the podcast medium.[132]

The intimacy and voice at the heart of podcasting has made audiences more comfortable with the postmodern blurring of journalism and storytelling/drama, or of news and entertainment. The further implications of how podcasting is breaking down this dichotomy suggest that the lack of censorship of the medium in general and the extreme overreach for market share via the entertainment draw (as with *Caliphate*) have created a kind of rhetorical Wild West amid an industrial land grab for this digital space. This dynamic is at the core of this book's assertion that podcasting is therefore actively transforming journalistic principle with each new challenge and innovation (as illustrated by *Ear Hustle*), with achievements as spectacular as its failures.

Intimacy and storytelling drive not only right-leaning podcasts but are also integral to left-leaning programming. As the next chapter demonstrates, diverse and marginalized populations leveraging the podcast medium indeed share these essential affordances of the medium. However, the following analysis demonstrates that the predisposition toward diversity tends to broaden the spectrum of voices and perspectives represented on progressive shows. The range of interests, identities, and personal narratives is more varied on left-leaning shows, whose listener ethos is anathema to the self-described "ditto-head" mentality of the followers of figures like Limbaugh and Bongino. Conservative hosts in this tradition often aim to generate homogeneity in their audiences' views rather than seeking out plurality. The distillation of the views of listeners toward monolithic perspectives that conforms to a rigid ideological code thus characterizes right-leaning podcasts associated with some segments of the Republican Party. Advocacy is pitched differently for liberal hosts, specifically to aid silenced and marginalized communities. Broadness and diversity contribute to more moderate content for progressive podcasts, despite the presence of extremist liberal shows. Podcasts align with the Right's (Republican Party coalition) function as an ideological movement compared to the big-tent nature of the political Left (Democratic Party coalition), whose impulse lies not in consensus building or rallying around a narrow set of views but in appealing to as many groups as possible. This pattern of political sensibilities in podcasting reflects the larger reality of political party organization in the United States, which Matt Grossman and David A. Hopkins describe in *Asymmetric Politics*.[133]

CHAPTER SIX

Voices from the Margins

Black, Hispanic, Asian, and LGBTQIA+ podcasts have skyrocketed in popularity since 2010, opening avenues for candid treatment of race and gender issues typically marginalized from coverage in the mainstream media industry. In 2021 Nielsen reported that 41 percent of podcast listeners were non-white, a figure reflecting the increasing diversity of audio media. The most rapid growth occurred within the Hispanic audience, which exploded over the course of nine years, from 1.1 million in 2010 to six times that—6.8 million—in 2019. Black and Asian podcast audiences were five times larger in 2019 than in 2010. Expanding at a significantly slower rate were white audiences, which grew fourfold over the same period.[1] This changing complexion of the podcast market is characterized by an influx of shows addressing issues of race and gender ranging from humor and entertainment to politics and social justice. For the first time in media history, the non-white podcast listenership (at 41 percent) exceeded the overall minority population in the United States (at 39.5 percent) in 2019. As arguably the most diverse audience in digital publishing, the podcast listenership is thus diversifying at a greater rate than the non-white U.S. population itself, which saw its steepest ascent during the decade following the 2010 census, which measured it at 30 percent.[2] The dramatic expansion of non-white podcast listenership, however, has exposed the persistence of major labor inequities in both the podcast and radio news industries, particularly among local NPR affiliate stations. As recently as 2018, for example, an NPR self-study reported that 83 percent of all voices featured on weekday news programs were white, of which 67 percent were male.[3] NPR responded with a concerted effort to expand its reach into non-white and diverse gender communities with shows such as *Code Switch* and *Strange Fruit*. Such efforts coincided with a rise in the racial and ethnic diversity of NPR's staff from 20.4 to 29.1 percent between 2015 and 2019.[4]

Whereas the origins of podcasting as grassroots alternative media have directly served diverse and marginalized communities, mainstream audio media has shown much slower progress.[5] Research by Spinelli and Dann indicates that podcast audiences perceive the medium as safe digital space that does "not seem tainted by any sense of threat or insecurity."[6] This perception is reinforced by 60 percent of respondents who believed the "media industry" was "not sufficiently diverse," compared to a mere 11 percent who harbored this attitude toward the podcast ecosphere. Although the majority of respondents in this study "felt the podcast space was more diverse" and "felt an ownership of that space," few said this preference derived from hosts' gender and racial demographics matching their own.[7] Instead of demographic homophily, which risks funneling listeners into information silos, "podcasts become the space where opposing views can co-exist, rather than the 'echo-chamber' associated so closely with social or mainstream media."[8] In this sense, podcast diversity is perhaps best measured as an organic experience characterized by an intersection of listeners drawn to similar interests, a dynamic that transcends top-down quotas, publisher's protocols, and regulatory policy aimed at artificially generating diversity. Due to the medium's consumption via participation in what Roshanak Kheshti calls the "aural imaginary," the formation of diverse communities is possible without the often delimiting visual signifiers inhibiting membership.[9]

Podcasts tend to defy broadcast radio's production practice whereby "the material nature of sound presumes an unnamed white listening ear," a pattern Marie Thompson associates with "white aurality" or sonic whiteness.[10] The whiteness of NPR, for example, has been perhaps most revealingly discussed from the perspective of non-white employees, whose success in the organization was implicitly measured according to their ability to mimic a white voice in cadence, intonation, and delivery.

The podcast medium's construction as safe digital space for expressing personal encounters with social injustice is exhibited by the sudden rise of *Code Switch* as one of NPR's top ranked podcasts in the wake of the George Floyd protests. Prior to its launch as a podcast in 2016, the show's blog offered an outlet for outspoken views on race, many of which did not reflect well on NPR's own standards for diversity. Chenjerai Kumanyika's testimony on the blog, for example, addressed the stultifying effects of "the whiteness of public radio," leading many, including himself, "to imitate the standard and hide the distinctive features of our own voice."[11] This reification of the hegemonic norms of radio production practice has been partially circumvented by the "experiential diversity" of the podcast ecosphere.[12] Although podcasting makes possible alternative racial representation, podcasters are still enmeshed in the wider corporate market, compromising the medium's relative freedom from such influence. Despite advances evident in the new wave of diverse voices, vestiges of inequity persist. The Gimlet Media debacle regarding the podcast company's hypocritical stand on diversity, for example, led to the cancellation of *Reply All*, a show dedicated to frank and candid discussions of toxic workplace environments. The show ended when *Reply All*'s second episode, "Test Kitchen," investigated the racist organizational infrastructure of the magazine *Bon Appetite*, in the process prompting serious scrutiny of Gimlet's (and, by extension, parent company Spotify's) own insufficiently diverse personnel and practices.

This chapter engages the question of how the ostensible progress toward increased audience diversity and representation of previously marginalized communities in the podcast ecosphere has been mitigated by workplace and labor inequities, particularly evident in corporate resistance to coverage of social justice issues. The industrial norm of white aurality is the focus of the next section, which explores how Black and Hispanic podcasts can circumvent the editorial resistance to diversity in audio journalism.[13] Shows dedicated to Hispanic, Black, and LGBTQIA+ topics generate an "aural imaginary" to foster intimacy through imagined physical presence.[14] Depending on production practice and representation, racial and gender difference can be authentically constructed or, conversely, can encourage exoticized consumption of marginalized and minority identities. The central argument claims that beyond technological developments that have made podcast consumption more convenient, accessible, and mobile, the medium offers access to the public sphere, particularly regarding issues pertinent to minority communities. In this sense, "the civic urge and ability to tell stories emanating from routinely marginalized lived experiences" animates the journalism created for and by diverse social groups.[15] News production methods transitioning from traditional terrestrial radio to more personalized reporting—that began with blogs (such as that associated with *Code Switch* prior to its release as a podcast in 2016) and evolved into longform narrative storytelling—now drive advocacy journalism on behalf of underrepresented communities. Case studies examine shows representative of the Black, Hispanic, and LGBTQIA+ sectors of the podcast industry. Episodes and topics analyzed include corporate resistance to Black podcasting's emergence from a niche media subculture into the mainstream via the Gimlet Media labor dispute and controversy surrounding *The 1619 Project* by the *New York Times*; Maria Martin's *Latino USA* on the transnational applications of the term *chollo* to ethnic and cultural identities; The Immigrant Defense Project's podcast series; and the queering of gender through audio for feminist and trans advocacy in shows such as *Strange Fruit*, *ShoutOut*, and *Burn It All Down*.

CIRCUMVENTING WHITE AURALITY

Podcasting's distinct departure from the stentorian broadcast voice that prevailed in the twentieth century on public radio has increasingly yielded to the Ira Glass model, made popular by Sarah Koenig on *Serial* and Brian Reed on *S-Town*. In the early 2010s, this "sensitive, hesitating, transparently liberal" voice decentered the authority intoned by public radio reporters conveyed through "affected, upper class, wasp, Ph.D. student-like" delivery.[16] To avoid alienating listeners with hosts who did not "sound like human beings over the air," Glass urged production to place "human narrators at its center."[17] Although the voices of longform documentary audio journalism in the early 2010s were mostly white and male, their openly progressive inclusion of silenced voices in programming opened another "possibility offered by the podcasting boom" whereby "other kinds of voices might more easily reach Americans' ears."[18] Embodying this potential is Pineapple Street Media, which first produced *Still Processing* hosted by *New York Times* culture critics Jenna Wortham and Wesley Morris, whose commentary on Black music and slavery is featured on the Pulitzer Prize–winning *1619 Project*. Unlike Gimlet Media, whose failure to maintain successful Black-hosted podcasts such as *The Nod* and *Reply All* stemmed in part from its acceptance of venture-capital investment, Pineapple has refused such investment in order to protect its editorial autonomy over such culturally sensitive shows. Pineapple earns corporate support by producing isolated projects specifically for companies including Morgan Stanley and Nike.[19] These companies therefore have no editorial leverage over Pineapple's content beyond those shows contracted by them.

With relative editorial autonomy, Pineapple prides itself on the fact that nearly all of its podcasts have featured hosts who are ethnic minorities, women, gay men, or members of other marginalized groups. As Rebecca Mead points out, the young and urban audience Pineapple has cultivated "is unlikely to tune into NPR over brunch."[20] This shift is due in part to a "move away from the voice-of-God newsman," which Gimlet has also abandoned, but without fully embracing diversity in a substantive sense. In addition to Gimlet's controversial firing of host Ngofeen Mputubwele, originally hired as the face of its new commitment to diversity in late 2015, twenty-four of the company's twenty-seven employees were white.[21] Mputubwele tweeted in June of 2020, "the thing about being Black in podcasting, in my experience, is constantly being told your pitches don't work and wondering whether it's you or a systemic lack of cultural competency and knowledge of experiences outside of whiteness."[22]

The model of journalistic transparency Michael Barbaro has described as "a kind of soul-searching way of telling a story, where you embrace your confusion and you experience the quest for an answer" that has prevailed over podcast journalism does not automatically equate with diversity, equity, and inclusion.[23] However, the method of "constant, ever-evolving explanation while simultaneously undermining the concept of certainty around the news generated by and for the Trump era" can be leveraged for social justice.[24] Activist audio journalism's long history traces back to immigrant advocacy on mid-twentieth-century radio produced for California populations at risk for deportation. As discussed in chapter 4, Pedro Gonzáles hosted the most influential show produced in English and Spanish that connected listeners and enabled collective, strategic methods of evading racist immigration policy in addition to combating social isolation and cultural alienation. The current wave of podcasts hosted in dialects unique to marginalized communities represent the legacy of English–Spanish language radio that served as a public advocate and channel for organizing and connecting listeners.[25]

Despite the surge in the non-white podcast audience and number of shows made for and by marginalized social groups, public radio continues to be mired in production practices geared toward a white audience under financial pressure to avoid alienating lucrative financial sources. White aurality in audio media manifests itself as a production practice standard to which many aspiring minority media professionals have either consciously or unconsciously aspired. An employee of a local NPR affiliate, for example, commented that "whenever we do public-facing, marketing," the approach is "very much signaling to a college-educated, middle- to upper-class white audience."[26] The majority of reporters pitching stories that potentially made white listeners uncomfortable or uncentered received direct resistance. "The audience is always unnamed," but when invoked, "it is always white and middle-aged or older."[27]

Public radio NPR affiliates tend to avoid topics that podcasts specializing in race-related issues routinely embrace. Eric Eddings and Brittany Luse's podcast *The Nod*, for example, delved into the history of artificially flavored grape drinks marketed to Blacks in the South. During the Great Migration, the products suddenly became available in the Northern urban cities where African Americans and their families relocated. In many Northern regions, the drinks were not available, and thus took on a nostalgic significance, reminding many of home in the South. The episode's historical specificity—marked by an interview with an expert on artificial flavor, who discusses methyl anthranilate's history that intersects with the coal and transportation industries—is matched by its personal narrative flourishes uniquely connected to the Black community's collective past and its link to this otherwise obscure product.[28] Such a story likely would not have been produced for local radio, where editors rejected similar topical approaches to Black culture, including a piece on Black hair. The reporter noted that the editor's trivialization of the story suggested "a lack of understanding of the depth of racial history."[29] In this and other instances within the production process, white aurality is actively enforced not as an ahistorical monolithic concept but as one rooted in conditions that shape the perceptual schema. Those forces include "Eurological histories, practices, ontologies, epistemologies, and technologies of sound."[30] As Anjuli Joshi Brekke aptly observes, "much of sonic whiteness in the realm of radio and podcasting goes unnamed" despite these contextualizing influences existing in traditions and beliefs that shape production practice toward an overall audio aesthetic designed with a white audience in mind.[31]

Such podcasts exploring the collective consciousness of the Black community share with immigrant advocacy podcasts and *Latino USA* an understanding of audience that transcends the limitations of white aurality. These shows do not repress content that may strike white audiences as uncomfortable or disturbing but instead highlight and investigate them thoroughly. Although podcast producers may project a radical independence from market forces and industrial norms built on the infrastructure of sonic whiteness, "cultural production is progressively 'contingent on,' that is, *dependent on* a select group of powerful digital platforms," which include Google, Apple, Facebook, Microsoft, and Amazon.[32] Platforms are imbedded with social and cultural biases, against which podcasts representing marginalized communities must contend. The major platforms of Apple Podcasts and Spotify, in addition to Soundcloud and Acorn, "control the lists of podcasts that would fit each listener's preferences" mainly through algorithms that conceal important executive decisions made by such digital empires.[33] Crucially, algorithms reinforce and extend racial and social inequalities by automating them through digital data processing.[34] Humans have been replaced as gatekeepers of creative cultural industry online with artificial intelligence operating in their place "with no guarantee that systems of representation or equality are addressed."[35] Through their algorithms, these platforms directly contribute to the construction of a white audience for podcasting that can then prompt editorial self-censorship like that routinely practiced in the public radio sector.

Although complete escape from the pervasive reach of sonic whiteness may seem a quixotic ideal of techno-utopianism, the podcast medium offers producers and audiences more opportunities as a relatively safe and autonomous digital space. Notwithstanding the institutional racism of companies such as Gimlet, companies such as

Pineapple and digital publications such as *Latino USA* have opened space for more diverse producers and listeners. Podcasts have diversified faster, therefore, than older media such as terrestrial public radio, which is held captive by its white, highly educated core of listeners, managers, and editors unlikely to cede what Laura Garbes calls "their entitlement to these airwaves," a situation in which "the relationship of NPR member stations to their employees of color will continue to be parasitic."[36] Crucially, diverse and marginalized communities have escaped this environment in a mass exodus from terrestrial radio to on-demand digital audio. The sixfold increase in the Latino podcast listenership from 2010 to 2020 exemplifies how "people whose perspectives are already sorely lacking will leave for spaces with more opportunities to tell stories to their own communities."[37] Furthermore, platform influence through podcast rankings is not entirely unresponsive to the political moment. The protest following George Floyd's murder resulted in a sea change on the Apple Podcast charts, as podcasts about race or featuring race as its main theme dramatically rose in the ranks in June of 2020. That month, *1619* by the *New York Times*, *Code Switch* by NPR, and *Pod Save the People* by Crooked Media ascended to the 5 through 7 spots. *Code Switch*'s breakthrough into the top ten, however, left then-host Shereen Meraji feeling conflicted about the success. She noted, "It's very strange that we now have all these eyes and ears on what we're doing because a number of very horrific things happened back to back," particularly Floyd's murder. She still found reason to be "glad that people are here and that they're open to listening to what we've been saying on the podcast for the last four years."[38] Partisan polarization, however, is evident in charting conservative shows during this time, which makes podcasts about race more prominent.

Podcasts represent an alternative to local radio's editorial practice, which conforms to financial pressure to appease white donors and listeners. One local radio reporter pitching a story on Confederate monuments, for example, urged that the piece would be meaningful to Black listeners from the South like him. "How does this matter to you? You were never a slave," was the editor's icy reply.[39] Roughly one-third of reporters surveyed in 2020 avoided pitching stories dealing with racial issues, citing that they "didn't feel valued or seen." The formidable resistance has led many reporters to seek less controversial topics of a lighter nature. When stories occasionally treat racial issues, they typically are framed as comforting triumphal tales of progress rather than exposing tensions signaling larger social discord and political strife. One story on refugees at a local high school, for example, originally aimed to cover their experience through their artwork. The reporting, however, revealed "overt instances of racism among white boys targeting the girls of color," details the editor refused to include, instead suggesting to cast the incidents as "challenges."[40] Public radio's audience and donor base harbors expectations for uplifting narratives rather than critical inquiries, thus constraining editorial decisions. Rather than glossing over or trivializing tension, podcasts produced for ethnically diverse audiences instead tend to highlight and investigate inequities and politically contentious aspects of stories. In the process of seeking safe digital spaces without such restrictions on content, ethnically diverse audiences have turned to podcasts as a form of what Sarah Florini calls cocooning, a form of retreat from hegemonic white spaces via alternative media enclaves.[41]

Such media enclaves are protected from "the mainstream gaze."[42] This alternative space fosters a substantial form of community and public engagement within marginalized and ethnic groups themselves, rather than leveraging the aural imaginary to commoditize and reify otherness for white audiences. As Brekke points out, in cocooning, "listening then becomes an act of resistance" engaged by marginalized audiences and not a performance of race for a mainstream listenership.[43] In this way podcasts can become spaces of solidarity for marginalized social groups. The practice of cocooning serves as evidence supporting how, "although sonic whiteness pervades the airwaves, communities of color have developed various strategies for subverting this soundscape."[44]

BLACK PODCASTING

The intimate audio space of Black podcasting can create bonds among listeners and hosts to help promote community formation. Florini has compared these discursive spaces, which encourage free-flowing uncensored conversation about a range of topics from popular culture to politics and society, to "historically significant Black social spaces like barber/beauty shops and churches."[45] Similar to these public spaces that offer a means of civic engagement and opportunity for community building, podcasts "reproduce a sense of being in Black social spaces."[46] As with the gendered divisions separating voices heard at barber and beauty shops, podcasts also can also be gender-exclusive. But with male–female host teams of such influential Black shows as *The Read*, *The Nod*, and *Still Processing*, the industry has progressed toward more gender-inclusive programming. "Despite the obvious gendered parameters of this aspect of the podcasts as community spaces," as Photini Vrikki and Sarita Malik show, "these spaces first and foremost create bonds and strong homophilic tendencies between the hosts, irrespective of their gender."[47] Due to the podcast medium's affordance of offering listeners full access free from any self-inhibiting restrictions generated by visual markers of race, class, and gender, cocooning should be understood as a social practice marked by greater gender fluidity through the podcast medium than the embodied discursive spaces of barber shops and beauty salons characterized by gender exclusion and heterosexual normativity.

Historically, podcasts containing both humor and in-depth analysis of Black identity predate what Davy Sims describes as the bandwagon effect of *Serial*. "Podcasting had difficulty reaching a mass generalist market," he explained, "because it lacked a leading brand," and was instead characterized by a wide variety of niche programming catering to the narrow interests of select subcultures in the long tail of digital media products. The "phenomenal success of *Serial*" then established "a bandwagon to jump on, something for people to talk about, and suddenly people wanted to know about podcasting."[48] The *Serial* bandwagon effect may have aided the ascent of Black podcasting as it did the industry in general, but its signature genres arose of out the grassroots TWiB! (This Week in Blackness!) network beginning in 2008. Unlike *Serial*'s brand of true crime, African American podcasts at the time consisted of variations of extended chat formats featuring current affairs and historical analysis of Black identity and culture.

Elon James White founded *TWiB!* in 2008, which began as a Web series of the same title hosted on YouTube. "In early 2009 we launched a short run of a weekly show, *Blacking It Up* hosted by me and Bassey Ikpi," White recalled in private correspondence with media scholar Kim Fox, who has coauthored several studies on Black podcasting with me.[49] Due to what he felt was poor quality, he ceased production but attempted a return the next year. The show then adopted a Monday through Thursday schedule, added two new cohosts, Syreeta McFadden and Jon Pitts-Wiley, and continued broadcasting for roughly one month. "For the next year," James noted, "people kept referencing our month of shows and begged us to return."[50] White then committed to a regular schedule in January of 2011, starting on Martin Luther King Jr. Day. Although podcasts did not fully come of age for a full decade following the release of the iPod in 2001, Black audiences were already well established to capitalize on the transition to longer and richer podcast content enabled by the introduction of the smartphone in 2007, communication policy changes in 2011, and 4G LTE technology in 2012.[51] With the decline of Black urban radio stations that began with the Telecommunications Act of 1996, Black disc jockeys such as Lynn Tolliver Jr. of WZAK in Cleveland, Ohio, turned to BlogTalkRadio in 2010 to maintain and cultivate their existing audiences. Blogging thus combined with radio to fuel the network of Black podcasts self-described as the "Chitlin' Circuit," a historical allusion to segregation. Shortly after the initial 2008 launch of *TWiB!*, *The Combat Jack Show*, another successful early Black podcast, appeared in 2010. Hosted by music attorney Reggie Ossé, roundtable discussions featured high-profile hip-hop artists. Topics centered on the lives of Black celebrities, often merging with racial politics and current affairs. The show's more than four hundred episodes produced over the course of four years engaged concerns related to social justice shared by its Black listenership.[52]

The grassroots origins of Black podcasting epitomize how "digital media, and specifically podcasts, cannot contribute to social progress until there is a sustained resistance to the racialized power structures that govern them."[53] Beginning in the late 2000s, the Chitlin' Circuit proved that "podcasts can make audible struggles for representation, challenge institutional colonialisms, and traverse both the political landscape and lived experiences of racialized oppression."[54] In this sense, the digital space of early Black podcasting distinguished itself from the mainstream creative cultural industry through what Vrikki and Malik describe as the medium's "culture of flexible production."[55] This production practice is characterized as "self-organized, low-budget, content-led, and operating outside traditional regulatory structures," which also aptly describes that of *TWiB!* This podcast ecosphere was conducive to the production of narratives "that oppose exclusionary forms of representation and politics found in talk radio, opinion journalism, and current affairs programming" associated with the mainstream media industry, particularly public radio.[56] As Florini notes, the development of Black digital networks shows how "users of color can program their digital and social media spaces with cultural logics and communication strategies that negotiate, and to varying degrees, resist neoliberal regimes of race and technology."[57] Illustrating such use of digital space is Elon James White's establishment of the Black Podcasters United group on Facebook in 2014.[58]

Storytelling featuring personal narrative, which was central to early Black podcasting, has been identified as a powerful discursive form in audio media.[59] Whereas confessional storytelling speaking to the inner emotional life of individuals plays a key role in Black podcasts, content tends to address a larger communal experience defining Black identity within culture. Programming stems from intellectual culture via analytical discourse, a phenomenon perennially sidelined in traditional news media. For example, Brittany Luse and Eric Eddings originally hosted the podcast *For Colored Nerds* for three years (2014–2016) prior to receiving an offer to join Gimlet Media, which at the time was a relatively unknown independent startup prior to its acquisition by Spotify. From the start, "Our conversations were always deep and intense," Eddings recalled.[60] Launched in 2017, *The Nod* built on their original principle behind *For Colored Nerds*, which focused on "the conversations that Black people have when white people aren't in the room." As Larson points out, "these are valuable conversations for everyone to hear," and not just the Black audience.[61] The key difference between the two shows was the storytelling component, as *The Nod* featured "better production, segmentation, and reporting."[62] Along with this new standard for professional production, *The Nod* continued the original approach of *For Colored Nerds* by foregrounding Black intellectual culture from diverse perspectives on gender, countering the traditional exclusion of women's views.[63]

In the fall of 2021, months after the debacle with Gimlet/Spotify over *Reply All*, Luse and Eddings returned to their roots by relaunching *For Colored Nerds*, which predated *The Nod*, with an independent contract with Stitcher on SiriusXM. Luse and Eddings maintained full possession of the IP address, the host interface identification, and location address while sharing an undisclosed portion of the show's revenue with Stitcher. It is telling of the importance of the first wave of podcasts, particularly their autonomy, do-it-yourself culture, and relative freedom from corporate influence that Eddings would elect to return to the original principles of his podcast aesthetic with *For Colored Nerds*. It is significant that ascendant figures of Luse and Eddings's caliber in the world of podcasting would return to these original principles of the genre. Luse explained, "The industry is going to have to bend toward a situation where there are organizations that are providing institutional support to people who want to make quality audio without demanding that they also hand over all of their ownership."[64] With Gimlet/Spotify, the hosts' creative and financial rights were severely restricted and exploitative compared to the autonomy and revenue sharing built into the Stitcher contract. The "ability to share in the fruits of the creative labor and maybe even exploit it on your own or stay with it either financially or creatively if it becomes something bigger . . . yes, that's definitely been an issue," according to Eddings.[65]

Eddings's decision to rejoin his female cohost—rather than forging a career as a solo podcaster—resonates with the gender-inclusive collective labor economy of Black podcasting. The gender-inclusive nature of the current Black podcast culture contrasts sharply with the Black intellectual tradition at the turn of the twentieth century that was dominated by men such as W.E.B. Dubois and Booker T. Washington. "We do not often hear what the African American club women were doing and saying at this time," as Gwendolyn D. Pough points out.[66] More than a century later, the more inclusive gender fluidity of the Black podcast medium helps answer the call "for Black feminist theory to contribute to the work of the Black public intellectual dealing with Black popular cultures."[67] Shows addressing Black culture tend to create and condition a sense of community that includes the Black female perspective. The critical and analytical thrust of many Black-themed podcasts raises the question of whether Black intellectual culture represents a distancing from the Black community. Some critics view the cultural type of the blerd (short for "Black nerd," self-reflexively and humorously invoked in shows like *For Colored Nerds*) "as a mode of policing appropriate blackness."[68] Intellectual discourse in Black podcasts, however, is not always performed self-consciously. This is apparent in the examples of *Still Processing* and *BhD: Black and Highly Dangerous*, a podcast showcasing powerful Black intellectuals' voices in academia driving the national conversation on social justice and diversity.

In addition to offering a channel for the development of Black intellectual culture, pioneer Black podcasts such as *The Read* feature unscripted informal content capturing the Black vernacular in organic settings. The move toward more structure and edited content in Black podcasting mirrors the development of the improvisational interaction of *For Colored Nerds* into the thoroughly reported research of *The Nod*. In describing his transition from *For Colored Nerds* to *The Nod*, cohost Eric Eddings recalled how learning the process of sound editing, reporting, and writing introduced him to "a different *form* of podcasting," which cohost Brittany Luse captured in a word, *storytelling*, indicative of the new standard of narrative audio journalism they had achieved.[69] The careers of Eddings and Luse illustrate how independent podcasters are motivated to launch programs due to technological/media affordances, content motives (i.e., "filling an un-served niche market"), and interpersonal desires.[70] Crucially, content motives include "promoting people" according to Kris Markman's schema, and interpersonal motives aim to foster "community networks and relationships."[71] It is important to underscore, however, that community building in podcasts by African Americans is not often stated as an explicit proscriptive objective. Instead, a sense of community organically emerges from the programs in a noncoercive manner. African American podcasters are less concerned with performing Black identity than in discussing and deconstructing it in the culture. This relative freedom from identity performance as the sole means for engaging African American topics through mass media is a major departure from the audio convention, dating back to the mid-twentieth century, of white hosts performing Black roles in radio skits. The wildly popular *Amos & Andy* show, for example, was a radio version of minstrel entertainment that performed Black identity through coarsely racist comedic content trivializing issues such as unfair labor practices, wages, and police treatment.[72]

Following the 2008 launch of *TWiB!*, the next milestone in the development of Black podcasting occurred with the appearance of *The Read* in 2013. *The Read* spoke to audiences seeking content on contemporary popular culture, filling the niche of entertainment news and off-the-cuff, often humorous commentary about celebrities in the music industry. Missing from *The Read*, however, was context, historical reportage, and immersion journalism, areas later addressed in 2017 by *The Nod*. For example, to illustrate the relative scarcity of African American–produced consumer goods, such as the FUBU (For Us, By Us) brand's hip-hop clothing line, *The Nod* featured an episode in which the hosts engaged in a contest to see who could purchase the most products made exclusively by Black companies. This journalistic immersion served as an experiment in consumerism designed to unmask brand culture and the racial pretensions of many marketers. Cohost Brittany Luse's professional experience in marketing and political campaigns informed this episode's deep market analysis. Such programming raises awareness of the Black community's range of consumer choices and the racial politics of brand messaging, drawing listeners into the experience of the Black consumer.[73] Such editorial latitude, however, ceased for Eddings with his attempt to shift the focus of *Reply All* onto the racial politics of his publisher's labor practices. On June 8, 2020, Eddings tweeted, "The pres of a podcast company accused me of lying at an all-staff about diversity numbers his own HR rep had shared with me shortly before." The proposal to cast the same critical eye from *Bon Appetit* in "The Test Kitchen" episode of *Reply All* onto Gimlet's organizational infrastructure was met with a tirade directed at Eddings. He recalled that Gimlet's president "later yelled at me asking 'If diversity is so bad here, why are you still here?'" He noted that his experience was not unique since "the gaslighting and disregard is in every part of media," including the podcast world.[74]

In the podcast world, the subjective, confessional approach to journalism can be a deterrent rather than a catalyst for engaging the topic of race. *Serial*, for example, has been criticized for its narrow focus on the drama of Koenig's investigation and reporting along with the question of accused murderer Adnan Syed's guilt or innocence for the death of his eighteen-year-old ex-girlfriend Hae Min Lee at the expense of the more pressing issue of racial justice.[75] *Serial*'s horizontal storytelling method presented an ideal opportunity—however unrealized—for engaging more difficult social questions. Narrative journalistic approaches that eschew the inverted pyramid model of news writing for more human-focused, creative approaches to storytelling can invite contextually nuanced appreciation of sociopolitical issues, in the process fostering greater identification with particular social groups.[76] The intimate and personal style of podcasting serves as a richer and more expressive mode for communicating the complexity of racial issues.[77] Narrative and slow journalism has been touted as more effective for reporting on immigration and race than fragmented methods blind to the complexity of such large issues.[78] Coverage of race exclusively through catastrophic breaking news such as arrests, raids, and demonstrations squanders the opportunity for in-depth explanation and thorough investigations featuring narratives humanizing the subjects themselves.[79]

These affordances suggest that podcast journalism can affect the listener's political subjectivity, a measure of listener engagement that reveals the degree to which they participate in the democratic process.[80] Whereas platformization and the commercialization of podcasting may privilege white aurality, thus disadvantaging independent startup amateur podcasters of color, the sharp increase in non-white podcast listeners indicates that the current gatekeeping system has not silenced voices from marginalized communities. Alternative voices have now become valued in diverse sectors of the market, encouraging political engagement and action. Although research shows that the commercialization of podcasting has made discovering and developing new audiences more difficult for startup podcast producers, and that equity suffers when commercial practice cultivates audience expectation privileging certain voices over others, alternative voices have migrated into mainstream media space.[81] The professionalization of Black podcasting now exposes industrywide inequities. In addition to Gimlet's silencing of Eddings on *Reply All*, among the most highly visible examples of resistance to the mainstreaming of Black podcasting is Nikole Hannah-Jones's *1619*.

Listed by the *Washington Post* among the top-ten best works of journalism from 2010 to 2020, The 1619 Project's five-part podcast was hailed as a "formal reimagining of what an audio essay can be, embracing aesthetic fluidity and a vivid sense of atmosphere in the service of historical remembering."[82] Episode 1, "The Fight for a True Democracy," of the show, which *New York* ranked second among the best podcasts of 2019, is a repackaging of Hannah-Jones's Pulitzer Prize–winning essay for the project. Following the same trajectory of the essay in keeping with the *Times*'s overall transmediation strategy, beginning with reflections on her father's insistence on flying the American flag as a frame for rumination on the political economy of sharecropping, the piece answers the need for nuance in discussions of race.[83] Compared to conventional historical perspectives on race in America, Hannah-Jones provides a much longer view of the institution of slavery reaching back four hundred years into American history, offering a powerful and provocative economic argument about the nation's reliance on slave labor.[84] Fashioned as a two-part feature profile story, the final episodes paint a portrait of the Provost family, who were dispossessed of their land beginning with the family's original Louisiana sugar cane planation 150 years after the U.S. government's promise of forty acres and a mule to every African American. Hannah-Jones was not universally embraced by media or academic institutions. Her attempted hire with tenure at the University of North Carolina–Chapel Hill, for example, was denied under a firestorm of controversy by a cluster of white historians. The common fault alluded to in a dizzying array of allegations distilled down to Hannah-Jones's overstatement that the North—rather than some citizens of the North—supported the American Revolution in order to protect slavery. The statement continues to plague her. "I should have been more careful with how I wrote that," Hannah-Jones confessed, "because I don't think that any other fact would have given people the fodder that this has. I'm absolutely tortured by it."[85]

Although the University of North Carolina eventually recanted its denial of tenure to Hannah-Jones, she turned down the elite faculty position, electing to take her talents to Howard University in Washington, D.C., rather than offering them to a predominantly white university. As the most prominent of the historically Black colleges and universities in the United States, Howard University represents an environment conducive to journalistic training and production specifically aimed at fostering diverse storytelling addressing the Black experience. The decision to renounce North Carolina for Howard speaks to the importance of institutional context and financial support in the development of podcast journalism. Just as platforms influence the creative conditions for podcasters, institutions of higher education can also bear a similar impact. Hannah-Jones thus elected to launch her Center for Journalism and Democracy at Howard because "it was actually built for Black uplift and Black excellence" and not "in opposition to the work I want to do."[86]

LATINO PODCASTING

In the spirit of Milan Kundera's claim that "the struggle of man against power is the struggle of memory against forgetting," the 1619 Project's podcast joins the ranks of diverse shows such as *Latino USA* in producing journalism with a long historical perspective.[87] The 1619 Project's exploration of slavery's four-hundred-year influence contextualizes the present conditions of institutional inequities and counters the tendency of some media to "not provide the historical context necessary to understand where we are currently" in terms of race relations.[88] Racial inequity "is not new," and breaking news of it should not be covered as if it were the first time it has ever occurred, a point often overlooked by traditional media. Just as the current crisis of law enforcement's relationship with many Black citizens "is far better understood when we remember the laws and customs erected during the Jim Crow segregation era," current subcultures within the Latino community can be more richly represented from a longer historical perspective.[89] The podcast medium's longer, more intimate storytelling template encourages treatment of socially marginalized and disenfranchised communities from a broader historical perspective. The episode "I Am a Chollo" on *Latino USA*, for example, explores the origins of the term *chollo* according to a production aesthetic that powerfully illustrates how the audio medium "works best when [producers] broadcast the kind of lost or obscured voices, the kind of character-driven and emotionally rich stories, that plant ideas and facts more deeply in the memory."[90]

As a defector from the world of public radio, Maria Martin originally founded *Latino USA* to fulfill journalism's public service mission in a way that could more directly address the Latino community than her former position at National Public Radio allowed. As a child growing up on the border between the United States and Mexico, students in her school were routinely punished for speaking Spanish. In college Martin recalled that the African American civil rights movement inspired the social and political uplift of Mexican Americans and other Latinos. As a bicultural Latina, she had few role models in audio journalism to inspire her until she encountered KBBF 89.1 of Santa Rosa, California, the first Latino-owned and -operated public radio station in the United States. Broadcasting in both Spanish and English, the station regularly advocated for Latino women, openly offering advice regarding issues such as reproductive rights. Largely absent from other media at the time, such public service reporting addressed the immediate welfare of listeners. After taking a position at the station, Martin's impact on the lives of listeners included providing translation to hospital workers on behalf of one desperate woman suffering from an overdose. Building on this tradition, *Latino USA* thus advances Martin's belief in "the power of media to build bridges of cultural understanding."[91]

Martin identified two founding principles behind *Latino USA*, which she launched in the 1990s as an alternative to NPR's coverage of Latino communities.[92] The primary objective aimed to fulfill the Hutchins Commission's 1947 definition of media's responsibility to serve democracy through a "representative picture of the constituent groups in the society."[93] Also informing her visions was the Kerner Commission's finding in the 1960s that "the media's inaccurate portrayals and misrepresentations of the African American community contributed to racial divisions in our nation."[94] While with NPR, Martin became acutely aware of the news organization's limited knowledge of the complexity of the Latino experience, discovering that coverage cast "Hispanics as 'problem people,'" particularly through a preponderance of stories on undocumented immigration and gangs.[95] Dolors Palau-Sampio notes that the humans at the heart of immigration issues are often overlooked in news coverage, which instead casts migration "as a form of pollution or natural disaster" posing a threat to host countries.[96] To counter this view of Latinos as a monolithic group, Martin pursued an editorial agenda covering both individuals on the street and intellectuals, spotlighting the community's regional diversity from Los Angeles to Miami. She soon realized that the scope could still be broader. To establish "a place on public radio for Latinos to feel at home—where Puerto Ricans could learn about Mexican Americans and Cubans about Dominicans and Central Americans and vice-versa," Martin launched *Latino USA* with a distinct advocacy and public service mission.[97]

As safe digital space for Latino listeners, the podcast *Latino USA* deconstructs demonized and romanticized subcultural representations in mainstream media that fuel misperceptions. Answering to the infamous cultural mystique of the *chollo* identity associated with Los Angeles gangs and low riders, an image commodified and recirculated through cinema and the music industry for mass consumption, the episode "I Am a Chollo" thoroughly historicizes the term and deconstructs the stereotype. Through reportage that freely blends Spanish and English languages, the episode critically analyzes the appellation's multivalent applications via its hood and gangster associations in the United States and its original definition referring to an Indigenous person from the Andes of Peru. Slang in Spanish for *dog*, *chollo* originally referred to people of mixed origins, especially African and Indian, and later denoted those who were three-quarters native and one-quarter Spanish.[98] Used for centuries in the United States and Mexico, Chicano gang members reclaimed the derogatory moniker in the 1960s and 1970s, calling themselves *chollos* as a token of empowerment. Currently alluding to Mexican descendants born in the United States, the term *chollo*'s racist origins surface upon further investigation. According to expert interviews, positive reclamation of the term could have paradoxically become synonymous with gang life and criminality. Professor Al Valdez of the University of California, Irvine, a specialist in Mexican culture and society, noted that within Mexican mafia prison gang culture, many consider themselves Aztec warriors. These gangs, he explained, initially formed into organizations for protection because "with that grouping and solidarity comes a power base."[99] Many Latinos bear a complicated relationship with the term, which is often used as a label to designate a second-class citizen. For many Peruvians, it can denote a "dirty Indian," despite also signifying proud acknowledgment of Indigenous heritage in other contexts and usage.[100] Elsewhere in South America, *chollita* takes on entirely different connotations, particularly in Bolivia, where it is understood as an expression of Indigenous esteem. Its pejorative use derived from its application to native peoples who were assumed to be nonhuman because they did not follow Christianity.

The complex origins and alternate meanings of the *chollo* identity examined in the *Latino USA* podcast exhibit Martin's editorial dedication to the accurate representation of Latino identity. The dynamic and interconnected plurality of Latino identity emerges through the exploration of its historical origins, which effectively deconstructs monolithic understandings of the culture. Episodes frequently trace crosscurrents in the complex web between the United States and Latinidad. "A Family Conversation on Race in Latinidad," for example, profiles two Afro-Latino cousins whose mothers were raised in Panama. Navigation of their transcontinental cultural identities in this episode blurs boundaries commonly separating Latin American, African American, and South American communities.

The Immigrant Defense Project's podcast series titled *Indefensible* focuses on stories of people resisting deportation, "standing up and holding out, fighting to be with their families."[101] The narratives featured on *Indefensible* contain information about legal and political sources of support that would be of immediate use to certain immigrant listeners facing similar circumstances. Episode 1, for example, details the experience of Eddy Arias, an immigrant in Houston, Texas, who was targeted in a racially profiled traffic stop, jailed, and placed in solitary confinement—purportedly for his own protection because he indicated that he was gay during questioning—despite committing no crimes. Arias then stood up for his constitutional rights and those of thousands of immigrant families in Houston. The episode features interviews with several local activists who joined Arias in combating the 287(g) agreement whereby Immigration and Customs Enforcement could arrange to deport arrested individuals. The agreement encourages racial profiling, separates families, and is a source of fear in the community, as detailed in the opening episode of *Indefensible*.[102]

In this episode, the listener learns that Arias's encounter with the criminal justice system led him to form United We Dream, an organization designed to extend former President Barak Obama's DACA Act (Deferred Action for Childhood Arrivals). As the episode proceeds, host and producer Will Coley—whose podcast credits include production for *99% Invisible*, NPR News, and the BBC—recedes into the background as the narrative takes shape around Arias's quest to repeal 287(g). Edited sound on tape consisting of the spliced-together voices of Arias and other key figures in the story takes over with minimal scoping (i.e., interludes where the host narrates alone) at this juncture in the episode. Tension rises as we hear tape of the election debate between Houston Democratic sheriff candidate Ed Gonzalez and Republican incumbent Ron Hickman. The debate then cuts to a recorded interview with Gonzalez, who remarks on how Arias and his United We Dream immigrant advocacy organization inspired his run for office. Coley's voice-over narration then briefly reveals that Gonzalez would eventually win the election by more than 64,000 votes and end 287(g) that had allowed Houston law enforcement's collaboration with Immigration and Customs Enforcement. Emotional relief is then signaled through tape from Gonzalez's victory rally, where we hear an exuberant speaker address the audience. "We're celebrating our victory; an end to 287(g)!" he announces to a roar of approval. "This week we had some really, really good news after years of frustration."[103] Coley then sounds a sobering note alluding to victory's repercussions, which resulted in the withdrawal of all federal funding from the Trump White House. This and other stories in *Indefensible*'s five-episode series provide a public service to immigrants and their advocates by spotlighting progress and impediments in the struggle against "the deep harms of an immigration system that, by design, denies basic rights—such as the right to a fair trial and protection from excessive punishment."[104]

LBGTQIA+ PEOPLE AND THE FUTURE OF DIVERSE PODCAST PRODUCTION

The narrative arc of *Indefensible*'s first episode offers listeners a sense of satisfaction in Eddy Arias's redemption through the poetic and legislative justice of Ed Gonzalez's victorious campaign for sheriff that ended 287(g) in Houston. However, the jubilation is tempered by the reality that immigration reform is an ongoing struggle, especially as inequities became pronounced during the Trump presidency and continued to plague the Biden administration. LBGTQIA+ storytelling follows a similar arc, tracing and celebrating progress while also attending to political exigencies contributing to oppression, stigmatization, and denial of equal rights. In the podcasts *Burn It All Down* by Blue Wire and *Strange Fruit* by NPR, hosts use these digital spaces as discursive domains treating the spectrum of LBGTQIA+ issues. The episode "Trans Women and Trans Girls Belong in Women's Sports" represents *Burn It All Down*'s dedication to the intersection of racism and misogyny in women's sports established by Shireen Ahmed, sports activist on behalf of Muslim women. In this episode, Team USA Olympian Chris Mosier, who is the first transgender athlete to qualify for the Olympics in the gender they identify directs listeners to his website, Transathlete.com, and its Take Action page featuring a map of anti-trans bills.[105] Mosier explains that listeners can use the map to locate and contact their local elected officials and law makers, providing a clear channel for voicing opposition to this legislation. In this and other episodes on *Burn It All Down*, "patriarchal and gender hegemonic public spheres are circumvented and resisted" in a space where counter discourses are generated and circulated specifically as "oppositional interpretations of their identities, interests and needs."[106]

These digital spaces designed for the generation of LGBTQIA+ counter discourses are particularly well suited to the audio medium of podcasting. In a two-part analysis of audio and the queering of gender, Aria Bracci detailed the potentially liberating power of podcasting and broadcasting for transgender hosts.[107] *ShoutOut*, the United Kingdom's premier LBGTQIA+ music show hosted by Steffi Barnett, who is transgender, exhibits audio's freedom from visual signifiers typically relied upon to identify gender. Audio can highlight or obscure both gender and race, as Chenjerai Kumanyika noted of his "instinctually code-switching to assimilate to the existing sound of public radio," particularly its white aurality, discussed earlier in this chapter.[108] Since gender signaling through audio is limited to pitch, timbre, and accent, "gender can be ripe for misinterpretation" when based on voice alone, particularly in Barnett's experience. Audio excels at functioning as a metonymic signifier capable of conjuring scenes and experiences through vocal intonation—a richly polysemic signifier Roland Barthes located in "the grain of voice" used to distinguish quality among vocal performers—as well as ambient sounds.[109] But sound also is literally blind to visual cues crucial for identifying gender and race. Although voice alone can "confine a speaker to a box" that may not be accurate, it can also present opportunities. For nonbinary and transgender individuals, self-presentation disconnected from one's physical body "can bring a form of relief" and greater control over the attentional focus of the audience.[110]

The fluid, potentially androgynous gender ambiguity built into the disembodied podcast voice "can inherently present more opportunities because of how it removes the associated appearance of a character." This flexibility can provide trans women like Barnett liberation through the invisible workplace of audio, lending "increased confidence" compared to an embodied, highly visible workplace where she is "constantly tasked with proving her womanhood."[111] As Barnett's experience illustrates, misperception of transgender audio journalists is not necessarily threatening because "those who are more transient and not as familiar with the particulars of [her] life and identity are probably not paying any mind, since their focus is the music at the center of her shows" on *Shout-Out*.[112] In the case of podcasts centered on LGBTQIA+ politics, hosts might be more inclined to make their gender orientation known from the onset and assume that followers of the show will accurately identify them. Unlike with Barnett's hosting of *ShoutOut*, which is more about music than politics, the more politically engaged podcast *Strange Fruit* hosted by Jaison Gardner and Kaila Story spotlights race and gender. *Strange Fruit*'s topics, for example, include explorations of why young adult literature is so straight and white and why polyamory is viewed as exclusive to white people. The historical long view that brings deeper meaning to gender and identity as a means of contextualizing urgent current affairs is evident in an episode examining online homophobia, transphobia, and racism titled "The 'Jim Crow' Mentality and Social Media Trolls."[113] As an NPR podcast, the show represents the news organization's next most important social justice project since *Code Switch*, its first blockbuster in that category to reach the coveted top ten of Apple's podcast chart. The success of *Strange Fruit* suggests that NPR's investment pattern will continue on its current trajectory toward podcasts treating identity that encompass not only race but also gender. It should be noted that the journalistic prowess of *Code Switch* is evidenced in its development into the premier show about race and identity in America, an achievement that landed its cofounder, Shereen Marisol Meraji, a prestigious Harvard Nieman Fellowship among twenty-two of the world's best journalists, after which she will assume a faculty position at the University of California–Berkeley's School of Journalism.

The relatively liberating space of podcasting presents Black, Hispanic, and LGBTQIA+ producers with a complex predicament in which they "are both willingly and unwillingly imbricated in the wider corporate media environment."[114] This predicament problematizes the production of counter discourses through media designed to circumvent hegemonic values and normativity associated with traditional news formats. In particular, the pressures of the wider corporate media environment—in which local radio continues to be conditioned by white aurality—"casts doubt on the seemingly uncompromised freedom that podcasters appear to have, even based on some of their own assertions," such as Barnett's referenced above.[115] However, one of the strengths of the podcast medium, especially for traditionally marginalized groups, lies in the fact that it is untethered from social media. Unlike reporters publishing screen-based digital journalism, podcasters are not necessarily expected to maintain program-specific forums for audience discussion. Listeners often host their own forums developed independently on a variety of platforms, from Facebook fan pages and Twitter hashtags to Reddit threads. *Still Processing*, for example, is notable for its lack of official, producer-hosted forums for listener discussion.[116] The show generates a great deal of online discussion, all of which is decentralized and organic. Benefits accrue to podcasters from such a flexible relationship to social media, particularly by allowing producers to meet the demands of community development primarily through the podcast itself. Podcasters enjoy their relative liberation from social media, which they claim is often time-consuming to maintain; often inappropriate for expressing rigorous, serious opinions; and vulnerable to dissenters bent on lifting and spreading select comments out of context.[117] As Kim Fox and colleagues note, the podcast medium deters trolls because its longform audio format is less prone to searching and excerpting—particularly for those seeking samples to support confirmation bias—compared to that of online written text.[118]

Although podcasts appear to have the potential to foster "a future for digital media that foregrounds a multiplicity of voices, marking a departure from the culture of instantaneous dominant mainstream communication and reactionary social media one-liners," the medium nonetheless continues to be enmeshed "within the power structures and forms of marginalization that prevail in digital cultural industries."[119] To excel as a progressive medium worthy of its colossal ambitions, well-intended principles, and skyrocketing audience base, podcasts featuring marginalized voices must be vigilant of "the commodified, corporatized and managed processes," especially platformization and pressure to conform editorial content to the ideological agendas of financial supporters.[120] Despite impediments such as labor inequities like those raised by Eric Eddings in *Reply All*, which illustrate the consequences of white aurality through corporate media structures, tangible progress toward increasingly diverse journalism is evident in the podcast sector of digital publishing. Fox and colleagues' argument that Black podcasts open "discourse on the meaning of blackness in U.S. culture to an audience of unprecedented scope and diversity" now equally applies to Hispanic and LBGTQIA+ podcasts, introducing what has arguably become the most sophisticated public discourse on race and gender in media history.[121]

Building on this and the previous chapter's focus on the use of narrative journalism by the political Right and Left, the following chapter explores how commercial interests are represented in the digital audio space by corporate brands that have assumed the role of media producers. As with the podcasts of the Far Right and those showcasing diverse voices from the margins, the persuasive intimacy of the medium informs branded podcasts. With content designed around personal storytelling, the narrative journalism of brands takes on an array of purposes and tones, from humorous stunts to earnest public service missions. It is to the expanding market for branded podcasts and their intersection with the journalistic role that attention now turns.

CHAPTER SEVEN

The Profit Motive

Brands as Publishers

In the hotly contested race for market share in the digital publishing industry, news organizations have dramatically expanded the commercial business side of operations, in many cases adopting the function of advertising agents, marketers, and strategic communicators conscripted to amplify brands. Not only have major legacy newspapers such as the *Wall Street Journal* and the *New York Times* increased investment in production studios dedicated to generating sponsored content for brands and corporations, smaller upstart news organizations have also sold their reporting and writing to companies to serve their marketing needs. WSJ Custom Studios, rebranded The Trust in 2019, operates as a custom content studio like the *Times*'s T Brand Studio, which also specializes in sponsored content production. Such brand studios have increased in number and size since 2010 due to publishers making them a fiscal priority.[1] Among start-ups, journalism's pivot toward content marketing and brand amplification is evident in the fate of news outlets such as Dose. Originally founded by Emerson Spartz in 2014, Dose featured viral news consisting of lists and click-bait headlines designed for wide circulation through social media. Through mercenary tactics some critics described as arbitrage, Dose exploited price differences between disparate markets such as the book trade Spartz drew from—often without attribution— for some of his platform's most popular content.[2] Dose has since transformed into a digital market research firm. In keeping with Spartz's training in business rather than journalism, the company's initial focus on developing viral news shared many of the core functions of its subsequent dedication to marketing target groups through personalized messages featured on social media feeds designed to garner authentic, unfiltered user feedback. While many aggressively commercial online news organizations such as Dose have abandoned the guise of journalism to fully embrace a marketing role, an influx of brands have begun to produce their own journalistic content. Digital storytelling produced by brands now builds on the tradition of John Deere's *The Furrow*, a magazine simultaneously promoting the iconic farm equipment manufacturer and featuring original reporting on the agricultural industry. Since its debut in 1895 as a compendium of colorful feature writing and technical information to supplement relatively dry farmers' almanacs, the publication now boasts a circulation of 1.5 million in forty countries and twelve languages. Described as "an agrarian version of *Rolling Stone*," *The Furrow* now has its own podcast.[3]

Over a century since the publication of *The Furrow*, and through asynchronous on-demand digital audio media ideally suited for mobile users, podcasting now represents the new frontier for brands to tell their stories. The influence of advertising on the podcast industry in the early 2020s cannot be underestimated, as witnessed in Spotify's colossal 627 percent year-over-year increase in podcast advertising revenue as of August 2021.[4] As brands increasingly become publishers across the media ecosphere, podcasting's intimacy takes on greater commercial significance. Yet with "more potential to generate empathy and to humanize the deeply marginal," as Spinelli and Dann aptly observe, the podcast "also holds a potentially troubling capacity for manipulation."[5] The question of journalistic integrity in brand storytelling for podcasts becomes more concerning in light of the lack of accountability and the evasiveness of the audio medium, which is more difficult to fact-check in the absence of transcripts. Brand-produced podcasts effectively invert the conventional business model for podcast journalism predicated on the notion that revenue from advertising, merchandise, and crowdfunding are only possible once a project has generated a large audience. Digital journalism carries promotional purposes insofar as it communicates the publishers' news brand as it circulates on the internet. Native advertising is another tactic that converges editorial and commercial sides of news organizations, particularly as "a form of paid content marketing, where the commercial content is delivered adopting the form and function of editorial content with the attempt to recreate the user experience of reading news instead of advertising content."[6] In podcasting, traditional advertisements are considered incongruous and disruptive when placed in the middle of shows. Media scholar Larry Rosin points out that "although prerecorded slots are still used, the preferred format, that bakes in the content and prevents the audience from skipping through to the next section, is to have the presenter personally endorse the product."[7]

Unlike native advertising well known in most podcasts—which can take the form of an interview with a representative of the sponsor, an endorsement by a user, or a segment where the host discusses the benefits and uses of the product—entire shows can function as a type of commercial advertisement in the form of branded podcasts. Unlike hosts hawking the products of sponsors or strategically mentioning them during the course of their shows, producers of branded podcast journalism are not in the business of selling their audience's listening time—and, thus, their trust—to third-party advertisers. Branded podcasts therefore do not suffer from the awkward intrusion of product pitches, which can introduce jagged dissonance into an otherwise carefully edited sound design. Host endorsements violate "an implied contract between the independent podcaster and their listener," which aligns directly with that of an independent journalist working for an autonomous news organization, operating on the "understanding that they are saying what they are saying because they chose to."[8] Similarly, agency becomes veiled and potentially problematic when podcasts engage in product placement akin to that of the cinema and television industries. In sharp contrast to news outlets that "do not boldly push for transparency and instead remain ambiguous" in disclosing native ads, no such ambiguity plagues branded podcasts.[9] The marketing agenda in branded podcasts is explicit rather than hidden, camouflaged or baked in to a larger product. The appearance of an advertising-free media product is well suited to podcasting's development of "human-scale sensibilities" whose honest and authentic intent are ironically not without their commercial appeal.[10] "Selling your authenticity" is thus the paradox of podcast production that reaches its apotheosis in brand-produced podcasts, raising the question of commercial influence on core public radio values so vital to the production aesthetic of podcast journalism.[11] Siobhán McHugh notes that veteran U.S. public radio figure Jay Allison's lament for "podcasting's blurring of the lines between content and paid copy" indicated that "advertisers are trading on this" development Ira Glass identified in his infamous declaration that "public radio is ready for capitalism."[12] But is journalism ready for nonjournalistic organizations—trading in products and services from hair salons to pet food—to become news producers, particularly in the podcast medium, which ranks among the most empathic and intimate forms of reportage?

This chapter centers on the question of how brands have hijacked journalistic roles for nonfiction podcast production to serve their commercial advertising protocols. Corporate efforts to produce content that appears as a viable channel for civic participation exploits journalism's process of "transitioning from a more or less coherent industry to a highly varied and diverse range of practices."[13] Any public service benefits of sponsored podcasts are designed to directly serve strategic communication goals while appearing to operate as journalism. While appropriating the styles and discursive norms of journalism in order to draw on its authority, sponsored podcasts are anathema to the principle of independence that distinguishes a free press and authorizes it to hold power to account as a watchdog or guardian on behalf of the public interest. Despite performances of transparency, no tension or strife within the companies producing these shows is disclosed, all in keeping with their strategic communication aims. The growing appeal of journalism operating at the intersection of entertainment and public interest—particularly in the relatively low-cost podcast medium—has been discovered by brands as a means for serving their financial goals. Although community and public service functions might be highlighted in the storytelling of these podcasts, they ultimately remain a form of strategic communication for three reasons: (1) They undermine the notion of a free and independent press, (2) which prevents them from performing the watchdog function, and they (3) prioritize corporate profit over public interest. Brands may make a show of comforting the afflicted through stories about their products changing consumers' lives. However, such marketing sharply contrasts with—and can actively undercut—monitorial journalism whose top priority is to afflict the comfortable.

The following section demonstrates the shifts in journalistic digital publishing that encouraged corporations to invest in producing their own podcasts. This discussion provides the aesthetic and industrial framework for the ensuing case studies on the Coca-Cola Company's *Total Refresh*, the McDonald's Corporation's *The Sauce*, and the Trader Joe's Company's *Inside Trader Joe's*. The chapter concludes with consideration of how sponsored content produced by podcast companies differs significantly from shows published by nonmedia brands. Specifically, Gimlet Media's sponsored content will be examined in terms of its aim to achieve both commercial and journalistic value.

BEYOND PODCAST JOURNALISM

The standard definition of news is understood as "new information about a subject of some public interest that is shared with some portion of the public." Journalism is therefore defined as "the activity of collecting, presenting, interpreting, or commenting on the news for some portion of the public."[14] These relatively stable understandings aptly explain what news is and what journalists do. The question of who qualifies as a journalist and where journalistic production occurs, however, has been in radical flux since the advent of the digital revolution when journalism associated with traditional newsroom production practice began yielding to a growing wave of new storytelling forms. Untrained producers either working for upstart news organizations or as independent bloggers during the early 2000s and 2010s inaugurated the citizen journalism movement. Figures like Nate Silver and Bill Simmons leveraged blogs to gain respective positions with the *New York Times* and ESPN. Joining this influx of citizens into journalism, brands increasingly engaged in reporting and nonfiction storytelling online. With audio teams lacking formal training in journalism, brand-produced podcasts raise similar questions to those broached by alternative and prosumer creators whose production practice changed fundamental digital journalism principles. These transformed principles include gatekeeping (who gets to decide what is newsworthy), citizen journalism (user-generated content), and news values (what is considered news).[15] Such changes enticed brands to migrate into digital space.

Although some critics reject brands as credible producers of journalism, calling them mercenary and untrustworthy, nonmedia companies have escalated production of journalistic podcasts that aim to provide various levels of information and entertainment through sales messages that purport to serve both the profit motive and the public interest.[16] Investors argue that brand-produced podcast journalism can enrich the diversity of media coverage of political and historical events. Conversely, because brand-produced podcasts operate outside professional norms of journalistic production, their content can suffer from distortion. Additionally, the rise of native advertising has presented the Federal Trade Commission in the United States with the challenge of regulating attempts to deceive audiences, one complicated by the blurring of editorial and advertising boundaries. The failed efforts of the FTC have exposed government's inability to control content of this nature whose advertising function places it outside the parameters of journalism.[17] Yet such regulation would not provide a panacea for deceptive advertising, which is already prevalent even in advertising that conspicuously presents itself as a commercial sales message. By contrast, traditional news organizations employ editors to regulate data collection, media professionals to double check the facts, and lawyers to make sure published stories are not libelous.[18] The risks of brand-produced podcast journalism, which are analogous to those of citizen journalism, thus severely limit the potential for this genre of audio storytelling to enable richer forms of narrative. Proponents of sponsored podcasts argue that they can potentially augment traditional journalism's mission to inform the public.

Brand journalism shares many basic characteristics of traditional news production teams, as evidenced in content marketing studios staffed by legacy media reporters, including T Brand Studios (*New York Times*), The Trust (*Wall Street Journal*), and WP BrandStudio (*Washington Post*). Like many news organizations, brands' production practice bears the characteristics of "content with value, newsworthiness and interest for them and their audiences; being distributed by their own media; and using journalistic work processes, tools, principles, and formats."[19] Whereas news organizations have leveraged the rhetoric of transparency as a metajournalistic performance designed to add credit and legitimacy to the publisher, brands bear different nonjournalistic identities less concerned with legitimating reportorial credentials.[20] Although legacy media's performance of transparency can be dissembling and self-promotional as in the case of *Caliphate* by the *New York Times*, it bears the advantage over brands of harboring serious concern for the reportorial process. Instead of using transparency in the manner of news organizations seeking "to proudly advertise the quality of their performance" and "market merits of their journalistic identity to potential audiences" by lifting the veil on the process of production, brands deploy the trope of transparency to bring listeners a more direct, intense, and intimate experience of their goods and services.[21] Narrative plays a crucial role in expressing the company's brand values, particularly through empathic and charismatic hosts inclined toward self-disclosure.

With the primary rhetorical objective shifting from defending journalistic legitimacy, nonjournalistic podcast producers instead aim to promote their brand values through a news product that is simultaneously entertaining and informative. Such podcasts as *The Sauce* by McDonalds and *Inside Trader Joe's* thus pivot the metajournalistic performance of transparency toward the publisher's primary product, particularly its process of production. Listeners are invited into the stocking, pricing, personnel, and warehousing management decisions of the Trader Joe's grocery store chain, for example, just as they are offered a behind-the-scenes view of the executive strategy for the release of McDonald's Szechuan sauce. Disclosure, authenticity, and transparency are thus selling points emphasized in many brand-produced podcasts, only without concern for reinforcing traditional definitions of journalism. Instead, branded podcasts place emphasis on the quality of the company's products and consumer experience. Since insights are funneled into marketing imperatives, fallacious or intentionally deceptive reporting threatens to mar the content.

The actions and attitudes traditionally defining journalism according to an ideal standard often view the profession as "providing a public service; being objective, fair and (therefore) trustworthy; working autonomously, committed to an operational logic of actuality and speed (preeminent in concepts such as reporting on breaking news, getting the story first); and having social responsibility and ethical sensibility."[22] Corporations have taken notice of how these standards defining the journalistic role have undergone profound transformation since the digital revolution. As Matt Carlson observes, even from its origin, journalism has always been characterized as "a varied cultural practice embedded within a complicated social landscape. Journalism is not a solid, stable thing to point to, but a constantly shifting denotation applied differently depending on context."[23] The point aptly describes the shifting meaning of journalism when brands engage in journalistic podcast production. No longer confined to newsrooms and governed by a closed and strict set of principles and practices, journalism appears across a variety of platforms, often in media bearing primary entertainment functions. The pivot to video in the early to mid-2010s positioned online documentaries as the future of content marketing, a period when gamification and interactives, often featuring rigorous reporting, became increasingly journalistic. This was "a measure designed to entice users to take them more seriously as editorial content rather than peripheral—and thus distracting and ephemeral—sales messages."[24] The delivery of information on relevant issues and current events coalesces with the brand messages, particularly addressing the company's broader ethos, cultural positioning, and perspective toward lifestyle-defining values. Content marketing is defined as storytelling that precedes or is strategically blended with the sales message.[25] Podcasting is an audio extension of digital longform journalism that functions as both story and advertisement to promote the company that produced it. The conflation of editorial and advertising functions is evident in *Animal Planet*'s "Blood and Water," a dramatic online interactive documenting efforts to combat the illegal whaling trade. The piece won both a Webby, recognizing "general excellence on the internet," and an ADDY award from the American Advertising Federation for outstanding advertisements.[26] Advertising has reached sophisticated, almost Zen-like levels of storytelling as its content has achieved recognition for transcending the once ghettoized genre of commercials cordoned off from legitimate forms of nonfiction storytelling and stigmatized as promotional content for marketing purposes only.[27]

The spread of journalism production beyond newsrooms and their trained staff to citizens and brands has been described as the "postindustrial" condition of digital news publishing.[28] The "liquid" nature of journalistic production practice in the digital age has prompted brands to leverage, for competitive advantage, journalism's ongoing transformation as "a profession in a permanent process of becoming."[29] Ambiguity arises when protocols for media companies and nonmedia companies alike aim to integrate the social public service mission into the broader objective of accruing profit. Brands increasingly capitalize on how this ambiguity is largely recognized and tolerated by podcast producers as well as their listeners, who are not likely to follow twentieth-century definitions of journalism "in terms of limited newsroom conceptions [that] jettison any considerations of journalism's poetic or its ambitious forms."[30] As products whose evolution has been fueled by the relatively rich funding resources of the free market, branded and sponsored longform podcasts are self-consciously crafted to represent these more ambitious forms of journalism. The important role of advertising as "the financial lynchpin supporting independent media" has developed beyond a necessary evil or, worse, an abhorrent distraction polluting editorial content.[31] Compared to government subsidies and paid subscriptions, advertising has historically provided much more consistent and substantial financial support for independent news and entertainment media.[32] As online advertising investment has grown, opportunities for storytelling have opened with the new fluid process of journalism's ongoing transformations and myriad iterations across media. Since journalism is neither a stable nor consistent entity, either as a coherent and unified profession or as a canonized set of texts, publishers have found creative entries into journalist discourse. In the process, increasingly ambitious storytelling is undergirded by the richer financial resources of the free market beyond third-party advertising and government subsidies alone. As Christopher William Anderson and colleagues note, "journalism may be dead as an industry, but journalism exists in many places," a point not to be confused with its use as strategic communication explicitly crafted for corporate profit.[33]

Debate surrounding journalism's boundaries traditionally has been viewed as a dichotomy of insiders and outsiders. Podcasts produced by brands, however, pose a new question precisely because disclosure of promotional intent is typically overt compared to its more surreptitious nature in native advertising. That open disclosure, both on the screen interface and through the audio content, can be understood as a means of redrawing the boundaries of journalism, particularly by refashioning them according to larger strategic communication goals. Insofar as objects of journalism have been shown to visualize boundary work to demarcate the nature of principle of the producers' journalism practice, "objects of journalism embedded in native ads have an ontological interpretive power for an audience to decide whether a piece is news or advertising" and thus "can be used to establish the visual boundaries of journalism," particularly in screen-based online news.[34] Podcasts can embed native advertising in deceptive forms, especially through product placement in documentary longform works.

Given the soaring popularity of nonfiction podcasts, brands bear a financial incentive to build trust in their audience. But such trust bears more on establishing brand loyalty for marketers than for journalists. Amid the flurry of divergent actors rushing into the journalistic field, corporate entities have entered the fray. Nikki Usher notes that "digital news products as objects of journalism are also sites where power is negotiated among the actors that use them, the actors that make them, and by the objects themselves, and in turn, invoke different claims about trust."[35] The boundaries of journalism are constantly being contested by the introduction of new technologies, actors, and forms.[36] Brands are at the forefront of the wave of intrusion onto the journalistic terrain. Gatekeepers can accept migration into journalistic online space by brands and other interlopers as an opportunity for boundary expansion. Conversely, they can reject it in an effort to expel them as deviant actors who might be perceived as a threat to journalism, particularly in the separation of business from editorial operations in newspapers.[37] Corporate marketers have thus taken advantage of the redrawing of journalistic boundaries by social movements and the many prominent publications in the news media industry who have endorsed interlopers, particularly in light of the new urgent need for social justice.

The rise of sponsored podcasts can be understood in part as the strategic corporate entrance into digital storytelling enabled by broadening definitions of journalism within the profession itself. According to Mark Deuze and Tamara Witschge, the "modernist dream of coherence and consensus"—particularly conspicuous in studies of the early 2010s—attempted to bring stability back to the profession by leveraging narrow definitions through massive surveys in an effort to render a static portrait of journalists and their practice.[38] Yet emerging genres and formats of journalism continued to proliferate across industries and platforms. Further, the lack of consensus in the news industry regarding what counts as journalism became particularly evident inside of legacy media newsrooms, which appeared far less coherent and stable than it is made to appear.[39] Thus, the notion of insiders harboring a clear and mutually understood professional identity that contrasts with interlopers attempting to gain approval from the periphery became undermined by inconsistencies, contradictions, and tensions among legacy media reporters themselves regarding the journalistic role. Brands rapidly capitalized by donning the journalistic role to serve their financial interests while appearing to be civic-minded supporters of the public interest.

Podcasting's roots in do-it-yourself (DIY) culture and indie media position it in opposition to commercial, profit-driven media production. The tendency of podcast producers "to avoid association with commercial media and its considerations" is underscored by the chorus of dissent elicited by Ira Glass's aforementioned claim that public radio was prepared to embrace capitalism.[40] In keeping with self-representation that aligns with hand-made, artisanal, DIY culture, podcasters tend to emphasize passion over profit and crowdfunding over advertising. The culture of podcast production is inclined toward keeping operating budgets discretely out of public view; hosts even of the largest mainstream audience commanding massive corporate commercial investment relish the opportunity to present their work as anathema to industrial settings and logics. As discussed in chapter 1, Ira Glass relished the opportunity to sound this anti-industrial keynote of podcasting as a deeply personal practice in posting a photo of himself recording barefoot in his closet with his wardrobe parted to form a tiny makeshift studio during the first outbreak of the pandemic in 2020. Similarly, Sarah Koenig and Dana Chivvis describe the production of *Serial* as taking place in a basement "rather than framing it as part of a hugely successful radio franchise" produced on an industrial scale for a mass audience.[41] The leveraging of new audio media technology to circumvent the so-called mainstream media is integral to the alternative, oppositional identity of podcasting's roots in fringe, indie culture. Corporate production studios funded by advertising thus undermines this nostalgic narrative at the heart of podcasters' self-definition. According to this cultural predilection, the incursion of brands into this DIY space represents the apotheosis of the corporate hijacking of the podcast medium.

The emergence of the once fringe podcast culture into big-tech industrial-scale production is captured not only in the ascendance of *Serial*, which led to the acquisition of Serial Productions by the *New York Times* in 2020, but also in Alex Blumberg and Matt Lieber's startup company, Gimlet Media. Founded prior to *Serial*'s 2014 success, the company represents the first podcast-specific deliberate attempt to corporatize and commodify the medium's DIY space. Gimlet's business model draws revenue from holding the rights to its published shows rather than granting them to the producer. By stripping producers of their financial and creative autonomy, Gimlet (and its parent company, Spotify) have alienated celebrity hosts such as Eric Eddings and Brittany Luse, who left the company in pursuit of more equitable terms and conditions of production with Stitcher on SiriusXM (as detailed in chapter 6). Thus, boundary work should be conceived of as occurring not only between journalism and advertising but also between DIY indie podcast culture and corporate media. This complicates and crosscuts the conception of journalism in a straightforward, dichotomous relation with commercial interests, commonly referred to as church and state, according to newsroom parlance. When journalism's age-old tension between editorial and business sides is recast in the context of new digital media such as podcasting, that dynamic complicates profoundly, particularly in light of podcasting's recent emergence from its former grassroots identity into the corporate realm dominated by big-tech firms like Apple and Spotify. Blumberg and Lieber's achievement of their goal to monetize podcasting is evident in the expansion of the initial investment of $1.5 million in 2014 to $15 million two years later in 2016. Advertising and brand partnerships were integral to the business model since the company's founding, as seen in the branded podcasts produced by Gimlet Creative, its studio dedicated to sponsored content. Gimlet's branded podcasts support brands across a vast array of industries ranging from digital media platforms and tools (Squarespace, Tinder, Microsoft, Lyft, eBay, WeWork, and Adobe) and athletic apparel (Reebok and New Balance) to cooking (Blue Apron) and venture capitalism (Virgin Atlantic).

Once a cottage industry offshoot of public radio, podcasting's roots in storytelling on shows like Jay Allison's *The Moth Radio Hour* now appear more calculated to win market share. Allison recalled that in the early days of the Transom Story Workshop, dedicated to training audio producers, "It used to be that I would say to the students, 'Look, we are going to train you to do this public-media storytelling, and I know you may have to make a vow of poverty, but it does have meaning, and it does create change in your community.'" He noted that since the corporatization of podcasting, "Now they come here, and, pretty much as soon as they leave, they can get a job that pays pretty well."[42] Although start-ups increasingly face longer odds for success in the face of fewer companies owning a greater share of the most popular shows, the overall economic scale of the industry has expanded dramatically, making employment opportunities more plentiful. Dreams of producing and hosting one's own show may not be as attainable, but employment on production teams in supporting roles is on the rise. The open, startup-driven market characterizing the competitive scramble of the first wave of podcasting during the early 2000s has now yielded to a corporate marketplace with more ancillary and intermediary positions available in support of large-market shows. The real limitations to the success of startups in the wake of corporatization are the result of the mainstreaming of podcasting in blockbuster shows such as Spotify's *The Joe Rogan Experience*.

Spotify's podcast advertising revenue increase of 627 percent year-over-year, announced in the second quarter of 2021, not only signifies gargantuan profits for the company but also points to the influx of advertisers in the on-demand digital audio space. Spotify CEO Daniel Ek noted that "the continued out-performance is currently limited only by the availability of our inventory," which the company has solved. The explosion of ad revenue is exhibited in Ek's reflection that "the days of our ad business accounting for less than ten percent of our total revenue are behind us, and going forward, I expect ads to be a substantial part of our revenue mix."[43] Behind this astronomical leap in advertising revenue for Spotify was the introduction of "streaming ad insertion" technology, which proved instrumental in generating sales of ad space. Concurrent with this rise in ad revenue is a dramatic increase in listenership, which grew in terms of monthly active users by 30 percent year-over-year on a per user basis.[44] Importantly, this industrial sea change brings advertising brands closer to the storytelling process. In the case of branded podcasts, commercial marketers assume complete editorial control over the content, often in consultation with a podcast publisher who may supply a hired production team, as in the case of Gimlet. News work, in this sense, clearly operates outside of the newsroom, despite appearing to engage in production practices associated with traditional journalism. Although branded podcasts, like other digital media produced outside of newsrooms, are not "necessarily free of the constraints and structures traditionally provided by the institutional arrangement of journalism," they should not be confused with an independent press operating in the public interest.[45]

Neoliberal individualism's influence on enterprise journalism is consonant with newsrooms' embrace of sponsored content. Branded podcasts place podcast producers squarely in the role of strategic communications specialists generating advertising copy. Market pressures have increasingly influenced content decisions within newsrooms, leading to the formation of podcast content marketing studios such as Gimlet Creative. Although "the notion of the enterprising or entrepreneurial individual extends beyond the creative industries," it is important to note that "the emergence of the enterprising professional in journalism is a relatively recent phenomenon, coinciding with a gradual breakdown of the wall between commercial and editorial sides of the news organization."[46] With branded podcasts, that wall has altogether vanished. In the case of screen-based native advertising, market pressures have led to increasingly ambiguous presentation, which may mislead readers into identifying native ads as distinct from editorial content.[47] Recent findings show that "although coinciding and disclosing objects could be used to maximize transparency, native ads use coinciding objects to camouflage ads as much as possible and disclosing objects only to a minimal extent."[48] For native ads, news organizations tend to lean toward ambiguity rather than transparency, in part due to power asymmetries between marketers and news organizations. This pressure "to integrate commercial and editorial content without clearly disclosing it" is circumvented entirely when brands publish stand-alone media products, which have an incentive to signal the corporate brand early in each piece in order to forge the optimal impression on the reader.[49]

Native advertising only discloses authorship (whether a company, news organization, or a person) in roughly half (54 percent) of native ads.[50] Sponsored podcasts aim for greater legitimacy through disclosure of identifying authorship information, which has been proven to (1) build trust in news audiences, (2) positively influence the credibility of the news website, and (3) make users more amenable to storytelling by brands.[51] As such, they attempt to win trust through explicit brand identification.

MARKETING PUBLIC SERVICE

Corporate marketers have discovered that their strategic communication goals can be reached more easily through podcasts for both consumer-based companies and through producers of B2B (business-to-business) products. The B2B software maker Alpha UX is a tech company that uses podcasting to promote its brand. The podcast *This Is Product Management* features extended interviews with product leaders, authors, and executives who share their best insights on research, leadership, and innovation. Storytelling centered on fostering customer relationships is the focus of the Zendesk podcast. As an alternative to traditional B2B promotional campaigns, the episodes of Zendesk's podcast resonate with the company's customer relationship software. For marketers, podcasts bear the advantages of attracting listeners through powerful narratives rather than more aggressively direct product messaging through conventional advertising or product promotion through the tactic of native advertising. The more deeply engaged the listener, the more likely they will be inclined "to view the brand in a positive light."[52] The profusion of brands becoming podcast publishers serves the needs of marketers while appearing to celebrate how "beautiful radio is being produced in the least likely of places."[53]

Although the ostensible "remit of commercial-funded media networks is to accrue profit, rather than act in fulfillment of any broader social mission," it is often designed to appear wedded to journalistic civic purpose in branded podcasts.[54] In the hands of brands and corporate partners, nonfiction storytelling has never been better funded. The tropes of public service journalism are appropriated to converge with entertainment media in serving the marketing needs of companies in the music and food industries as well as the medical field. Some of the clearest examples of branded podcasts pantomiming public interest journalism are produced by medical companies. Abbott Laboratories, which develops biomedical health technologies, sponsors an episode on the podcast *CES Tech Talk* dedicated to "Tech Solutions for the Greatest Health Challenges," including neuromodulation. In addition to isolated sponsored episodes, the Abbott Newsroom publishes *Health Tech on the Horizon*, a show in the health and fitness category on medical inventions that foreshadows the future of health care. Interviews of the inventors and users of such technology communicate the significance of Abbott's medical products.[55] The podcast reinforces the company's strategic communication of its advances in AIDS research through personal storytelling that showcases the experience of survivors of the disease who have directly benefited from the company's pharmaceutical products and technologies. Abbott's podcast illustrates how the use of audio journalistic reporting tropes appear to advance beyond a dichotomous relationship with strategic communication for promotional purposes.

Perhaps the most powerful example of a branded podcast designed to amplify its corporation's own civic engagement through the appropriation of a social movement is the Starbucks series *Upstanders*. Its two ten-episode seasons launched in 2016 were conceived in direct response to the wave of political hostility that coincided with the Trump presidential campaign, one fueled by news coverage of social divisions and conflict occasioned by the coarsening of public discourse. In keeping with its brand's identity as not only a producer of beverages but also a provider of public space for civil discourse linked to a long history tracing back to the coffee houses of colonial America, Starbucks' statement of purpose for *Upstanders* serves as a counter to "the divisiveness and cynicism currently fueling our national discourse."[56] The aim is not just civility and mutual respect but to harness the talents and energy of the citizenry for the benefit of the greater good. The podcast episodes, which also appear as digital news stories and videos, all coalesce around the aim to issue a "reminder that ordinary citizens can create extraordinary impact by refusing to be bystanders." This first original content series produced by Starbucks positions the brand itself as an upstanding citizen in the communities it serves, particularly by providing space to plan the sort of public service projects showcased in the series. The project marked a milestone in the company's community outreach efforts, which led to the establishment of the Starbucks Foundation Neighborhood Grants awarded in 2021. "Coffee has the power to fuel human connection," a brand value that resonates with the company's 2,500 grants awarded to neighborhood organizations from 2019 to 2020. All U.S. states and Canadian provinces participated in the program across more than 3,500 stores in North America. The organizations supported are grassroots and community-led nonprofit groups that directly benefited from catalytic investments ranging from $1,000 to $10,000. The aim of mounting sustained local impact to attract partner engagement is strategically aligned with several socially efficacious fronts, from inclusion, diversity, and racial equity to fighting hunger, supporting social services, empowering youth, and addressing homelessness.[57]

In the *Upstanders* podcast, storytelling in the public interest is showcased in all episodes, including one detailing how a community in Michigan united and organized to provide every one of its high school students a college scholarship. This alternative collective economy is consonant with the spirit of altruistic giving as a gesture of public service, one that runs directly counter to the logics of radically individualistic, profit-oriented entrepreneurialism associated with free-market enterprise. Interestingly, *Starbucks Stories and News*, which functions as the company's current online publication of media content, engages in long-form storytelling of a personal nature as well as shorter headline-driven pieces, each one subtly reinforcing the brand's location at the heart of neighborhoods and communities as a space for collaboration, planning, and social cohesion. "Scholarships for Every Student" reflects this editorial vision, which directly translates into the podcast's production aesthetic. The episode inheres an aesthetic at once artful and journalistic, leveraging emotion through the power of compassion within the community of Baldwin, Michigan. Plagued by low income and food insecurity, 95 percent of Baldwin's public school students quality for free and reduced-price lunches. Prior to the initiative, only 30 percent of students attended college following high school graduation, as the narrator explains. A pause follows this alarming statistic, generating a sense of intrigue in how the community responded. "But something fascinating has occurred in the village of Baldwin," signals a shift in tone toward unmistakably hopeful energy shot through with collective ambition.[58]

Listeners learn of the vision of Ellen Kerans, a retired schoolteacher and resident of Baldwin who had learned of community scholarships through the Kalamazoo Promise, which offered students full tuition to any Michigan public university through funds donated by anonymous sources. Kerans made a pitch for donations from several corporations in the state in 2007, but most demurred. She then learned from Rick Simonson, a Baldwin native and legislative staffer and lobbyist in Michigan, that a law had been passed creating "promise zones" requiring startup funds of only several hundred thousand dollars—rather than the $3 million they originally assumed they needed—to qualify for a share of annual property tax revenue to sustain the scholarships over time. Dramatic tension escalates as the challenge of raising several hundred thousand dollars appears out of reach for the economically challenged community, with most residents on welfare and "living paycheck to paycheck," without surplus capital to spare.[59] The verbal cadence of the narration matches Kerans's slow accretion of funds leading toward the goal, which initially appears unlikely to succeed. She "began to knock on doors. Her neighbors. Churches. The Rotary Club. The police station and the fire station." After a long pause, the emotionally charged revelation emerges. "Everyone gave." Schoolteachers, staff, and custodians contributed, and a roadside barbecue restaurant raised $500 in a collection jar. Some grandparents, the listener learns, pledged $20 per month. The historical long view of the region surrounding Baldwin from the Jim Crow era to the 1960s details the socioethnic origins of its cohesive integration against the socially corrosive tide of segregation.

Aesthetics are defined as "the way things show themselves, together with the reasons for preferring one way of showing itself to another," variables that include both the creator's and the audience's perspectives.[60] "Scholarships for Every Student" reflect an ear for production aesthetics that stems from the journalistic prowess of hosts and producers Howard Schultz, who is Starbucks' CEO, and Rajiv Chandrasekaran, the company's executive producer who previously served as senior editor at the *Washington Post*. The piece's journalistic integrity is evident in the sourcing via carefully edited interviews from Kerans to student recipients of the scholarships, such as Da'Ron Copeland, and meticulous historical research into Baldwin's cultural situation within a region beleaguered by racial strife.[61] Strategic communication is cloaked by the selection of details and emphasis that place *Upstanders* on the continuum of news forms "between the extremes of straightforward, matter-of-fact, plain style news item and multisensory stimulating art experiences, evoking various degrees of (emotional) response towards coexisting factual and felt truths."[62] As such, the piece strategically communicates legislative and community advocacy opportunities to support underprivileged youth in achieving their career goals as a means of advancing its marketing agenda. It of course carries this information through the empathic intimacy unique to the podcast medium in a narrative structure that follows the contours of well-crafted fiction as well as absorbing journalistic feature writing. Starbucks' brand value of community and sociality are evident in subtle shadings and hues, particularly in a tableau of Black and white students seated together "in classrooms and at lunch tables, not in separate groups."[63] Coffee never explicitly enters the narrative as a product for sale, but the ethos of integration and outreach pervades the episode, even in the contributions to the collection jar at the roadside barbecue—clearly not a Starbucks but an establishment performing public service to the community in the spirit of the ubiquitous coffeehouse chain from Seattle.

Starbucks opportunistically positions its podcast storytelling as a reprieve from the overwhelmingly negative coverage in mainstream news media highlighting social division and animosity. The public service commitment is strategically communicated by working against the grain of dominant trends in journalistic storytelling. Brands place a high premium on originality in the storytelling of the content marketing, including those who employ content production studios run by legacy media such as the *New York Times*'s T Brand Studio. A study by the Tow Center for Digital Journalism and Columbia University recently found that staff working in branded content studios for news publishers consistently cited originality as the most common demand of their clients. "Clients, our interviewees constantly told us, always ask for something that 'has never been done.'"[64] This "demand for novelty forces news organizations to pitch campaigns that are closely aligned with what journalists" rather than advertisers "are producing, because other marketing channels cannot offer their clients this association."[65] The presence of a former *Washington Post* editor among Starbucks' top-ranking executives ideally positions the company to straddle both advertising and journalistic functions in its podcast. Starbucks enjoys a built-in advantage with a legacy news media veteran of Chandrasekaran's caliber that most brands lack. Brands thus seek legacy media content studios for precisely such expertise in journalistic production practice while also seeking to reflect credit on their product through the news organization's prestige. A former *Times* T Brand Studio employee noted pressure from clients to produce branded stories "that are 'Times-ian'" by adopting "the same tone as the publication's newsroom."[66] Chandrasekaran's storytelling acumen developed at the *Washington Post* is evident in *Upstanders*, particularly in its clear opposition to the Trump administration's hostile rhetoric.

Novelty is similarly invoked as a trope rhetorically leveraged to validate *Upstanders* as content marketing. As Chandrasekaran notes, "*Upstanders* is a unique set of stories told in a unique way," specifically by redrawing journalistic boundaries to dissociate from the effect of being "inundated with stories of discord and dysfunction." His most deceptive move, however, occurs when he describes such storytelling explicitly as journalism rather than strategic communication. He urges that "journalism" produced by the Starbucks brand will approach news from another angle to emphasize "people who are courageously, selflessly, collaboratively, and thoughtfully creating positive change." The impetus is "to share their stories, which are often ignored by traditional news organizations, with millions of our fellow Americans through Starbucks' unparalleled platform."[67] The effort here is to reimagine journalism—as it were, with the category of strategic communication carefully hidden from view—from a fresh perspective unique to the brand identity, one that the company defines explicitly in lieu of partnering with a legacy media publisher to gain prestige by association. To complete the marketing of public service under the guise of a new media producer, Starbucks' "unparalleled platform" thus intends not to be "Times-ian" in its aesthetic feel but to project an altogether singular image—colored by a defiant, socially aware optimism in the potential for disparate groups to cohere and achieve shared goals—through audio storytelling.

CASE STUDIES IN BRANDED PODCASTS: COCA-COLA, MCDONALD'S, AND TRADER JOE'S

Across news media, there are many instances in which "publishers actively work with bands that are antithetical to their missions" and editorial outlook, as in the case of *The Atlantic*'s content production on behalf of the Church of Scientology.[68] The incongruity is perhaps best explained by the financial power imbalance between advertisers and news organizations. Thus, companies such as Coca-Cola capable of investing in their own media production carry a competitive advantage of operating independent journals without third-party mitigation. Like Starbucks, Coca-Cola's *Total Refresh* podcast series performs strategic communication by insinuating itself into journalistic boundary work as a brand demarcating its unique "reportorial" method and production practice as distinct from so-called mainstream media, a rhetorical tactic that simultaneously allows for product differentiation over and against competing brands.[69] In an attempt to establish credibility through the metajournalistic performance of transparency, episode 1 announces, "We are pulling back the curtain and turning internal communications inside out," a nod to podcasting's signature authenticity and self-disclosure.[70] The Netflix documentary series *Inside*, produced by Bloomberg (which covers Chipotle and McDonald's among other companies), makes a similar appeal to audience fascination with the inner workings of a massive, multinational corporation. Rather than an investigative team of journalists exposing tensions within the company, these shows make a rhetorical performance of transparency that carefully avoids any potentially unflattering topics, such as the environmental impact of industrial-scale production, labor issues, and the question of nutrition. Such strategic communication is thus incapable of the monitorial watchdog function due to the maintenance of its prevailing profit motive.

Although the turning of internal communications inside out may promise to lift the veil obscuring the entire process of production, only select portions are strategically displayed. As with *Caliphate*, the *New York Times* true crime podcast that was discredited when the testimony of its main source was revealed to be fabricated, branded podcasts purporting to offer full revelations of the inside of institutions, organizations, or companies often veiled in secrecy can be deceiving based on what

The Profit Motive   195

producers decide to reveal and conceal.[71] The journalistic genre of feature profile writing can be divided into two types (which overlap in some instances): the adversarial investigation exposing misdeeds contrary to the company's public relations interests and the laudatory portrait aimed at elevating and ennobling the status of the subject. Just as transparency is leveraged by journalists, brands also attempt to show they can be trusted and that the story is true in keeping with the "culture of journalism" rooted in the principle of bearing witness in person, the norm of objectivity, and the practice of verifying information.[72] Transparency is highlighted in the story promoting *Total Refresh* on Coca-Cola's "News" menu of their main website, an article designed to promote the podcasts, which itself is a work of content marketing. Within this promotional funhouse mirror of reflections of reflections of the company's main product, rhetorical performances of transparency draw legitimacy by embracing valued production practice standards in journalistic culture. For brands, this entails creating the appearance of total audience immersion in the product's process of production, which in Coca-Cola's case depends on the (re)construction of internal company communications behind the scenes of its beverages. The promise of the podcast is to deliver nothing less than the audio equivalent of privately circulated emails—personal confessions of those inside the network of strategic communications for one of the world's most powerful and recognizable companies.

Coca-Cola executives interviewed on *Total Refresh* engage in the strategic communication equivalent of what Carlson calls metajournalism.[73] This metalevel discourse is what "journalists engage in when discussing their work in the news," and transparency can be considered a "a form of journalism about journalism that occurs within a news product."[74] Similarly, *Total Refresh* is a form of strategic communication about strategic communication that occurs within a (branded) news product. As a podcast, this branded news product seizes the opportunity to build trust and intimacy with listeners, simultaneous to being potential customers, through the authenticity of unscripted personal narrative. By facing doubts, these executives can "reinvigorate their own faith in their professional authority" in addition to restoring the audience's trust in that authority.[75] A brand like Coca-Cola faces unique challenges to re-instill waning trust in the face of criticism of multinational corporations as a major culprit in Western global economic dominance and exploitation fueled by rampant, runaway capitalism. The tactical use of personal confession, which Rosalind Coward notes is concomitant to the rise of personized and intimate journalism, is foregrounded in promotion of *Total Refresh* as candid, honest conversations.[76] The podcast's website insists, "Nothing was scripted, leaders were not briefed, and no questions were off the table." The faux air of tension thus sets the stage for executives to reconcile with challenges, if only to neatly resolve them in triumphalist narratives. Such performances of transparency align with the two manifestations of personal and subjective journalism identified by Mia Lindgren. The first is "by journalists . . . participating in the story and sharing their own experiences" and "second, by journalists taking a narrative approach to the development of their journalism, emphasizing the personal experiences of subjects of the story."[77] To this end, executives including Coca-Cola North America president Jim Dinkins reflect on their career paths and leadership styles.[78]

Total Refresh host Jamal Booker explained that the personal narratives of these executives will establish trust with the company's lower-level employees, thus bringing an internal communication agenda to add to the show's ostensible external message to consumers. "We hope employees come away from each episode with a sense that these leaders at one point faced some of the same challenges they're currently facing," he urged, noting that "we tried to dig into each leader's personal story and try to understand their decision making processes at different points in their career."[79] Interestingly, Booker and his cohost are not identified as reporters or journalists, despite clearly assuming the journalistic role, but are described as "Coca-Cola communications colleagues," an oblique disclosure of their positions as paid employees of the beverage company.[80] Through "intimate and transparent dialogue," the show strives to embody how "the best corporate podcasts are unafraid to get real." Episodes include an interview with Dagmar Boggs, the first female to lead national retail sales for Coca-Cola North America. Boggs underscores the pattern of performative transparency designed to build employee and consumer trust with her comment, "I have probably four or five stories where I've taken a risk at Coke, where I've learned that most of the time they worked and when they don't, guess what—the company still wakes up the next day and we go on." The podcast goes on to offer those stories of risk-taking, which are possible and even encouraged according to the master narrative, given the size of the company.[81]

Coca-Cola's tentative first steps into the podcast terrain are far less confident than the imaginative PR stunt of *The Sauce* by McDonald's, which showcases a knowing ear for investigative documentary conventions of the form, including ponderous music, self-reflexive narration, dramatization of the reportorial process, and emphasis on the tenuous semantic foundation of evidence. True crime documentary podcasts repeating those conventions have made the genre ripe for satire. McDonald's seized this opportunity when the company failed to meet demand for its teriyaki-flavored Szechuan sauce, which led to a consumer revolt online in the form of 45,000 signatures on Change.org insisting on replenished supplies. The ensuing podcast set out to solve the mystery of what went wrong to lead to such a catastrophe, intoned in a pitch-perfect mockumentary whose production values reveal a deep awareness of the many clichés and hackneyed signature moves of the documentary podcast. Gizmodo produced the piece that the *New York Times* described as distinct from an advertisement but instead as "subtle, brand-building efforts that intend to entertain as well as persuade." Host Catherine LeClair listened to past episodes of *Serial* as she composed the script for *The Sauce* with the Gizmodo production team. Her highly attuned ear for *Serial*'s idiosyncrasies evident in the script derived from her own role as a fan of the show. "To try to emulate that was almost like an honor," she said of her masterful mockumentary.[82]

Launched the same year as *The Sauce* in 2017, *Inside Trader Joe's* reached the fifth spot out of 750,000 podcasts on iTunes' top 100 chart. Host Matt Sloan's promise in the opening episode that "this isn't going to be a commercial" is overtly disingenuous, as the show is more advertisement than public service. The promotion of food items via hosts oozing over their favorite products (as in the episode "A Trader Joe's Shopping List to Add Sparkle to Your Summer") and obsequious discussion of why the staff are so friendly (in "Why Is Everyone So Nice?") serve as persuasive rhetoric driving toward commercial goals identical with those of advertisements. The show's five-star rating on iTunes suggests that the commercial agenda has not been a deterrent to attracting eager listeners. The practice of playing the podcast in some stores while customers shop suggests the show's function according to how "propaganda—which is after all what this is—tends to slide into our consciousness without our quite perceiving it."[83] The show epitomizes how companies can leverage the podcast medium to create their own platform for strategic communication rather than surreptitiously baking their sales message into another product.

The massive listening audience of *Inside Trader Joe's*—essentially a longform advertisement—is the large overlap between the demographic of its customers and the typical podcast consumer, both of whom are relatively young, educated, and affluent.[84] Also consonant with nonfictional longform podcast listeners is this segment of consumers' "growing preference for smaller stores that provide individualized service to the community in which they are located."[85] This preference aligns with the resurgence of independent bookstores, a reaction against online booksellers and big-box chains such as Barnes and Noble that led to the increase of independents by 40 percent from 2009 to 2018.[86] In keeping with the design of the shopping experience, *Inside Trader Joe's* is quirky and sophisticated, blending elements of humor in product names and staff clad in Hawaiian shirts. "Episode 16: Produce" matches this playful and mindful tone, as evidenced in the discussion of terminal markets, which performs effectively as explanatory journalism.[87] The listener learns through an interview with Trader Joe's category manager for produce—whose thick Boston brogue, wit, and clearly conveyed specialized knowledge echoes that of Tom and Ray Magliozzi of NPR's *Car Talk* (1987–2012)—that the company refuses to buy their produce from terminal markets, where "suppliers don't have a home for their goods." He explains that "we don't buy from there because we lose control over where it's been harvested." His next point would be of particular interest to educated listeners concerned with consuming responsibly produced goods. "We're loyal to a supplier. We pay a fair price for the product. We become a very desired account and we can leverage that into getting things that we want, like social responsibility." This major problem in the produce industry has "no easy solutions," he allows, but he affirms the company's aim to "deal with companies that treat their workers fairly," a point punctuated by upbeat music transitioning to a discussion of new varieties appearing in the produce case.[88] As such, all insights are funneled toward product sales.

As the most successful pairing of the podcast medium with a brand, *Inside Trader Joe's* epitomizes how companies can engage with creative, in-depth storytelling without risking alienating potential consumers. The crucial role of the intimate parasocial host–listener relationship that is the signature of podcast journalism and a major appeal of individual shows mitigates the dubious ethical terrain otherwise trammeled by native advertising and product placement. Sirrah notes that most native advertisements lack bylines, allowing "journalists at a publisher to write commercial content without readers knowing."[89] This trend has encouraged former journalists, freelancers, and legacy media studio producers "to leverage their skill sets in advertising departments across major newspapers."[90] Brands that tell stories through podcasts typically do so through hosts that carry a high profile in the company itself or through their own producers who perform the role of reporting journalists under the name of communication colleagues, as with Coca-Cola's *Total Refresh*. This transparency, however, does not necessarily elevate branded podcasts to the plane of impeccable journalistic principle, as fact-checking, source verification, and holding power to account are investigative measures that brands are unlikely to apply to their own business practices unless the outcome serves PR protocol. Such self-investigation ended abruptly at Gimlet Media, for example, when Eric Eddings's proposed exploration of its workplace inequities was deemed incongruous with its brand.

Since branded podcasts are themselves commercial storytelling, they carry no spot advertising, offering the listener uninterrupted storytelling. The irony, of course, lies in the notion that advertising-free news and entertainment is being facilitated by media products that are themselves longer, more immersive advertisements. Podcast journalism and strategic communication has become increasingly characterized by three distinct business models: Brands that make use of journalistic styles to promote their goods and services; startup news and commentary podcasts on platforms such as Spotify that generate revenue through streaming ad insertion; and the loss leader (or soft paywall) model of ad-free (or ad-light) podcast journalism produced by legacy media.[91] Many legacy publications carry multiple shows "to link their podcast footprint to their overall brand and increase paywall participation from loyal podcast listeners."[92] Bloomberg, for example, carries more than twenty podcasts, including *Businessweek*, to drive listeners to its monetizing site. For sponsored podcasts, although authorship is transparent through host and brand identification, the tenuous status of source verification remains inherent in the relatively evasive and ephemeral audio medium.

As the last three chapters have shown, the expressive power of the podcast medium has attracted not only producers advancing political views and interests from the Right and Left but also corporate brands seeking to leverage this highly persuasive digital space. Narrative journalism's capacity to inform and persuade is tantamount to that of the human voice itself, which forms the nucleus of linguistic expression, at once remediating and extending verbal and written communication in the podcast form. In the process, the products at the leading edge of the industry have attracted serious consideration as literary art. The function of podcasts as literary journalism thus constitutes the focus of the following epilogue, which coalesces this book's central concern for narrative journalism in an assessment of the aural nonfiction novel and the audio essay as viable literary forms, among the newest of the twenty-first century.

Epilogue
Podcasting as Digital Literary Journalism

Creative nonfiction in the audio medium has reached a new register in the podcast medium. Throughout this book, in each iteration of podcast journalism—whether the narrative-driven extended chat of news commentary shows, the genre of true crime, or the cultural form of the branded podcast—elements of essayistic and creative nonfiction storytelling are at the heart of the medium. The rise of the video essay as a cultural form now sees its counterpart in nonfiction podcasts such as *1619*, which has been designated one of the top shows of 2019 for its "formal reimagining of what an audio essay can be."[1] As digital literary journalism, the podcast inheres the flexibility to both stand alone and expand stories rather than repeating them across multiple platforms. Podcasts now have become the main text, spawning transmedia storytelling to augment them. The skyrocketing success of *The Daily* podcast by the *New York Times*, for example, prompted the development of the television production *The Weekly*, which builds both directly and indirectly on the podcast's related commentary and stories that further broaden the scope of the publisher's digital newsletter *Race/Related* on social justice issues.[2] The 1619 Project originally appeared in an issue dedicated to the four-hundred-year history of American slavery in the *New York Times Magazine*, published with the Sunday print edition, as a multigenre gallery of nonfictional literary journalism featuring the nation's best minds on the topic of race across a variety of formats. Nikole

Hannah-Jones's essay contribution to the issue lays the foundation for the podcast, which takes creative license afforded by audio storytelling to humanize and develop key characters in the story. The twelve core stories of the magazine content are compressed into episodes running from thirty to forty-four minutes in length, placing each contribution into a uniquely personal and animated collection of interrelated contributions.

In the podcast version of the original print essay, Hannah-Jones's narrative historical method both condenses and expands on the original print contributions with respect to quantity while engaging sound design documentary and narrative production practice aesthetics unique to podcasting. Wesley Morris's highly cerebral and abstract criticism of the Black influence on popular music becomes liberated from its formal constraints in the audio medium, which animates his discussion to "make underlying issues relatable and digestible." Morris's vocal delivery adds to the piece the missing dimensions not only of his own personality but also a more nuanced version accompanied by clips from popular music to rework his original writing into a symphonic piece of documentary journalistic artistry.[3] Fluid production aesthetics thus expand and enrich the original print version through a new array of storytelling techniques not available in the print medium. Digital literary journalism as a screen-based medium has typically found in its best productions a richer range of conventions drawing from cinema, digital interactives, and documentary video to enrich its print counterparts. The feature profile genre of print journalism lends itself well to longform scroll-activated storytelling in pieces such as *Firestorm* by the *Guardian*. The personal, conversational, and contextualizing nature of podcasting now allows for a different type of storytelling enabling greater comprehension of topics through the immediacy of the spoken word that can fulfill the public service function of journalism.

The evidence of the Pulitzer foundation generating a new category for its coveted prize in 2020 for audio reporting speaks to the importance of narrative journalism as an emerging aesthetic form rooted in both the literary world of creative nonfiction and reportorial fact. The convergence of the worlds of journalism and nonfiction creative writing are epitomized in *This American Life*'s "The Out Crowd," which was awarded the first Pulitzer Prize for audio reporting. It displays both journalism's dedication to reportorial truth-telling also associated with hard news coverage and creative nonfiction's attention to felt-detail and compassionate rendering of vivid atmosphere, character, and scene-setting. "The Out Crowd," like the public radio origins of *99% Invisible*, describes this distinct trajectory toward a more layered, self-referential mode of storytelling complexity. This moment of podcasting's ascent has invited many attempts at blockbusters, such as *Caliphate*, that have strained beyond their limits to capture "a change in journalistic ethics in which truth-telling has been extended to include greater transparency."[4] Whereas the processing and gathering of news backstage has been carefully concealed from audiences in traditional formats such as TV news, the revelation of that process can boost accountability and legitimacy. Now the front stage of "distribution and presentation" in podcast journalism showcases the messy practice of determining and shaping the final news story.[5] As such, a greater range of vocal presentation beyond the staid formality of daily news reports can emerge. The public-facing persona of the host has expanded to include a wider variety of scenes in which that host is cast. Voice-of-God narration in the documentary cinema tradition of the mid-twentieth century has similarly yielded to methods that place the journalist in the heart of the narrative as an active and influential character shaping the course of events, as in the work of *National Geographic* photographer and Oscar-winning documentarian Louie Psihoyos and stunt immersion journalist Morgan Spurlock. Consumers are now invited backstage, where the drama of the production practice itself becomes central to the storytelling and where the reporter "can let down their guard, relax, and show their true nature."[6]

In addition to self-reflexivity and the blending of popular *making-of* paratextual footage (commonly published as an accessory to the main publication) into the main text itself, the distinctly literary turn in journalistic audio storytelling enabled by the podcast medium has been marked by efforts to democratize a previously elitist sound inherited from public radio. In 2010 NPR began in earnest to alter content in response to audience perceptions that its programs are "stuffy sounding," upscale, highly educated, predominantly white, and thus elitist.[7] Podcasts such as *Code Switch* were instrumental to NPR's movement toward richer diversity in their content production, shows fueled by personal narrative woven together with carefully contextualized reportage. Shows reflecting this move drew upon the longer tradition of *This American Life*, particularly its compassionate storytelling focused on marginalized groups and culture. Strengthening the diversity of voices and views has been instrumental to the surge in listenership of podcasts, many of which are produced by NPR. Pew reports that the podcast audience has "substantially increased over the last decade," as only 7 percent reported listening to a podcast within the previous week in 2013, rising to 24 percent by 2020 and 28 percent by 2021. Perhaps more impressive was the measurement of monthly use at 9 percent in 2008, which dramatically expanded to 37 percent in 2020 and 41 percent in 2021.[8] The increasing popularity of longform narrative audio journalism is further evidenced in the precipitous rise of weekly unique users who download NPR-produced podcasts such as *Fresh Air* and *Up First*, shows that rank in the top ten of the Apple Podcasts charts. That number rose from 11.3 million in 2019 to 14 million in 2020, according to NPR's data.[9]

Such a strong presence in the digital ecosphere suggests that NPR's influence on journalistic reporting and writing has successfully leveraged the podcast medium to shed its reputation from the 1990s–2010 as stuffy, elitist, and detached.[10] The charge for NPR producers "to make shows that are more lively and conversational" while enabling a more diverse range of listeners "to hear themselves in the programming," specifically by reverting what previously seemed like "a private party" to "a party where everyone's included."[11] The influence of literary journalism on the current audio media revolution spearheaded by podcasting is pervasive, particularly in light of its origin from the NPR model initiated by Ira Glass. Fifteen of the twenty top U.S. podcasts are associated with public radio publishers, each of which uniquely reflecting its production values, narrative structure, and intimacy codes.[12] With respect to daily news coverage, the shift in consumption toward podcasts with richer analysis is evident in shows such as *The Current*, featuring seventy-five minutes of intelligent conversation and strong journalistic analysis by NPR political correspondents examining the latest headlines of the day.[13] High-quality production is also a mainstay of *The Daily* by the *New York Times*, which instead offers a deep dive into the most salient development of the day, tapping the zeitgeist through *Times* reporters covering those stories as well as their most important sources. By casting the latest news in greater relief, the slow journalistic tenets of rich context and nuanced attention to narrativity undergirded by rigorous fact-checking and reporting describe this brand of audio literary journalism.

The emergence of audio literary journalism is central to questions raised by this book addressing the new spaces for social and political discourse opened by the podcast medium. The current trend toward greater diversity among podcasting as it evolves beyond the sonic whiteness of NPR of the 2000s suggests that a vast new array of voices is being heard and presented. The podcast medium's predilection for personal narrative, as detailed by Mia Lindgren, has been vital to this development.[14] Despite the emergence of such a rich tapestry of voices, the industry continues to become more homogenized as fewer shows increasingly absorb greater market share. Fewer publishers such as the *New York Times*, the BBC, NPR, and Gimlet Media have become dominant forces in the podcast industry, attracting the vast majority of publicity. Equally important is Apple's role as tastemaker in this process, whose charts predominantly drive listening habits. Yet the flexibility of the podcast medium suggests that even Apple's own gargantuan influence over listener preference can be mitigated by the long-tail economics of the internet. Specifically, a new and growing genre of podcasts are now dedicated to reviewing and promoting other podcasts, in effect offering a more sophisticated channel for listeners to navigate their options. This development may represent what Spinelli and Dann identify as an attempt by public broadcasters "to reclaim for themselves the position of arbiters of 'quality' media," which may represent a movement toward a "broader and deeper culture of well-defined audio arts criticism."[15] As podcast journalism evolves on its distinctly humanistic literary arc across the many genres addressed in this book—from Faulknerian true crime to the intellectual culture of science and history—the rise of critical discourse about podcasting is evident in the growth of academic research on the topic and general interest as evidenced in launch of *Podcasting Magazine: Beyond the Microphone*. In this full-form digital version of a print magazine, rising demand for podcast criticism is met through stories on podcasts, podcast culture, and the industry's leading podcasters. The magazine targets a readership embodied precisely by the hybrid territory identified by Henry Jenkins as the "aca-fan," operating at the intersection of intellectual inquiry and celebrity interest.

This epilogue considers the immediate answers and future directions raised throughout the course of this book to define the impact of the podcast medium on journalistic storytelling specifically in terms of its development as a form of literary nonfiction. The new accountability of journalism that moves away from traditional standards of objectivity and toward transparency is considered with respect to the new forms of storytelling podcasting has introduced. The COVID-19 pandemic's transformation of digital culture and the larger podcast ecosphere sets the stage for a discussion of true crime's literary prowess that may have contributed to its journalistic liabilities. The effect of podcasting as digital literary journalism on intellectual culture is then addressed with respect to platformization. Far Right uses of podcasting, the influx of diverse voices, and the migration of brands into this digital space all bear significantly on the future of audio narrative as literary journalism.

NEWS IN A NEW LANGUAGE

Journalism's professional expectation of objectivity and distance has been radically revised in recent years, particularly in the wake of the social justice movements following the murder of George Floyd in 2020. The urgency of the current social movement for racial justice moved key figures in the industry to question the viability of objectivity as quasi-impartiality typically reflective of a mostly white, male editorial perspective. Margaret Sullivan of the *Washington Post*, for example, voiced her dissent against journalists as stenographers or uncritical scribes operating at the service of newsmakers. Homer Bigart, known for exposing inconsistencies in claims of U.S. military officials at press conferences during the Vietnam War, deplored such "clerkism" as the unquestioning reporting of official views that failed to advocate for soldiers on the front lines.[16] Sullivan suggests that "it's more than acceptable that [journalists] should stand up for civil rights—for press rights, for racial justice, for gender equity and against economic inequality."[17] Although journalists should respect the limits of advocacy by refraining from serving on political campaigns simultaneous to their reporting work, "neutering journalists' best instincts" to fight for justice suppresses their "admirable impulses to improve society."[18] Podcasting now presents itself as a less contested space than print or television for outspoken journalism dedicated to social justice issues, as seen in the precipitous rise of Black and Latino podcasting. Further, podcasts organically situate reporters as narrators with the potential of elevating their craft to the level of literary art, especially in a medium driven by ancient oral storytelling practices met with advanced digital audio recording and editing technology.

As Karin Wahl-Jorgensen and Thomas Schmidt aptly observe, an inherent tension lies at the heart of the current "narrative turn" in the journalism industry.[19] This is in part because the narrative qualities of news have traditionally been viewed "as posing problems for journalists" at the least, if not representing tendencies entirely anathema to the profession.[20] Subjectivity can be construed as a strength insofar as it engages the audience but a liability in that it can endanger journalism's claim to truth, as reflected in a host of research on narrative journalism.[21] Yet the reconciliation of the novelist's flair for constructing causally linked scenes driven by characters in specific settings is perhaps better suited to podcasting than any other form of news media. Podcasting like that of The 1619 Project epitomizes the definition of literary journalism that Josh Roiland posits as "a form of nonfiction writing that adheres to all of the reportorial and truth-telling covenants of conventional journalism, while employing rhetorical and storytelling techniques more commonly associated with fiction."[22] The migration of journalism into the world of aesthetics and creative expression associated with art and literature nonetheless raises concern, especially given the fact that "journalistic storytelling is a narrative practice housed in a professional practice, creating a permanent tension between the demand for objectivity and distance and the need to tell more compelling stories."[23] Precisely the same resistance voiced in opposition to Sarah Koenig's storytelling method on *Serial* in 2014 was also raised against the innovative New Journalists who rebelled against the narrow, staid conventional nature of objective journalism. The currently well-established premium on transparency in podcast journalism prompted in large part by Koenig's self-questioning method helps to answer criticism regarding the deception of the listener. John Tulloch specifically notes that news consumers can easily be deceived into taking the first person use of "I" in a story to be an observer or witness rather than a narrator reflecting on personal experience.[24] A principled producer will of course disclose that role from the outset, whereas a host with compromised ethics may be disinclined to do so, especially if engaging a highly politicized or partisan topic.

Despite arguments that journalism schools are failing in their duty to inculcate objectivity in the latest generation of reporters, "a mentality that's killing trust in our profession," as one critic alleged, there is a growing tide of practitioners and academics whose views resonate with *New York Times* journalist Wesley Lowery's claim that "the mainstream has allowed what it considers objective truth to be decided almost exclusively by white reporters and their mostly white bosses."[25] Truth and moral clarity, Lowery argues, should prevail over two-side-ism, which is one of the strategic rituals designed to obtain objectivity and thus journalistic authority.[26] Two-side-ism can be defined as "the illusion of fairness by letting advocates pretend in your journalism that there is a debate about the facts when the weight of truth is clear."[27] This deconstruction of objectivity exposes the gap between journalistic ideals and the exigencies of production practice in daily reporting. A key difference, for example, exists between the objectivity that *Times* editor Dean Baquet envisions and the way it is practiced by reporters such as Lowery, who conceive of their work as a form of advocacy. This distinction is what Claudia Mellado defines as the gap between *role perception* and *role performance*.[28] Professional principle is an ideal that can differ from the reality of praxis. Digital audio and video recording technology increasingly bear an advocacy function analogous to that of Jacob Riis's innovative use of flash photography to illuminate the slums New York City during the Progressive Era, thus exposing the plight of its most impoverished citizens to crusade for economic justice. Such advocacy and use of personal narrative and subjectivity, as in the *Latino USA* podcast, does not preclude adherence to the truth covenant of conventional journalism. Instead, it discloses the cultural situatedness of the host-as-reporter in a more candid and forthright manner than that of TV news, whose interests (financial or otherwise) in crafting any given story typically remain undisclosed.

The human voice as the primary storytelling tool enables narrative journalism through the as-told-to method by which citizens tell their own stories. The patchwork assemblage of citizen stories recalls photo essay and longform as-told-to documentary journalism such as Stephen G. Bloom's *The Oxford Project* and *New York Magazine*'s "One

Block," both works that capture the soul of local communities. Interviews are typically opportunities for subjects to describe their situation, motives for protesting, and perhaps something about their past and current affiliations. The pastiche of voices and experience of the community—its fear, sorrow, and rage—reflects social justice podcasting's empathic, citizen-focused inclination that aims to transform demonstrators without access to media into reporters themselves. "Journalists who practice narrative storytelling, particularly when they want to produce an accurate representation of a misunderstood or little understood reality, realize in the storytelling, consciously or not, the basic principles of an empathic approach to gaining readers' understanding."[29] News appears in a new language altogether when produced by subjects themselves, as exhibited in the San Quentin prisoner-produced Radiotopia podcast *Ear Hustle*. Compassion for their circumstances arises from the podcasts' function as "important vehicles for the personalization of journalism" combined with their emphasis on the host-reporter and sources' expertise and credibility.[30]

Podcasting thus delivers news in a new language, one both informed and informal.[31] It invites "the audience as knowing participants in the conversation," as questions between hosts and sources can also be aimed at listeners.[32] This invokes the parasocial relationship addressed throughout this book, in which listeners are drawn into the sense of a social relationship with podcasters. If executed in the interest of advancing listeners' capacity for civic engagement, this dynamic can generate high levels of political efficacy from listeners. The "informalization of news" in podcasts not only allows for greater user engagement but also builds on understandings of the nature of knowledge as occurring by accretion rather than in one final draft. Facts transform over time in their significance when new information enters the picture, a pattern serialized podcasts allow for in alignment with digital journalism's capacity "not only to update news on a continual basis, but to do so cumulatively," with each new episode displaying "progress toward journalistic understanding."[33] Verbal discourse can engage intellectual concepts through both highly specialized and informal language on a continuum in podcasting not tolerated in traditional print and broadcast journalism. As such, the informed specialist speaking in a voice ranging from highly technical and abstract to colloquial and direct can potentially access greater depth into intellectual concepts. "Using a narrative template with recognizable characters," as research results show, "is seen as a powerful means to a) increase the audience's understanding of society in all its complexities and b) enhance the audience's sense of being part of that society," the latter providing a service to democracy through civic engagement. Multiple studies have shown that "topics about minority groups and social, cultural, or racial injustice lend themselves particularly well to be covered in a narrative style that renders critical voices."[34] This point is illustrated by the humorous social critique established in Elon James White's digital network that spearheaded the first wave of Black podcasting in the late 2000s.

Podcasting is vital to the societal role of narrative journalism, particularly as a force that can function as a discursive guide for what Kim Fox and colleagues call "a curriculum for blackness" functioning as a means of building both the Black community and educating outsiders on its core concerns and values.[35] The many voices from the margins that have gained significant audiences through podcasting leverage narrative techniques to develop a sense of social cohesion. Mutual understanding of oppression and marginalization open channels of creativity for resistance, achievement, and ambition. The narratives driving podcasts such as *The Nod*, *Still Processing*, and *The Read* perform a similar social role to the South African magazine *Drum*, whose literary journalistic storytelling offered Black readers in the early years of apartheid "an attitude to take, an identity to occupy, a language they could use to describe their world."[36] Podcasts are uniquely powerful at conveying the many diverse inflections and dialects of the Black idiom. They can showcase highly abstract intellectual exchanges as well as colloquial free-flowing public conversation akin to a finely written scene from a novel not unlike the porch conversations in Zora Neale Hurston's *Their Eyes Were Watching God*. Hurston's anthropological background drew her to such public settings recreated with her finely attuned ear for the local vernacular of the mid-twentieth-century Black experience in the rural South. In all of its rich variety, contemporary Black culture speaks for itself in podcasts that themselves showcase such informal free-flowing exchanges representing nuanced scene-setting, character development, and tension-building previously limited to the genius of novelists such as Hurston to recreate such voices and their communities. As Siobhán McHugh aptly observes, "when the audio medium is added to the arsenal of narrative journalism, its impact is hugely amplified."[37]

McHugh's coproduction of *Wrong Skin* about Aboriginal culture in Australia reveals precisely how the podcast medium can leverage narrative journalism by showcasing the voices of the subjects themselves.[38] "A mainstream audience would have difficulty understanding the uniquely Aboriginal way of speaking English (often a third or fourth language) in this remote community," she notes of the production aesthetic, "yet we felt it was vital that these so often marginalized voices be literally heard."[39] Editing to provide scripted narration around the subjects' voices, which often are presented in excerpts and fragments, was integral to the narrative strategy for maintaining as much authenticity of expression while still maintaining coherence. Maria Martin notes a similar technique used in *Latino USA* whereby Spanish-speaking interviewees are allowed to express their complete thought before entering English-language voice-over. Although this may take 10 to 12 seconds or longer, this technique "validates the dignity of the person whose voice is part of the production and whose story I'm telling," Martin explains. News in a new language from Martin's perspective—particularly as a former NPR host whose editors during the 1990s systematically silenced such voices—bears this responsibility, which in turn upholds media's duty to democracy. This method allows the "non-English language to breathe," or, in McHugh's case, the Australian Aboriginal English dialect to breathe, to "show respect for the increasing number of Americans who speak Spanish and other languages, and who—more and more each day—are becoming part of our audience."[40]

TRUE CRIME IN THE AGE OF COVID-19

With podcast listenership already on the ascent, boosted by milestone productions of *Serial* in 2014 and *S-Town* and *The Daily* in 2017, the onset of the pandemic in the spring of 2020 raised several questions. Would this industry suffer in the way of music, performing arts, and other media relying on live production? Could the podcast industry survive the loss of its coveted commuter listeners, whose peak times of consumption formed a predictable and steady source of revenue from advertisers?

Longform narrative storytelling, it seemed, might be construed as less relevant than breaking hard news and public service journalism, forcing the genre to take a back seat to more pressing affairs such as quarantine mandates, masking, contact tracing, and health care availability. Industry insiders openly expressed concern for the medium's capacity to weather this global crisis. Yet podcasting's inherent flexibility displayed an uncanny ability to adapt to the circumstances, emerging not only stronger in terms of overall listenership but also capable of adapting reportage for longform narrative and deep-dive storytelling to media's new public service mission in response to the global health emergency. Digital and quarantine cultures were well suited to longer, crafted stories, many of which featured COVID-19 victims of marginalized cultures. Indeed, when life in quarantine become life online, not only the producers of Zoom content benefited but the podcast medium actually expanded listenership simultaneous to embracing an unprecedented journalistic seriousness and urgency, as discussed in chapter 1, through shows such as *Solvable*, published by Pushkin Industries. Demand for breaking news and updates on shifting COVID-19 protocols was met by legacy media and startup publishers alike as a wave of pandemic-specific shows cropped up across the podcast ecosphere. With listeners literally captive and podcasts already at the forefront of digital culture as the fastest-growing medium in digital publishing, podcasting reached a new level of journalistic maturity to match its already well-established business acumen as entertainment media.

    The true crime genre's literary repertoire evolved significantly into storytelling driven toward deeper knowledge about the pandemic, particularly through profiles of victims and frontline workers. *The Daily* offered frequent coverage that epitomized how podcasting could deliver the type of affective impact on audiences to elicit more nuanced comprehension as well as compassion for subjects. Freedom from the staid and detached delivery associated with terrestrial broadcast radio enabled podcasts to deliver a reexamination of current affairs with an emotional import previously limited to television news dramas. Like well-crafted TV dramas based on current affairs, podcast journalism can perform as a vehicle "of sensemaking and may outperform traditional journalism in establishing meaningful connections between politics and audience members."[41] This is accomplished through the performance of information rather than rote, detached delivery according to the genre conventions of traditional radio broadcasting. The method, like longform television dramas, can be construed as "public affairs narratives" that bring forth more sophisticated understandings of topics "by constructing complicated, at times holistic, social worlds, populated by richly conceptualized characters who face true, if scripted, social, political, and economic challenges."[42] Podcasts thus emerged as the standard-bearer of narrative journalism through the global health crisis of the COVID-19 pandemic and the social justice movement in the wake of George Floyd's murder. Digital culture provided the space and media for citizens to process these crises both cognitively and emotionally as well as offering a mode of civic engagement.

The evolution of true crime from *Serial*, whose name draws from Victorian-era crime dramas serialized in the periodical press and in the form of novels, to this more urgent public service mission is evident in the show's evolution toward civic concerns and social injustice. Whereas the original *Serial* podcast has been criticized for evading issues of race and inequality raised by the murder cases it investigates, the third season specifically engages in structural biases against people of color and the working class in the Cleveland municipal court system. The show's ruminations on democracy and the tensions between diversity and unity are signaled in episode 1 through the poetic—almost Whitmanesque—catalog celebrating the vast range of human and cultural identity showcased in the accoutrement of items on the bodies of people she observes in the elevator. An elevator in a government building, she notes, is "one of the few places in our country where different kinds of people are forced into proximity." This sense of hope in our democracy is embodied in the scene metaphorically through our capacity to "stand so close to one another, with our sensible heels, and Timberland boots, and American flag lapel pins, and fake eye lashes, and Axe cologne, and orthopedic inserts, and teardrop tattoos, and to-go coffees." As with Whitman's "Crossing Brooklyn Ferry," the catalog in celebration of the populace intimates a miraculous instance of communion amid radical diversity in an otherwise volatile cocktail of tension. "And when the elevator doors open up, spilling us out onto our floor, the fact that no one is bloodied or even in tears, it's a small, pleasing reminder that we're all in this together."[43] The podcast medium has opened space for not only narrativity but also such reflective and poetic ruminations that mark podcasting's entrance into the realm of literary journalism.

The official accreditation of podcasting as serious journalism occasioned by its eligibility for the Pulitzer Prize in 2020 coincided with a wave of critical consideration of audio journalism as a form of literature. At a moment when journalism itself appears across a broader range of digital forms than ever in media history, it also has become widely recognized as literary by a variety of arbiters and gatekeepers adjudicating canonization. Just as the world of popular music produced the first Nobel Prize for literature when it was awarded to the folk-rock icon Bob Dylan, podcast industry insiders and academics embrace audio reporting as a literary form. Much of the discourse surrounding the literary potential of podcast journalism was originally devoted to *S-Town*.[44] This was largely because the show openly aligned itself with the prose fictional subjects and styles of William Faulkner, whose works similarly explore the inner reaches of Southern culture and psychological interiority of specific characters in it. Arranged in chapters rather episodes, the podcast "arc evolves from classic reporter-detective story and treasure hunt to personal quest and biography" as the plot pivots away from the quest to resolve an unsolved murder and psychological mystery of the show's main character, who tragically takes his own life.[45] Intolerance for homosexuality in Southern culture, which *S-Town* addresses, is also a concern in Faulkner's fiction, as in the character of Homer Baron in "A Rose for Emily." Faulkner's treatment of the rural South and its cultural predilections intersect with the exploration of the deceased John C. McLemore's plight and the inner demons that plagued him.

S-Town has been described as an "unnaturally sophisticated creation for the medium, an inventive and emotionally rich step forward that reconfigures the value of its immediate peer group."[46] *Slate*'s review lauded the production team at *This American Life* for its unprecedented discovery of "a mode that transcends pulpy entertainment and edges into literary beauty." The review claimed that "if *Serial*'s first season pioneered a new genre of emotionally sensitive true crime podcasting, *S-Town* marks an exhilarating turn toward something more like aural literature."[47] The Peabody Award jury was especially emphatic about the work's literary merits, describing the show as "the first true audio novel, a nonfiction biography constructed in the style and form of a seven-chapter novel."[48] As a digital audio version of the nonfiction novel associated with the New Journalism, podcasts were first considered worthy of literary status in the wake of *Serial*. As early as 2015, James Tierney noted the medium's capacity to elicit in the listener "enrapturement typically associated with the experience of reading a novel."[49] Tierney was commenting on the implications of a *New York Times* opinion piece by James Atlas that made a case for audio as literature, yet with serious qualifications. "There are obvious limits to the podcast as a literary genre," Atlas allows, particularly in "keeping track of all those voices" and the way in which "the dialogue can feel slack." He notes, however, that "at best, it has the tension of those nonfiction classics of an earlier era—Truman Capote's *In Cold Blood* or Norman Mailer's *Executioner's Song*."[50] Missing from these early considerations is the piece recognized by McHugh regarding the unique qualities of audio-based media technology that greatly enhance rather than delimit the audience's experience.[51] As Ella Waldmann points out, "Narrative nonfiction podcasts in general, and *S-Town* in particular, are not prototypical popular culture products; they are a case in point in the debate around new media textualities in a mass-mediated popular culture."[52] To this point, *S-Town* not only functions as literature but "also lends itself to an (audio)narratological analysis, which takes into account nonverbal clues, such as music, sound effects, fading, silence, and pauses."[53]

These silences, pauses, and sound effects are particularly powerful in the sound design of the otherwise reportorially flawed *Caliphate* by the *New York Times*. Host Rukmini Callimachi applies standards of the New Journalism to narrative podcast reportage. Podcasters' use of the devices of fiction to tell true stories is cogently defined by McHugh as a process by which "the real people they depict are developed as characters and interviews are quoted as conversations; deep research and analysis is conveyed as plot and reconstructed scenes; and the writer employs fresh, descriptive language to place the reader at various locations."[54] *Caliphate* follows precisely this approach while also adhering to the foundational tenets of Alex Blumberg's Gimlet Media. *StartUp*, Blumberg's self-referential podcast detailing what initially appeared as a quixotic launch of Gimlet Media specializing in longform podcast storytelling, depicted the former NPR *Planet Money* host pitching his "narrative journalism and storytelling" business to prospective venture capitalist investors. The common reason cited among those rejecting the proposal was that he was "swimming upstream" against the trend for shorter and shorter content, as seen in the rise of Snapchat, Twitter, TikTok, and other short messaging service platforms. Undeterred, Blumberg marshaled his faith in the evidence of *This American Life*'s success and refused to cater to short attention spans, instead developing his podcasting publishing startup on the assumption that "maybe we *want* to pay attention."[55] The gambit showed potential in *The Daily*'s August 2017 success as a deep-dive podcast for the *New York Times*. But the *Times* had yet to develop a blockbuster leveraging its journalistic brand for the podcast audience. In the *Times*'s case for *Caliphate*, *performing* preempted the importance of *informing* the listening audience according to the journalism of verification rooted in accuracy, the first and most foundational of all journalistic principles, according to Bill Kovach and Tom Rosensteil's *The Elements of Journalism*. At stake in the revelation of its main source, who claimed to have been a member of ISIS, as an impostor was the *Times*'s reputation as a trusted, venerable news brand. *The Daily* host Michael Barbaro's efforts to mitigate the damage through a strategic yet highly secretive public relations campaign suggests the importance of podcast journalism to the publisher's reputation. The stratospheric ascent of Blumberg's Gimlet attracted the attention of Spotify, which acquired the company. *The Times*, at the writing of this epilogue, continues to dominate the daily news podcast competition and has returned to serialized storytelling with *The Trojan Horse Affair*, a large-scale investigative podcast.

THE BUSINESS OF AUDIO NARRATIVE

The rise of content marketing in digital media has encouraged brands to seek the fastest-growing online publishing markets to tell their stories. Due to the rise of podcasting as a promotional tool, consumers now have better access to brands and their core values than previously in the history of promotional and strategic communication. Brands now seek to develop media such as originally reported podcasts, representing a move away from the production of audio and video advertising as background or, worse, an interruption to another larger podcast. A major finding of this book is that hosts mentioning sponsors is far less effective than stand-alone sponsored podcasts. The intrusion of sponsors and their products in the space of regular content violates the listeners' trust and severs the parasocial bond with the host. As Julie Shapiro of Radiotopia told McHugh, a podcaster's comment on their personal relationships with sponsors' products on shows is anathema to the enthralling, novelesque storytelling mode nonfiction podcasts aim to achieve.[56] "No one loves it. Listeners don't love hearing it. Podcasters don't love talking about companies before they start," despite the economic necessity all parties recognize in the use of this convention.[57] Circumventing that necessity altogether are branded podcasts, many of which deploy humor, as in the satirical spinoff of *Serial* in McDonald's *The Sauce*. Rather than background material or an awkward intrusion into the narrative flow of another unrelated podcast, branded podcasts can function as "fully authored creative works" of narrative documentary news.[58]

The liberation of the podcast medium comes at a cost, particularly for startups whose personnel were formerly in radio broadcasting. John Biewen, who directs the Center for Documentary Studies, told McHugh that the benefits nonetheless outweighed the cost in "the loss of audience numbers." The advantages he cited centered on creative freedom, particularly the unleashing of production practice aesthetics from the tyranny of "broadcast gatekeepers and formats," allowing him "to produce work in the tone and at the length that I choose," a freedom he calls "priceless."[59] The authored documentary and crafted feature has now emerged from its stigma as mere entertainment to occupy the realm of serious journalism. Literary journalism in the audio form is no longer a financial sacrifice for refugees from the terrestrial radio sector or an outlet for creative license for those seeking to expand their repertoire. The influx of brands into narrative storytelling would indicate that nuanced podcast reportage is good business. Of vital importance in understanding the evolution of the podcast medium is the confluence of capitalism, particularly its emergence as a viable competitor in digital publishing, and its capacity to function like a novel, as Brain Reed described *S-Town*. Much commentary has been made about Ira Glass's proclamation that public radio, particularly longform documentary narrative of the sort *This American Life* produces, was ready for capitalism.[60] The literary dimensions of podcasting have also attracted critical attention.[61] But the two forces of capitalism and literature are typically seen as mutually exclusive entities, as in Biewen's commentary. The economics of literary audio journalism has been a major focus of this book, one that positions podcasting as the technological successor of the nonfiction novel in the twentieth century, a form equally generated by economic forces and shifts in news consumption patterns. Upon the granting of its coveted award to Brian Reed, the Peabody committee's praise for *S-Town* took on a distinctly literary feel. Any literary advances associated with the show should be understood in conjunction with its commercial success. Thus, it is not by coincidence that the literary achievement of *S-Town* occurred simultaneously to its record listenership that dwarfed *Serial*'s following.

The aesthetic concern for how podcasting "has breathed new life into established . . . tropes and forms" has often been blind to the ways in which larger consumer patterns and market shifts have been instrumental in their adoption.[62] The aforementioned insight of Blumberg to invest in longform audio storytelling was chided by venture capitalists who claimed that media formats were increasingly shrinking, along with attention spans in the highly distracting digital landscape, dominated by products brokered on speed and impact. Yet documentary video's rise—which traces back to longform PBS documentaries by Ken Burns in the 1990s, later packaged as DVDs suitable for binge watching—and its development into the Netflix streaming on-demand television model that reaffirmed the hunger for chapter-driven serialized storytelling describes a different scenario. Blumberg's own industrial situation as a longform storytelling producer of audio for *Planet Money* and as a market analyst ideally positioned him to capitalize on these patterns in consumption. As mentioned in the introduction of this book, the diagnosis of narrative depravation in digital culture was overestimated in the early 2000s as a force capable of overwhelming, and even superannuating, demand for longform. The movement toward immersive longform storytelling in the twentieth century has a long history reaching back well before the advent of the twentieth-century nonfiction novel associated with Tom Wolfe, Truman Capote, and New Journalism. The original movement toward nonfiction storytelling as a potentially more potent and politically efficacious form of traditional news can be located in the weekly press of the early nineteenth century, which fanned the flames of the Civil War in the United States with the moving abolitionist writings of Harriet Beecher Stowe and the labor advocacy work of Rebecca Harding Davis. Central to the ascent of such figures and the weekly press—particularly as a generator of novelized nonfiction and nonfictional novels—were economic transformations in the publishing industry enabled by new technologies for production (the double-cylinder steam press) and distribution (the railroad).

The producers of *This American Life* and *Serial* conjoined the forces of capitalism and aesthetics specifically through market-savvy production practice catering to the rising demand for its mode of longform, distinctly literary storytelling with *S-Town*. The investment clearly paid dividends in the form of the *New York Times*'s acquisition of the company at a moment when the newspaper's editorial staff was struggling to gain market share in serialized documentary journalism. *Caliphate*, the *Times*'s solo foray into longer investigations than *The Daily* format could offer, had met with a spectacular failure matched only by the colossal ambition and expectation of its star investigative reporter, Rukmini Callimachi. The *Times* had determined that it was ready for capitalism based on the stratospheric success of *The Daily* and thus turned to the most potent producer in the market, which was Serial Productions. Rather than attempting again to decipher the formula for a blockbuster success in isolation and risk another failure on the scale of *Caliphate*, the *Times* operated according to the tenets of Spotify and Apple through acquisition rather than original production. When the *Times* acquired Serial Productions, it acquired the genetic code for the most potent form of literary journalism in the twenty-first century, thereby making a statement to the journalistic world. The aforementioned reception of *S-Town* had cemented the *Times*'s desire to make literary audio journalism its prize investment, as all accolades for the podcast center on its capacity to elevate reporting to the realm of art.

The literary dimensions were indeed so pronounced in the show's production aesthetics that some critics found them a slight overreach. "The writing stretches a little too far for an inspired metaphorical connection; a motif of clocks recurs throughout the podcast, which would have been a more elegant device were the association not been so literal," Nick Quah noted.[63] But the leitmotif of clocks is hardly ham-fisted in its delivery in *S-Town* but instead directly invokes Faulkner more specifically as its literary heir, particularly his haunting ruminations on the demons plaguing the zeitgeist of a deeply broken and flawed social fabric of the Deep South. As Waldmann points out, the critical community was overwhelmingly unanimous in identifying *S-Town* as a work of aural literature based on its nomenclature's saturation with literary critical concepts and terminology.[64] The recognition of its status as a work of literature, rather than as mere reporting bearing stylistic flourishes borrowed from the literary world, was generated by the show's unmistakable intimation of its own mode of consumption *as literature*. Narrative audio journalism's aesthetic and financial origins in Ira Glass and the *Times*'s acquisition of Serial Productions signals the emergence of journalism into the literary realm through the understanding that "it takes a sound realist to make a convincing symbolist," as the poet D. J. Enright said.[65] Now brands and marginalized social groups can leverage podcasting's capacity for expression at the nexus of realism and symbolism, precisely in lending the literal and phenomenological world more meaningful. Podcast drama's roots in terrestrial serialized radio drama of the 1940s signal a clear demand for narrative as fictional and role-play shows have established a passionate following. The market's embrace of this mode of storytelling bears a greater experiential influence on the listenership. Despite the shrinking number of shows and publishers garnering attention due to the domination of the market by fewer companies, it has become clear to conglomerates and tech giant platforms alike that diversity is good business not only on principle but as a means of reaching untapped audiences.

As digital longform publications such as *The Athletic* continue to attract massive investments in audio narrative journalism, the market shift toward more political and socially diverse coverage extends to the world of sports. Podcasts such as *Burn It All Down* have exploded due to their showcasing of gender inequities in women's athletics. Such shows do not dilute their intellectual content but instead deploy an intersectional feminist approach with a team of hosts that include accomplished academics. The ascent of *Burn It All Down* and Bill Simmons's *The Ringer* have prompted digital longform publishers like *The Athletic* to dramatically increase investment in podcasting. *The Athletic*'s podcast expansion into multiple national and localized markets signals the audio ambitions of born-digital narrative journalism. The publication's investment of $95 million in 2020 and 2021, committed mainly to the development of its podcast offerings, is designed to attract an acquirer at the price of $750 million. As the arc of Simmons's career at the top of sports broadcasting shows, the move toward audio is consonant with an editorial palette steeped in sophisticated content, drawing on the tradition established by ESPN's "The Long, Strange Trip of Doc Ellis," the first multimedia feature delivered in chapters in the history of digital publishing. Podcasting's future suggests that longer, more immersive content will continue to usher categories of journalism into intellectual culture. The instance of news workers raising their artistic voice is particularly conducive to the podcast medium, marking a distinct departure from the most basic form of journalism's descriptive style found in the matter-of-fact news brief.

Sports podcasts are increasingly hosted by athletes themselves, who have leveraged the internet's decentralization of sports journalism publishing to produce their own shows. NBA star Kevin Durant is among many who have discovered podcasting, like Derek Jeter's screen-based *Player's Tribune*, as an appealing "space for storytelling" capable of "disrupting traditional flows of information." Free from mainstream media gatekeepers, athletes can reach a wide audience directly, without being screened by often arbitrary and structurally inequitable management. As a result, "players have grown infatuated with sharing their perspectives in real time, in direct, unfiltered ways," with "triumphs flecked with pain are self-doubt" as "stars openly shared their traumas." Figures like Kendrick Perkins, whom ESPN did not compensate for one year during his employment there, find relative freedom on the podcast medium. As Hua Hsu points out, the "fallacy that athletes should 'stick to sports'" is "a call that has grown almost in direct proportion to Black players speaking out about police brutality and abuse."[66] *Deadspin*'s dissolution similarly came at the behest of new ownership who similarly demanded that reporters stick to sports and depoliticize their commentary. Podcasting represents a circumventing medium to evade such restrictions endemic to the perpetuation of structural inequality. As with marginalized and silenced voices representing minority gender and ethnic groups, the objectification of athletes by fans who could previously view them at a distance "as avatars that they could manipulate" is profoundly disrupted upon "listening to players talk about what they actually value," a process that "upends this theatre, destabilizing the role that sports play in our lives."[67]

INTELLECTUAL CULTURE

Just as podcasting has opened space beyond the traditional information flows of sports media for players to speak of their values and experience, it has also created similar opportunities for diverse groups. Within those groups, intellectuals now have a platform through podcasting to showcase their work and engage a wide range of listening publics. If journalism, according to Mark Deuze and Tamara Witschge, "is in a permanent process of becoming," it is clear that the confluence of art and journalism found in news photography, print-based literary journalism, and reportage illustration now extends to audio.[68] The aural nonfiction novel may be the form that *S-Town* set out to invent, but nonfictional literary journalism also engages a form of analysis and cultural criticism, a type of intellectual discourse that may include cause-effect, scene-based sequencing of events but more emphatically interprets its subjects. Such social and cultural criticism has performed as literature featured in the periodical press dating back to the works of Henry David Thoreau and Ralph Waldo Emerson, particularly in the pages of the *New-York Tribune*. Progressive intellectual voices were featured there as its editor, Horace Greeley, openly advocated for progressive causes by featuring leading-edge intellectuals. Now the podcast medium supports journalism's movement beyond its obsession with fact collection and transcription in pursuit of what Mitchell Stephens calls *wisdom journalism*.[69] Various forms of media can fulfill journalism's duty to democracy. Intellectual discourse, which often appeared in "interpretive blogging" as a forerunner to podcasting, can indeed deliver content that Stephens describes as informed, intelligent, interpretive, insightful, and illuminating. Black podcasting arose from blogging as a means of circumventing restrictions to Black-hosted terrestrial radio shows, thus opening space for marginalized voices.

The promise of podcasting's function as journalism is also its greatest liability, particularly to the forces of subjectivity. As chapter 5 on the podcasting of the Far Right shows, the highly personal nature of the medium can lend itself to the journalism of affirmation associated with the sort spearheaded by Rush Limbaugh on conservative talk radio in the 1980s. Subjective journalism is generally viewed as a problem associated with the trivialization of the news, its dumbing down, and sensationalism, particularly as fuel for partisan fulmination. Dan Bongino has officially accepted the role of carrying on Limbaugh's legacy, contributing to broader criticism of the state of the news. Bongino and other pundits are often cited to support "the thesis that objective, fact-based, knowledgeable reportage has given way to sensationalist, partisan, and trivial concerns not just in the tabloids, but in the broadsheets."[70] The argument typically notes a lack of funding for quality journalism to counter this tide, particularly journalism of a less personal and subjective nature. The problem, however, cannot be laid at the door of personal journalism, which itself can be accurate and well-researched. As Rosalind Coward astutely observed, "That readers and consumers are attracted to—and engaged by—a journalism which is more subjective and transparent should be pause for thought, rather than seen as the cause of establishment journalism's decline."[71] We now see a distinct "turning towards different, more personalized forms of communication" no longer limited to younger generations, "where they can get access to groups with shared interest, argue directly with opinions when they encounter them, engage with personalities who interest them, and explore intimate themes of relationships, emotions, and health when they need to."[72] Most importantly, personal journalism "can be extraordinary and powerful," a type of journalism "we remember and cherish, that helps us through our personal journeys and dilemmas." Podcasting's ascent epitomizes how, through the spoken word, whether scripted or improvised, this mode of storytelling "widens the reach of journalism and humanizes it."[73]

Podcast journalism has not evolved on a preset path according to technological determinism but, as this book has shown, has been intentionally adopted, constructed, and reconfigured by producers seeking to serve their vision of societal needs. Not only has personal narrative been restored to journalism through podcasting, but the medium has also enabled critical analysis of social systems and structures as well as the nuances of its cultural lexicon. Rich, precisely crafted cultural critique was on display in the examination of the term *chollo* by Maria Martin's *Latino USA* just as the early grassroots immigration advocacy of Latino radio in California occasioned *New Yorker* contributor and Harvard University historian Jill Lepore's investigation in her podcast *The Last Archive*. "In parallel to New Journalism's critique of professional values," particularly pretentions to objectivity as a timeless-universal-human truth of journalism somehow unconnected from the political reality of the reporter's context, "women journalists began their own challenge to lofty claims of objectivity and detachment."[74] Advocacy becomes *more* potent when the standard of balance is jettisoned for moral clarity, as Wesley Lowery of the *New York Times* noted in response to a Tom Cotton op-ed during the protests prompted by the murder of George Floyd in 2020. Now voices from the margins can adopt this form of journalism, continuing the rewriting of the newspaper that began in the twentieth century.

The shortcomings of the brief history of podcast journalism are all too visible in the bad actors, ideologues, capitalists, and big tech companies angling for domination through the nuanced art of platformization. Even progressive, well-intended publishers such as the *New York Times* could not capitalize on the success of *The Daily* in longform documentary podcasting with *Caliphate*. But as the rise of Black podcasting illustrates, listeners now have access to the richest and most nuanced discourse on race in the history of mass media. Watchdog journalism has seen a renaissance through the more progressive sectors of the true crime podcast industry. Continuing the movement that Thomas Schmidt locates in the Style section of the *Washington Post* during the mid-twentieth century, podcast journalism also engages in that original project by reconfiguring the medium "to establish a novel, if not unprecedented, form of news," in the process "actively shifting culturally determined genre conventions, allowing reporters to experiment with literary forms that challenged traditional forms of news writing."[75] As audio reporting evolves, the medium will continue to shape the message as podcasting's emergence into maturity writes the next chapter of journalism's narrative turn.

Epilogue

Notes

INTRODUCTION

1. On the "golden age of podcasting," see Richard Berry, "Serial and Ten Years of Podcasting: Has the Medium Grown Up?," in *Radio, Sound and Internet*, Proceedings of the Net Station International Conference, ed. M. Oliveira and F. Ribeiro, 299–309 (Braga, Port.: LASICS, University of Minho, 2015).
2. R. Winn, "Podcast Stats and Facts (New Research from Dec 2019)," *Podcast Insights*, December 11, 2019.
3. Nic Newman, with Richard Fletcher, Anne Schulz, Simge Andı, Craig T. Robertson, and Rasmus Kleis Nielsen, *Reuters Institute Digital News Report 2021*, 10th ed. (Oxford: Reuters Institute for the Study of Journalism, 2021); and Nic Newman, "Inspired by The Daily, Dozens of Daily News Podcasts Are Punching Above Their Weight," *NiemanLab*, December 3, 2019.
4. Newman, "Inspired by The Daily."
5. Mark Frary, "Power to the Podcast: Podcasting Is Bringing a Whole New Audience to Radio and Giving Investigative Journalism a Boost," *Index on Censorship*, 46, no. 3, (2017): 24–27.
6. Mariel Soto Reyes, "Pulitzer's New 'Audio Reporting' Category Will Bring More Journalists to Podcasting," *Business Insider*, December 9, 2019.
7. J. Panyard, "Back from the Grave: The Evolution of Longform Writing," *Medium*, December 14, 2016; and Siobhan McHugh, "Radiodoc Review: Developing Critical Theory of the Radio Documentary and Feature Form," *Australian Journalism Review* 35, no. 2 (2014): 23.

8. Guy Starkey, "The New Kids on the Block: The Pictures, Text, Time-Shifted Audio, and Podcasts of Digital Radio Journalism Online," in *The Routledge Companion to Digital Journalism Studies*, ed. Bob Franklin and Scott A. Eldridge II (New York: Routledge, 2017).
9. On podcasting's "deeply personal nature," see Joe Amditis, "An Ethical Analysis of *Serial*," *Medium*, December 23, 2016.
10. Ashley Carman, "The Nod Hosts Ditch Spotify to Relaunch Their Original Show," *The Verge*, August 2, 2021.
11. David B. Nieborg and Thomas Poell, "The Platformization of Cultural Production: Theorizing the Contingent Cultural Commodity," *New Media & Society* 20, no. 11, (2018); and Patricia Aufderheide, David Lieberman, Atika Alkhallouf, and Jiji Majiri Ugboma, "Podcasting as Public Media: The Future of U.S. News, Public Affairs, and Educational Podcasts," *International Journal of Communication* 14 (February 2020): 1683–1704.
12. Ashley Carman, "The Next Big Thing in Podcasts Is Talking Back," *The Verge*, October 12, 2021.
13. Aufderheide et al., "Podcasting as Public Media"; and Martin Conboy, "Journalism and the Democratic Market Society: Decline and Fall?," *Journalism Studies* 18, no. 10 (2017): 1263–1276.
14. Carman, "The Next Big Thing."
15. Daniel Savage, "Marshall McLuhan," on *Something Savage, Al Jazeera*, Vimeo, 2017, https://vimeo.com/206112739.
16. Nic Newman and Nathan Gallo, *Daily News Podcasts: Building New Habits in the Shadow of Coronavirus* (Oxford: Reuters Institute for the Study of Journalism 2020); and Kevin Moloney, "All the News That's Fit to Push: The New York Times Company and Transmedia Daily News," *International Journal of Communication* 14 (2020).
17. Reyes, "Pulitzer's New 'Audio Reporting' Category."
18. Frary, "Power to the Podcast."
19. Commission on Freedom of the Press, *A Free and Responsible Press: A General Report on Mass Communication: Newspapers, Radio, Motion Pictures, Magazines, and Books* (Chicago: University of Chicago Press, 1947).
20. "SPJ Code of Ethics," *Society of Professional Journalists*, https://www.spj.org/ethicscode.asp.
21. Commission on Freedom of the Press, *A Free and Responsible Press*.
22. Rebecca Mead, "Binge Listening: How Podcasts Became a Seductive—and Sometimes Slippery—Mode of Storytelling," *New Yorker*, November 12, 2018.
23. Jillian DeMair, "Sounds Authentic: The Acoustic Construction of *Serial*'s Story World," In *The Serial Podcast and Storytelling in the Digital Age*, ed. E. McCracken, 24–38 (New York: Routledge 2017); and Mia Lindgren, "Personal

Narrative Journalism and Podcasting," *Radio Journal: International Studies in Broadcast & Audio Media* 14, no. 1 (2016): 23–41.

24. Frary, "Power to the Podcast"; and Dario Llinares, "Podcasting as Liminal Praxis: Aural Mediation, Sound Writing and Identity," in *Podcasting: New Aural Cultures and Digital Media*, ed. Dario Llinares, Neil Fox, and Richard Berry, 123–146 (New York: Palgrave Macmillan, 2018).

25. Alix Spiegel, "Variations in Tape Use and the Position of the Narrator," in *Reality Radio: Telling True Stories in Sound*, ed. John Biewen and Alexa Dilworth (Chapel Hill: University of North Carolina, Press 2017), 44.

26. Llinares, "Podcasting as Liminal Praxis."

27. James Curran, "What Democracy Requires of the Media," in *Institutions of American Democracy: The Press*, ed. Kathleen Hall Jamieson and Geneva Overholser, 120–140 (New York: Oxford University Press 2005); James Curran, *Media and Democracy* (London: Routledge 2011); and Robert Entman, "The Nature and Sources of News," in *Institutions of American Democracy: The Press*, ed. Kathleen Hall Jamieson and Geneva Overholser, 48–65 (New York: Oxford University Press, 2005).

28. Frary, "Power to the Podcast."

29. "The Podcast Consumer, 2018," *Edison Research*, April 19, 2018.

30. "The Podcast Consumer, 2019," *Edison Research*, March 6, 2019.

31. Kris M. Markman, "Everything Old Is New Again: Podcasting as Radio's Revival," *Journal of Radio & Audio Media* 22, no. 2 (2015): 240–43; and Jonathan Kern, *Sound Reporting: The NPR Guide to Audio Journalism and Production* (Chicago: University of Chicago Press, 2008).

32. Eric Nuzum, "The Year of the DIY Podcast Network," *NiemanLab*, December 15, 2018.

33. Newman, "Inspired by The Daily."

34. Martin Spinelli and Lance Dann, *Podcasting: The Audio Media Revolution* (New York: Bloomsbury, 2019).

35. Newman, "Inspired by The Daily."

36. Susan Douglas, *Listening in: Radio and the American Imagination* (Minneapolis: University of Minnesota Press, 2004), 30.

37. Lene Bech Sillesen, Chris Ip, and David Uberti, "Journalism and the Power of Emotions," *Columbia Journalism Review*, May 11, 2015.

38. Newman et al., *Reuters Institute Digital News Report 2021*; and Newman, "Inspired by The Daily."

39. Amy Mitchell, Galen Stocking, and Katerina Eva Matsa, "Long-Form Reading Shows Signs of Life in Our Mobile News World," Pew Research Center, May 5, 2016; David O. Dowling, "Toward a New Aesthetic of Digital Literary Journalism: Charting the Fierce Evolution of the 'Supreme Nonfiction,'" *Literary*

Journalism Studies 9, no. 1, (2017): 101–116; and Susan Jacobson, Jacqueline Marino, and Robert Gutsche, "The Digital Animation of Literary Journalism," *Journalism* 17, no. 4 (2016): 527–546.

40. Kim Fox, David O. Dowling, and Kyle Miller, "A Curriculum for Blackness: Podcasts as Discursive Cultural Guides, 2010–2020," *Journal of Radio & Audio Media* 27, no. 2, (2020): 298–318.

41. Sarah Florini, "The Podcast 'Chitlin Circuit': Black Podcasters, Alternative Media, and Audio Enclaves," *Journal of Radio & Audio Media* 22, no. 2 (2015): 209–219.

42. Walter Benjamin, "The Storyteller," in *Illuminations* (1936; repr. New York: Schocken, 1968).

43. Jessica Helfand and John Maeda, *Screen: Essays on Graphic Design, New Media and Visual Culture* (Princeton, N.J.: Princeton Architectural Press, 2001).

44. Kern, *Sound Reporting*; and Bob Lochte, "U.S. Public Radio: What Is It—and for Whom?," in *More than a Music Box: Radio Cultures and Communities in a Multi-Media World*, ed. Andrew Crisell, 39–56 (New York: Berghahn, 2004).

45. David O. Dowling, *Immersive Longform Storytelling: Media, Technology, Audience* (New York: Routledge, 2019).

46. James G. Webster, *The Marketplace of Attention: How Audiences Take Shape in a Digital Age* (Cambridge, Mass.: MIT Press, 2016).

47. Jenny Odell, *How to Do Nothing: Resisting the Attention Economy* (Brooklyn, N.Y.: Melville House, 2019), 181.

48. John Biewen and Alexa Dilworth, *Reality Radio: Telling True Stories in Sound*, 2nd ed. (Chapel Hill: University of North Carolina Press, 2017).

49. Tiffanie Wen, "Inside the Podcast Brain: Why Do Audio Stories Captivate?," *Atlantic*, April 15, 2015; Jonah Weiner, "The Voices: Toward a Critical Theory of Podcasting," *Slate*, December 14, 2014; and Helfand and Maeda, *Screen*.

50. Jayanta Panda, "Impact of Media Convergence on Journalism: A Theoretical Perspective," *Pragyaan: Journal of Mass Communication* 12, nos. 1–2 (2014): 14–21; Nikki Usher, *Interactive Journalism: Hackers, Data, and Code* (Champaign: University of Illinois Press, 2016); and Dowling, *Immersive Longform Storytelling*.

51. Biewen and Dilworth, *Reality Radio*, 178; and Michele Hilmes, *Only Connect: A Cultural History of Broadcasting in the United States*, 4th ed. (Boston: Wadsworth, 2014).

52. David O. Dowling and Kyle J. Miller, "Immersive Audio Storytelling: Podcasting and Serial Documentary in the Digital Publishing Industry," *Journal of Radio & Audio Media* 26, no. 1 (2019): 167–184.

53. On video on-demand, see Biewen and Dilworth, *Reality Radio*. On personal narrative, see Lindgren, "Personal Narrative Journalism and Podcasting." On a liminal space, see Dario Llinares, Neil Fox, and Richard Berry, eds., *Podcasting: New Aural Cultures and Digital Media* (New York: Palgrave Macmillan, 2018).

54. Meriano Cebrián, quoted in Carmen Peñafiel Saiz, "Radio and Web 2.0: Direct Feedback," in *Radio Content in the Digital Age: The Evolution of a Sound Medium*, ed. Angeliki Gazi, Guy Starkey, and Stanislaw Jedrzejewski (Chicago: Intellect, University of Chicago Press, 2011), 69.

55. On new genre conventions, see Siobhán McHugh, "How Podcasting Is Changing the Audio Storytelling Genre," *Radio Journal—International Studies in Broadcast and Audio Media* 14, no. 1 (April 2016): 65–82. On motivations for consumption of true crime, see Kelli S. Boling and Kevin Hull, "*Undisclosed* Information—*Serial* Is *My Favorite Murder*: Examining Motivations in the True Crime Podcast Audience," *Journal of Radio & Audio Media* 25, no. 1 (2018): 92–108. On the intersection with radio, see Berry, "Serial and Ten Years of Podcasting"; Richard Berry, "Podcasting: Considering the Evolution of the Medium and Its Association with the Word 'Radio,'" *Radio Journal: International Studies in Broadcast and Audio Media* 14, no. 1 (2016): 7–22; Christopher Cwynar, "More Than a 'VCR for Radio': The CBC, the Radio 3 Podcast, and the Uses of an Emerging Medium," *Journal of Radio & Audio Media* 22 (2015): 190–199; Markman, "Everything Old Is New Again"; Yi Mou and Carolyn A. Lin, "Exploring Podcast Adoption Intention Via Perceived Social Norms, Interpersonal Communication, and Theory of Planned Behavior," *Journal of Broadcasting & Electronic Media* 59, no. 3 (2015): 475–493; and Kyle Wrather, "Making 'Maximum Fun' for Fans: Examining Podcast Listener Participation Online," *Radio Journal: International Studies in Broadcast & Audio Media* 14 (2016): 43–63, http://doi.org/10.1386/rjao.14.1.43_1. On approaches to longform audio journalism, see McHugh, "RadioDoc Review." On convergence, see Panda, "Impact of Media Convergence on Journalism."

56. Hilmes, *Only Connect*. See also Dowling and Miller, "Immersive Audio Storytelling."

57. Scott A. Eldridge II, *Online Journalism from the Periphery: Interloper Media and the Journalistic Field* (New York: Routledge, 2018).

58. Matthew Freeman and Renira Rampazzo Gambarato, eds. *Routledge Companion to Transmedia Studies* (New York: Routledge, 2019).

59. Siobhán McHugh, "The Narrative Podcast as Digital Literary Journalism: Conceptualizing S-Town," *Literary Journalism Studies* 13, nos. 1 and 2 (June and December 2021): 100–129.

60. Nicholas Quah, "Should Spotify Be Responsible for What Joe Rogan Does?," *New York*, November 3, 2020.

61. Andrew J. Bottomley, "Podcasting: A Decade in the Life of a 'New' Audio Medium: Introduction," *Journal of Radio & Audio Media* 22, no. 2 (2015): 164–169; and Jessica Abel, *Out on the Wire: The Storytelling Secrets of the New Masters of Radio* (Portland: Broadway Books, 2015).

62. Biewen and Dilworth, *Reality Radio*, 1; and Jeff Porter, *Lost Sound: The Forgotten Art of Radio Storytelling* (Chapel Hill: University of North Carolina Press, 2016).
63. Lindgren, "Personal Narrative Journalism and Podcasting," 27.
64. Sillesen et al., "Journalism and the Power of Emotions."
65. Dowling and Miller, "Immersive Audio Storytelling"; and Kelli S. Boling, "True Crime Podcasting: Journalism, Justice, or Entertainment?" *Radio Journal: International Studies in Broadcast & Audio Media* 17, no. 2 (2019): 161–178.
66. Sarah Weinman, "The NYPD Wants in on the True Crime Journalism Boom," *Columbia Journalism Review*, December 11, 2019.
67. Bill Kovach and Tom Rosenstiel, *Blur: How to Know What's True in the Age of Information Overload* (New York: Bloomsbury, 2011), 27.
68. Weinman, "The NYPD Wants in on the True Crime Journalism Boom."
69. Corey Atad, "*In the Dark* Host Madeleine Baran Explains How the Year's Best True-Crime Podcast Was Made," *Esquire*, November 2016.
70. Stephen J. Berry, *Watchdog Journalism: The Art of Investigative Reporting* (New York: Oxford University Press, 2009).
71. Llinares, "Podcasting as Liminal Praxis," 129.
72. Llinares, "Podcasting as Liminal Praxis," 129.
73. Newman, "Inspired by The Daily."
74. Lukasz Swiatek, "The Podcast as an Intimate Bridging Medium," in *Podcasting: New Aural Cultures and Digital Media*, ed. Dario Llinares, Neil Fox, and Richard Berry, 173–188 (New York: Palgrave Macmillan, 2018), 177.
75. Mead, "Binge Listening," 50.
76. Newman, "Inspired by The Daily."
77. Jennifer Rauch, *Slow Media: Why Slow Is Satisfying, Sustainable, and Smart* (New York: Oxford University Press, 2018).
78. Mead, "Binge Listening," 51. See also Rauch, *Slow Media*.
79. Mead, "Binge Listening," 51. See also Bottomley, "Podcasting."
80. Robert McChesney, *Rich Media, Poor Democracy: Communication Politics in Dubious Times* (New York: New Press, 2015).
81. Thomas Schmidt, *Rewriting the Newspaper: The Storytelling Movement in American Print Journalism* (Columbia: University of Missouri Press, 2019).
82. Berry, "Podcasting," 22.
83. Ros Coward, *Speaking Personally: The Rise of Subjective and Confessional Journalism* (New York: Palgrave, 2013).
84. On metajournalistic discourse, see Matt Carlson, "Metajournalistic Discourse and the Meanings of Journalism: Definitional Control, Boundary Work, and Legitimation," *Communication Theory* 26, no. 4 (2016): 349–368. On metajournalistic discourse of conservative media, see Eldridge, *Online Journalism*

from the Periphery; and Benjamin Krämer and Klara Langmann, "Professionalism as a Response to Right-Wing Populism? An Analysis of a Metajournalistic Discourse," *International Journal of Communication* 14 (2020): 5643–5662.
85. Florini, "The Podcast 'Chitlin Circuit'"; and Photini Vrikki and Sarita Malik, "Voicing Lived Experience and Anti-Racism: Podcasting as a Space at the Margins for Subaltern Counterpublics," *Popular Communication* 17, no. 44 (2019): 273–287.
86. "The Podcast Consumer, 2019"; and Winn, "Podcast Stats and Facts."
87. Florini, "The Podcast 'Chitlin Circuit'"; and Melissa Harris-Lacewell, *Barbershops, Bibles, and BET: Everyday Talk and Black Political Thought* (Princeton, N.J.: Princeton University Press, 2006).
88. Spiegel, "Variations in Tape Use."
89. "Top 25 Black Podcasts You Must Follow in 2020," *Feedspot* (2020); and Florini, "The Podcast 'Chitlin circuit,'" 210.
90. Beatriz García, "Five Latin Podcasts That Would Deserve a Pulitzer," *Al Día*, December 9, 2019.
91. Swiatek, "The Podcast as an Intimate Bridging Medium," 180.
92. Duncan Stewart, Mark Casey, and Craig Wigginton, "The Ears Have It: The Rise of Audiobooks and Podcasting," *Deloitte*, December 9, 2019.
93. Stephen J. Dubner, "Should America Be Run by . . . Trader Joe's?," *Freakonomics*, episode 359, November 28, 2018.
94. David Yaffee-Bellany, "Welcome to McDonald's. Would You Like a Podcast with That?," *New York Times*, August 20, 2019.
95. Michael Canyon Meyer, "Should Journalism Worry about Content Marketing?," *Columbia Journalism Review*, March 2, 2015; and Mara Einstein, *Black Ops Advertising: Native Ads, Content Marketing, and the Covert World of the Digital Sell* (New York: OR Books, 2016).
96. Boling, "True Crime Podcasting."
97. Spinelli and Dann, *Podcasting*, 194.
98. Arthur Miller, "Why I Wrote *The Crucible*," *New Yorker*, October 13, 1996.
99. Janet Blank-Libra, *Pursuing an Ethic of Empathy in Journalism* (New York: Routledge, 2017).
100. On New Journalism, see Schmidt, *Rewriting the Newspaper*. On the digital longform movement, see James Bennet, "Against 'Long-Form Journalism,'" *Atlantic*, December 12, 2013; and Jonathan Mahler, "When 'Long-Form' Is Bad Form," *New York Times*, January 24, 2014.
101. Ayana Mathis, quoted in David O. Dowling, *A Delicate Aggression: Savagery and Survival in the Iowa Writers' Workshop* (New Haven, CT: Yale University Press), 327.
102. Josh Roiland, "Derivative Sport: The Journalistic Legacy of David Foster Wallace," *Literary Journalism Studies* 10, no. 1 (2018): 176. See also James

Tierney, "Literary Listening: The Rise of the Podcast as Literary Form," *Kill Your Darlings*, January 21, 2015.
103. Sillesen et al., "Journalism and the Power of Emotions"; Karin Wahl-Jorgenson, "The Strategic Ritual of Emotionality: A Case Study of Pulitzer Prize-Winning Articles," *Journalism* 14, no. 1 (2013): 129–145; and Coward, *Speaking Personally*.
104. Lilah Raptopoulos, "This American Life's First Spinoff Podcast: 'I don't know where it will end,'" *Guardian*, October 10, 2014.

1. PODCASTING THE PANDEMIC

1. Dylan Matthews, "Coronavirus Could Lead to the Highest Unemployment Levels Since the Great Depression," *Vox*, April 1, 2020.
2. Don Lemon, "Interview with Trymaine Lee," MSNBC, March 29, 2020.
3. Henry Jenkins, "Revenge of the Origami Unicorn: Seven Principles of Transmedia Storytelling," *Confessions of an Aca-Fan*, December 12, 2009; Renira Rampazzo Gambarato, "The Sochi Project: Slow Journalism within Transmedia Space," *Digital Journalism* 4, no. 4 (2016): 445–61; and Renira Rampazzo Gambarato, "Transmedia Journalism," in *The Routledge Companion to Transmedia Studies*, ed. Matthew Freeman and Renira Rampazzo Gambarato, 90–98 (New York: Routledge, 2019).
4. Trymaine Lee, "Into Coronavirus for the Uninsured," in *Into America*, episode 5, NBC News Network, podcast audio, YouTube, March 26, 2020.
5. Lee, "Into Coronavirus for the Uninsured."
6. Rashawn Ray, "Why Are Blacks Dying at Higher Rates from COVID-19?," *Brookings*, April 9, 2020.
7. Martin Spinelli and Lance Dann, *Podcasting: The Audio Media Revolution* (New York: Bloomsbury, 2019), 179–85; and Mia Lindgren, "Personal Narrative Journalism and Podcasting," *Radio Journal: International Studies in Broadcast & Audio Media* 14, no. 1 (2016): 23–41.
8. James Curran, "What Democracy Requires of the Media," in *Institutions of American Democracy: The Press*, ed. Kathleen Hall Jamieson and Geneva Overholser, 120–40 (New York: Oxford University Press 2005); James Curran, *Media and Democracy* (London: Routledge 2011); Robert McChesney, *Rich Media, Poor Democracy: Communication Politics in Dubious Times* (New York: New Press, 2015); and David Ryfe, *Journalism and the Public* (Cambridge: Polity, 2017). See also "SPJ Code of Ethics," *Society of Professional Journalists*, https://www.spj.org/ethicscode.asp.
9. Matt Carlson and Seth Lewis, "Boundary Work," in *The Handbook of Journalism Studies*, ed. Karin Wahl-Jorgenson and Thomas Hanitzsch, 123–35 (New

York: Routledge, 2020), 131. On declining public trust in the news media, see Nic Newman, Richard Fletcher, Antonis Kalogeropoulos, and Rasmus Kleis Nielsen, eds., *Reuters Institute Digital News Report 2019* (Oxford: Oxford University Reuters Institute, 2019).
10. Amy Mitchell and J. Baxter Oliphant, *Americans Immersed in COVID-19 News; Most Think Media Are Doing Fairly Well Covering It*, Pew Research Center, March 18, 2020.
11. Howard Saltz, "Removing Paywalls on Coronavirus Coverage Is Noble. It also Makes No Sense," *Poynter*, April 6, 2020.
12. Saltz, "Removing Paywalls"; Leonard Downie Jr. and Michael Schudson, "The Reconstruction of American Journalism," *Columbia Journalism Review*, November/December 19, 2009; and Christopher William Anderson, Emily Bell, and Clay Shirky, *Post-Industrial Journalism: Adapting to the Present* (New York: Tow Center for Digital Journalism, 2012): 32–123.
13. Nic Newman, "Inspired by The Daily, Dozens of Daily News Podcasts Are Punching Above Their Weight," *NiemanLab*, December 3, 2019.
14. Nicholas Quah, "Podcasts about Race Are Climbing the Charts, and Coronavirus Shows Drop Out," *Nieman Lab*, June 9, 2020.
15. Richard Berry, "Serial and Ten Years of Podcasting: Has the Medium Grown Up?," in *Radio, Sound and Internet*, Proceedings of the Net Station International Conference, ed. M. Oliveira and F. Ribeiro, 299–309 (Braga, Port.: LASICS, University of Minho, 2015), http://sure.sunderland.ac.uk/id/eprint/5759/.
16. Lukasz Swiatek, "The Podcast as an Intimate Bridging Medium," in *Podcasting: New Aural Cultures and Digital Media*, ed. Dario Llinares, Neil Fox, and Richard Berry, 173–188 (New York: Palgrave Macmillan, 2018), 182.
17. Victor Picard, "Coronavirus Is Hammering the News Industry. Here's How to Save It," *Jacobin*, April 20, 2020.
18. Eric Nuzum, "The Year of the DIY Podcast Network," *NiemanLab*, December 15, 2019.
19. Nuzum, "The Year of the DIY Podcast Network."
20. John Sullivan, "Podcast Movement: Aspirational Labor and the Formalisation of Podcasting as a Cultural industry," in *Podcasting: New Aural Cultures and Digital Media*, ed. Dario Llinares, Neil Fox, and Richard Berry, 35–56 (New York: Palgrave Macmillan, 2018).
21. Timothy Havens and Amanda Lotz, *Understanding Media Industries* (New York: Oxford University Press, 2016).
22. Richard Berry, "A Golden Age of Podcasting? Evaluating *Serial* in the Context of Podcast Histories," *Journal of Radio and Audio Media* 22, no. 2 (2015): 170–78.
23. Jacqueline Marino, Susan Jacobson, and Robert Gutsche Jr., "Scrolling for Story: How Millennials Interact with Longform Journalism on Mobile Devices," white

paper for Donald W. Reynolds Journalism Institute, University of Missouri, August 1, 2016.

24. Guy Starkey, "The New Kids on the Block: The Pictures, Text, Time-Shifted Audio, and Podcasts of Digital Radio Journalism Online," in *The Routledge Companion to Digital Journalism Studies*, ed. Bob Franklin and Scott A. Eldridge II (New York: Routledge, 2017). See also Joe Amditis, "An Ethical Analysis of *Serial*," *Medium*, December 23, 2016; Joyce Barnathan, "Why *Serial* Is Important for Journalism," *Columbia Journalism Review*, November 25, 2016; Lindgren, "Personal Narrative Journalism and Podcasting"; and Siobhán McHugh, "How Podcasting Is Changing the Audio Storytelling Genre," *Radio Journal—International Studies in Broadcast and Audio Media* 14, no. 1 (April 2016): 65–82.
25. Starkey, "The New Kids on the Block."
26. Newman, "Inspired by The Daily."
27. Spinelli and Dann, *Podcasting*, 194.
28. Spinelli and Dann, *Podcasting*, 195.
29. Amy Mitchell, Jesse Holcom, and Rachel Weisel, *State of the News Media 2016*, Pew Research Center, June 1, 2016; and Newman et al., *Reuters Institute Digital News Report 2019*.
30. Havens and Lotz, *Understanding Media Industries*.
31. Lindgren, "Personal Narrative Journalism and Podcasting."
32. Nicholas Quah, "Pandemic Watch: April 7, 2020," *Hotpod*, April 7, 2020.
33. Tomás Aragón, "Shelter in Place: Order of the Health Officer No. C19-07," City and County of San Francisco, Department of Public Health, March 16, 2020.
34. Brian Stelter, "Reliable Sources," *CNN Business*, March 15, 2020.
35. Will Leitch, "5 Ways Joe Biden Can Make His Bad Podcast Better," *Intelligencer*, April 7, 2020.
36. Berry, "Serial and Ten Years of Podcasting."
37. Berry, "Serial and Ten Years of Podcasting."
38. Karen McIntyre, "Solutions Journalism: The Effects of Including Solution Information in News Stories about Social Problems," *Journalism Practice* 13, no. 1, (2019): 16–34.
39. Jacob Weisberg, "Solvable Presents: Help in a Crisis," in *Solvable*, Pushkin Industries, podcast audio, April 3, 2020; and Molly Wood, "Startup Helps Feed Bank Account of Food Stamps Recipients," *Marketplace Tech*, April 15, 2020.
40. Weisberg, "Solvable Presents."
41. Weisberg, "Solvable Presents."
42. Ira Glass, "Harnessing Luck as an Industrial Product," in *Reality Radio: Telling True Stories in Sound*, 2nd ed., ed. John Biewen and Alexa Dilworth, 54–66 (Chapel Hill: University of North Carolina Press, 2017).
43. Glass, "Harnessing Luck as an Industrial Product," 70.

44. "Don't Stand So Close to Me: How Social Distancing Has Shifted Spotify Streaming," *Newsroom Spotify*, March 30, 2020.
45. Nicholas Quah, "Should Spotify Be Responsible for What Joe Rogan Does?" *New York*, November 3, 2020.
46. Acast, "Acast Announces 2019 Financial Results, Doubling Revenue to 361MSEK," *Acast Tech*, April 2, 2020.
47. Newman et al., *Reuters Institute Digital News Report 2019*, 60.
48. Newman et al., *Reuters Institute Digital News Report 2019*, 60.
49. Newman, "Inspired by The Daily."
50. SimilarWeb, "newyorktimes.com March 2020 Traffic Overview," *SimilarWeb*, March 31, 2020, www.similarweb.com.
51. Newman, "Inspired by The Daily."
52. Newman, "Inspired by The Daily."
53. Newman, "Inspired by The Daily."
54. David O. Dowling, "Toward a New Aesthetic of Digital Literary Journalism: Charting the Fierce Evolution of the 'Supreme Nonfiction,'" *Literary Journalism Studies* 9, no. 1 (2017): 101–16.
55. SimilarWeb, "newyorktimes.com March 2020 Traffic Overview."
56. Newman, "Inspired by The Daily."
57. Jessica Abel, *Out on the Wire: The Storytelling Secrets of the New Masters of Radio* (Portland: Broadway Books, 2015); and Rob Moran, "New Podcast from Serial Makers, S-Town, Breaks Download Records," *Sydney Morning Herald*, April 3, 2017.
58. Amy Mitchell, Galen Stocking, and Katerina Eva Matsa, "Long-form Reading Shows Signs of Life in our Mobile News World," *Pew Research Center*, May 5, 2016.
59. Bob Lochte, "U.S. Public Radio: What Is It—and For Whom?" in *More than a Music Box: Radio Cultures and Communities in a Multi-Media World*, ed. Andrew Crisell, 39–56 (New York: Berghahn, 2004); and Jeff Porter, *Lost Sound: The Forgotten Art of Radio Storytelling* (Chapel Hill: University of North Carolina Press, 2016).
60. Lindgren, "Personal Narrative Journalism and Podcasting."
61. David O. Dowling and Kyle J. Miller, "Immersive Audio Storytelling: Podcasting and Serial Documentary in the Digital Publishing Industry," *Journal of Radio & Audio Media* 26, no. 1, (2019): 167–184.
62. Dowling, "Toward a New Aesthetic of Digital Literary Journalism."
63. Newman et al., *Reuters Institute Digital News Report 2019*.
64. Newman, "Inspired by The Daily."
65. Kate Lacey, *Listening Publics: The Politics and Experience of Listening in the Media Age* (New York: John Wiley, 2013), 7.

66. Ana Serrano Telleria, "Transmedia Journalism: Exploring Genres and Interface Design," *Tripodos* 38 (2016): 68.
67. James G. Webster, *The Marketplace of Attention: How Audiences Take Shape in a Digital Age* (Cambridge, Mass.: MIT Press, 2016).
68. Oliver Grau, *Virtual Art: From Illusion to Immersion* (Cambridge, Mass.: MIT Press, 2003), 7.
69. Newman, "Inspired by The Daily."
70. Newman, "Inspired by The Daily."
71. Newman, "Inspired by The Daily."
72. John Biewen and Alexa Dilworth, *Reality Radio: Telling True Stories in Sound*, 2nd ed. (Chapel Hill: University of North Carolina Press, 2017), 82.
73. Nicholas Carr, *The Shallows: What the Internet Is Doing to Our Brains* (New York: Norton, 2011).
74. Carl Therrien, "Immersion," in *The Routledge Companion to Video Game Studies*, Mark J. P. Wolf and Bernard Perron (New York: Routledge, 2014), 451.
75. Therrien, "Immersion," 452.
76. Biewen and Dilworth, *Reality Radio*, 2.
77. Jonathan Kern, *Sound Reporting: The NPR Guide to Audio Journalism and Production* (Chicago: University of Chicago Press, 2008), 3.
78. Kern, *Sound Reporting*.
79. Kern, *Sound Reporting*, 12.
80. Biewen and Dilworth, *Reality Radio*, 2.
81. Ralph Schroeder, *Social Theory after the Internet: Media, Technology, and Globalization* (London: UCL Press, 2018), 88.
82. Bob Witmer and Michael Singer, "Measuring Presence in Virtual Environments: A *Presence* Questionnaire," *Presence: Teleoperators and Virtual Environments* 7, no. 3, (1998): 225–40.
83. Witmer and Singer, "Measuring Presence in Virtual Environments," 226.
84. Lindgren, "Personal Narrative Journalism and Podcasting," 38.
85. Janet Blank-Libra, *Pursuing an Ethic of Empathy in Journalism* (New York: Routledge, 2017).
86. Spinelli and Dann, *Podcasting*, 180.
87. Ryan Engley, "The Impossible Ethics of *Serial*: Sarah Koenig, Foucault, Lacan," in *The* Serial *Podcast and Storytelling in the Digital Age*, ed. Ellen McCracken, 87–100 (New York: Routledge, 2017).
88. Ira Glass, as quoted in Spinelli and Dann, *Podcasting*, 180.
89. Leitch, "5 Ways Joe Biden Can Make His Bad Podcast Better."
90. Leitch, "5 Ways Joe Biden Can Make His Bad Podcast Better."

91. Travis Vogan and David Dowling, "Bill Simmons, Grantland.com, and ESPN's Corporate Reinvention of Literary Sports Writing Online," *Convergence* 22, no. 1 (2016): 18–34.
92. Henry Jenkins, *Convergence Culture: Where Old and New Media Collide* (New York: New York University Press, 2006).
93. Glass, "Harnessing Luck as an Industrial Product."
94. Lee, "Into Coronavirus for the Uninsured."
95. Lemon, "Interview with Trymaine Lee."
96. "Introducing Into America," *Into America*, podcast, NBC News Network, February 20, 2020.
97. Glass, "Harnessing Luck as an Industrial Product," 70.
98. Commission on Freedom of the Press, *A Free and Responsible Press: A General Report on Mass Communication: Newspapers, Radio, Motion Pictures, Magazines, and Books* (Chicago: University of Chicago Press, 1947).
99. Spinelli and Dann, *Podcasting*, 196.
100. Spinelli and Dann, *Podcasting*, 196.
101. Lee, "Into Coronavirus for the Uninsured."
102. Gambarato, "Transmedia Journalism," 91.
103. Jenkins, "Revenge of the Origami Unicorn"; and Gambarato, "Transmedia Journalism."
104. "Good Luck, Everybody," in *All Told*, podcast, *Washington Post*, April 3, 2020.
105. "Will Coronavirus Tenant Protections Really Help Renters?," in *The California Report*, KQED, podcast audio, March 31, 2020.
106. Quah, "Podcasts about Race Are Climbing the Charts."
107. Spinelli and Dann, *Podcasting*, 184.
108. Spinelli and Dann, *Podcasting*, 184.
109. Quah, "Podcasts about Race Are Climbing the Charts."
110. Rachel Riederer, "New York City's Empty Streets," *New Yorker*, April 7, 2020.
111. David Remnick, "Special Update: The Coronavirus Crisis," *New Yorker: The Daily*, April 25, 2020.
112. Robert Dalleck, *Franklin D. Roosevelt: A Political Life* (New York: Penguin, 2017).

2. THE PERILS AND PROMISE OF TRUE CRIME PODCAST JOURNALISM

1. Elahe Izadi and Paul Farhi, "The New York Times Could Not Verify ISIS Claims in Its 'Caliphate' Podcast. Now It's Returning a Prestigious Award," *Washington Post*, December 18, 2020.

2. Matthew Schneier, "The Voice of a Generation: Michael Barbaro Made the New York *Times* Podcast a Raging Success. Or Is It the Other Way Around?," *New York*, January 21, 2020.

3. Kylie Jarrett, "Private Talk in the Public Sphere: Podcasting as Broadcast Talk," *Communication, Politics and Culture* 42, no. 2 (2009): 116–135; Nic Newman, "Inspired by The Daily, Dozens of Daily News Podcasts are Punching Above their Weight," *NiemanLab*, December 3, 2019; and Nic Newman and Nathan Gallo, *Daily News Podcasts: Building New Habits in the Shadow of Coronavirus* (Oxford: Reuters Institute for the Study of Journalism 2020).

4. Gabriella Perdomo and Philippe Rodrigues-Rouleau, "Transparency as Metajournalistic Performance: *The New York Times' Caliphate* Podcast and New Ways to Claim Journalistic Authority," *Journalism* 23, no. 11 (2021): 2311–2327, http://dx.doi.org/10.1177/1464884921997312.

5. On journalistic principles for sourcing, see Robert Entman, "The Nature and Sources of News," in *Institutions of American Democracy: The Press*, ed. Kathleen Hall Jamieson and Geneva Overholser, 48–65 (New York: Oxford University Press, 2005); James Curran, "What Democracy Requires of the Media," in *Institutions of American Democracy: The Press*, ed. Kathleen Hall Jamieson and Geneva Overholser, 120–40 (New York: Oxford University Press 2005); and James Curran, *Media and Democracy* (London: Routledge 2011). On confidence in journalism, see Arjen Van Dalen, "Journalism, Trust, and Credibility," in *The Handbook of Journalism Studies*, 2nd ed., ed. Karin Wahl-Jorgensen and Thomas Hanitzsch (New York: Routledge 2020): 356–371; and Raghavan Mayur, "Do Americans Still Trust Established Media Outlets?," *Tipp Insights*, March 9, 2021.

6. Kevin Moloney, "All the News That's Fit to Push: The New York Times Company and Transmedia Daily News," *International Journal of Communication* 14 (2020): 4683–4702.

7. Schneier, "The Voice of a Generation."

8. Nicholas Quah, "L'Affaire Caliphate," *Hot Pod*, episode 287, January 5, 2021.

9. "Most Listened to Podcasts of 2020," *Edison Research*, February 9, 2021.

10. Peter Libbey, "The Latest Entry in the True Crime Serial Market: Copcasts," *New York Times*, November 3, 2019; Chandler Hodo, "Why Podcasting Is the Next Wave of Journalism and True Crime Reporting," *Local Profile*, September 22, 2019; and Charley Locke, "How True Crime Podcasts Perpetuate the Myth of an Effective Criminal Justice System," *Hot Pod*, episode 262, June 16, 2020.

11. Locke, "How True Crime Podcasts Perpetuate the Myth."

12. Kelli S. Boling and Kevin Hull, "*Undisclosed* Information—*Serial* Is My Favorite Murder: Examining Motivations in the True Crime Podcast Audience," *Journal of Radio & Audio Media* 25, no. 1 (2018): 106.

13. James G. Webster, *The Marketplace of Attention: How Audiences Take Shape in a Digital Age* (Cambridge, Mass.: MIT Press, 2016).
14. Kelli S. Boling, "True Crime Podcasting: Journalism, Justice, or Entertainment?" *Radio Journal: International Studies in Broadcast & Audio Media* 17, no. 2 (2019): 164.
15. Boling, "True Crime Podcasting," 164.
16. Dylan Taylor-Lehman, "The Grisly Murder That Launched a Podcast Star," *Narratively*, September 26, 2017; and David O. Dowling and Kyle J. Miller, "Immersive Audio Storytelling: Podcasting and Serial Documentary in the Digital Publishing Industry," *Journal of Radio & Audio Media* 26, no. 1, (2019): 167–184.
17. Molly Snead, "2020 AAN Awards Winners Announced," *Association of Alternative Newsmedia*, September 18, 2020.
18. Boling and Hull, "*Undisclosed* Information," 106.
19. Boling and Hull, "*Undisclosed* Information," 105.
20. Libbey, "The Latest Entry in the True Crime Serial Market."
21. Boling and Hull, "*Undisclosed* Information," 99–100.
22. Boling and Hull, "*Undisclosed* Information," 105.
23. Michael Barbaro, "An Examination of 'Caliphate'," in *The Daily, New York Times*, podcast audio, December 18, 2020.
24. Quah, "L'Affaire Caliphate."
25. Jean Murley, *The Rise of True Crime: Twentieth Century Murder and American Popular Culture* (Westport, Conn.: Praeger, 2008).
26. Quah, "L'Affaire Caliphate."
27. Murley, *The Rise of True Crime*; and Ian Case Punnett, *Toward a Theory of True Crime Narratives: A Textual Analysis* (Routledge: New York, 2018).
28. Punnett, *Toward a Theory of True Crime Narratives*, 93.
29. Boling, "True Crime Podcasting," 168.
30. Boling, "True Crime Podcasting," 168.
31. Amy Mitchell, Mark Jurkowitz, J. Baxter Oliphant, and Elsa Shearer, "Americans Who Get their News on Social Media Are Less Engaged, Less Knowledgeable," *Pew Research Center: Journalism and Media*, July 30, 2020.
32. Steen Steensen, "The Intimization of Journalism," in *The Sage Handbook of Digital Journalism*, ed. Tamara Witschge, Christopher William Anderson, David Domingo, and Alfred Hermida, 115–133 (Thousand Oaks, CA: Sage 2016), 122.
33. Rasmus Kleis Nielsen, "Economic Contexts of Journalism," in *The Handbook of Journalism Studies*, 2nd ed., ed., Karin Wahl-Jorgensen and Thomas Hanitzsch, 324–340 (New York: Routledge 2020), 328.
34. Van Dalen, "Journalism, Trust, and Credibility," 359.
35. Van Dalen, "Journalism, Trust, and Credibility," 359–360. See also Andie Tucher, *Froth and Scum: Truth, Beauty, Goodness, and the Ax Murder in*

America's First Mass Medium (Chapel Hill: University of North Carolina Press, 2000).
36. Tim Vos and Ryan Thomas, "The Discursive Construction of Journalistic Authority in a Post-Truth Age," *Journalism Studies* 19, no. 13 (2018): 2001–2010; and Boling, "True Crime Podcasting," 164.
37. Quoted in Jon Allsop, "*Caliphate*, The 1619 Project, *The Times*, and Culture," *Columbia Journalism Review*, October 14, 2020.
38. Allsop, "*Caliphate*, The 1619 Project, *The Times*, and Culture."
39. Entman, "The Nature and Sources of News," 54.
40. Curran, "What Democracy Requires of the Media."
41. Entman, "The Nature and Sources of News," 54.
42. Barbaro, "An Examination of *Caliphate*."
43. Barbaro, "An Examination of *Caliphate*."
44. Barbaro, "An Examination of *Caliphate*."
45. Barbaro, "An Examination of *Caliphate*."
46. Izadi and Farhi, "The New York Times Could Not Verify ISIS Claims."
47. Izadi and Farhi, "The New York Times Could Not Verify ISIS Claims."
48. Barbaro, "An Examination of *Caliphate*."
49. Izadi and Farhi, "The New York Times Could Not Verify ISIS Claims."
50. Perdomo and Rodrigues-Rouleau, "Transparency as Metajournalistic Performance," 2.
51. Rebecca Nee and Arthur Santana, "Podcasting the Pandemic: Exploring Storytelling Formats and Shifting Journalistic Norms in News Podcasts Related to the Coronavirus," *Journalism Practice* 16, no. 8 (2021): 1559–1577, http://dx.doi.org/10.1080/17512786.2021.1882874.
52. Punnett, *Toward a Theory of True Crime Narratives*.
53. Nee and Santana, "Podcasting the Pandemic."
54. Nee and Santana, "Podcasting the Pandemic," 1569.
55. E. J. Dickinson, "Judge Allows Lawsuit to Proceed Against *S-Town* Podcast Makers," *Rolling Stone*, March 25, 2019.
56. Dickinson, "Judge Allows Lawsuit to Proceed Against *S-Town* Podcast Makers."
57. Dowling and Miller, "Immersive Audio Storytelling."
58. "Lawsuit Over Popular S-Town Podcast Dismissed," Associated Press, May 20, 2020.
59. Nee and Santana, "Podcasting the Pandemic."
60. Perdomo and Rodrigues-Rouleau, "Transparency as Metajournalistic Performance."
61. Nee and Santana, "Podcasting the Pandemic," 1570.
62. Mark Coddington and Seth Lewis, "*Caliphate* and the Limits of Performative Transparency," *NiemanLab*, March 10, 2021.

63. Laith Zuraikat, "The Parasocial Nature of the Podcast," in *Radio's Second Century: Past, Present, and Future Perspectives*, ed. John Allen Hendricks, 39–52 (New Brunswick, N.J.: Rutgers University Press, 2020).
64. Elihu Katz, John Durham Peters, Tamar Liebes, and Avril Orloff, *Canonic Texts in Media Research: Are There Any? Should There Be? How About These?* (Cambridge: Polity, 2003): 138–139, quoted in Zuraikat, "The Parasocial Nature of the Podcast," 40.
65. Zuraikat, "The Parasocial Nature of the Podcast," 43.
66. Zuraikat, "The Parasocial Nature of the Podcast," 43.
67. Richard van der Wurff and Klaus Schönbach, "Between Profession and Audience," *Journalism Studies* 12, no. 4 (2011): 418.
68. Perdomo and Rodrigues-Rouleau, "Transparency as Metajournalistic Performance," 4.
69. David Ryfe, *Can Journalism Survive? An Inside Look at Newsrooms* (Cambridge: Polity, 2012).
70. David S. Allen, "The Trouble with Transparency: The Challenge of Doing Journalism Ethics in a Surveillance Society," *Journalism Studies* 9, no. 3 (2008): 323–340.
71. David Ryfe, *Journalism and the Public* (Cambridge: Polity, 2017).
72. David Dowling and Travis Vogan, "Can We Snowfall This? Digital Longform and the Race for the Tablet Market," *Digital Journalism* 3, no. 2 (2015): 209–224.
73. Damali Ayo, "What Did She Just Say?," in *Reality Radio: Telling True Stories in Sound*, ed. John Biewen and Alexa Dilworth, 76–85 (Chapel Hill: University of North Carolina Press, 2017), 82.
74. Ryfe, *Can Journalism Survive?*
75. Perdomo and Rodrigues-Rouleau, "Transparency as Metajournalistic Performance," 5.
76. Perdomo and Rodrigues-Rouleau, "Transparency as Metajournalistic Performance."
77. Perdomo and Rodrigues-Rouleau, "Transparency as Metajournalistic Performance," 7.
78. Bob Franklin and Scott A, Eldridge II, *The Routledge Companion to Digital Journalism* (New York: Routledge, 2017).
79. Perdomo and Rodrigues-Rouleau, "Transparency as Metajournalistic Performance," 14.
80. Perdomo and Rodrigues-Rouleau, "Transparency as Metajournalistic Performance," 8.
81. Rukmini Callimachi, "Chapter 9: Prisoners, Part 1," in *Caliphate*, New York Times, podcast audio, aired May 24, 2018.

82. Callimachi, "Chapter 9."
83. Matt Carlson and Seth Lewis, "Boundary Work," in *The Handbook of Journalism Studies*, ed. Karin Wahl-Jorgenson and Thomas Hanitzsch, 123–35 (New York: Routledge, 2020).
84. Callimachi, "Chapter 9."
85. Callimachi, "Chapter 9."
86. Callimachi, "Chapter 9."
87. Callimachi, "Chapter 9."
88. Callimachi, "Chapter 9."
89. Callimachi, "Chapter 9."
90. Rukmini Callimachi, "I am fiercely proud . . ." @rcallimachi, Twitter, December 18, 2020.
91. Mats Hyvönen, Maria Karlsson, and Madeleine Erikkson, "The Politics of True Crime: Vulnerability and Documentaries on Murder in Swedish Public Radio's *P3 Documentary*," in *Vulnerability in Scandinavian Art and Culture*, ed. Adriana Margareta Dancus, Mats Hyvönen, and Maria Karlsson, 291–314 (New York: Palgrave), 310.
92. Hodo, "Why Podcasting Is the Next Wave."
93. Locke, "How True Crime Podcasts Perpetuate the Myth."
94. Locke, "How True Crime Podcasts Perpetuate the Myth."
95. Locke, "How True Crime Podcasts Perpetuate the Myth"; and Kathleen M. Donovan and Charles F. Klahm, "The Role of Entertainment Media in Perceptions of Police Use of Force," *Criminal Justice and Behavior* 42, no. 12 (2015): 1261–1281.
96. Liam O'Donoghue, "Podcasts Could Spark a New Golden Age of Investigative Journalism," *Bello Collective*, November 5, 2018.
97. Madeleine Baran, "The Crime," in *In the Dark*, American Public Media Reports, podcast audio, season 1, episode 1, September 7, 2016.
98. Elon Green, "Q&A: Madeleine Baran on Reinvestigating the Jacob Wetterling Abduction," *Columbia Journalism Review*, December 22, 2016.
99. Boling, "True Crime Podcasting."
100. Boling, "True Crime Podcasting," 170.
101. O'Donoghue, "Podcasts Could Spark a New Golden Age."
102. Locke, "How True Crime Podcasts Perpetuate the Myth."
103. Jay Allison, "Afterword: Listen," in Biewen and Dilworth, *Reality Radio: Telling True Stories in Sound*, 2nd ed., ed. John Biewen and Alexa Dilworth, 183–196 (Chapel Hill: University of North Carolina Press, 2017), 185.
104. Allison, "Afterword," 184.
105. Ayo, "What Did She Just Say?," 82.
106. Locke, "How True Crime Podcasts Perpetuate the Myth."

3. INTELLECTUAL CULTURE

1. Nic Newman, Richard Fletcher, Antonis Kalogeropoulos, and Rasmus Kleis Nielsen, eds., *Reuters Institute Digital News Report 2019* (Oxford: Oxford University Reuters Institute, 2019).
2. Dario Llinares, "Podcasting as Liminal Praxis: Aural Mediation, Sound Writing and Identity," in *Podcasting: New Aural Cultures and Digital Media*, ed. Dario Llinares, Neil Fox, and Richard Berry, 123–46 (New York: Palgrave Macmillan, 2018), 125.
3. Antonio Gramsci, *Selections from the Prison Notebooks of Antonio Gramsci*, (London: International Publishers 1972).
4. David O. Dowling, *Immersive Longform Storytelling: Media, Technology, Audience* (New York: Routledge, 2019).
5. Lukasz Swiatek, "The Podcast as an Intimate Bridging Medium," in *Podcasting: New Aural Cultures and Digital Media*, ed. Dario Llinares, Neil Fox, and Richard Berry, 173–188 (New York: Palgrave Macmillan, 2018).
6. Swiatek, "The Podcast as an Intimate Bridging Medium."
7. Mia Lindgren, "Personal Narrative Journalism and Podcasting," *Radio Journal: International Studies in Broadcast & Audio Media* 14, no. 1 (2016): 23–41.
8. Llinares, "Podcasting as Liminal Praxis," 125.
9. Newman et al., *Reuters Institute Digital News Report 2019*, 27.
10. Newman et al., *Reuters Institute Digital News Report 2019*, 27.
11. Martin Spinelli and Lance Dann, *Podcasting: The Audio Media Revolution* (New York: Bloomsbury, 2019), 22.
12. Spinelli and Dann, *Podcasting*, 22–23.
13. Michael Brüggemann and Sven Engesser, "Beyond False Balance: How Interpretive Journalism Shapes Media Coverage of Climate Change," *Global Environmental Change* 42 (January 2017): 58–67.
14. Brüggemann and Engesser, "Beyond False Balance," 58.
15. Brüggemann and Engesser, "Beyond False Balance"; and Kris M. Wilson, "Drought, Debate, and Uncertainty: Measuring Reporters' Knowledge and Ignorance About Climate Change," *Public Understanding of Science* 9, no. 1 (2000): 1–13.
16. Faith Kearns, *Getting to the Heart of Science Communication: A Guide to Effective Engagement* (Washington, D.C.: Island Press, 2021).
17. Kate Yoder, "The Conventional Wisdom About How to Talk About Climate Change? It's Wrong," *Grist*, May 4, 2021.
18. David Dowling, "Sailing into Sandy: Media and the Moral Wreckage of the HMS Bounty," *Journal of American Culture* 37, no. 3 (2014): 269–281.
19. Kearns, *Getting to the Heart of Science Communication*.
20. Kearns, *Getting to the Heart of Science Communication*.

21. Philip J. Pauly, *Biologists and the Promise of American Life: From Meriwether Lewis to Alfred Kinsey* (Princeton, N.J.: Princeton University Press 2000).
22. Pauly, *Biologists and the Promise of American Life*.
23. Pauly, *Biologists and the Promise of American Life*.
24. Alix Spiegel, "Variations in Tape Use and the Position of the Narrator," in *Reality Radio: Telling True Stories in Sound*, ed. John Biewen and Alexa Dilworth (Chapel Hill: University of North Carolina, Press 2017), 43.
25. Spiegel, "Variations in Tape Use," 51.
26. Spiegel, "Variations in Tape Use," 51–52.
27. Spiegel, "Variations in Tape Use," 44.
28. Spiegel, "Variations in Tape Use," 45.
29. Spiegel, "Variations in Tape Use," 46.
30. Lulu Miller and Alix Spiegel, "Entanglement," in *Invisibilia*, podcast audio, January 29, 2015.
31. Spiegel, "Variations in Tape Use," 49.
32. Spiegel, "Variations in Tape Use," 51.
33. Spiegel, "Variations in Tape Use," 51.
34. Miller and Spiegel, "Entanglement."
35. Joanna Thornborrow, *The Discourse of Public Participation Media: From Talk Show to Twitter* (London: Routledge, 2015); and Paddy Scannell, *Radio, Television and Modern Life* (Cornwall, UK: Blackwell, 1996).
36. Laith Zuraikat, "The Parasocial Nature of the Podcast," in *Radio's Second Century: Past, Present, and Future Perspectives*, ed. John Allen Hendricks, 39–52 (New Brunswick, N.J.: Rutgers University Press, 2020), 49.
37. Swiatek, "The Podcast as an Intimate Bridging Medium," 177.
38. Robert C. McDougall, *Digination: Identity, Organization, and Public Life in the Age of Small Digital Devices and Big Digital Domains* (Madison, N.J.: Fairleigh Dickinson University Press 2012), 178.
39. McDougall, *Digination*, 179.
40. Henry A. Giroux, "The Crisis of Public Values in the Age of the New Media," *Critical Studies in Media Communication* 28, no. 1 (2011): 21.
41. Giroux, "The Crisis of Public Values," 25.
42. Swiatek, "The Podcast as an Intimate Bridging Medium," 180.
43. Karen Elizabeth McIntyre and Kyser Lough, "Toward a Clearer Conceptualization and Operationalization of Solutions Journalism," *Journalism* 22, no. 6 (2019), https://doi.org/10.1177/1464884918820756.
44. Swiatek, "The Podcast as an Intimate Bridging Medium," 178.
45. Adam Smith, "Donna Strickland," in *Nobel Prize Conversations*, podcast audio, March 3, 2021.
46. Spinelli and Dann, *Podcasting*, 23.

47. Spinelli and Dann, *Podcasting*, 28.
48. Spinelli and Dann, *Podcasting*, 21–22.
49. Spiegel, "Variations in Tape Use," 33, 46.
50. Spinelli and Dann, *Podcasting*, 39–40.
51. Mike Pesca, "Cold, Hard Facts with Wendy Zukerman," in *The Gist*, episode 703, *Slate*, podcast audio, March 20, 2017.
52. Maxwell T. Boykoff and Jules M. Boykoff, "Balance as Bias: Global Warming and the U.S. Prestige Press," *Global Environmental Change* 14, no. 2 (2004): 125–136, https://doi.org/10.1016/j.gloenvcha.2003.10.001.
53. Brüggemann and Engesser, "Beyond False Balance," 60.
54. Jill Lepore, *The Last Archive*, Pushkin Industries, podcast audio (2021).
55. Michael Schaub, "'These Truths' Looks at America Through the Promises of Its Beginning," NPR, September 18, 2018.
56. Michael Schudson, *Why Democracies Need an Unlovable Press* (Cambridge: Polity, 2008), 88.
57. Schudson, *Why Democracies Need an Unlovable Press*, 88.
58. Roy Peter Clark, "Explanatory Journalism Is Entering a Golden Age in the Middle of the Coronavirus Pandemic," *Poynter*, May 8, 2020.
59. Clark, "Explanatory Journalism Is Entering a Golden Age."
60. Lepore, *The Last Archive*.
61. Lepore, *The Last Archive*.
62. Lepore, *The Last Archive*.
63. Lepore, *The Last Archive*.
64. Lepore, *The Last Archive*.
65. Lepore, *The Last Archive*.
66. Spinelli and Dann, *Podcasting*, 70.
67. Vann R. Newkirk II, *Floodlines*, *Atlantic*, podcast audio (2020).
68. Newkirk, *Floodlines*.
69. Nicholas Quah, "Pandemic Watch: April 7, 2020," in *Hotpod*, April 7, 2020.
70. Newkirk, *Floodlines*.
71. Newkirk, *Floodlines*.
72. Jason Salzman, "Michael 'Heck've a Job' Brown, of Katrina Fame, Won't Take Covid Vaccine," *Colorado Times Recorder*, May 20, 2020.
73. Newkirk, *Floodlines*.
74. Newkirk, *Floodlines*.
75. Jessa Crispin, "America Is Losing Its Mind. Again. With Chelsey Weber Smith," *Public Intellectual with Jessa Crispin*, podcast audio, December 7, 2020.
76. David O. Dowling, "Toward a New Aesthetic of Digital Literary Journalism: Charting the Fierce Evolution of the 'Supreme Nonfiction,'" *Literary Journalism Studies* 9, no. 1 (2017): 101–116.

77. Alan Lightman, "The Role of the Public Intellectual," *MIT Communication Forum*, December 2, 1990, http://web.mit.edu/comm-forum/legacy/papers/lightman.html.
78. Spencer Bailey and Andrew Zuckerman, "Bill McKibbon on COVID-19's Impact and the Climate Crisis," in *At a Distance*, podcast audio, April 2, 2020.
79. Bailey and Zuckerman, "Bill McKibbon on COVID-19's Impact."
80. Bailey and Zuckerman, "Bill McKibbon on COVID-19's Impact."

4. SOUND TRANSACTIONS

1. Nick Geidner and Denae D'Arcy, "The Effects of Micropayments on Online News Story Selection and Engagement," *New Media & Society* 17, no. 4 (2015): 613.
2. Martin Conboy, "Journalism and the Democratic Market Society," *Journalism Studies* 18, no. 10 (2017): 1263–1276.
3. Jacob Weisberg, "Solvable Presents: Help in a Crisis," in *Solvable*, Pushkin Industries, podcast audio, April 3, 2020.
4. Nic Newman with Richard Fletcher, Anne Schulz, Simge Andı, Craig T. Robertson, and Rasmus Kleis Nielsen, *Reuters Institute Digital News Report 2021*, 10th ed., (Oxford: Reuters Institute, 2021), 14.
5. Kevin Moloney, "All the News That's Fit to Push: The New York Times Company and Transmedia Daily News," *International Journal of Communication* 14 (2020): 4696.
6. Weisberg, "Solvable Presents."
7. Weisberg, "Solvable Presents."
8. Nicholas Carr, *The Shallows: What the Internet Is Doing to Our Brains* (New York: Norton, 2011).
9. Weisberg, "Solvable Presents."
10. Weisberg, "Solvable Presents."
11. Peter Laufer, *Slow News: A Manifesto for the Critical News Consumer* (Corvallis: Oregon State University Press, 2014); see also Jennifer Rauch, *Slow Media: Why Slow Is Satisfying, Sustainable, and Smart* (New York: Oxford University Press, 2018).
12. David Dowling, "The Business of Slow Journalism: Deep Storytelling's Alternative Economies," *Digital Journalism* 4, no. 4 (2018): 530–546.
13. John MacArthur, "False Idol: The Scrooge of 'Digital Correctness,'" *Columbia Journalism Review*, July/August 2014.
14. MacArthur, "False Idol."
15. MacArthur, "False Idol"; and David O. Dowling, *Immersive Longform Storytelling: Media, Technology, Audience* (New York: Routledge, 2019).

16. David García-Marín, "Mapping the Factors that Determine Engagement in Podcasting: Design from the Users and Podcasters' Experience," *Communication & Society* 33, no. 2 (2020), https://doi.org/10.15581/003.33.2.49-63; Michael Barthel, Amy Mitchell, Dorene Asare-Marfo, Courtney Kennedy, and Kirsten Worden, *Measuring News Consumption in a Digital Era*, Pew Research Center, December 8, 2020; and Sara Fischer, "The Podcast Paywall Wars Have Arrived," *Axios*, April 27, 2021.
17. Fischer, "The Podcast Paywall Wars Have Arrived."
18. García-Marín, "Mapping the Factors."
19. Barthel et al., "Measuring News Consumption in a Digital Era."
20. David B. Nieborg and Thomas Poell, "The Platformization of Cultural Production: Theorizing the Contingent Cultural Commodity," *New Media & Society* 20, no. 11 (2018): 4275–4292; and Patricia Aufderheide, David Lieberman, Atika Alkhallouf, and Jiji Majiri Ugboma, "Podcasting as Public Media: The Future of U.S. News, Public Affairs, and Educational Podcasts," *International Journal of Communication* 14 (February 2020): 1683–1704.
21. Amy Mitchell, Leah Christian, and Tom Rosenstiel, *News Is Valued but Willingness to Pay Is Low*, Pew Research Center, October 25, 2011.
22. Felicia Greiff, "Ira Glass: 'Public Radio Is Ready for Capitalism,'" *Ad Age*, April 30, 2015.
23. Sylvia Chan-Olmsted and Rang Wang, "Understanding Podcast Users: Consumption Motives and Behaviors," *New Media & Society* 24, no. 3 (2020): 687.
24. Chan-Olmsted and Wang, "Understanding Podcast Users," 689.
25. Kyung-Ho Hwang, Sylvia M. Chan-Olmsted, Sang-Hyun Nam, and Byeng-Hee Chang, "Factors Affecting Mobile Application Usage: Exploring the Roles of Gender, Age, and Application Types from Behaviour Log Data," *International Journal of Mobile Communications*, 14, no. 3 (2014): 256–272; and Kelli S. Boling and Kevin Hull, "*Undisclosed* Information—*Serial* Is *My Favorite Murder*: Examining Motivations in the True Crime Podcast Audience," Journal of Radio & Audio Media 25, no. 1 (2018): 92–108.
26. Dowling, *Immersive Longform Storytelling*.
27. Henry Jenkins, *Convergence Culture: Where Old and New Media Collide* (New York: New York University Press, 2006).
28. Richard Berry, "Podcasting: Considering the Evolution of the Medium and Its Association with the Word 'Radio,'" *Radio Journal: International Studies in Broadcast and Audio Media* 14, no. 1 (2016): 7–22; and Lars Nyre, "Urban Headphone Listening and the Situational Fit of Music, Radio and Podcasting," *Journal of Radio & Audio Media* 22, no. 2 (2015): 279–298.
29. Kris M. Markman, "Everything Old Is New Again: Podcasting as Radio's Revival," *Journal of Radio & Audio Media* 22, no. 2 (2015): 240–243.

30. Chan-Olmsted and Wang, "Understanding Podcast Users."
31. Boling and Hull, *"Undisclosed* Information."
32. Mia Lindgren, "Personal Narrative Journalism and Podcasting," *Radio Journal: International Studies in Broadcast & Audio Media* 14, no. 1 (2016): 38.
33. Lindgren, "Personal Narrative Journalism and Podcasting," 38.
34. Thomas Schmidt, *Rewriting the Newspaper: The Storytelling Movement in American Print Journalism* (Columbia: University of Missouri Press, 2019).
35. Dowling, *Immersive Longform Storytelling*.
36. Rebecca Mead, "Binge Listening: How Podcasts Became a Seductive—and Slippery—New Mode of Storytelling," *New Yorker*, November 19, 2018.
37. Barthel et al., "Measuring News Consumption in a Digital Era," 21.
38. Barthel et al., "Measuring News Consumption in a Digital Era," 21.
39. Barthel et al., "Measuring News Consumption in a Digital Era," 21.
40. Siobhán McHugh, "How Podcasting Is Changing the Audio Storytelling Genre," *Radio Journal—International Studies in Broadcast and Audio Media* 14, no. 1, (April 2016): 71.
41. "Pew Finds More Americans Are Turning to Podcasts for News," *Inside Radio*, December 14, 2020.
42. Moloney, "All the News That's Fit to Push."
43. Barthel et al., "Measuring News Consumption in a Digital Era," 5.
44. Clay Shirky, *Here Comes Everybody: The Power of Organizing Without Organizations* (New York: Penguin 2008).
45. Barthel et al., "Measuring News Consumption in a Digital Era," 24.
46. Moloney, "All the News That's Fit to Push."
47. Chan-Olmsted and Wang, "Understanding Podcast Users," 692.
48. Alan M. Rubin and Elizabeth M. Perse, "Audience Activity and Television News Gratifications," *Communication Research* 14, no. 1 (1987): 58–84.
49. McHugh, "How Podcasting Is Changing the Audio Storytelling Genre," 72.
50. McHugh, "How Podcasting Is Changing the Audio Storytelling Genre," 72.
51. Chan-Olmsted and Wang, "Understanding Podcast Users."
52. Chan-Olmsted and Wang, "Understanding Podcast Users," 691.
53. Berry, "Podcasting," 12.
54. *The Nielsen Total Audience Report 2021* (2021), https://www.nielsen.com/insights/2021/total-audience-advertising-across-todays-media/; and "The Podcast Consumer, 2019," *Edison Research*, March 6, 2019.
55. Nic Newman and Nathan Gallo, *Daily News Podcasts: Building New Habits in the Shadow of Coronavirus* (Oxford: Reuters Institute for the Study of Journalism 2020), 24.
56. Newman and Gallo, *Daily News Podcasts*, 24.
57. Newman and Gallo, *Daily News Podcasts*, 5.

58. Newman and Gallo, *Daily News Podcasts*, 5.
59. Newman and Gallo, *Daily News Podcasts*, 9; and Flamingo, *How Young People Consume News and the Implications for Mainstream Media* (Oxford: Reuters Institute for the Study of Journalism 2019).
60. Newman and Gallo, *Daily News Podcasts*, 24.
61. Newman and Gallo, *Daily News Podcasts*, 25.
62. Newman and Gallo, *Daily News Podcasts*, 25.
63. Brittany Faison, "Westwood One 2021 Audioscape: 5 Things to Know About the Podcast Audience," *Westwood One*, January 11, 2021.
64. Newman and Gallo, *Daily News Podcasts*, 27.
65. Carr, *The Shallows*.
66. Chan-Olmsted and Wang, "Understanding Podcast Users," 698.
67. Chan-Olmsted and Wang, "Understanding Podcast Users," 699.
68. George P. Slefo, "Spotify and Pandora Duke It Out for Podcasting Prominence," *Ad Age*, January 23, 2019.
69. Chan-Olmsted and Wang, "Understanding Podcast Users," 690.
70. Rachel L. Pavelko and Jessica Gall Myrick, "Muderinos and Media Effects: How the My Favorite Murder Podcast and Its Social Media Community May Promote Well-Being in Audiences with Mental Illness," *Journal of Radio & Audio Media* 27, no. 1 (2020): 151–169; and Laith Zuraikat, "The Parasocial Nature of the Podcast," in *Radio's Second Century: Past, Present, and Future Perspectives*, ed. John Allen Hendricks, 39–52 (New Brunswick, N.J.: Rutgers University Press, 2020).
71. Jessica Moore and Olivia Moore, "After a Breakout Year, Looking Ahead to the Future of Podcasting," *TechCrunch*, August 21, 2019; and Chan-Olmsted and Wang, "Understanding Podcast Users," 687.
72. Nieborg and Poell, "The Platformization of Cultural Production"; and Aufderheide, et al., "Podcasting as Public Media."
73. Nieborg and Poell, "The Platformization of Cultural Production"; and Aufderheide, et al., "Podcasting as Public Media."
74. Nieborg and Poell, "The Platformization of Cultural Production"; and Aufderheide, et al., "Podcasting as Public Media."
75. Spinelli and Dann, *Podcasting*, 166.
76. Kris M. Markman, "Doing Radio, Making Friends, and Having Fun: Exploring the Motivations of Independent Audio Podcasters," *New Media & Society* 14, no. 4, (2012): 547–565.
77. Spinelli and Dann, *Podcasting*, 162.
78. Robert C. McDougall, *Digination: Identity, Organization, and Public Life in the Age of Small Digital Devices and Big Digital Domains* (Madison, N.J.: Fairleigh Dickinson University Press 2012).

79. Nieborg and Poell, "The Platformization of Cultural Production"; and Aufderheide, et al., "Podcasting as Public Media."
80. McDougall, *Digination*.
81. Laufer, *Slow News*.
82. Weisberg, "Solvable Presents."
83. MacArthur, "False Idol."
84. John MacArthur, "Publisher's Letter," *Harper's*, October 2013.
85. Ravi Somaiya, "Harper's Publisher Standing Firm in His Defense of Print and Paywall," *New York Times*, August 10, 2014.
86. Fischer, "The Podcast Paywall Wars Have Arrived."
87. Fischer, "The Podcast Paywall Wars Have Arrived."
88. Fischer, "The Podcast Paywall Wars Have Arrived."
89. Laufer, *Slow News*; and Rauch, *Slow Media*.
90. John V. Pavlik, "Global Journalism in the Digital Age," in *Global Communication: A Multicultural Perspective*, 3rd ed., ed. Yahya R. Kamalipour, 211–238 (Lanham, Md.: Rowman and Littlefield 2020), 224.

5. CHARTING THE FAR RIGHT

1. Rich Barlow, "The Obituary Rush Limbaugh Deserves," *Cognoscenti*, WBUR Boston, February 18, 2021.
2. Brian Rosenwald, *Talk Radio's America: How an Industry Took Over a Political Party That Took over the United States* (Cambridge, Mass.: Harvard University Press 2019).
3. Kylie Jarrett, "Private Talk in the Public Sphere: Podcasting as Broadcast Talk," *Communication, Politics and Culture* 42, no. 2 (2009): 116–135; Matt Sienkiewicz, and Deborah L. Jaramillo, "Podcasting, the Intimate Self, and the Public Sphere," *Popular Communication* 17, no. 4 (2019): 268–272, http://dx.doi.org/10.1080/15405702.2019.1667997; and Jonathan Sterne, Jeremy Morris, Michael Brendan Baker, and Ariana Moscote Freire, "The Politics of Podcasting," *Fibreculture Journal* 13 (2008).
4. Mia Lindgren, "Personal Narrative Journalism and Podcasting," *Radio Journal: International Studies in Broadcast & Audio Media* 14, no. 1 (2016): 38.
5. Walter Lippmann, *Liberty and the News* (1920; repr., Mineola, N.Y.: Dover, 2010).
6. Michele Hilmes, *Only Connect: A Cultural History of Broadcasting in the United States*, 4th ed. (Boston: Wadsworth, 2014).
7. Patricia Aufderheide, David Lieberman, Atika Alkhallouf, and Jiji Majiri Ugboma, "Podcasting as Public Media: The Future of U.S. News, Public Affairs, and Educational Podcasts," *International Journal of Communication* 14

(February 2020): 1683–1704; and Robert McChesney, *Rich Media, Poor Democracy: Communication Politics in Dubious Times* (New York: New Press, 2015).
8. Hilmes, *Only Connect*, 129.
9. John F. Barber, "The *War of the Worlds* Broadcast: Fake News or Engaging Storytelling," in *Radio's Second Century: Past, Present, and Future Perspectives*, ed. John Allen Hendricks, 96–118 (New Brunswick, N.J.: Rutgers University Press 2020).
10. Richard J. Hand, *Terror on the Air! Horror Radio in America, 1931–1952* (Jefferson, N.C.: MacFarland, 2006).
11. Michael Barbaro, "The Legacy of Rush Limbaugh," in *The Daily, New York Times*, podcast audio, February 22, 2021; and Rosenwald, *Talk Radio's America*.
12. Brian Flood, "Rush Limbaugh, Conservative Radio Pioneer, Dead at 70," *Fox News*, February 17, 2021.
13. Allyson Chiu, "Rush Limbaugh on Coronavirus: The 'Common Cold' That's Being 'Weaponized' Against Trump," *Washington Post*, February 25, 2020.
14. Daniel Villarreal, "Rush Limbaugh Compares Capitol Hill Riot to American Revolution," *Newsweek*, January 7, 2021.
15. Rosenwald, *Talk Radio's America*; and Anthony Nadler and A. J. Bauer, eds., *News on the Right: Studying Conservative News Cultures* (Oxford: Oxford University Press 2019).
16. Barbaro, "The Legacy of Rush Limbaugh."
17. Rush Limbaugh, "Address to Incoming House GOP Freshmen," *American Rhetoric*, December 10, 1994, https://www.americanrhetoric.com/speeches/rushlimbaughhousegop.htm.
18. Limbaugh, "Address to Incoming House GOP Freshmen."
19. Matthew Levendusky and Neil Malhorta, "Does Media Coverage of Partisan Polarization Affect Political Attitudes?," *Political Communication*, no. 33 (2016): 283.
20. Ros Coward, *Speaking Personally: The Rise of Subjective and Confessional Journalism* (New York: Palgrave, 2013).
21. Rebecca Nee and Arthur Santana, "Podcasting the Pandemic: Exploring Storytelling Formats and Shifting Journalistic Norms in News Podcasts Related to the Coronavirus," *Journalism Practice* 16, no. 8 (2021): 1559–1577, http://dx.doi.org/10.1080/17512786.2021.1882874; and Kevin Loker, "Confusion About What's News and What's Opinion Is a Big Problem, But Journalists Can Help Solve It," *American Press Institute*, September 19, 2018, https://www.americanpressinstitute.org/publications/reports/survey-research/confusion-about-whats-news-and-whats-opinion-is-a-big-problem-but-journalists-can-help-solve-it/.
22. Nee and Santana, "Podcasting the Pandemic," 12.

23. Nee and Santana, "Podcasting the Pandemic," 12.
24. Nic Newman and Nathan Gallo, *Daily News Podcasts: Building New Habits in the Shadow of Coronavirus* (Oxford: Reuters Institute for the Study of Journalism 2020).
25. David B. Nieborg and Thomas Poell, "The Platformization of Cultural Production: Theorizing the Contingent Cultural Commodity," *New Media & Society* 20, no. 11, (2018): 4275–4292; and McChesney, *Rich Media, Poor Democracy*.
26. Yonghwan Kim, Hsuaun-Ting Chen, Homero Gil de Zúñiga, "Stumbling upon News on the Internet: Effects of Incidental News Exposure and Relative Entertainment use on Political Engagement," *Computers in Human Behavior* 29, no. 6 (2013): 2607–2614.
27. James Curran, "What Democracy Requires of the Media," in *Institutions of American Democracy: The Press*, ed. Kathleen Hall Jamieson and Geneva Overholser, 120–40 (New York: Oxford University Press 2005); Anthony Nadler, *Making the News Popular: Mobilizing U.S. News Audiences* (Urbana: University of Illinois Press 2016); David O. Dowling, *Immersive Longform Storytelling: Media, Technology, Audience* (New York: Routledge, 2019); David O. Dowling, *The Gamification of Digital Journalism: Innovation in Journalistic Storytelling* (New York: Routledge 2021); and Scott A. Eldridge II, *Online Journalism from the Periphery: Interloper Media and the Journalistic Field* (New York: Routledge, 2018).
28. Lindgren, "Personal Narrative Journalism and Podcasting."
29. Newman and Gallo, *Daily News Podcasts*, 13.
30. Bill Kovach and Tom Rosenstiel, *Blur: How to Know What's True in the Age of Information Overload* (New York: Bloomsbury, 2011).
31. Anthony Nadler, A. J. Bauer, and Magda Konieczna, *A Report on the Values and Practice of Online Journalists on the Right* (New York: Tow Center for Digital Journalism: A Tow/Knight Report 2020), https://doi.org/10.7916/d8-z16z-1g80.
32. Kovach and Rosenstiel, *Blur*, 49.
33. Ed Pilkington, "The Strange Case of Fox News, Trump, and the Death of Young Democrat Seth Rich," *Guardian*, August 7, 2017, https://www.theguardian.com/media/2017/aug/07/seth-rich-trump-white-house-fox-news.
34. Limbaugh, "Address to Incoming House GOP Freshmen."
35. Kate Lacey, *Listening Publics: The Politics and Experience of Listening in the Media Age* (New York: Wiley, 2013), 15.
36. Lacey, *Listening Publics*, 15.
37. Kovach and Rosenstiel, *Blur*, 40.
38. Bill Kovach and Tom Rosenstiel, *The Elements of Journalism: What Newspeople Should Know and the Public Should Expect* (New York: Three Rivers Press, 2014).

39. Kovach and Rosenstiel, *Blur*, 44.
40. Rosenwald, *Talk Radio's America*.
41. Kovach and Rosenstiel, *Blur*, 42.
42. Nadler et al., *A Report on the Values and Practice*.
43. Newman and Gallo, *Daily News Podcasts*, 13.
44. Nee and Santana, "Podcasting the Pandemic."
45. Nic Newman, "Inspired by The Daily, Dozens of Daily News Podcasts Are Punching Above Their Weight," *NiemanLab*, December 3, 2019.
46. Nee and Santana, "Podcasting the Pandemic," 2; for more on podcasting's transformation of journalistic norms, see Siobhán McHugh, "How Podcasting Is Changing the Audio Storytelling Genre," *Radio Journal—International Studies in Broadcast and Audio Media* 14, no. 1 (April 2016): 65–82; and Kobie van Krieken and José Sanders, "What Is Narrative Journalism? A Systematic Review and an Empirical Agenda," *Journalism* 22, no. 6 (2021): 1393–1412.
47. Nee and Santana, "Podcasting the Pandemic," 2.
48. David O. Dowling and Kyle J. Miller, "Immersive Audio Storytelling: Podcasting and Serial Documentary in the Digital Publishing Industry," *Journal of Radio & Audio Media* 26, no. 1 (2019): 167–184.
49. Martin Spinelli and Lance Dann, *Podcasting: The Audio Media Revolution* (New York: Bloomsbury, 2019), 193–194.
50. John Biewen and Alexa Dilworth, *Reality Radio: Telling True Stories in Sound*, 2nd ed. (Chapel Hill: University of North Carolina Press, 2017).
51. Kimberly Meltzer, *From News to Talk: The Expansion of Opinion and Commentary in U.S. Journalism* (Albany: SUNY Press 2020); and Biewen and Dilworth, *Reality Radio*.
52. Levendusky and Malhorta, "Does Media Coverage," 296.
53. Newman and Gallo, *Daily News Podcasts*, 23.
54. Elizabeth M. Perse and Jennifer Lambe, *Media Effects and Society* (New York: Routledge 2017).
55. Perse and Lambe, *Media Effects and Society*, 62.
56. Perse and Lambe, *Media Effects and Society*, 62.
57. Judd Legum and Tesnim Zekeria, "The Dirty Secret Behind Ben Shapiro's Extraordinary Success on Facebook," *Popular Information*, June 25, 2020, https://popular.info/p/the-dirty-secret-behind-ben-shapiros.
58. Nieborg and Poell, "The Platformization of Cultural Production"; and McChesney, *Rich Media, Poor Democracy*.
59. Aufderheide, et al., "Podcasting as Public Media," 1689.
60. Nieborg and Poell, "The Platformization of Cultural Production."
61. James Curran, *Media and Democracy* (London: Routledge 2011); Curran, "What Democracy Requires of the Media"; and David O. Dowling, "Toward a New

Aesthetic of Digital Literary Journalism: Charting the Fierce Evolution of the 'Supreme Nonfiction,'" *Literary Journalism Studies* 9, no. 1 (2017): 101–116.
62. Aufderheide, et al., "Podcasting as Public Media."
63. McChesney, *Rich Media, Poor Democracy*.
64. Brett Schafer, "How Spotify Can Lead the Podcast Market," *Motley Fool*, November 4, 2020, https://www.fool.com/investing/2020/10/29/how-spotify-can-lead-the-podcast-market/.
65. Aufderheide, et al., "Podcasting as Public Media."
66. Joe Rogan, "Alex Jones and Tim Dillon," episode 1555, in *The Joe Rogan Experience*, podcast audio, October 27, 2020.
67. Nicholas Quah, "Should Spotify Be Responsible for What Joe Rogan Does?," *New York*, November 3, 2020.
68. Andrew Marantz, *Antisocial: How Online Extremists Broke America* (New York: Pan Macmillan, 2019); Andrew Marantz, "Why Facebook Can't Fix Itself," *New Yorker*, October 20, 2020; and Aufderheide, et al., "Podcasting as Public Media."
69. Quah, "Should Spotify Be Responsible."
70. Aimee Morrison, "An Impossible Future: John Perry Barlow's 'Declaration of the Independence of Cyberspace,'" *New Media & Society* 11, no. 1–2 (2009): 53–71.
71. Nadler and Bauer, *News on the Right*.
72. Julia Alexander, "YouTube Bans Steven Molyneux, David Duke, Richard Spencer, and More for Hate Speech," *The Verge*, June 29, 2020.
73. Crystal Tellis, "Anchor Platform Redefines Podcast Potential to Independent Creators," *Medium*, January 15, 2019.
74. Schafer, "How Spotify Can Lead."
75. Schafer, "How Spotify Can Lead."
76. Schafer, "How Spotify Can Lead."
77. Schafer, "How Spotify Can Lead."
78. Travis Vogan and David Dowling, "Bill Simmons, Grantland.com, and ESPN's Corporate Reinvention of Literary Sports Writing Online," *Convergence* 22, no. 1 (2016): 18–34.
79. Nicholas Quah, "Bill Simmons Just Wants to Win," *New York*, May 19, 2020.
80. Vogan and Dowling, "Bill Simmons, Grantland.com."
81. Aufderheide, et al., "Podcasting as Public Media," 1692.
82. Aufderheide, et al., "Podcasting as Public Media."
83. Rachel Sussman-Wander Kaplan, "The Fandom of Howard Stern and Its Relationship to His Success: The King of All Media and a Dynamic Audience," in *Radio's Second Century: Past, Present, and Future Perspectives*, ed. John Allen Hendricks, 82–95 (New Brunswick, N.J.: Rutgers University Press 2020).
84. Ira Glass, "We Just Won the First-Ever Pulitzer for Audio Journalism!," *This American Life*, May 4, 2020.

85. Nicholas Quah, "The Left Right Game," *HotPod*, November 17, 2020.
86. Rush Limbaugh, *The Rush Limbaugh Show*, Premiere Networks, podcast audio, (2021).
87. Quah, "The Left Right Game."
88. Kevin Roose, "Dan Bongino Has No Idea Why Facebook Loves Him," *New York Times*, October 29, 2020.
89. Laith Zuraikat, "The Parasocial Nature of the Podcast," in *Radio's Second Century: Past, Present, and Future Perspectives*, ed. John Allen Hendricks, 39–52 (New Brunswick, N.J.: Rutgers University Press, 2020).
90. Quah, "The Left Right Game."
91. Quah, "The Left Right Game."
92. Aufderheide, et al., "Podcasting as Public Media," 1688.
93. Quah, "The Left Right Game."
94. Dan Bongino, "About Yesterday," in *The Dan Bongino Show*, Westwood One, podcast audio, January 7, 2021.
95. Bongino, "About Yesterday."
96. Bongino, "About Yesterday."
97. Bongino, "About Yesterday."
98. Bongino, "About Yesterday."
99. Bongino, "About Yesterday."
100. Roose, "Dan Bongino Has No Idea."
101. Roose, "Dan Bongino Has No Idea."
102. Roose, "Dan Bongino Has No Idea."
103. Roose, "Dan Bongino Has No Idea."
104. Benedict Nicholson, "These Were the Top Publishers on Facebook in August 2020," *NewsWhip*, September 17, 2020.
105. Legum and Zekeria, "The Dirty Secret."
106. Legum and Zekeria, "The Dirty Secret."
107. Emma Vickers, Joe Carroll, and Tom Maloney, "Billionaire Fracking Brothers Hammered by Permian Holdings," *Financial Post*, November 21, 2019.
108. Vickers et al., "Billionaire Fracking Brothers."
109. Ben Shapiro, "The Worst Day in Modern American Political History," in *The Ben Shapiro Show*, The Daily Wire, podcast audio, January 7, 2021.
110. Shapiro, "The Worst Day."
111. Shapiro, "The Worst Day."
112. "Far-Right Digital Media Paved the Way for the Riot in Washington," *Economist*, January 7, 2021.
113. "Far-Right Digital Media."
114. Anna Bauman and Meghna Chakrabarti, "How Right-Wing Media Fuels the Political Divide," *On Point*, WBUR Boston, November 23, 2020.

115. Bauman and Chakrabarti, "How Right-Wing Media."
116. Bauman and Chakrabarti, "How Right-Wing Media."
117. Bauman and Chakrabarti, "How Right-Wing Media."
118. Bauman and Chakrabarti, "How Right-Wing Media."
119. Bauman and Chakrabarti, "How Right-Wing Media."
120. Bauman and Chakrabarti, "How Right-Wing Media."
121. Michael M. Grynbaum, "Where Will Rush Limbaugh's 50 Million Listeners Go Now?," *New York Times*, February 20, 2021.
122. Grynbaum, "Where Will Rush Limbaugh's."
123. Nikolas Lanum, "Rush Limbaugh Praised by Dan Bongino: He Was 'What Conservatism Was About,'" *Fox News*, February 18, 2021.
124. Joseph A. Wulfsohn, "Dan Bongino to Take Over Rush Limbaugh's Radio Time Slot," *Fox News*, March 18, 2021.
125. Wulfsohn, "Dan Bongino to Take Over."
126. Wulfsohn, "Dan Bongino to Take Over"; and Meltzer, *From News to Talk*.
127. Jeremy W. Peters, "Rush Limbaugh's Legacy of Venom: As Trump Rose, 'It All Sounded Familiar,'" *New York Times*, February 17, 2021.
128. Rosenwald, *Talk Radio's America*.
129. Peters, "Rush Limbaugh's Legacy of Venom."
130. Manoel Horta Ribeiro, Raphael Ottoni, Robert West, Virgílio A. F. Almeida, and Wagner Meira, "Auditing Radicalization Pathways on YouTube," *FAT* '20: Proceedings of the 2020 Conference on Fairness, Accountability, and Transparency*, general chairs, Mireille Hildebrandt and Carlos Castillo, 131–141 (New York: Association for Computing Machinery, January 2020), https://doi.org/10.1145/3351095.3372879.
131. David Ryfe, *Journalism and the Public* (Cambridge: Polity, 2017).
132. Matt Carlson, *Journalistic Authority* (New York: Columbia University Press 2017); and David O. Dowling, Patrick Johnson, and Brian Ekdale, "Hijacking Journalism: Legitimacy and Metajournalistic Discourse in Right-Wing Podcasts," *Media and Communication* 10, no. 3 (2022): 17–27.
133. Matt Grossman and David A. Hopkins, *Asymmetric Politics: Ideological Republicans and Group Interest Democrats* (Oxford: Oxford University Press 2016).

6. VOICES FROM THE MARGINS

1. *The Nielsen Total Audience Report 2021* (2021), https://www.nielsen.com/insights/2021/total-audience-advertising-across-todays-media/.
2. Elizabeth Jensen, "New On-Air Source Diversity Data for NPR Show Much Work Ahead," *NPR Public Editor*, December 17, 2019.

3. Elizabeth Jensen, "NPR Staff Diversity Numbers, 2019," *NPR Public Editor*, November 19, 2019.
4. Jensen, "NPR Staff Diversity Numbers."
5. Kim Fox, David O. Dowling, and Kyle Miller, "A Curriculum for Blackness: Podcasts as Discursive Cultural Guides, 2010–2020," *Journal of Radio & Audio Media* 27, no. 2 (2020): 293–318.
6. Martin Spinelli and Lance Dann, *Podcasting: The Audio Media Revolution* (New York: Bloomsbury, 2019), 136.
7. Spinelli and Dann, *Podcasting*, 136.
8. Photini Vrikki and Sarita Malik, "Voicing Lived Experience and Anti-Racism: Podcasting as a Space at the Margins for Subaltern Counterpublics," *Popular Communication* 17, no. 44 (2019): 279.
9. Roshanak Kheshti, "Touching Listening: The Aural Imaginary in the World Music Culture Industry," in *Sound Clash: Listening to American Studies*, ed. Kara Keeling and Josh Kun, 267–288 (Baltimore: Johns Hopkins University Press, 2012).
10. Anjuli Joshi Brekke, "The Sound of Yellow Rain: Resisting Podcasting's Sonic Whiteness," in *Radio's Second Century: Past, Present, and Future Perspectives*, ed. John Allen Hendricks, 173–190 (New Brunswick, N.J.: Rutgers University Press 2020); and Marie Thompson, "Whiteness and the Ontological Turn in Sound Studies," *Parallax* 23, no. 3 (2017): 266–282.
11. Chenjerai Kumanyika, "Challenging the Whiteness of Public Radio," *NPR: Code Switch*, January 29, 2015.
12. Spinelli and Dann, *Podcasting*, 134.
13. Thompson, "Whiteness and the Ontological Turn."
14. Kheshti, "Touching Listening," 268.
15. Vrikki and Malik, "Voicing Lived Experience and Anti-Racism," 274.
16. Rebecca Mead, "Binge Listening: How Podcasts Became a Seductive—and Slippery—New Mode of Storytelling," *New Yorker*, November 19, 2018; and Mia Lindgren, "Personal Narrative Journalism and Podcasting," *Radio Journal: International Studies in Broadcast & Audio Media* 14, no. 1 (2016): 28.
17. Ira Glass, "RadioLab: An Appreciation by Ira Glass," *Transom* 11, no. 6 (November 8, 2011), https://transom.org/wp-content/uploads/2011/09/Ira_Glass-Transom_Review2.pdf.
18. Mead, "Binge Listening."
19. Mead, "Binge Listening."
20. Mead, "Binge Listening."
21. Katherine Rosman and Reggie Ugwu, "What Really Happened at 'Reply All?,'" *New York Times*, March 10, 2021.

22. Nicholas Quah, "Podcasts About Race Are Climbing the Charts, and Coronavirus Shows Drop Out," *Nieman Lab*, June 9, 2020.
23. Matthew Schneier, "The Voice of a Generation: Michael Barbaro Made the New York *Times* Podcast a Raging Success. Or Is It the Other Way Around?," *New York*, January 21, 2020.
24. Schneier, "The Voice of a Generation."
25. Dolores Inés Casillas, *Sounds of Belonging: U.S. Spanish-Language Radio and Public Advocacy* (New York: New York University Press 2014).
26. Laura Garbes, "'I Just Don't Hear It': How Whiteness Dilutes Voices of Color at Public Radio Stations," *American Prospect*, August 18, 2020.
27. Garbes, "'I Just Don't Hear It.'"
28. Sarah Larson, "'The Nod,' A Playful and Serious Podcast About Blackness," *New Yorker*, September 28, 2017.
29. Garbes, "'I Just Don't Hear It.'"
30. Thompson, "Whiteness and the Ontological Turn," 274.
31. Brekke, "The Sound of Yellow Rain."
32. David B. Nieborg and Thomas Poell, "The Platformization of Cultural Production: Theorizing the Contingent Cultural Commodity," *New Media & Society* 20, no. 11, (2018): 4276, emphasis in original.
33. Vrikki and Malik, "Voicing Lived Experience and Anti-Racism," 274.
34. Virginia Eubanks, *Automating Inequality: How Hi-Tech Tools Profile, Police, and Punish the Poor* (New York: St. Martin's, 2018).
35. Vrikki and Malik, "Voicing Lived Experience and Anti-Racism," 274.
36. Garbes, "'I Just Don't Hear It.'"
37. Garbes, "'I Just Don't Hear It.'"
38. Justine Goode, "Listen Up: 12 Podcasts About Race, Social Justice, and Black History," *Vanity Fair*, February 8, 2021.
39. Garbes, "'I Just Don't Hear It.'"
40. Garbes, "'I Just Don't Hear It.'"
41. Sarah Florini, "The Podcast 'Chitlin Circuit': Black Podcasters, Alternative Media, and Audio Enclaves," *Journal of Radio & Audio Media* 22, no. 2 (2015): 209–219.
42. Florini, "The Podcast 'Chitlin Circuit,'" 214.
43. Brekke, "The Sound of Yellow Rain," 177.
44. Brekke, "The Sound of Yellow Rain," 177.
45. Florini, "The Podcast 'Chitlin Circuit,'" 210.
46. Florini, "The Podcast 'Chitlin Circuit,'" 210.
47. Vrikki and Malik, "Voicing Lived Experience and Anti-Racism," 279.
48. Davy Sims, Podcasting interview, *Davy Sims*, July 30, 2017, https://www.davysims.com/2017/07/podcasting-interview/.

49. Kim Fox, Twitter correspondence with Elon James White, February 6, 2020.
50. Fox, Twitter correspondence with Elon James White.
51. Andrew J. Bottomley, "Podcasting: A Decade in the Life of a 'New' Audio Medium: Introduction," *Journal of Radio & Audio Media* 22, no. 2 (2015): 164–169; and Fox et al., "A Curriculum for Blackness."
52. Fox et al., "A Curriculum for Blackness."
53. Vrikki and Malik, "Voicing Lived Experience and Anti-Racism," 275.
54. Vrikki and Malik, "Voicing Lived Experience and Anti-Racism," 276.
55. Vrikki and Malik, "Voicing Lived Experience and Anti-Racism," 276.
56. Vrikki and Malik, "Voicing Lived Experience and Anti-Racism," 276; and Garbes, "'I Just Don't Hear It.'"
57. Sarah Florini, *Beyond Hashtags: Racial Politics and Black Digital Networks* (New York: New York University Press, 2019), 13.
58. Florini, *Beyond Hashtags*, 39.
59. Lindgren, "Personal Narrative Journalism and Podcasting."
60. Larson, "'The Nod.'"
61. Larson, "'The Nod.'"
62. Larson, "'The Nod.'"
63. Gwendolyn D. Pough, *Check It While I Wreck It: Black Womanhood, Hip-Hop Culture, and The Public Sphere* (Lebanon, N.H.: University Press of New England 2004); and Johnnetta Betsch Cole and Beverly Guy-Sheftall Cole, *Gender Talk: The Struggle for Women's Equality in African-American Communities* (New York: One World 2009).
64. Ashley Carman, "The Nod Hosts Ditch Spotify to Relaunch Their Original Show," *The Verge*, August 2, 2021.
65. Carman, "The Nod Hosts Ditch Spotify."
66. Pough, *Check It While I Wreck It*, 56.
67. Pough, *Check It While I Wreck It*, 73; see also Cole and Guy-Sheftall, *Gender Talk*.
68. Johnathan Charles Flowers, "How Is It Okay to Be a Black Nerd?," in *Age of the Geek: Depictions of Nerds and Geeks in Popular Media*, ed. Kathryn E. Lane, 169–192 (London: Palgrave Macmillan, 2018), 171.
69. Larson, "'The Nod.'"
70. Kris M. Markman, "Doing Radio, Making Friends, and Having Fun: Exploring the Motivations of Independent Audio Podcasters," *New Media & Society* 14, no. 4 (2012): 556.
71. Markman, "Doing Radio, Making Friends," 556.
72. Clint C. Wilson II, Félix Guttiérrez, and Lena M. Chao, *Racism, Sexism, and the Media: Multicultural Issues in the New Communications Age* (Los Angeles: Sage 2013); and Juan Gonzalez and Joseph Torres, *News for All the People: The Epic Story of Race and the American Media* (New York: Verso 2011).

73. Brittany Luse and Eric Eddings, "Ready, Set . . . Buy Black," in *The Nod*, podcast audio, Gimlet Media, November 27, 2017.
74. Quah, "Podcasts about Race."
75. Charli Valdez, "*Serial's* Aspirational Aesthetics and Racial Erasure," in *The Serial Podcast and Storytelling in the Digital Age*, ed. Ellen McCracken, 101–113 (London: Taylor & Francis Group 2017).
76. Kobie van Krieken and José Sanders, "What Is Narrative Journalism? A Systematic Review and an Empirical Agenda," *Journalism* 22, no. 6 (2021): 1393–1412; Geoffrey Baym, "Journalism and the Hybrid Condition: Long-Form Television Drama at the Intersection of News and Narrative," *Journalism* 18, no. 1 (2017): 11–26; and Mary Beth Oliver, James Price Dillard, Keunmin Bae, and Daniel J. Tamul, "The Effect of Narrative News Format on Empathy for Stigmatized Groups," *Journalism & Mass Communication Quarterly* 89, no. 2 (2012): 205–224.
77. Fox et al., "A Curriculum for Blackness."
78. Megan Le Masurier, "What Is Slow Journalism?" *Journalism Practice* 9, no. 2 (December 2014): 1–15; Erik Neveu, "Revisiting Narrative Journalism as One of the Futures of Journalism," *Journalism Studies* 15, no. 5 (2014): 533–542; and Roberto Suro, Introduction to *Writing Immigration: Scholars and Journalists in Dialogue*, ed. Marcelo Suarez-Orozco, Vivian Louie, and Roberto Suro, 1–18 (Berkeley: University of California Press 2011).
79. Carol Pauli, "Whole Other Story: Applying Narrative Mediation to the Immigration Beat," *Cardozo Journal of Conflict Resolution* 18 (2016): 23–70; and Dolors Palau-Sampio, "Reframing Central American Migration from Narrative Journalism," *Journal of Communication Inquiry* 43, no. 1 (2019): 93–114.
80. David García-Marín, "Mapping the Factors that Determine Engagement in Podcasting: Design from the Users and Podcasters' Experience," *Communication & Society* 33, no. 2 (2020): 22, https://doi.org/10.15581/003.33.2.49-63.
81. Tiziano Bonini, "The Second Age of Podcasting: Reframing Podcasting as a New Digital Mass Medium," *Quaderns del CAC* 41 (2015): 23–33; and Caroline Crampton, "The Problem with the Inconsequential Quest," *Hot Pod News*, October 6, 2020.
82. Nicholas Quah, "The Best Podcasts of 2019," *Vulture*, December 5, 2019.
83. Kevin Moloney, "All the News That's Fit to Push: The New York Times Company and Transmedia Daily News," *International Journal of Communication* 14 (2020): 4683–4702.
84. Nikole Hannah-Jones, "The Fight for a True Democracy," in *1619*, podcast audio, *New York Times*, August 23, 2019.
85. Tom Jones, "A Deeper Look into the Controversy of The New York Times' '1619 Project,'" *Poynter*, October 14, 2020.

86. Deepa Shivaram, "Nikole Hannah-Jones Chose Howard Over UNC. HBCUs Hope It's the Start of a New Era," *NPR*, July 13, 2021.

87. Milan Kundera, quoted in Stephen Smith, "Living History," in *Reality Radio: Telling True Stories in Sound*, 2nd ed., ed. John Biewen and Alexa Dilworth, 182–193 (Chapel Hill: University of North Carolina Press 2017), 190.

88. Earnest L. Perry, "Teaching History in the Age of Black Lives Matter: Embracing the Narratives of the Long Struggle for Civil Rights," *American Journalism* 33, no. 4 (2016): 467, 468.

89. Kundera, quoted in Stephen Smith, "Living History," 190.

90. Smith, "Living History," 193.

91. Maria Martin, "Crossing Borders," in *Reality Radio: Telling True Stories in Sound*, 2nd ed., ed. John Biewen and Alexa Dilworth, 204–211 (Chapel Hill: University of North Carolina Press 2017), 206.

92. Martin, "Crossing Borders."

93. Commission on Freedom of the Press, *A Free and Responsible Press: A General Report on Mass Communication: Newspapers, Radio, Motion Pictures, Magazines, and Books* (Chicago: University of Chicago Press, 1947), 26.

94. Martin, "Crossing Borders," 207.

95. Martin, "Crossing Borders," 207.

96. Palau-Sampio, "Reframing Central American Migration from Narrative Journalism," 93.

97. Martin, "Crossing Borders," 207.

98. Emilce Quiroz, "I Am a Cholo," in *Latino USA*, podcast audio, PRX, June 11, 2021.

99. Quiroz, "I am a Cholo."

100. Quiroz, "I am a Cholo."

101. Will Coley, "Episode 1: Land of the Free, But Only for Some," in *Indefensible*, podcast audio, Immigration Defense Project, January 18, 2017.

102. Coley, "Episode 1."

103. Coley, "Episode 1."

104. Mizue Aizeki, "'Indefensible': Stories of Resilience in the Face of Deportation," *Medium*, May 25, 2017.

105. Jessica Luther, Shireen Ahmed, and Lindsay Gibbs, "Trans Women and Trans Girls Belong in Women's Sport," episode 195, in *Burn It All Down*, podcast audio, Blue Wire, March 2, 2021.

106. Vrikki and Malik, "Voicing Lived Experience and Anti-Racism," 280; and Nancy Fraser, "Rethinking the Public Sphere: A Contribution to the Critique of Actually Existing Democracy," in *Habermas and the Public Sphere*, ed. Craig J. Calhoun, 109–142 (Boston: MIT Press 1992), 123.

107. Aria Bracci, "Audio and the Queering of Gender, Part I–II," *Hot Pod*, episodes 331 and 332, June 22 and 29, 2021.

108. Bracci, "Audio and the Queering of Gender, Part I–II."
109. Roland Barthes, *Image, Music, Text* (New York: Hill and Wang, 1977).
110. Bracci, "Audio and the Queering of Gender, Part I–II."
111. Bracci, "Audio and the Queering of Gender, Part I–II."
112. Bracci, "Audio and the Queering of Gender, Part I–II."
113. Jaison Gardner and Kaila Story, "The 'Jim Crow Mentality' of Social Media Trolls," in *Strange Fruit*, podcast audio, Louisville Public Media, November 10, 2020.
114. Vrikki and Malik, "Voicing Lived Experience and Anti-Racism," 274.
115. Vrikki and Malik, "Voicing Lived Experience and Anti-Racism," 274.
116. Fox et al., "A Curriculum for Blackness."
117. Vrikki and Malik, "Voicing Lived Experience and Anti-Racism," 282.
118. Fox et al., "A Curriculum for Blackness."
119. Vrikki and Malik, "Voicing Lived Experience and Anti-Racism," 283.
120. Vrikki and Malik, "Voicing Lived Experience and Anti-Racism," 283.
121. Fox et al., "A Curriculum for Blackness," 3.

7. THE PROFIT MOTIVE

1. Brandon R. Einstein, "Reading Between the Lines: The Rise of Native Advertising and the FTC's Inability to Regulate It," *Brooklyn Journal of Corporate, Financial & Commercial Law* 10, no. 1 (2015).
2. Andrew Marantz, "The Virologist," *New Yorker*, January 5, 2015.
3. David Yaffee-Bellany, "Welcome to McDonald's. Would You Like a Podcast with That?," *New York Times*, August 20, 2019.
4. Nicholas Quah, "Apple and Spotify Are Ready to Take Your Podcast Money," *New York*, April 17, 2021.
5. Martin Spinelli and Lance Dann, *Podcasting: The Audio Media Revolution* (New York: Bloomsbury, 2019), 71.
6. Raul Ferrer-Conill, "Camouflaging Church as State: An Exploratory Study of Journalism's Native Advertising," *Journalism Studies* 17, no. 7 (2016): 905.
7. Larry Rosin, quoted in Spinelli and Dann, *Podcasting*, 180.
8. Spinelli and Dann, *Podcasting*, 212.
9. Raul Ferrer-Conill, Erik Knudsen, Corinna Lauerer, and Aviv Barnoy, "The Visual Boundaries of Journalism: Native Advertising and the Convergence of Editorial and Commercial Content," *Digital Journalism* 9, no. 7 (2020): 946.
10. Siobhán McHugh, "How Podcasting Is Changing the Audio Storytelling Genre," *Radio Journal—International Studies in Broadcast and Audio Media* 14, no. 1 (April 2016): 75.
11. Spinelli and Dann, *Podcasting*, 212.

12. McHugh, "How Podcasting Is Changing," 75; and Felicia Greiff, "Ira Glass: 'Public Radio Is Ready for Capitalism,'" *Advertising Age*, April 30, 2015.
13. Mark Deuze and Tamara Witschge, "Beyond Journalism: Theorizing the Transformation of Journalism," *Journalism* 19, no. 2 (2018): 168.
14. Mitchell Stephens, *Beyond News: The Future of Journalism* (New York: Columbia University Press, 2014), xii, xiii.
15. Peter Bro and Filip Wallberg, "Gatekeeping in a Digital Era: Principles, Practices and Technological Platforms," *Journalism Practice* 9, no. 1 (2015): 92–105; Melissa Wall, "Citizen Journalism: A Retrospective on What We Know, an Agenda for What We Don't," *Digital Journalism* 3, no. 6 (2015): 797–813; and Tony Harcup and Deirdre O'Neill, "What Is News? News Values Revisited (Again)," *Journalism Studies* 18, no. 12 (2017): 1470–1488.
16. Einstein, "Reading Between the Lines"; and Ferrer-Conill et al., "The Visual Boundaries of Journalism."
17. Einstein, "Reading Between the Lines."
18. Gabe Mythen, "Reframing Risk: Citizen Journalism and the Transformation of News," *Journal of Risk Research* 13, no. 1 (2010): 45–58.
19. Ángel Arrese and Francisco J. Pérez-Latre, "The Rise of Brand Journalism," in *Commercial Communication in the Digital Age: Information or Disinformation?*, ed. Gabriele Siegert, Björn von Rimscha, and Stephanie Grubenmann, 121–139 (Berlin: De Gruyter Mouton, 2017), 124.
20. Gabriella Perdomo and Philippe Rodrigues-Rouleau, "Transparency as Metajournalistic Performance: *The New York Times' Caliphate* Podcast and New Ways to Claim Journalistic Authority," *Journalism* 23, no. 11 (2021): 2311–2327, http://dx.doi.org/10.1177/1464884921997312.
21. Richard van der Wurff and Klas Schönbach, "Between Profession and Audience," *Journalism Studies* 12, no. 4 (2011): 418.
22. Deuze and Witschge, "Beyond Journalism," 167; see also Mark Deuze, "What Is Journalism? Professional Identity and Ideology of Journalists Reconsidered," *Journalism* 6, no. 4 (2005): 442–464.
23. Matt Carlson, Introduction to *Boundaries of Journalism: Professionalism, Practices and Participation*, ed. Matt Carlson and Seth Lewis, 1–18 (Abingdon, N.Y.: Routledge 2015), 2.
24. David O. Dowling, *The Gamification of Digital Journalism: Innovation in Journalistic Storytelling* (New York: Routledge 2021), 43.
25. Keith Hernandez, "Introduction to Content Marketing with BuzzFeed," *Google Small Business*, YouTube video, May 28, 2015; and Mara Einstein, *Black Ops Advertising: Native Ads, Content Marketing, and the Covert World of the Digital Sell* (New York: OR Books, 2016).

26. David Dowling and Travis Vogan, "Longform Narrative Journalism: 'Snow Fall' and Beyond," in *The Routledge Companion to Digital Journalism Studies*, ed. Bob Franklin and Scott A. Eldridge II, 478–486 (New York: Routledge 2017).
27. David O. Dowling, *Immersive Longform Storytelling: Media, Technology, Audience* (New York: Routledge, 2019).
28. Christopher William Anderson, Emily Bell, and Clay Shirky, *Post-Industrial Journalism: Adapting to the Present* (New York: Tow Center for Digital Journalism, 2012).
29. Deuze and Witschge, "Beyond Journalism," 177; see also Mark Deuze, "The Changing Context of News Work: Liquid Journalism for a Monitorial Citizenry," *International Journal of Communication* 2 (2008): 848–865.
30. G. Stuart Adam, "Notes Towards a Definition of Journalism: Understanding an Old Craft as an Art Form," in *Journalism: The Democratic Craft*, ed. G. Stuart Adam and Roy Peter Clark (New York: Oxford University Press 2006), 345.
31. Bill Kovarik, *Revolutions in Communication: Media History from Gutenberg to the Digital Age*, 2nd ed. (New York: Bloomsbury 2016), 218.
32. Kovarik, *Revolutions in Communication*, 218.
33. Anderson, et al., *Post-Industrial Journalism*, 76.
34. Ferrer-Conill et al., "The Visual Boundaries of Journalism," 5.
35. Nikki Usher, "Re-Thinking Trust in the News: A Material Approach through 'Objects of Journalism,'" *Journalism Studies* 19, no. 4 (2018): 572.
36. Matt Carlson and Seth Lewis, "Boundary Work," in *The Handbook of Journalism Studies*, ed. Karin Wahl-Jorgenson and Thomas Hanitzsch, 123–35 (New York: Routledge, 2020), 126.
37. Carlson and Lewis, "Boundary Work," 126–127.
38. Deuze and Witschge, "Beyond Journalism," 168.
39. Matt Carlson and Seth Lewis, eds., *Boundaries of Journalism: Professionalism, Practices and Participation* (Abingdon, N.Y.: Routledge 2015); and Chris Paterson and David Domingo, eds., *Making Online News: The Ethnography of New Media Production*, 2 vols. (New York: Peter Lang 2011).
40. Spinelli and Dann, *Podcasting*, 217.
41. Spinelli and Dann, *Podcasting*, 217.
42. Rebecca Mead, "Binge Listening: How Podcasts Became a Seductive—and Slippery—New Mode of Storytelling," *New Yorker*, November 19, 2018.
43. Quah, "Apple and Spotify Are Ready."
44. Quah, "Apple and Spotify Are Ready."
45. Deuze and Witschge, "Beyond Journalism," 166–167.
46. Deuze and Witschge, "Beyond Journalism," 174–175.
47. Ferrer-Conill et al., "The Visual Boundaries of Journalism."
48. Ferrer-Conill et al., "The Visual Boundaries of Journalism," 18.

49. Ferrer-Conill et al., "The Visual Boundaries of Journalism," 18.
50. Ferrer-Conill et al., "The Visual Boundaries of Journalism," 12.
51. Simone Krouwer, Karolien Poels, and Steve Paulussen, "Moving Towards Transparency for Native Advertisements on News Websites: A Test of More Detailed Disclosures," *International Journal of Advertising* 39, no. 1 (2020): 51–73.
52. Jerry Ascierto, "How Brands Can Find New Audiences Through Podcasts," *Social Shake Up*, July 10, 2017.
53. Jessica Abel, *Out on the Wire: The Storytelling Secrets of the New Masters of Radio* (Portland: Broadway Books, 2015), 10.
54. Spinelli and Dann, *Podcasting*, 217.
55. Mike Rugnetta, "Advancing the Tech of Diabetes Decision-Making," in *Health Tech on the Horizon*, podcast audio, Abbott, December 11, 2020.
56. "Strengthening Communities Through the Starbucks Neighborhood Foundation Grants," *Starbucks Stories and News*, June 8, 2021.
57. "Strengthening Communities."
58. Howard Schultz and Rajiv Chandrasekaran, "Scholarships for Every Student," in *Upstanders*, podcast audio, *Starbucks Stories and News*, September 15, 2016.
59. Schultz and Chandrasekaran, "Scholarships for Every Student."
60. Arthur C. Danto, *What Art Is* (New Haven, Conn.: Yale University Press 2013), 136.
61. Schultz and Chandrasekaran, "Scholarships for Every Student."
62. Stijn Postema and Mark Deuze, "Artistic Journalism: Confluence in Forms, Values, and Practices," *Journalism Studies* 21, no. 10 (2020): 1311.
63. Schultz and Chandrasekaran, "Scholarships for Every Student."
64. Ava Sirrah, "Guide to Native Advertising," *Tow Center for Digital Journalism*, September 6, 2019.
65. Sirrah, "Guide to Native Advertising."
66. Sirrah, "Guide to Native Advertising."
67. Schultz and Chandrasekaran, "Scholarships for Every Student."
68. Sirrah, "Guide to Native Advertising."
69. Carlson and Lewis, "Boundary Work."
70. Jamal Booker, "Jim Dinkins—Writing Our Next Chapter Together," in *Total Refresh*, podcast audio, Coca-Cola Company, July 8, 2019. See also Perdomo and Rodrigues-Rouleau, "Transparency as Metajournalistic Performance."
71. Perdomo and Rodrigues-Rouleau, "Transparency as Metajournalistic Performance."
72. David Ryfe, *Can Journalism Survive? An Inside Look at Newsrooms* (Cambridge: Polity, 2012).
73. Matt Carlson, "Metajournalistic Discourse and the Meanings of Journalism: Definitional Control, Boundary Work, and Legitimation," *Communication Theory* 26, no. 4 (2016): 349–368.

74. Perdomo and Rodrigues-Rouleau, "Transparency as Metajournalistic Performance," 5.
75. Perdomo and Rodrigues-Rouleau, "Transparency as Metajournalistic Performance," 5.
76. Ros Coward, *Speaking Personally: The Rise of Subjective and Confessional Journalism* (New York: Palgrave, 2013).
77. Mia Lindgren, "Personal Narrative Journalism and Podcasting," *Radio Journal: International Studies in Broadcast & Audio Media* 14, no. 1 (2016): 24.
78. Booker, "Jim Dinkins."
79. Jamal Booker, "Coca-Cola Executives Open Up About Leadership, Growth, and More in Company's First Podcast Series," *Coca-Cola Company News*, April 9, 2019.
80. Booker, "Coca-Cola Executives Open Up."
81. Booker, "Jim Dinkins."
82. Catherine LeClair, "Good Intentions," in *The Sauce*, podcast audio, McDonald's, January 13, 2021.
83. Yaffee-Bellany, "Welcome to McDonald's."
84. Claus Ebster and Riem Khalil, "Trader Joe's: An Experiential Discount Retailer Conquers the Culinary Seas," in *Fallstudien aus der Österreichischen Marketingpraxis*, no. 8, ed. Udo Wagner, Heribert Reisinger and Karl Akbari, 15–28 (Vienna: Facultas, 2018).
85. Ebster and Khalil, "Trader Joe's," 25.
86. Ebster and Khalil, "Trader Joe's," 25.
87. Tara Miller and Matt Sloan, "Episode 16: Produce," in *Inside Trader Joe's*, podcast audio, July 22, 2019.
88. Miller and Sloan, "Episode 16: Produce."
89. Sirrah, "Guide to Native Advertising."
90. Sirrah, "Guide to Native Advertising."
91. Frank Racioppi, "How Podcasts Have Changed in the Last Decade (and Predictions for the Future)," *Discover Pods*, July 31, 2019.
92. Racioppi, "How Podcasts Have Changed."

EPILOGUE

1. Nicholas Quah, "The Best Podcasts of 2019," *Vulture*, December 5, 2019.
2. Kevin Moloney, "All the News That's Fit to Push: The New York Times Company and Transmedia Daily News," *International Journal of Communication* 14 (2020): 4688.
3. Moloney, "All the News That's Fit to Push," 4689.

4. Brad Clark and Archie Mclean, "Revenge of the Nerds: How Public Radio Dominated Podcasting and Transformed Listening to Audio," in *Radio's Second Century*, ed. John Allen Hendricks, 207–230 (New Brunswick, N.J.: Rutgers University Press 2020), 213.
5. Michael Karlsson, "The Immediacy of Online News, the Visibility of Journalistic Processes and a Restructuring of Journalistic Authority," *Journalism* 12, no. 13 (2011): 282.
6. Clark and Mclean, "Revenge of the Nerds," 213.
7. Jon Friedman, "NPR: Don't Give Us the 'Elitist' Label," *MarketWatch*, October 20, 2010, https://www.marketwatch.com/story/you-can-call-npr-stuffy-but-not-elitist-2010-10-20.
8. Elisa Shearer and Jacob Liedke, "Audio and Podcasting Fact Sheet," Pew Research Center, June 29, 2021.
9. Shearer and Liedke, "Audio and Podcasting Fact Sheet."
10. John Mark Dempsey, "'A More Inclusive Public Service': Can NPR Serve All of America?," in *Radio's Second Century*, ed. John Allen Hendricks, 154–172 (New Brunswick, N.J.: Rutgers University Press 2020).
11. "NPR Audience Opportunity Study: Summary of Key Takeaways," *Current*, Summer 2010, https://www.readkong.com/page/audience-opportunity-study-summary-of-key-takeaways-2261010; and Karen Everhart, "Study Sees Growth if NPR Loosens Up, Sounds Less Elite," *Current*, September 20, 2010.
12. Clark and Mclean, "Revenge of the Nerds," 218.
13. Clark and Mclean, "Revenge of the Nerds," 225.
14. Mia Lindgren, "Personal Narrative Journalism and Podcasting," *Radio Journal: International Studies in Broadcast & Audio Media* 14, no. 1 (2016): 23–41.
15. Martin Spinelli and Lance Dann, *Podcasting: The Audio Media Revolution* (New York: Bloomsbury, 2019), 229.
16. Bill Kovach and Tom Rosenstiel, *Blur: How to Know What's True in the Age of Information Overload* (New York: Bloomsbury, 2011), 30.
17. Margaret Sullivan, "What's a Journalist Supposed to Be Now—an Activist?" *Washington Post*, June 7, 2020.
18. Sullivan, "What's a Journalist Supposed to Be Now."
19. Karin Wahl-Jorgensen and Thomas Schmidt, "News and Storytelling," in *The Handbook of Journalism Studies*, ed. Karin Wahl-Jorgensen and Thomas Hanitzsch, 261–276 (New York: Routledge, 2020), 261.
20. Barbie Zelizer, *Taking Journalism Seriously: News and the Academy* (Thousand Oaks, Calif.: Sage, 2004), 130.
21. Kobie van Krieken and José Sanders, "What Is Narrative Journalism? A Systematic Review and an Empirical Agenda," *Journalism* 22, no. 6 (2021):

1393–1412; Isabel Soares, "Where Travel Meets Literary Journalism," *Literary Journalism Studies* 1, no. 1 (2009): 17–30; and Kate Willman, "Unidentified Narrative Objects: Approaching Instant History Through Experiments with Literary Journalism in Beppe Sebaste's *H. P. Lady Diana's Last Driver* and Frédéric Beigbeder's *Windows on the World*," *Journalism* 21, no. 7 (2020): 1007–1022.

22. Josh Roiland, "By Any Other Name: The Case for Literary Journalism," *Literary Journalism Studies* 7, no. 2 (2015): 71.
23. Wahl-Jorgensen and Schmidt, "News and Storytelling," 261; see also Stijn Postema and Mark Deuze, "Artistic Journalism: Confluence in Forms, Values, and Practices," *Journalism Studies* 21, no. 10 (2020): 1305–1322.
24. John Tulloch, "Ethics, Trust and the First Person in the Narration of Long-Form Journalism." *Journalism* 15, no. 5 (2014): 629–638.
25. Michael Blanding, "Where Does Activism End and Journalism Begin?," *Nieman Reports*, August 21, 2018; and Wesley Lowery, "A Reckoning over Objectivity, Led by Black Journalists," *New York Times*, June 23, 2020.
26. Lowery, "A Reckoning over Objectivity"; see also Møller Hartley and Tina Askanius, "Activist-Journalism and the Norm of Objectivity: Role Performance in the Reporting of the #MeToo Movement in Denmark and Sweden," *Journalism Practice* 15, no. 6 (2021): 860–877; and Gaye Tuchman, "Objectivity as Strategic Ritual: An Examination of Newsmen's Notions of Objectivity," *American Journal of Sociology* 77, no. 4 (1972): 660–679, https://doi.org/10.1086/225193.
27. Alex S. Jones, *Losing the News: The Future of the News that Feeds Democracy* (New York: Oxford University Press, 2009), 83, quoted in Lowery, "A Reckoning over Objectivity."
28. Claudia Mellado, "Professional Roles in News Context: Six Dimensions of Journalistic Role Performance," *Journalism Studies* 16, no. 4 (2015): 596–614.
29. Janet Blank-Libra, *Pursuing an Ethic of Empathy in Journalism* (New York: Routledge, 2017), 109–110.
30. Angela Smith and Michael Higgins, *The Language of Journalism*, 2nd ed. (New York: Bloomsbury, 2020), 185.
31. Smith and Higgins, *The Language of Journalism*, 185.
32. Smith and Higgins, *The Language of Journalism*, 189.
33. Smith and Higgins, *The Language of Journalism*, 193.
34. van Krieken and Sanders, "What Is Narrative Journalism?," 1404.
35. Kim Fox, David O. Dowling, and Kyle Miller, "A Curriculum for Blackness: Podcasts as Discursive Cultural Guides, 2010–2020," *Journal of Radio & Audio Media* 27, no. 2, (2020): 298–318.
36. Lesley Cowling, "Echoes of an African Drum: The Lost Literary Journalism of 1950s South Africa," *Literary Journalism Studies* 8, no. 1 (2016): 26.

37. Siobhán McHugh, "Subjectivity, Hugs, and Craft: Podcasting as Extreme Narrative Journalism," *Nieman Storyboard*, October 8, 2019.
38. McHugh, "Subjectivity, Hugs, and Craft."
39. McHugh, "Subjectivity, Hugs, and Craft."
40. Maria Martin, "Crossing Borders," in *Reality Radio: Telling True Stories in Sound*, 2nd ed., ed. John Biewen and Alexa Dilworth (Chapel Hill: University of North Carolina Press, 2017), 208.
41. van Krieken and Sanders, "What Is Narrative Journalism?," 1404.
42. Geoffrey Baym, "Journalism and the Hybrid Condition: Long-Form Television Drama at the Intersection of News and Narrative," *Journalism* 18, no. 1 (2017): 23.
43. Sarah Koenig, *Serial*, Season 3, podcast audio, Serial Productions (2018).
44. Kylie Cardell, "'Like a Novel': Literary Aesthetics, Nonfiction Ethics, and the S-Town Podcast," *Australian Literary Studies* 36, no. 1 (2021), https://doi.org/10.20314/als.079241fcb6; and Ella Waldmann, "From Storytelling to Story*listening*: How the Hit Podcast *S-Town* Reconfigured the Production and Reception of Narrative Nonfiction," *Ex-Centric Narratives: Journal of Anglophone Culture, Literature, and Media*, no. 4 (2020): 28–42.
45. Cardell, "'Like a Novel.'"
46. Nicholas Quah, "S-Town Podcast Transcends the True Crime of Serial," *Vulture*, March 1, 2017.
47. Katy Waldman, "The Gorgeous New True Crime Podcast S-Town Is Like Serial But Satisfying," *Slate*, March 1, 2017.
48. "*S-Town*: Serial and This American Life," *Peabody Awards* (2017), https://peabodyawards.com/award-profile/s-town/.
49. James Tierney, "Literary Listening: The Rise of the Podcast as Literary Form," *Kill Your Darlings*, January 21, 2015.
50. James Atlas, "Hearing Is Believing," *New York Times*, January 11, 2015.
51. McHugh, "Subjectivity, Hugs, and Craft."
52. Waldmann, "From Storytelling to Story*listening*," 30.
53. Waldmann, "From Storytelling to Story*listening*," 37.
54. McHugh, "Subjectivity, Hugs, and Craft."
55. Atlas, "Hearing Is Believing."
56. McHugh, "How Podcasting Is Changing," 75.
57. McHugh, "How Podcasting Is Changing," 75.
58. McHugh, "How Podcasting Is Changing," 73.
59. McHugh, "How Podcasting Is Changing," 77.
60. Felicia Greiff, "Ira Glass: 'Public Radio Is Ready for Capitalism,'" *Advertising Age*, April 30, 2015.
61. Tierney, "Literary Listening"; McHugh, "Subjectivity, Hugs, and Craft"; Siobhán McHugh, "The Narrative Podcast as Digital Literary Journalism: Conceptualizing

S-Town," *Literary Journalism Studies* 13, nos. 1 and 2 (June and December 2021): 100–129; Waldmann, "From Storytelling to Story*listening*"; and Tierney 2021

62. Kris M. Markman, "Everything Old Is New Again: Podcasting as Radio's Revival," *Journal of Radio & Audio Media* 22, no. 2 (2015): 241.
63. Nick Quah, "*S-Town* Transcends the True Crime of *Serial*," *New York*, March 28, 2017.
64. Waldmann, "From Storytelling to Story*listening*," 32.
65. Jeremy Page, "What They Said . . .," *Frogmore Papers*, no. 12 (August 1986), http://poetrymagazines.org.uk/magazine/record00d3.html?id=11044.
66. Hua Hsu, "Game Over: How Athletes Began Telling a New Story About Sports," *New Yorker*, April 5, 2021.
67. Hsu, "Game Over."
68. Mark Deuze and Tamara Witschge, "Beyond Journalism: Theorizing the Transformation of Journalism," *Journalism* 19, no. 2 (2018): 165.
69. Mitchell Stephens, Beyond News: The Future of Journalism (New York: Columbia University Press, 2014), 10
70. Ros Coward, *Speaking Personally: The Rise of Subjective and Confessional Journalism* (New York: Palgrave, 2013), 8.
71. Coward, *Speaking Personally*, 9.
72. Coward, *Speaking Personally*, 9.
73. Coward, *Speaking Personally*, 9.
74. Coward, *Speaking Personally*, 64.
75. Thomas Schmidt, *Rewriting the Newspaper: The Storytelling Movement in American Print Journalism* (Columbia: University of Missouri Press, 2019).

Selected Bibliography

Allsop, Jon. "*Caliphate*, The 1619 Project, *The Times*, and Culture." *Columbia Journalism Review*, October 14, 2020.
Aufderheide, Patricia, David Lieberman, Atika Alkhallouf, and Jiji Majiri Ugboma. "Podcasting as Public Media: The Future of U.S. News, Public Affairs, and Educational Podcasts." *International Journal of Communication* 14 (February 2020): 1683–1704.
Bailey, Spencer, and Andrew Zuckerman. "Bill McKibbon on COVID-19 and the Climate Crisis." In *At a Distance*, April 2, 2020. Audio podcast.
Baran, Madeleine. "The Crime." In *In the Dark*, September 7, 2016. Audio podcast.
Barbaro, Michael. "An Examination of *Caliphate*." In *The Daily*, December 18, 2020. Audio podcast.
——. "The Legacy of Rush Limbaugh." In *The Daily*, February 22, 2021. Audio podcast.
Berry, Richard. "A Golden Age of Podcasting? Evaluating *Serial* in the Context of Podcast Histories." *Journal of Radio and Audio Media* 22 no. 2 (2015): 170–80.
——. "Podcasting: Considering the Evolution of the Medium and Its Association with the Word 'Radio.'" *Radio Journal: International Studies in Broadcast and Audio Media* 14, no. 1 (2016): 7–22.
Biewen, John, and Alexa Dilworth. *Reality Radio: Telling True Stories in Sound*. 2nd ed. Chapel Hill: University of North Carolina Press, 2017.
Boling, Kelli S. "True Crime Podcasting: Journalism, Justice, or Entertainment?" *Radio Journal: International Studies in Broadcast & Audio Media* 17, no. 2 (2019): 161–178.

Boling, Kelli S., and Kevin Hull. "*Undisclosed* Information—*Serial* Is *My Favorite Murder*: Examining Motivations in the True Crime Podcast Audience." *Journal of Radio & Audio Media* 25, no. 2 (2018): 92–108.

Bongino, Dan. "About Yesterday." In *The Dan Bongino Show*, January 7, 2021. Audio podcast.

Booker, Jamal. "Jim Dinkins—Writing Our Next Chapter Together." In *Total Refresh*, July 8, 2019. Audio podcast.

Bottomley, Andrew J. "Podcasting: A Decade in the Life of a 'New' Audio Medium: Introduction." *Journal of Radio & Audio Media* 22, no. 2 (2015): 164–169.

Brekke, Anjuli Joshi. "The Sound of Yellow Rain: Resisting Podcasting's Sonic Whiteness." In *Radio's Second Century: Past, Present, and Future Perspectives*, ed. by John Allen Hendricks, 173–189. New Brunswick, N.J.: Rutgers University Press, 2020.

Callimachi, Rukmini. *Caliphate*, May 24, 2018. Audio podcast.

Cardell, Kylie. "'Like a Novel:' Literary Aesthetics, Nonfiction Ethics, and the S-Town Podcast." *Australian Literary Studies* 36, no. 1 (2021): 1–17.

Carlson, Matt. *Journalistic Authority*. New York: Columbia University Press, 2017.

Casillas, Dolores Ines, *Sounds of Belonging: U.S. Spanish-Language Radio and Public Advocacy*. New York: New York University Press, 2014.

Chan-Olmsted, Sylvia, and Rang Wang. "Understanding Podcast Users: Consumption Motives and Behaviors." *New Media & Society* 24, no. 3 (2020): 684–704.

Coley, Will. "Episode 1: Land of the Free, But Only for Some." In *Indefensible*, January 18, 2017. Audio podcast.

Crispin, Jessa. "America Is Losing Its Mind. Again. With Chelsey Weber Smith." In *Public Intellectual with Jessa Crispin*, December 7, 2020. Audio podcast.

Curran, James. *Media and Democracy*. London: Routledge, 2011.

———. "What Democracy Requires of the Media." In *Institutions of American Democracy: The Press*. Ed. by Geneva Overholser and Kathleen Hall Jamieson, 120–124. New York: Oxford University Press, 2005.

Cwynar, Christopher. "More Than a 'VCR for Radio:' The CBC, the Radio 3 Podcast, and the Uses of an Emerging Medium." *Journal of Radio & Audio Media* 22 (2015): 190–199.

Demair, Jillian. "Sounds Authentic: The Acoustic Construction of *Serial*'s Story World." In *The Serial Podcast and Storytelling in the Digital Age*. Ed. by Ellen McCracken, 24–38. New York: Routledge, 2017.

Dempsey, John Mark. "A More Inclusive Public Service: Can NPR Serve All of America?" In *Radio's Second Century: Past, Present, and Future Perspectives*. Ed. by John Allen Hendricks, 154–172. New Brunswick, N.J.: Rutgers University Press, 2020.

Deuze, Mark, and Tamara Witschge. "Beyond Journalism: Theorizing the Transformation of Journalism." *Journalism* 19, no. 2 (2018): 168–181.

Dowling, David O. *Immersive Longform Storytelling: Media, Technology, Audience.* New York: Routledge, 2019.

Dowling, David O., Patrick Johnson, and Brian Ekdale. "Hijacking Journalism: Legitimacy and Metajournalistic Discourse in Right-Wing Podcasts." *Media & Communication* 10, no. 3 (2022): 17–27.

Dowling, David O., and Kyle Miller. "Immersive Audio Storytelling: Podcasting and Serial Documentary in the Digital Publishing Industry." *Journal of Radio & Audio Media* 26, no. 1 (2019): 167–184.

Dowling, David, and Travis Vogan. "Longform Narrative Journalism: 'Snow Fall' and Beyond." In *The Routledge Companion to Digital Journalism Studies*. Ed. by Bob Franklin and Scott A. Eldridge II, 478–486. New York: Routledge, 2017.

Einstein, Mara. *Black Ops Advertising: Native Ads, Content Marketing, and the Covert World of the Digital Sell.* New York: OR Books, 2016.

Eldridge, Scott A., II. *Online Journalism from the Periphery: Interloper Media and the Journalistic Field.* New York: Routledge, 2018.

Florini, Sarah. *Beyond Hashtags: Racial Politics and Black Digital Networks.* New York: New York University Press, 2019.

Fox, Kim, David O. Dowling, and Kyle Miller. "A Curriculum for Blackness: Podcasts as Discursive Cultural Guides, 2010–2020." *Journal of Radio & Audio Media* 27, no. 2 (2020): 298–318.

García-Marín, David. "Mapping the Factors that Determine Engagement in Podcasting: Design from the Users and Podcasters' Experience." *Communication & Society* 33, no. 2 (2020): 49–63.

Gardner, Jaison, and Kaila Story. "The 'Jim Crow Mentality' of Social Media Trolls." In *Strange Fruit*, November 10, 2020. Audio podcast.

"Good Luck, Everybody." In *All Told*, April 2, 2020. Audio podcast.

Hannah-Jones, Nikole. "The Fight for a True Democracy." In *1619*, August 23, 2019. Audio podcast.

Harcup, Tony, and Deidre O'Neill. "What Is News? News Values Revisited (Again)." *Journalism Studies* 18, no. 12 (2017): 1470–1488.

Kern, Jonathan. *Sound Reporting: The NPR Guide to Audio Journalism and Production.* Chicago: University of Chicago Press, 2008.

Koenig, Sarah. *Serial*, Season 3, 2018. Audio podcast.

Kovach, Bill, and Tom Rosenstiel. *The Elements of Journalism: What Newspeople Should Know and the Public Should Expect.* 4th ed. New York: Three Rivers, 2021.

LeClair, Catherine. "Good Intentions." In *The Sauce*, January 13, 2021. Audio podcast.

Lee, Trymaine. "Into Coronavirus for the Uninsured." In *Into America*, March 27, 2020. Audio podcast.

Lepore, Jill. *The Last Archive*, 2021. Audio podcast.

Lindgren, Mia. "Personal Narrative Journalism and Podcasting." *Radio Journal: International Studies in Broadcast & Audio Media* 14, no. 1 (2016): 23–49.

Limbaugh, Rush. *The Rush Limbaugh Show*, 2021. Audio podcast.

Llinares, Dario. "Podcasting as Liminal Praxis: Aural Mediation, Sound Writing and Identity." In *Podcasting: New Aural Cultures and Digital Media*. Ed. by Dario Llinares, Neil Fox, and Richard Berry, 123–145. New York: Palgrave Macmillan, 2018.

Luse, Brittany and Eddings, Eric. "Ready, Set . . . Buy Black." In *The Nod*, November 27, 2017. Audio podcast.

Luther, Jessica, Shireen Ahmed, and Lindsay Gibbs. "Trans Women and Trans Girls Belong in Women's Sport." *Burn It All Down*, March 2, 2021. Audio podcast.

Markman, Kris M. "Everything Old Is New Again: Podcasting as Radio's Revival." *Journal of Radio & Audio Media* 22, no. 2 (2015): 240–243.

McHugh, Siobhán. "How Podcasting Is Changing the Audio Storytelling Genre." *Radio Journal: International Studies in Broadcast and Audio Media* 14, no. 1 (2016): 65–82.

———. "The Narrative Podcast as Digital Literary Journalism: Conceptualizing S-Town." *Literary Journalism Studies* 13, nos. 1 and 2 (2021): 100–129.

Miller, Lulu, and Alix Spiegel. "Entanglement." In *Invisibilia*, January 29, 2015. Audio podcast.

Miller, Tara, and Matt Sloan, Matt. "Episode 16: Produce." In *Inside Trader Joe's*, July 22, 2019. Audio podcast.

Moloney, Kevin. "All the News That's Fit to Push: The New York Times Company and Transmedia Daily News." *International Journal of Communication* 14 (2020): 4683–4702.

Nee, Rebecca C., and Arthur D. Santana. "Podcasting the Pandemic: Exploring Storytelling Formats and Shifting Journalistic Norms in News Podcasts Related to the Coronavirus." *Journalism Practice* 16, no. 8 (2021): 1559–1577.

Newkirk, Vann R. *Floodlines*, 2020. Audio podcast.

Newman, Nic, and Nathan Gallo. *Daily News Podcasts: Building New Habits in the Shadow of Coronavirus*. Oxford: Reuters Institute for the Study of Journalism, 2020.

Nieborg, David B., and Thomas Poell. "The Platformization of Cultural Production: Theorizing the Contingent Cultural Commodity." *New Media & Society* 20, no. 11 (2018): 4275–4292.

Perdomo, Gabriele, and Philippe Rodrigues-Rouleau. "Transparency as Metajournalistic Performance: *The New York Times' Caliphate* Podcast and

New Ways to Claim Journalistic Authority." *Journalism* 23, no. 11 (2021): 2311–2327.

Postema, Stijn, and Mark Deuze. "Artistic Journalism: Confluence in Forms, Values, and Practices." *Journalism Studies* 21, no. 10 (2020): 1305–1322.

Punnett, Ian Case. *Toward a Theory of True Crime Narratives: A Textual Analysis*. New York: Routledge, 2018.

Quiroz, Emilce. "I Am a Cholo." In *Latino USA*, June 11, 2021. Audio podcast.

Rauch, Jennifer. *Slow Media: Why Slow Is Satisfying, Sustainable, and Smart*. New York: Oxford University Press, 2018.

Rogan, Joe. "Alex Jones and Tim Dillon." In *The Joe Rogan Experience*, October 27, 2020. Audio podcast.

Rosenwald, Brian. *Talk Radio's America: How an Industry Took over a Political Party That Took over the United States*. Cambridge, Mass.: Harvard University Press, 2019.

Rugnetta, Mike. "Advancing the Tech of Diabetes Decision-Making." In *Health Tech on the Horizon*, December 11, 2020. Audio podcast.

Ryfe, David. *Journalism and the Public*. Cambridge, UK: Polity, 2017.

Schultz, Howard, and Rajiv Chandrasekaran. "Scholarships for Every Student." In *Upstanders*, September 15, 2016. Audio podcast.

Schroeder, Ralph. *Social Theory After the Internet: Media, Technology, and Globalization*. London: UCL Press, 2018.

Shapiro, Ben. "The Worst Day in Modern American Political History." In *The Ben Shapiro Show*, January 7, 2021. Audio podcast.

Sienkiewicz, Matt, and Deborah L. Jaramillo. "Podcasting, the Intimate Self, and the Public Sphere." *Popular Communication* 17, no. 4 (2019): 268–272.

Smith, Adam. "Donna Strickland." In *Nobel Prize Conversations*, March 3, 2021. Audio podcast.

Spiegel, Alix. "Variations in Tape Use and the Position of the Narrator." In *Reality Radio: Telling True Stories in* Sound. Ed. by John Biewen and Alexa Dilworth, 42–53. Chapel Hill: University of North Carolina Press, 2017.

Spinelli, Martin, and Lance Dann. *Podcasting: The Audio Media Revolution*. New York: Bloomsbury, 2019.

Starkey, Guy. "The New Kids on the Block: The Pictures, Text, Time-Shifted Audio, and Podcasts of Digital Radio Journalism Online." In *The Routledge Companion to Digital Journalism*. Ed. by Bob Franklin and Scott A. Eldridge II, 469–477. New York: Routledge, 2017.

Sterne, Jonathan, Jeremy Morris, Michael Brendan Baker, and Ariana Moscote Freire. "The Politics of Podcasting." *Fibreculture Journal* 13 (2008).

Sullivan, John L. "Podcast Movement: Aspirational Labor and the Formalisation of Podcasting as a Cultural Industry." In *Podcasting: New Aural Cultures and*

Digital Media. Ed. by Dario Llinares, Neil Fox, and Richard Berry, 35–56. New York: Palgrave Macmillan, 2018.

Swiatek, Lukasz. "The Podcast as an Intimate Bridging Medium." In *Podcasting: New Aural Cultures and Digital Media*. Ed. by Dario Llinares, Neil Fox, and Richard Berry, 173–187. New York: Palgrave Macmillan, 2018.

van Krieken, Kobie, and Jose Sanders. "What Is Narrative Journalism? A Systematic Review and an Empirical Agenda." *Journalism* 22, no. 6 (2021): 1393–1412.

Wahl-Jorgensen, Karin, and Thomas Schmidt. "News and Storytelling." In *The Handbook of Journalism Studies*. Ed. by Karin Wahl-Jorgensen and Thomas Hanitzsch, 261–276. New York: Routledge, 2020.

Waldmann, Ella. "From Storytelling to Story*listening*: How the Hit Podcast *S-Town* Reconfigured the Production and Reception of Narrative Nonfiction." *Ex-Centric Narratives: Journal of Anglophone Culture, Literature, and Media*, no. 4 (2020): 28–42.

"Will Coronavirus Tenant Protections Really Help Renters?" In *The California Report*, March 31, 2020. Audio podcast.

Index

Abbott Laboratories, 190
aca-fans, 206
Acast (global podcast company), 33
accuracy, as journalistic standard, 56
Acorn, white aurality and, 155
advertising: deceptive, 180, 181; influence on podcast industry, 119, 176; native advertising, 177; as revenue source, 99–101; on screen-based digital news, 121; streaming ad-insertion technology, 4
advocacy journalism, 151, 207
aesthetics, definition of, 192
affinity spaces, 135
affirmation, journalism of, 19, 128–132, 146, 223–224
Against the Rules (podcast), 36
Ahmed, Shireen, 170–171
algorithms, 110, 129–130, 155
All Told (*Washington Post*), 14, 29, 44
Allison, Jay, 178, 187
Alpha UX (B2B software maker), 189
Always Take Notes (podcast), 75
Amazon Prime, 133

American Press Institute, 127
American Public Media, *In the Dark*, 15–16
Amos & Andy (radio show), 162
analytical discourse, 160
Anchor company, 117, 135–136
Anderson, Christopher William, 183
Animal Planet, "Blood and Water," 182
Apple: *Apple News Today* (news platform), 110, 111; Apple Podcast Subscriptions, 102, 113–117; Apple Podcasts, white aurality and, 155; dominance of, 186; podcast market domination, 102, 122–123, 133, 135–136, 206; as podcast platform, 133
apps, Apple's Podcasts app, 113
Arias, Eddy, 169–170
Art and Copy (documentary), 77
"Art in the Age of Mechanical Reproduction" (Benjamin), 61
assertion, journalism of, 129, 130, 146
Astronomy Cast (science podcast), 78
Asymmetric Politics (Grossman and Hopkins), 148

asynchronicity of podcast listening, 18, 31
At a Distance (podcast, earlier *Time Sensitive*), 96–97
athletes in podcasting, 221–223
Athletic, The (podcast), 221–222
Atlantic, The (magazine): Church of Scientology, content production for, 195; explanatory journalism and, 91; *Floodlines*, 74, 94–95
Atlas, James, 216
attention economy, 35
audiences: audience-publisher exchange value, 119–123; Black and Asian, growth of, 149; demographics of, 105; depth of, 104; engaged time of, 104; genre and, in true crime podcast journalism, 51–55; Hispanic, growth of, 149; intentional selection, 108–109; Latino, growth of, 156; location of, 109; mobile audiences, 29; modes of listening, 108; nonfictional longform podcast listeners, 199; non-white podcast listenership, size of, 149; overlap of, for radio and podcasts, 121–122; paid podcast listening, normalization of, 113–119; political knowledge of, 55; routine of, 104–105; size of, 205; streaming music listeners, 112; for true crime podcasts, 51–52; understanding of, 155; width of, 104; younger, for podcasts, 110–111
audio: audio immersion, description of, 38; audio journalism as form of literature, 215; audio literary journalism, emergence of, 206; audio media, immersive quality of, 35–36; audio narrative, business of, 217–223; audio reporting, as new Pulitzer Prize category, 3, 203; audio reporting, as platform for intellectual culture, 74; creative nonfiction in, 202; editorial techniques for, 89; immersive audio storytelling, 36–39. *See also* podcast journalism (generally)
Audm, *New York Times*'s acquisition of, 121
aural imaginary, 150, 151
authorship information, identification of, 189

balance, as journalistic norm, 79, 90
Baldwin, Michigan, Starbucks and, 191–193
bandwagon effect, 158
Baquet, Dean, 52, 57–58, 209
Baran, Madeleine, 2, 16, 54, 68–70
Barbaro, Michael: Baquet and, 57–58; *Caliphate* disclaimer by, 67, 216; *Caliphate* fall and, 52; emotional states, 61; on journalistic transparency, 153; methodology of, 132; as podcast host, 26, 41; on podcasting, 6; recognition of, 27
Barlow, John Perry, 135
Barnett, Steffi, 171–172
Barnum, P. T., 126
Barstool Sport (podcast network), 27
Barthes, Roland, 40, 171
Basu, Shumita, 110
Ben Shapiro Show, The (*Daily Wire*), 9, 129, 132, 138–139, 142–143
Benjamin, Walter, 1, 10, 61
Bennett, Christian, 34
Berners-Lee, Tim, 115
Berry, Richard, 27, 28, 31
Berry, Stephen J., 16

Beyond the Microscope (podcast), 75, 76, 89
BhD: Black and Highly Dangerous (podcast), 11, 76, 162
Biden, Joe, 40
Biewen, John, 108–109, 218, 219
Bigart, Homer, 15, 207
Bill Simmons Podcast, The (Simmons), 41
binge listening, 18, 108
Black Podcasters United group, 160
Blacking It Up (podcast), 158–159
Black podcasting: Black community, consumer choices by, 163; blerds (Black nerds), 161; curriculum for blackness, 211; discussion of, 157–166; origins of, 223; professionalization of, 164; Elon James White and, 20
"Blood and Water" (*Animal Planet*), 182
Bloom, Stephen G., 209–210
Bloomberg, Michael, 42
Bloomberg company, 200–201
Blumberg, Alex, 186, 216, 219
Boggs, Dagmar, 197
Boling, Kelli S., 54, 70, 105
Bon Appétit (magazine), 151
Bongino, Dan, 140–142; Limbaugh, homage to, 145–146; as Limbaugh's successor, 224; Parler, co-ownership of, 145; as podcast host, 2, 19, 128; popularity of, 138–139
Booker, Jamal, 197
bookstores, independent, 199
Boreing, Jeremy, 142
Borenstein, Erik, 1
Bracci, Aria, 171
brands as publishers, 175–201; branded podcasts, 218; Coca-Cola's branded podcasts, 194–198; conclusions on, 200–201; introduction to, 21–22, 175–179; McDonald's branded podcasts, 198; podcast journalism, locus of, 179–189; public service, marketing of, 189–194; Trader Joe's branded podcasts, 198–200
Break in the Case (true crime podcast), 50, 68, 69
breathless edits, 89
Brekke, Anjuli Joshi, 155, 157
broadcasters, publishers versus, 9, 36
broadcasting, critical discourse on, 206
Brookings Institute, 6, 25
Brown, Michael, 94–95
Burn It All Down (Blue Wire), 44, 170–171, 221
Burns, Ken, 219
BuzzFeed, 53

cable TV packages, 107
Caliphate (longform documentary podcast): as attempted blockbuster, 204; breach of journalistic principles, 52–53; Callimachi and, 48; fall of, 49, 52, 56, 119, 195, 216, 220, 225; financial pressures on, 56; performance of transparency by, 63–68, 181; reporting ethics, sacrifice of, 15; sound design of, 216
Callimachi, Rukmini: ambition of, 220; *Caliphate* fall and, 52, 54, 55, 58; career overview, 48; context for reporting by, 72; inexperience with true crime genre, 53; journalistic principles, breaking of, 56; performance of transparency by, 63–68; reportage style, 216; rise of, 49
Camerer, Colin, 78
capitalism, in podcast medium, 218

Carlson, Matt, 182, 196
Carr, Nicholas, 97
Carson, Rachel, 96, 98
Carville, James, 40
Casillas, Dolores Inés, 92–93
Castbox, 102
Center for Journalism and Democracy (Howard University), 166
CES Tech Talk (podcast), 190
Chandrasekaran, Rajiv, 192, 194
Chan-Olmsted, Sylvia, 105, 108, 109, 112
Chartable (podcast analytics platform), 38
Chaudhry, Shehroze: credibility, question of, 49, 52; failure of, 55; falsehoods by, 57–58, 65; as interviewee, 48; opportunism of, 68
Chen, Jimmy, 31–32
Chitlin' Circuit, 159
Chivvis, Dana, 185
chollo, as term, 166
Church of Scientology, 195
cinema, monetization model for, 106
Citations Needed (podcast), 75
citizen journalism movement, 46, 179
citizen stories, 209–210
citizens' rights advocacy, 70
civic engagement, 18, 51, 211
civilization, science's importance to, 81
Clark, Christopher J., 76
clerkism, 15, 207
Cleveland, Ohio, municipal court system, 16
climate crisis, 79, 97–98
Coca-Cola's branded podcasts, 194–198, 200
Code of Ethics (Society for Professional Journalists), 6

Code Switch (podcast), 7, 150, 151, 156, 172
Coley, Will, 169–170
color television, 10–11
Columbia University, study on branded content studios, 193
Combat Jack Show, The (podcast), 159
commercialization, impact of, 164
community building, 162
compassion, 85
confirmation bias, 49, 56, 57, 62, 66–67, 68
conservatism: conservative media ecosystem, 19; conservative news media producers, loss of journalistic credibility among, 144; conservative podcasting, platformization and, 132–137; conservative podcasts, examples of, 138; conservative rhetoric, liberal rhetoric versus, 147–148; radicalization of, 144. *See also* Far Right podcasts
constructive journalism, 77
content: citizen stories, 209–210; content expansion (drillability), 43; content marketing, 182, 217; content marketing studios, 22, 188; creative content, regulation of, 137
copcasts (true crime subgenre), 50
Copeland, Courtney, 71
Copeland, Da'Ron, 193
Coughlin, Charles, 125
Coulter, Ann, 145
COVID-19 pandemic, 24–47; audio storytelling, immersive, 36–39; conclusions on, 45–47; growth of podcast industry during, 110; impact on media employees, 30; introduction to, 14–15, 24–26; NPR principles, in coronavirus age,

39–45; podcast industry, theorization of, 27–30; remote podcast production, 30–36; response to, 97–98; true crime in age of COVID-19, 212–217
Coward, Ros, 197, 224
Craigslist, 100
creative nonfiction, in audio medium, 202
Crime Junkie (true crime podcast), 50, 68, 69
criminal justice systems, investigations of, 69–71
Crispin, Jessa, 77, 95–96
"Crossing Brooklyn Ferry" (Whitman), 214
cross-platform transmedia publication, 107
culture: audio reporting as platform for intellectual culture, 74; Cold War culture, 22; digital culture, 5–8, 122, 219; Mexican mafia prison gang culture, 168; podcast culture, factors affecting, 5; quarantine culture during COVID-19 pandemic, 33, 45–46; Reddit, digital culture of, 127; Southern culture, 215; Twitter, digital culture of, 127. *See also* intellectual culture
The Current (NPR), 205
current affairs, gatekeepers for public information on, 139
curriculum for blackness, 211

DACA (Deferred Action for Childhood Arrivals) Act, 169
Daily, The (*New York Times*): audience size, 136; *Caliphate* fall and, 52; on *Caliphate* scandal, 56–58; during COVID-19 pandemic, 213; format for, 34; listenership of, 35; as model for podcast journalism, 26; narrative methods of, 29, 32; popularity of, 48, 202, 212, 217; production team for, 34; quality of, 205
daily podcasts: daily news podcasting, growth of, 26; NPR genre conventions, adoption of, 28; pedigrees of, 27; rise of, 32
Daily Wire, The (online news publication), 133, 142–144
Dan Bongino Show, The (podcast),138, 140–142
Dann, Lance: on journalism, 22, 29; mentioned, 88; on podcasts, challenges facing, 176; on podcasts, journalism in, 9; on podcasts, perceptions of safety of, 150; on podcast-specific intimacy, 93; on role of public broadcasters, 206; on tape-tape transitions, 89
data mining, 137
Dateline NBC (podcast), 42
Davis, Rebecca Harding, 220
De Correspondent (news startup), 101
Deadspin (podcast), 222
"Declaration of the Independence of Cyberspace, A" (Barlow), 135
deep audio storytelling, 28
deep dives. *See* longform journalism and longform content
Deferred Action for Childhood Arrivals (DACA) Act, 169
democracy: media in service of, 2, 167, 212; science's importance to, 81
DeSantis, Ron, 124
Deuze, Mark, 184, 223
digital culture, 5–8, 122, 219
digital ecosystem, capitalist competition un, 35

digital journalism: homogenization of, 18; promotional purposes, 176
digital literary journalism, podcasting as, 202–225; audio narrative, business of, 217–223; intellectual culture and, 223–225; introduction to, 202–207; new language of podcasting, 210–212; objectivity and distance and, 207–210; sports podcasts, 222–223; true crime in age of COVID-19, 212–217
digital longform journalism, 28, 182
digital publishing industry, minority voices in, 20–21
Dinkins, Jim, 197
disinformation, 92, 95
distraction, technologies of, 35
ditto-heads, 126, 147
diversity: diverse podcast production, future of, 172–174; in podcasting, increase in, 206; as principle of journalism, 43. *See also* marginalized groups, voices from
documentaries: documentary longform podcasting, 131; documentary videos, rise of, 219; online, as future of content marketing, 182
Doherty, Peter, 87
Dose (news outlet), 175–176
double articulation, 86
Douglass, Frederick, 96
Dowling, David, 211
driveway moments, 11, 39
Drum (South African magazine), 211
Durant, Kevin, 222
Dylan, Bob, 23, 215

Ear Hustle (Radiotopia), 7, 13, 29, 71, 72, 210
Eddings, Eric, 154, 160–163, 174, 186

Edison Research, 8
editing: of podcasts versus radio broadcasts, 93; of scientific podcasts, 76
ehollo, as identity marker, 168–169
Ek, Daniel, 134, 187
Eldridge, Scott, II, 12–13
Electronic Frontier Foundation, 135
elevators in government buildings, 214
Emerson, Ralph Waldo, 82, 96, 223
empathy, in historically focused podcasts, 93–94, 95
engaged time, of podcast audiences, 104
Engley, Ryan, 40
Enright, D. J., 221
entertainment media, journalistic content, 128–129
Epic Games, 114
episodic storytelling, 23
ethnicity, cultural impact of, 20
explanatory (analytic) journalism, 77, 91
extended chats and chat podcasts, 129, 130, 137

Facebook: Bongino and, 141; disinformation on, 134; impact on publishers, 121; Live Audio Rooms, 5; right-wing publishers on, 133
Fairness Doctrine, 125–126
false balance reporting, 90
"Family Conversation on Race in Latinidad, A," (*Latino USA*), 169
fandoms, importance of, 115
Far Right podcasts, 124–148; affirmation, journalism of, 128–132; *Ben Shapiro Show*, 142–143; conservative podcasting, platformization and, 132–137; *Dan Bongino Show*,

140–142; false balance reporting and, 90; future of, 143–148; introduction to, 19, 124–125; origins of, 125–128; right-wing podcast industry, 137–140
Fauci, Anthony, 97
Faulkner, William, 215, 220–221
feature profile writing, types of, 196
Federal Communications Commission, purpose of, 92
Federal Trade Commission, 180
feedback loop of disinformation, 95
FEMA, Hurricane Katrina and, 94–95
fiction: rhetorical devices of, 80; serialization of, 106
fireside chats, 46
Firestorm (*Guardian*), 203
Fix Solutions Lab (digital publication), 79
Floodlines (*The Atlantic* magazine), 16, 74, 77, 94–95
Florini, Sarah, 157, 160
Flowers, Curtis, 19
Floyd, George, impact of murder of, 156, 207, 214, 225
Folkenflik, David, 52
food stamp system, 31–32
For Colored Nerds (podcast), 160, 161, 162
Fortnite (video game), 114
Fox, Kim, 158, 173, 174, 211
Fox News, Limbaugh and, 124, 145
France, popularity of news podcasts in, 38
Franklin, Benjamin, 81
free press principle, violations of, 68
free speech, abuses of, 135
Fresh Air (NPR), 205
Fresh EBT (app), 31–32
FUBU (For Us, By Us) brand, 163

Fuller, Margaret, 96
Furrow, The (Deere), 176

Gab (platform), 143–144
Garbes, Laura, 156
Gardner, Jaison, 172
gender: gender inequities in women's athletics, 221; gender signaling through audio, 171–172; gender-exclusivity, of Black podcasts, 158; gender-inclusive labor economy of Black podcasting, 161; queering of, 171
Geraldino, Duarte, 110
Gimlet Media (podcast network): Black-hosted podcasts, failure of, 153; *Caliphate* and, 216; diversity issues, 151, 163; founding of, 186; Gimlet Creative, 186, 188; *Heavyweigtht*, 3; institutional racism of, 155; Luse and Eddings at, 160; mentioned, 5, 27; operating principles, 161; properties of, 111; self-investigation by, 200; Spotify's acquisition of, 133, 136, 217
Gingrich, Newt, 127
Giroux, Henry, 86–87
Gizmodo, 198
Gladwell, Malcolm, 14, 31, 36, 70, 90, 109
Glass, Ira: influence of, 73, 83; legacy of, 221; longform audio reportage by, 138; mentioned, 3; as model podcaster, 152; narrative reflexivity of, 40; NPR, model for, 205; on principles of audio reporting, 40; production space used by, 30; on public radio, monetization of, 104; on public radio and capitalism, 178, 185, 218; storytelling conventions, 32

GoDaddy, 144
Gonzáles, Pedro, 93–94, 153–154
Gonzalez, Ed, 170
Google: Google Play, 133; impact on publishers, 121
Gould, Stephen J., 96
Graham, Lindsey, 42
Gramsci, Antonio, 75
Grantland (website), 41, 136
grape drinks, artificially flavored, 154
Greeley, Horace, 223
Greenroom (Spotify), 4, 5
Greenwald, Glenn, 16, 36
Grier and Leitch (podcast), 30–31
Grist (online journal), 79
Grossman, Matt, 148
Guardian (news source): *The Guardian Science Weekly*, 78; listenership, 111; *Today in Focus*, 14, 28

Hannah-Jones, Nikole, 164–166, 202–203
Hannity, Sean, 145
Harper's magazine, 131
Harrison, Jaime, 42
Havens, Timothy, 28, 29
headphone listening, 86
Health Tech on the Horizon (Abbott Newsroom), 190
Heavyweight (podcast), 3–4
Helfand, Jessica, 10, 11
Helter Skelter (true crime podcast), 53
Hemingway, Ernest, 10
Hemmer, Nicole, 75, 144
Henry, William A., III, 127
Here's the Deal with Joe Biden (Biden), 40
Hickman, Ron, 170
Higher Ground productions, 133
Highly Relevant with Jack Rico (podcast), 20

Hilmes, Michele, 12, 125
historical podcasts, 77, 90–98
Hooked on Pop (podcast), 104
Hopkins, David A., 148
host-listener relationships, 114–116
Howard University, 165
Hsu, Hua, 222
Hull, Kevin, 105
humanistic journalism, characteristics of, 29
Hurricane Katrina, 94–95
Hurston, Zora Neale, 211
Hutchins Commission, 6, 22, 43, 167

"I Am a Chollo" (*Latino USA*), 166, 168–169
ideal intellectuals, 75
identity performance, 162
iHeartMedia, 145
iHeartRadio (podcast network), 27, 112
iHeartRadio First Taste Fridays with Coca-Cola, 21
Ikpi, Bassey, 158
immersive media: immersive audio storytelling, 36–39; immersive longform storytelling, popularity of, 9; immersive storytelling, podcasting as, 12
Immigrant Defense Project, 169
In Cold Blood (true crime podcast), 53
In Defense of Elitism (Henry), 127
In the Dark (Baran, American Public Media), 2, 15–16, 18, 19, 50, 68–70
Indefensible (Immigrant Defense Project), 169–170
independent bookstores, 199
information: information seeking, rise of podcasting and, 108, 109; information silos, dangers of, 18; performance of, 213–214

InfoWars (podcast), 129
Inside (documentary series), 195
Inside Radio (news source), 107
Inside Trader Joe's (podcast), 21, 181, 198–200
instrumental podcast listening, 108–109
insurrection. *See* January 6, 2021 insurrection
Integrity in Journalism Award (International Center for Journalists), 48
intellectual culture, 74–98; accessibility of, 11–12; Black intellectual culture, 161; conclusions on, 223–225; historical analysis and media criticism, 90–98; introduction to, 17–18, 74–77; science, communication of, 77–81; science podcasts, editorial craft of, 82–90
interactive audio, 4, 5
interactive storytelling, 29
Intercepted (Greenwald), 16, 36
interloper media, 12–13
International Center for Journalists, Integrity in Journalism Award, 48
International Consortium of Investigative Journalists, 53
interviews, longform podcast interviews, 131
intimacy, podcast-specific, 93
Into America (NBC News Media), 14, 24, 42–43
investigators, investigation of, 68–73
Invisibilia (podcast), 76, 83, 84–85, 88, 89
It's All Journalism (podcast), 7

January 6, 2021 insurrection, 120, 139, 140–141, 143
Jenkins, Henry, 42, 135, 206
Jeter, Derek, 222

"'Jim Crow' Mentality and Social Media Trolls, The" (*Strange Fruit*), 172
Joe Rogan Experience, The (Spotify), 134, 136, 187
John Deere company, 176
Jones, Alex, 129, 134
Journal, The (*Wall Street Journal*), 111
journalism: advocacy journalism, underrepresented communities and, 151; ambiguity in, 183; boundaries of, 184–185, 186; challenges faced by, 72–73; changing locus for, 179; constructive journalism, 77; definition of, 179; digital journalism, homogenization of, 18; emotion in, 23; explanatory journalism, 77, 91; ideological hijacking of, 19; narrative versus, 49–50, 53; opinion journalism, 131; solutions-based journalism, 77; Starbucks's reimagining of, 194; subjectivity in, 43, 197; traditional definition of, 181. *See also* reporting
journalism industry, narrative turn in, 208
journalism of affirmation, 19, 128–132, 146, 223–224
journalism of assertion, 129, 130, 146
journalism of verification, 130
journalism/storytelling dichotomy, break down of, 147
journalistic principles: branded podcasts and, 196; *Caliphate*'s breach of, 52–53, 54; compromising of, 2; diversity, 43; integrity, 176; NPR principles, in coronavirus age, 39–45; podcast's impact on, 3; profit motive as potential threat to, 2; transformation of, 179, 181; transparency and, 62; verification, 216

Index 287

journalistic storytelling, advances in digital design for, 35
journalistic transparency, 58–68
journalists: as experts, 59, 60; humanization of, 29; as narrators, 208; transparency and, 58–68

Kalamazoo Promise, 192
KBBF radio station, 167
Kearns, Faith, 79, 80
Keeping You Organized (branded podcast), 22
Kerans, Ellen, 192
Kern, Jonathan, 39
Kern, Lauren, 110
Kerner Commission, 167
Kheshti, Roshanak, 150
Kidder, Tracy, 54
Klein, Ezra, 100
Koenig, Sarah: background, 48; critiques of, 208; on episodic storytelling, 23; Glass model and, 152; importance, 73; journalistic values of, 53, 131; journalistic vulnerability, use of, 62; methodology of, 82, 132; narrow focus of, 163; self-critiques, 19; self-reflexivity, 40; on *Serial*, production of, 185; on *Serial*'s achievements, 106; on uncertainty, 72
Kovach, Bill, 129, 216
Kumanyika, Chenjerai, 151, 171
Kundera, Milan, 166

Larson, Sarah, 160
Last Archive, The (Lepore), 16, 75, 77, 90–92
Latina to Latina (podcast), 20
Latino podcasting, 156, 166–170
Latino USA (Martin and NPR): on *chollo*, as term, 224; discussion of, 166–169; importance, 20, 156; social justice and, 2; subjectivity in, 209; voices in, 212
Laufer, Peter, 97, 101, 119
LGBTQIA+ podcasting, 170–172
LeClair, Catherine, 198
Lee, Hae Min, 51, 163
Lee, Trymaine, 24–25, 41, 42
left (political). *See* marginalized groups, voices from
legacy media, development of digital spaces, 4
Leitch, Will, 41
Lepore, Jill, 75, 90–93, 109, 224–225
Lewis, Michael, 31, 36
liberal rhetoric, conservative rhetoric versus, 147–148
Libsyn, 8
Lieber, Matt, 186
Lightman, Alan, 96
Limbaugh, Rush, 19, 124–126, 129, 145–146
Lindgren, Mia, 30, 76, 197, 206
Lippmann, Walter, 81, 125
listeners and listening. *See* audiences
literary journalism: in audio form, 218; literary journalism movement, 105; nonfictional literary journalism, 223; Roiland on, 208; tone modulation in, 84
literature, Mathis on, 22
Little Village (magazine), 51
Liturgists, The (podcast), 29
Live Audio Rooms (Facebook), 5
Llinares, Dario, 75
Locke, Charley, 71
Lonely Idea, The (science podcast), 78
"Long, Strange Trip of Doc Ellis, The" (ESPN), 222

288 *Index*

longform journalism and longform content: documentary longform podcasting, 131; examples of, 34; experimentation in, 12; immersive longform storytelling, popularity of, 9; impact on true crime genre, 15; intellectual culture and, 17; longform investigative reporting, evolution toward, 6; longform narrative audio journalism, popularity of, 205; longform news podcasting, core journalistic skill set for, 9; longform podcast interviews, 131; longform serialized documentary, 129; longform storytelling, 25, 102, 219; pandemic's impact on, 14; in podcast journalism, 40; as slow medium, 18; ubiquity of, 11

Longform Podcast (podcast), 75

Longreads (digital longform aggregator), 44

long-tail economics, 21

Lotz, Amanda, 28, 29

Lowery, Wesley, 209, 225

loyals (long-term subscribers), 105

Luse, Brittany, 154, 160–161, 162, 186

MacArthur, John, 99

MacArthur, John R., 121

mainstreaming of podcast journalism, 1–23; digital culture, podcast journalism in, 5–8; introduction to, 1–5; narrative journalism, audio turn of, 13–22; new human journalism, 22–23; podcast consciousness for journalism, 9–13

Malik, Sarita, 158, 159

marginalized groups, voices from, 149–174; Black podcasting, 157–166; content produced by, 6; diverse podcast production, future of, 172–174; introduction to, 19–21, 149–152; Latino podcasting, 156, 166–170; LGBTQIA+ podcasting, 170–172; podcasts' intimacy and, 9–10; white aurality, circumventing of, 152–157

Mark Levin Show, The (podcast), 138, 139

Markman, Kris M., 105, 115, 162

Marshall Project, The, 70

Martin, Maria, 2, 166–167, 212, 224

Martinko, Michelle, 51

Mathis, Ayana, 22

Mazzetti, Mark, 57

McArthur, John, 101

McDonald's, *The Sauce*, 21, 181, 198, 218

McDougal, Robert C., 86

McFadden, Syreeta, 159

McHugh, Siobhán, 178, 212, 216, 218

McKibbon, Bill, 97–98

McLemore, John C., 18, 59–60, 215

McLuhan, Marshall, 5

McNabb, Donovan, 126

Mead, Rebecca, 153

media: critical perspectives on, 95–96; mainstream audio media, lack of diversity in, 150; media convergence, 42; media criticism, 75, 90–98; media framing, 80; slow media, 97

medical companies, podcasting by, 190

Megaphone (formerly Panoply), 133–134, 136

Mellado, Claudia, 209

Meltzer, Kimberly, 132

Mendez, Alicia, 20

Meraji, Shereen Marisol, 156, 172

metajournalism, 196

metanarrative self-reflexivity, 30

Index 289

Mexican mafia prison gang culture, 168
Michelle Obama Podcast, The, 133
microbulletins, 29, 34
Miller, Arthur, 22
Miller, Dennis, 132
Miller, Kyle, 211
Miller, Lulu, 82
Mills, Andy, 52, 60, 63, 64, 65
Minnesota Public Radio, *74 Seconds*, 15–16
mirror-touch synesthesia, 83, 84–85
mobile phone technology, 46
mockumentaries, 198
monitorial journalism, 178
Morris, Wesley, 37, 153, 203
Morrison, Herbert, 93
Mosier, Chris, 171
Moth Radio Hour, The (Allison), 187
Mputubwele, Ngofeen, 153
MSNBC, 24–25, 36
Murdoch, Rupert, 145
Murley, Jean, 53

Naked Scientist, The (science podcast), 78
narrative: audio narrative, business of, 217–223; in brand advertising, 181; journalism versus, 49–50, 53; narrative depravation, 10; narrative reflexivity, 40; narrative storytelling, 26, 210; narrative techniques, new methods of, 30; narrativity, credibility during COVID-19 pandemic, 45; narrativity, importance of, 211; personal narratives, 32, 78, 128–129, 160; public affairs narratives, 214; race and, 164; voice-of-God narration, 204. *See also* intellectual culture

narrative journalism: audio turn of, 13–22; challenges of, 18; industrial context for, 3; podcasts as standard-bearer of, 214; societal role of, 211. *See also* storytelling
Nation, The, 131
National Association of Broadcasters (NAB), 125
national emergencies, audio media's role during, 46
National Review, The, 131
Natisse, Kia Miakka, 82
native advertising, 180, 184, 188–189
NBC News Media, *Into America*, 14, 24, 42–43
Nee, Rebecca, 128
Nerdist (podcast), 21
Netflix, 77, 195, 219
new human journalism, 22–23, 29
New Journalism, 3, 105–106, 216
new language of podcasting, 210–212
New Republic magazine: Grier and Leitch podcast, 30–31; *The Politics of Everything*, 74
New York Ledger (newspaper), lack of advertising in, 106
New York Magazine, "One Block," 209–210
New York Times (news company): Audm, acquisition of, 121; investments in production studios, 175; New York Times Audio, description of, 4; podcasting by, 1–2, 131; Serial Productions, acquisition of, 49, 186, 220, 221; T Brand Studio, 175, 180, 193, 194. *See also Caliphate*; *The Daily*
New York Times Magazine, 1619 Project in, 202
New Yorker magazine: cartoon on COVID-19 pandemic, 45;

explanatory journalism and, 91; *Radio Hour* podcast episode on COVID-19 pandemic effects, 45
New Yorker Radio Hour, 90
Newkirk, Vann R., II, 94–95
Newman, Nic, 17, 34, 36–37, 38, 77
news: ambiguity of sources for, 107–108; commercialization of, 55; digital news publishing, postindustrial condition of, 182–183; entertainment versus, 8; informalization of, 210; new language for, 207–212; news labor, economy of, 56–58; news podcasts, 1, 17; news roundups, 29, 34; online news, paying for, 100; paid news, lack of recognition of, 107–108; in podcasting, categories of, 37; quality of, 100–102, 133; sensationalism of news coverage, 55; standard definition of, 179; TV news, 204
news media: core principles of, 25; public perceptions of, 25–26. *See also* journalism
Newsmax, 144
NewsWhip, 142
New-York Tribune (newspaper), 96, 223
Nielsen, report on podcast diversity, 149
Nobel Prize Conversations (podcast, formerly *Nobel Prize Talks*), 16, 74–76, 85–89
Nod, The (Gimlet Media), 20, 154, 160, 162, 163, 211
nonfiction novels, 29, 54, 219
nonfiction podcasts, binge consumption of, 18
nonfictional literary journalism, 223
non-profit organizations, podcasting by, 6
novel environments, characteristics of, 39

novels: aural nonfiction novels, 223; monetization model for, 106; nonfiction novels, 29, 54, 219
NPR: changing tone of, 204–205; long-form journalism, 14–15, 25; Martin and, 166–167; podcast subscription service, plans for, 121–122; principles of, in coronavirus age, 39–45; self-study on diversity, 150; template for journalistic storytelling, 32; whiteness of, 150

Obama, Barack, 130, 133, 169
Obama, Michelle, 133
objectivity and distance in podcasting, 207–210
Odell, Jenny, 11
On the Media (podcast), 7
One America News Network, 144
"One Block" (*New York Magazine*), 209–210
open-source software sharing, 115
opinion journalism, 131
original sin, in digital news industry, 99
Ossé, Reggie, 159
"Out Crowd, The" (*This American Life*), 138, 203–204
Oxford Project, The, (Bloom), 209–210

paid podcasts, 99–123; Apple podcast subscriptions, 113–117; introduction to, 19, 99–100; paid podcast listening, priming of, 110–113; paid-subscription model, 106; paywalls, historicization of, 100–103; podcast listeners, discussion of, 104–109; publisher-audience exchange value, 119–123; Spotify premium subscriptions, 117–119
Palau-Sampio, Dolors, 167

Index 291

pandemic. *See* COVID-19 pandemic
Pandora, investments in podcasts, 112–113
Panoply (later Megaphone), 133–134, 136
parasocial relationships, 112–113, 139, 200, 210, 218
Parcast, 136
Parler (platform), 143–144
partisan polarization, 156, 190
Patel, Nilay, 30
Pavlik, John V., 122
PayPal, 144
paywalls: during COVID-19 pandemic, 26; debates over, 99, 101–102, 120, 122; historicization of, 100–103; *WSJ* and, 111. *See also* paid podcasts
Peabody Award, 215–216, 219
Perkins, Kendrick, 222
personal confession, 40, 62, 160, 196, 197
personal journalism, 224
personal narratives, 32, 78, 160
Pew surveys: on audiences' political knowledge, 55; on payments for news, 102, 106; on podcast audience size, 205
Pierre-Louis, Kendra, 56
Pineapple Street Studios (formerly Pineapple Street Media), 53, 152–153, 156
Pitts-Wiley, Jon, 159
Planet Money (podcast), 219
platformization: of Apple's podcasts, 114–115; dangers of, 119, 173; impact of, 164, 225; Spotify and, 4
platforms, social and cultural biases in, 155
Player's Tribune (Jeter), 222
Pod Save the People (podcast), 156

podcast consciousness for journalism, 9–13
podcast industry: advertising revenue of, 21; platformization of, 102; theorization of, 27–30
podcast journalism (generally): brands as publishers, 175–201; COVID-19 pandemic and, 24–47; digital literary journalism, podcasting as, 202–225; Far Right podcasts, 124–148; intellectual culture and, 74–98; mainstreaming of, 1–23; marginalized groups, voices from, 149–174; paid podcasts, advent of, 99–123; true crime podcast journalism, 48–73
podcast journalism (specifics): business models for, 200; challenges faced by, 2, 3; deviations from traditional journalistic practice, 131; as digital literary journalism, 202; humanization of, 61; impact on listeners, 164; liminality of, 7; listening environments for, 11, 86; listening times for, 37; literary journalism, tone modulation in, 84; locus of, 179–189; paradox of, 7; popularity of, 8; rapid growth of, 29–30; script-tape transitions in, 83–84, 85; self-reflexivity of, 7, 38; as transmedia phenomenon, 13. *See also* podcasting; podcasts
podcasting: business model experimentation, 21; commercialization of, 27–28; core medium of, 39; corporatization of, 186–187; democratic function of, 124–125; importance of, 38; intimate confessional modes of, 40; low technological bar for entry, 31;

paradox of, 7; reporting standards, freedom from, 146–147; roots of, 185–186; transparency of, 40
Podcasting Magazine: Beyond the Microphone, 206
podcasts: as advertising, 62; audience size, impact of, 49–50; binge listening to, 18; branded podcasts, 177; content, quality of, 42; corporate hijacking of, 186; empathic intimacy of, 193; hosts, editorial power of, 145; impact of payment on quality of, 119–120; motivations for listening to, 51; as news sources, lack of recognition of, 108; podcast culture, factors affecting, 5; podcast ecosphere, experiential diversity of, 151; podcast networks, 8; as principled journalism, 43; as radically empathic aural literature, 22–23; radio versus, 105, 109; televised longform interviews versus, 137. *See also* Far Right podcasts; paid podcasts
polarization of the public, 127, 190
politics: political agency, objective of, 37; political knowledge of podcast audiences, 55; political subjectivity, 164; political violence, 140–141
PolitiFact, 142
Pough, Gwendolyn D., 161
Poynter (Poynter Institute), 91
principles, journalistic. *See* journalistic principles
produce industry, 199
production practices, 29–30, 83–84, 92, 159–160
profits, 56–57. *See also* brands as publishers
progressive true crime reporting, 16

propaganda, branded podcasts as, 199
Provost family, 165
Psihoyos, Louie, 204
public, the: civic engagement, 18, 51, 211; polarization of, 127, 190; public interest, sponsored podcasts and, 178; public life, pandemic's transformation of, 45; public pedagogy, *Nobel Prize Conversations* as, 86; public sphere, nature of, 37; public-service journalism, 27, 32, 44, 46, 47, 189–194
public broadcasting, success of, 35
Public Intellectual (Crispin), 16, 74, 77, 95–96
Public Media Marketing, 14, 44
publishers: broadcasters versus, 9, 36; publisher-audience exchange value, 119–123. *See also* brands as publishers
Punnett, Ian Case, 53
Pushkin Industries, 31, 36, 90, 91. *See also Solvable*

Quah, Nicholas, 94, 220

race and racism: COVID-19 and, 25; cultural impact of, 20; racial bias in criminal justice system, 71. *See also* Black people and Black podcasting; whiteness
radio: Black urban radio stations, 159; conservative talk radio, origins of, 126; creative power of, 93; disinformation and, 92; English–Spanish language radio, legacy of, 154; genre conventions of traditional radio broadcasting, 214; local radio, editorial practices of, 156–157; local radio, white aurality of, 173; online

radio (*continued*)
    radio, 111; original public service ideal of, 129; podcasts versus, 105, 109; public radio, 154, 156, 157; science programming on, 78; self-regulation in radio industry, 125; talk radio, signature convention of, 128; twentieth-century science radio programming, 88
Radiolab (podcast), 83–84, 89
Radiotopia (podcast network): *Ear Hustle*, 7, 13, 29, 71, 72, 210; mentioned, 5, 27
ranting monologues, 132
Rauch, Jennifer, 97
Read, The (podcast), 162–163, 211
Reagan, Ronald, 126
Reddit, 127, 135
Reed, Brian, 18, 59–60, 152, 218–219
remote podcast production, 30–36
Reply All (podcast), 151, 163, 174
reporters. *See* journalists
reporting: audio reporting, 3, 74; on climate change, 79; false balance reporting, 90; Glass on principles of audio reporting, 40; longform investigative reporting, evolution toward, 6; progressive true crime reporting, 16; reportorial subjectivity, foregrounding of, 14; traditional hard-news reporting, script-tape transitions in, 83. *See also* journalism
Republican Party, 126–127, 146
Republik online magazine, 78
Reuters, 33, 110
Reuters Digital News Project, 129, 130
Reveal (true crime podcast), 16, 50, 69
rhetorical devices, 80, 146
right (political). *See* Far Right podcasts

Riis, Jacob, 209
Ringer, The (podcast company), 136–137
Ringer, The (Simmons), 221
Ripley's Believe It or Not, 92
ritualized consumption of podcasts, 108
Road to Yuba City, The (Kidder), 54
Roberts, Cokie, 127
Rogan, Joe, 134
Roiland, Josh, 208
roles, role perception versus role performance, 209
Roose, Kevin, 142
Roosevelt, Franklin Delano, 46
Rosenstiel, Tom, 129, 216
Rosenwald, Brian, 146
Rosenworcel, Jessica, 30
Rosin, Larry, 177
RSS (Really Simple Syndication) feeds, 102, 116, 117, 118
Rudoren, Jodi, 100
Rush Limbaugh Show, The, 138
Ryfe, David, 61–62

Sagan, Carl, 96, 98
Salmon, Felix, 100
Santana, Arthur, 128
Sauce, The (McDonald's), 21, 181, 198, 218
Schmidt, Thomas, 208, 225
scholarship on podcasting, 12
"Scholarships for Every Student" (Starbucks), 191–193
Schudson, Michael, 91
Schultz, Howard, 192
science: communication of, through podcasts, 77–81; media outlets on, 89–90; public education, attitude toward, 96; question of objectivity

in, 81; science podcasts, editorial craft of, 82–90; science podcasts, examples of, 76–77
Science Magazine Podcast, The, (science podcast), 78
Science News Service, 81
Science Vs (podcast), 76, 89, 90
scientists: deficit model of communication by, 79–80; as public citizens, 80
Scopes Monkey Trial, 92
Scripps, E. W., 81–82
Secret History of the Future, The (podcast), 36
self-disclosure, 62
self-reflexivity, 7, 30, 38, 40, 58–59
sensory immersion, 38–39
Serial (true crime podcast): achievements, 106; changing methodology for, 71–72; Cleveland municipal court system and, 16; conventions used by, 131–132; impact of, 20; innovations in, 220; Koenig and, 19, 72; narrow focus of, 163; participatory practices, 51; Sims on, 158; source of name of, 214; success of, 35, 186, 212
serial documentaries, 28–29
Serial Productions: changing focus of, 70–71; *New York Times*'s acquisition of, 1–2, 4, 49, 186, 220, 221; suit against, 60
74 Seconds (Minnesota Public Radio), 15–16
Shapiro, Ben, 19, 119, 128, 140–142, 145
Shapiro, Julie, 218
Shaw, Yowei, 82
Sheffield, Matthew, 144, 145
Shirky, Clay, 107
shock jock radio, 125
ShoutOut (podcast), 171, 172

Silver, Nate, 100, 179
Simmons, Bill, 41, 131, 136–137, 179, 221, 222
Simonson, Rick, 192
Sims, Davy, 158
Singer, Michael, 39
SiriusXM (satellite radio), 107
Sirrah, Ava, 200
1619 Project (podcast), 153, 156, 164–165, 166, 202–203
Skeptic's Guide to the Universe, The (podcast), 11
Slate, 45, 215
Slate Plus (paid membership program), 100–101
Sloan, Matt, 21–22, 198
slow journalism, 136–137, 164
slow media, 97, 101
Slowdown, The (podcast), 77
Smith, Adam, 86, 87
"Snow Fall: The Avalanche at Tunnel Creek" (*New York Times*), 34
Snyder, Julie, 60
social justice movements, 207, 214
social media: news content on, 107; podcasts' flexible relationship with, 173
social representation, 6. *See also* marginalized groups, voices from
Society for Professional Journalists, Code of Ethics, 6
solutions journalism, 14, 26, 31, 77, 87, 91
Solvable (Gladwell and Weisberg), 14, 17, 31, 70, 91
Somebody (true crime podcast), 71
sonic whiteness (white aurality), 150, 152–157, 173, 174
sound transactions. *See* paid podcasts
Soundcloud, 155

Spartz, Emerson, 175–176
Spiegel, Alix, 82, 83, 84
Spinelli, Martin: on journalism, 22, 29; mentioned, 88; on podcasts, challenges facing, 176; on podcasts, journalism in, 9; on podcasts, perceptions of safety of, 150; on podcast-specific intimacy, 93; on role of public broadcasters, 206; on tape-tape transitions, 89
sponsored podcasts, 178, 217–218
sports journalism, Simmons and, 137
sports podcasts, 44, 221–223
Spotify: as Apple rival, 113, 117; business model, 134–135; challenges faced by, 4; core function of, 135; dominance of, 2, 102, 133–137, 186; featured shows on, 3; Gimlet Media, acquisition of, 133, 136, 217; Greenroom, 4, 5; growth of, 176; *Heavyweight*, acquisition of, 3–4; impact on podcast ecosystem, 122–123; *The Joe Rogan Experience*, 134, 136, 187; listenership, 187–188; microtargeting by, 129–130; on news podcasts, interest in, 33; operating principles, 161; platformization and, 4, 133; on podcast revenue, 2; podcasts, investments in, 112; problematic content on, 135; revenue, 176, 187; subscription podcast model, 102, 117–119; white aurality and, 155. *See also* Gimlet Media
Spurlock, Morgan, 204
Starbucks, 190–194
Starkey, Guy, 28
StarTalk (Tyson), 11
StartUp (podcast), 216
Stephens, Mitchell, 223
Stern, Howard, 137

sticky content, 29
Still Processing (podcast), 37, 162, 173, 211
Stitcher, 186
Stitcher Premium (app), 106, 160–161
Stone, Roger, 129
Stoneman, Drew, 111
Stop the Steal movement, 140
Story, Kaila, 172
storytelling: audio storytelling, immersive, 36–39; cognitive range of (*See* intellectual culture); conventions of, 32; deep audio storytelling, renaissance in, 28; episodic, 23; immersive longform storytelling, popularity of, 9; immersive storytelling, podcasting as, 12; journalism/storytelling dichotomy, break down of, 147; journalistic storytelling, advances in digital design for, 35; nonfiction storytelling, funding of, 189–190; online multimedia storytelling, 3; for science podcasts, 89; storytelling structures in digital longform journalism, 105; temporary demise of, 10; transmedia storytelling, core characteristics of, 24; true crime storytelling, 68. *See also* narrative journalism
Stowe, Harriet Beecher, 96, 220
S-Town (Serial Productions): audience size, 104; civic participation in, 18; critiques of, 220–221; discourse surrounding, 215–216; formats of, 13; *New York Times* and, 2; sonic synecdoche in, 89; success of, 35, 212
Strange Fruit (NPR), 150, 170, 172
Stranger Beside Me, The (true crime podcast), 53

Strickland, Donna, 87–88
subaltern counterpublics, 20
subjectivity in journalism, 43, 208, 224
subscriptions, 100–102, 106, 111, 113–119
Sullivan, John, 27–28
Sullivan, Margaret, 207
Suspicious Activity: Inside the FinCEN Files (true crime podcast), 53
Swiatek, Lukasz, 21, 76
Swisher, Kara, 45
Switched on Pop (podcast), 74
Syed, Adnan, 163

T Brand Studio (*New York Times*), 175, 180, 193, 194
Talese, Gay, 84
Taranto, Claudia, 107
technology: technological hubris, 98; technological innovation, sources of, 12–13
telegraphese, 10
Their Eyes Were Watching God (Hurston), 211
These Truths: A History of the United States (Lepore), 91
This American Life (Glass, Chicago Public Media), 3, 10, 30, 40, 138, 203–204, 220
This Day in Esoteric Political History (Hemmer), 75
This Is Product Management (Alpha UX), 189
This Week in Blackness (TWiB!, podcast network), 20
Thompson, Marie, 150
Thoreau, Henry David, 223
Tierney, James, 216
Time Sensitive (podcast, later *At a Distance*), 96–97

Tobin, Lisa, 52
Today, Explained (podcast), 29
Today in Focus (*Guardian*), 14, 28, 34
Tolliver, Lynn, Jr., 159
tone, in writing and speaking, 80
Tortoise Media, 78
Total Refresh (Coca-Cola), 195–198, 200
Tow Center for Digital Journalism, 193
Trader Joe's, 198–200
traditional hard-news reporting, script-tape transitions in, 83
"Trans Women and Trans Girls Belong in Women's Sports" (*Burn It All Down*), 170–171
Transathlete.com, 171
transmediation: of digital ecosystem, 107; transmedia journalism, 43; transmedia storytelling, core characteristics of, 24
Transom Story Workshop, 187
transparency: Apple's lack of, 115; of digital journalism, 29, 38; as metajournalism, 196; performance of, 58–68, 181, 195, 196–197; of podcasting, 6–7, 40; role of, 208
true crime genre: challenges facing, 49; as journalistic public interest documentary, question of, 60; medium-specificity of, 53; narrative conventions of, 59
true crime podcast journalism, 48–73; in age of COVID-19, 44, 212–217; audience for, 51–52; genre of, challenges facing, 52–55; introduction to, 15–17, 47, 48–51; investigators, investigation os, 68–73; journalistic transparency, 58–68; news labor, economy of, 56–58; structural bias of, 69
True Murder (Zupansky), 51

Trump, Donald and Trump administration, 97, 124, 138, 140, 143, 146
Trust, The (*Wall Street Journal*), 180
truth, death of, 90
Tulloch, John, 208
2020 Politics War Room (Carville), 41
TWiB! (This Week in Blackness!), 20, 158, 160
Twitch, 4
Twitter, 127, 135, 138, 140
287(g) Program, 169–170
two-side-ism, 209
Tyson, Neil deGrasse, 11

unemployment, 24
uninsured individuals, COVID-19's impact on, 25
United States: immigration reform in, 169–170; slave labor in, 165
United We Dream, 169–170
University of North Carolina, Hannah-Jones and, 165
Up First (NPR), 33–34, 205
Upstanders (Starbucks), 190–194
Usher, Nikki, 184

Valdez, Al, 168
video essays, 202
visual media, artifice of, 86
voices: of longform documentary audio journalism, 152; marginalized voices, 212; voice-of-God narration, 204; white aurality (sonic whiteness), 150, 152–157, 173, 174.
    See also marginalized groups, voices from
Vox (news source), as explanatory journalism, 91
Vox Media, 14, 27, 30, 44, 45
Vrikki, Photini, 158, 159

Wahl-Jorgensen, Karin, 208
Waldmann, Ella, 216, 221
Wall Street Journal (WSJ): investments in production studios, 175; podcasting by, 111
Wang, Rang, 105, 108, 109, 112
War of the Worlds (radio hoax), 125
Warner Music Group, 4
Washington Post: *All Told*, 14, 29, 44; WP BrandStudio, 180
watchdog journalism, 225
Watchdog Journalism (Berry), 16
Way Things Ought to Be, The (Limbaugh), 126–127
WBUR (radio station), 124
We Are the Champions (documentary), 77
Weber-Smith, Chelsey, 95–96
weekly press, 219–220
Weekly Standard, 131
Weisberg, Jacob, 17, 31, 36, 90–91, 99–101
Welles, Orson, 125
Wells, Shapearl, 71
Westwood One, 139
Wetterling, Jacob, 70
What's News (*Wall Street Journal*), 111
White, Elon James, 158–159, 160, 211
whiteness: objectivity and distance in podcasting and, 209; white aurality (sonic whiteness), 150, 152–157, 173, 174
Whitman, Walt, 214
Who? Weekly (podcast), 104
Wilks, Farris C., 142–143
Williams, Le-Ann, 94–95
Wingard, Penny, 25, 42
wisdom journalism, 223
Witmer, Bob, 39
Witschge, Tamara, 184, 223

Wolf, Rich, 78
Wolfe, Tom, 54
women: in STEM fields, 76, 87–88; women's athletics, gender inequities in, 221
Wondery (podcast network), 27
work-from-home orders, 30
Worldly (podcast), 74
"Worst Day in Modern American Political History, The" (Shapiro), 143
Wortham, Jenna, 37, 153
WP BrandStudio (*Washington Post*), 180
Wrong Skin (McHugh), 212

WSJ. See *Wall Street Journal*
WSJ Custom Studios (The Trust), 175
WTF (podcast), 29

XXI (subscription-only French magazine), 121

YouTube, 135

Zendesk podcast, 189
Zetland, 78
Zuckerberg, Mark, 134
Zukerman, Wendy, 89, 90
Zupansky, Dan, 51

Printed and bound by CPI Group (UK) Ltd, Croydon, CR0 4YY
11/06/2025
14688053-0002